By

SALLY CARRIGHAR

Moonlight at Midday (1958)

Icebound Summer (1953)

One Day at Teton Marsh (1947)

One Day on Beetle Rock (1944)

These are BORZOI BOOKS published in New York
by Alfred A. Knopf

Moonlight
AT
Midday

Moonlight
AT
Midday

SALLY CARRIGHAR

ALFRED A. KNOPF · NEW YORK · 1958

L. C. *Catalog card number: 58–10965*

© *Sally Carrighar, 1958*

THIS IS A BORZOI BOOK,
PUBLISHED BY ALFRED A. KNOPF, INC.

Published October 20, 1958
Second printing, December 1958

To

DR. CARL RENZ

❯❯❯-❯❯❯-❯❯❮❮❮-❮❮❮-❮❮❮❮

who still lives in the new lives
he gave to his patients

PREFACE

➤➤➤➤➤➤➤➤➤➤➤➤➤➤➤◀◀◀◀◀◀◀◀◀◀◀◀◀◀◀

The Forty-Ninth Star

BONFIRES ACROSS two thousand miles of the Northern wilderness —that would have been a spectacle if anyone could have seen all of them! Alaskans are not much given to shooting off firecrackers. They may feel that explosive noise-makers, however loud, have only a popgun effect in the silences of this vast, peaceful land. In such country, however, any bonfire will stir the emotions. A bonfire means human beings, other people, whose welcome is sure to be friendly. And a fire typifies life itself here, where for part of the year warmth is more immediately essential than food. It was natural, then, that Alaskans would celebrate the vote that admitted their Territory into the Union with bonfires.

In debates on Alaska statehood, here and there, it has sometimes been said that the residents might be reckless in managing their affairs. Were not most of the early settlers "rough, heedless characters" who were drawn to Alaska because of the feverish gold rush? The miners who have remained, the sourdoughs of today, are a class of men extraordinarily reasonable and gentle. Whatever they were when they came to the North, here, like the rest of the pioneers, they encountered the arctic climate.

That climate is a great disciplinarian. It forces a man to be realistic, and it teaches that those who do not stand together do not survive. Quickly learning those lessons, the gold-rush miners developed a practical outlook and consideration for others' needs. If, by August first, a prospector had not made a stake that would carry him through until spring, he was allowed to pan on the gold-bearing claim of any more fortunate neighbor. Today few Alaskans are seeking gold, but the climate is still the same, and so are the caution and kindliness. The arctic still bends a man's will. Other far-Northern countries, Norway, Sweden, Finland, and our well-balanced neighbor, Canada, all are known as among the best-governed lands in the world. For them too an austere climate probably is an influence. And there is evidence that in good sense, in thoughtfulness, and in social responsibility the state of Alaska will join them.

Those who have been fearful of recklessness might have looked at the record made by the Territorial government. It has been allowed to control only one per cent of Alaska's area (Washington has held 99 per cent); yet the services that the Territory provided have been a matter of pride with all residents.

In the Territory's last budget 51 per cent of its revenues were allocated to education; its teachers earn higher salaries than teachers anywhere else in the states. Alaska roads and airfields are efficiently engineered and maintained, in spite of the winter emergencies and the frozen soil. Utility systems have been designed that operate when the temperature is fifty degrees below zero. Traffic, the very small amount of juvenile delinquency, labor relations: problems like these all have been handled well.

In the humane Northern spirit, moreover, the Territory has seen its treatment of residents as calling for helpfulness that goes beyond justice, beyond what is merely fair. The ill, the aged of all races, dependent children, the handicapped, and unemployed are very adequately taken care of. No racial discrimination has been allowed in Alaska for fifteen years. Another example of social responsibility has been the Territorial help for some of the natives, who, many Alaskans believe, are badly mismanaged by the distant Indian Bureau. The Bureau has only one solution to the present economic dilemma of Northern natives: to move them to white-men's cities. Most of the white Alaskans view that plan as a tragedy for the Eskimos and Indians at this stage of their culture. Out of the limited Territorial revenues, therefore, Alaska has started to modernize native villages. Well-equipped workshops are being set up where the natives can practice civilized skills. Voluntarily, also, the Territory has taken over some poorly run Indian Bureau schools.

In providing these services, the Territorial government has not been extravagant. Its finances are in the black. However, much that the planning boards would have liked to do has necessarily been postponed. Many public services are still only a promise—but a promise that at last seems likely of early fulfillment.

As everyone now must know if he reads a newspaper or listens to broadcasts, Alaska, the state, may select from the public lands about 100,000,000 acres, or a fourth of its area. On these acres a much larger, permanent population will establish its homesteads and farms, its cities and industries. From these acres will be filled most of the people's needs, their food, fuel, and other supplies, and from them will come the revenues of the new state government.

Everyone must have heard, too, that the country is very rich in its known resources—timber, minerals, fish, and hydroelectric power—and even richer in its potentials, such as oil and gas, already found in commercial quantities. No state, surely, ever made a more promising start.

We lighted some of our bonfires for the federal agencies that have been especially helpful during our Territorial years—for the Civil Aeronautics Administration, always dependable in its guidance of pilots up in the arctic skies; for the Weather Bureau; the United States Public Health Service; and District Judges. To these, as well as some of the other officials, Alaskans will never forget that we owe our thanks.

Our appreciation should not be overshadowed by a listing of ways that have needed, and still need, a change in Washington policies. A few pieces of unfinished business have not been disposed of by making Alaska a state.

The first concerns salmon. Salmon, even in its depleted condition, is Alaska's most valuable resource. And yet the bill just passed deprived the state government of its management. From the earliest days of American settlement, Alaska has helplessly seen its salmon exploited by Stateside canneries—helplessly because the Territorial status permitted the federal government to control the wildlife. The canneries have been allowed to come into

Alaska's waters and build fish traps that prevent far too many salmon from getting into the rivers where they would spawn. The same kind of traps have long been outlawed in states where the canneries have their headquarters, and Alaskans have voted, seven to one, to condemn their use. That vote was ignored in Washington, where, under a program of perpetual "studies of salmon populations," the Fish and Wildlife Service has refused to abolish the Northern traps. Meanwhile the salmon runs have declined phenominally. The 1957 pack was the smallest in fifty years.

There is evidence that a large portion of the immense profits made from this source has been spent to defeat all the former bills proposing Alaska statehood. For the cannery-owners have known that a fully self-governing Alaska would never allow such a wanton waste of its principal resource. The canneries still seem to be able to influence persons high in the administration at Washington, since Alaska control of Alaska salmon was removed explicitly from the 1958 bill, until such time as the Secretary of the Interior, at his discretion, may grant it to the new state. Many Alaskans believe that even this bill would not have passed if that provision had not been included. The provision may be unconstitutional. We can hope that the United States Supreme Court will find it so before our last salmon is in a can. Otherwise we may have purchased our rights as citizens at the price of having Alaska salmon become extinct.

Freight rates, too, are a subject that has not been closed by the statehood vote. Alaska still is not guaranteed export-import tariffs on the United States railroads, a benefit granted to the Hawaiian Islands, although freight sent to Nome travels farther over the water than freight sent to Honolulu does. And the Alaska Railroad, owned by the federal government, is still free to set its freight rates as high as it will. They have been high enough in the past to allow the road an average annual profit of $2,000,000— charges for transportation that are added to retail prices paid by Alaskans for necessities such as milk. The road not only keeps its own rates very high, but it wars on private carriers that try to bring us our freight for less.

In one more way we should be glad to have the cooperation of Washington—in attracting ambitious residents to the new state.

During the last year 15,000 young businessmen, with their families, have emigrated from the United States to Northern Canada. They were recruited by the central Canadian government, which found them jobs or openings in small service industries and furnished them easy credit, special low rents and utility charges, and favorable banking arrangements. For investment capital, too, Canada provides tax incentives. The state of Alaska is planning similar offers—for example, free homesteads—but we cannot match Ottawa's inducements on the 73 per cent of our area that the federal government still controls.

The Territory has suffered some real injustices in the past. In this book I have said very little about them, but those pages have been allowed to remain. Although statehood will remove many of the difficulties, they should be understood widely, because such injustices occur in other parts of the country too, but not often so nakedly undisguised. For the authentic story in its completeness there is no better source than *The State of Alaska*, by Ernest Gruening, who was Governor of the Territory for thirteen turbulent years.

Some of us had begun to wonder if the discrimination against Alaska was going to be permanent. Its settlers had wanted citizenship for so long—not the forty-two years that Alaska has fought for statehood actively, but for the ninety-one years since the nation bought Alaska from Russia, and in the purchase treaty promised that Alaska's white residents would receive "all the rights, advantages and immunities of citizens of the United States." Among such rights, of course, would be the right to vote and to have representation in Congress. Ninety-one years, therefore, not forty-two, is the period that Alaska has waited for statehood.

In summer, during the time of the midnight sun, we have a most buoyant sense of release in our twenty-four hours of daylight. We go out into the lovely countryside, to fish, to gather the wild fruits, to watch and photograph animals, to pan gold, and (a favorite phrase) "just to live on the creeks." In those months we may seem almost pagan in our delight in this Northern land.

On the other side of the year—which we also enjoy—we have many hours of darkness in which to consider the serious questions of Northern living. It is then that we've most often dreamed of

organizing our own kind of government. That wish could only
be realized if we had statehood—but in the last years it has
seemed to many Alaskans that they had done all they could to
promote it, that even our selfless, devoted Congressional friends
could not go any further, and with our gratitude to them was
mixed something of fatalistic despair. A feeling had grown that
statehood must wait on a turn in our destiny, on impersonal
fortune.

In winter our moonlight at midday does not dim the stars; and
among them would Alaska's star ever rise? Where to place a new
star in the national flag seems a pressing question to citizens
whose state stars have been added much earlier. To Alaskans their
star has more importantly been a symbol—of the longing to build
their own practical and yet warmly human society in the North.

In ninety-one years many Alaskans have made their protests to
Washington, have been rebuffed, have learned to live with their
disappointments, and finally have died.

Through ninety-one years . . .

But now, look—the star!

WITH GRATITUDE

➤➤➤-➤➤➤-➤➤➤-➤➤➤-➤➤➤-➤➤➤-➤➤◄◄◄-◄◄◄-◄◄◄-◄◄◄-◄◄◄-◄◄◄

. . . I ACKNOWLEDGE THE KINDNESS of *The Saturday Evening Post*, *The Reader's Digest*, and *The Montrealer* in allowing me to reprint here material that they first published. Special thanks are due *The Saturday Evening Post* for permission to use the photograph credited to them.

Others also contributed photographs, and I hope they will take the credit lines as inadequate recognition.

So many Alaskans have helped to make this book a picture of arctic living that a list of them would include most of the Northerners I have met. All who knew I was writing about the country seemed eager to volunteer information and to tell about anything colorful they had witnessed or experienced. I only can say that this is their book too, and I hope I have transmitted accurately all the facts they have given me.

In coming, a novice, to so unfamiliar a land, I received special helpfulness from some who interpreted the strangeness, and who stood by during my first awkward efforts to become one of them. Of these I should like to mention especially: at Unalakleet, Frank and Eunice Ryan and Frank's three sisters, the Anawroks, Martha Nanouk, Fred Katchatag, Stefan Ivanof, David Paniptchuk, and Eric Accibuk; at Nome, Omie McCarthy, Margaret and Ben Mozee, James von der Heydt, Edith Bullock, Bessie Moses, Bertha Aukon, and Lela Oman; at Fairbanks, James and Florence Douthit and Dr. and Mrs. Kaare Rodahl; and many others, in all parts of Alaska, whose kindness will be evident from the contents of the book.

In ways that are less obvious I was assisted by Mr. and Mrs.

Frederick Machetanz, and by Lowell Sumner and George L. Collins.

Finally and importantly, I thank Alaska's Delegate to Congress, the Hon. E. L. Bartlett and his efficient staff. They found answers to uncounted questions, and "Bob" Bartlett read crucial parts of the book for errors, although he is not to be held responsible for any that have crept in.

Betty Wilson gave patient and intelligent help with the typing.

S.C.

CONTENTS

PART III

Alaska Summons Its Own

LIST OF ILLUSTRATIONS

➤➤➤-➤➤➤-➤➤➤-➤➤➤-➤➤➤-➤➤➤-➤➤◄◄◄-◄◄◄-◄◄◄-◄◄◄-◄◄◄-◄◄◄-◄◄◄

Following page 42

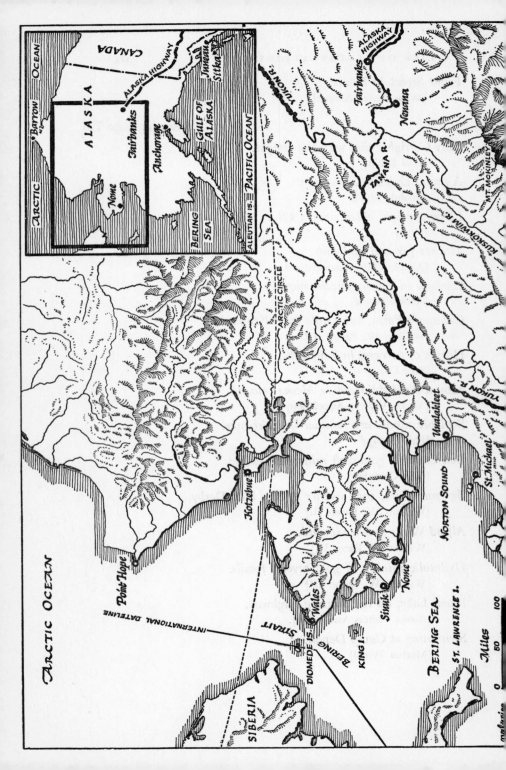

PART

I

A Fine, Complete People

NOTE: *The Eskimos refer to themselves as* Inuit, *or farther south often as* Yupik. *Both forms are usually translated as simply "the people," but the Eskimos themselves feel an emotional quality in the words, one of self-respect. If asked how to say it in English, they will tell you they mean the "right" or the "fine" or "complete" people.*

→»→»→» 1 «‹-«‹-«‹-

Stormy Route to a Quiet Mind

ONE WINTER NIGHT in the dining-room of the Bering Sea Club at Nome the juke box began to play *Far Away Places*. Could this be the scene the composer had in his mind? Outside the windows were limitless miles of snow-covered ice—a motionless, silent sea, white and sparkling under the Northern sky, which as usual blazed with stars. Inside, we were eating reindeer steaks, and the room was warm and comforting with the companionship that binds arctic-dwellers together. As the wishful sighs of the record ended, a bush pilot who was there smiled and said,

"We are the ones who don't have to sing that song . . . because we live at the farthest place." The farthest place—he was right; farthest, at least, on the North American continent.

The farthest places are not for everyone. Salesmen are sent to Nome, expensive salesmen to come so far, and if they arrive on a rainy day, sometimes they will stand, with their excellent haircuts and well-tailored topcoats, and look down the muddy length of Nome's unpretentious Front Street and murmur, "God, if this isn't the end of the world—"

And that is indeed what one reaches in northwest Alaska: the end of what seems the world to one reared in our kind of civilization. Beyond is the Bering Sea and beyond that is Siberia, only three miles from Alaska's Little Diomede Island. The end of the world, however, was not what the pilot meant. For him and a few hundred other white people, this coast is the farthest place, which is something different.

At the end of the world the distance from civilization is thought of in miles and hours of flying-time. At the farthest place the return view seeks for meanings, a long perspective on years one has lived and people that one has known—a perspective on civilization itself as one associates with the primitive natives, the Eskimos.

At the end of the world there's an annoying lack of momentum, as if everybody had lost his drive. But when it's the farthest place, the truth is that no one is pushing another, no one exerting pressure. Each lives at his own, individual tempo. Each is himself, uniquely, and little more will be asked of him except humane help at times. What he was before he came North is considered nobody's business.

The sky over the farthest shore is filled in the daytime with very clear, glossy light; at night with sheets of stars, so many that it is hard to distinguish the constellations. Because the sky is so much a part of the scene in the North, because we are always so conscious of it, our ties with the earth seem more tenuous than they do in a big and distracting city. Here we are, these few people out on the edge of the infinite, here for a little while: we see one another with different eyes now. We *see* one another, which in itself is a form of courtesy.

Nome is the take-off point for some of the Eskimo villages. They are not more remote geographically, but anyone might expect that they'd seem so. If a traveler stays long in one, he will, however, come to a period when this settlement does not seem "distant." He will pick up the Eskimos' attitude, that they are "the people"—and this is "the place." Eskimos do not see themselves in relation to New York City, Seattle, or even Nome. Many of them never have left the village where they were born, and so naturally they don't feel far away.

All of life that is really important is here—births and deaths;

young men and women setting up households; the concern with food, shelter, and fires for warmth; dancing and story-telling; and village government. Woven through these activities, all of them, are the Eskimos' creative kinds of relationships, which make their days not simple, really, but varied and rich. Why should they look to other places, or even think about them? The newcomer finds himself sharing that point of view for a while. New York is not more significant, he may soon decide—it is only *more*, and perhaps too much more.

It is not possible for a civilized person to become a real resident of "the place" and still try to hold in the front of his memory all of his complex past. Before any stranger can be a deep part of this immediate little sector of life, he will have to find something the Eskimos value highly—as they call it, "a quiet mind." A mind can't be quieted in a day, not without help. But I was fortunate —I did have assistance. I arrived in Unalakleet, the village where I was to live, with a mind at least partially quieted, and the new point of view was given to me gratuitously by a storm on the Bering Sea.

What the Eskimos mean by a quiet mind is picked up piece by piece:

"You never see ghosts if you don't have a quiet mind." "People with quiet minds wait till things happen at just the right time." Understatement is typical of the way that a quiet mind will express itself. The mountains behind Unalakleet, although nearly 4,000 feet high, are "hills." And of a boy with his kneecap blown off, someone said, "He is little bit hurt." "Little bit" is a phrase the Eskimos often use. They pronounce it as if it were one word, as perhaps the older, unschooled natives think that it is.

Another one of their favorite words is "maybe." It is the almost universal reply to a question. A more definite answer would be a commitment, and any commitment disturbs the quietness of a mind. Above all, the man with a quiet mind will be humble. If he wins in a game, he will say to the loser, "You are the better man. Too bad your foot slipped." To me he would say, "I will tell you what I know about seals, but I am not very good hunter. John Auliye is better. You ask him too."

When I arrived at Nome, near the end of my journey up to the land of the Eskimos, I was never further from having a quiet mind. To get myself there, with everything I might need through an arctic winter, had seemed to require the most intense planning and organizing. One with a quiet mind seldom plans; he waits till life gives him a cue and then acts decisively. But I wouldn't have thought of that, then, as a way to assemble supplies of every conceivable kind of medicine one might want in a year; sixty pounds of dried food to make the transition to whatever it was that the Eskimos ate; camera equipment and scientific apparatus— all specially lubricated with graphite because I'd been told that oil would congeal in the arctic cold; activity cages for captured animals; the warmest clothes made, which I'd purchased during some sizzling July days in California; source books, typewriter supplies, and dozens of items like hand lotion, ink, Kleenex— enough of each to last for twelve months. And when I arrived in Nome I found that everything, with the exception of scientific equipment, could have been secured there. The Nome brands of some things, like the clothing, would have been better.

Since that time I've seen dozens of research workers bring to the North, from as far away as New York sometimes, as many or more supplies that they could have bought locally. They arrive in a less harried state than I did, however, for most of them come from a university or museum where a staff aids in the planning. My own expedition was solitary, one naturalist who just wanted to know about arctic animals. The animals were discovered, observed, and written about, and that part of the project was largely carried out in the Eskimo way, receptively. But during the first stage, the preparation, I'd worked myself into a tension that would have been the worst possible mood in which to enter an Eskimo village.

The project was first conceived in the luminous mind of Dr.

Olaus J. Murie, biologist, conservationist, and director of the Wilderness Society. I was a guest of his family in Jackson Hole, a family whose own thinking and plans have the grandeur and sweep of their Wyoming landscape. Under the same roof at that time was also the brother of Olaus, Dr. Adolph Murie, partner in biological interests. Their wives (the two brothers married sisters) also write on biological subjects, and the several children had a veritable zoo of wild pets, from a kangaroo rat to a wolf. It was an atmosphere in which the ambitions of any visiting naturalist would bloom.

I had been staying farther out in the valley, writing a book about the animals in a Jackson Hole marsh. Previously I had written about the animals in a forest. What would my next subject be, Olaus asked one afternoon during a tea-break, while we all were gathered around a big square table, watching the jagged shadow of the high Teton crest move across the flat, mauve, snow-covered valley floor.

"The animals of a seashore," I told him.

"What shore? Where?" Olaus asked. I said that I thought it would be the coast of Maine. With a typical, inspired flash Olaus suggested,

"Why not the arctic coast? So little is known about the animals of the arctic."

The thought was electrifying—but where could I stay in order to watch those animals? I always wanted to be in a habitat for at least a year, to know all the seasons.

"Stay in an Eskimo village."

Would that be practical? The group thought it would. The two Murie women were reared in Fairbanks; the men had done field work in several parts of Alaska. Fairbanks, the tundra, the mountains where they had spent most of their time were not the coast, and they could not recommend a specific settlement. But they were sure that the difficulties would not be great. The Teton shadow was now climbing the slopes of the mountain range on the

eastern side of the valley. The sun was gone. Soon the stars
would expand the sky over the Teton peaks.

"I think I'll do that," I said. "I'll go and live with the Eskimos."

The most formidable obstacles went down the most easily: for
example, that of financing. Quickly, generously, the John Simon
Guggenheim Memorial Foundation provided funds. Now I could
make the plans definite. In my San Francisco apartment everything that I touched brought up the question: could I do without
this? Toothpaste, a clock, sheets, thermometer, matches, a gun
—in an Eskimo village would these be essential? The supplies
finally chosen filled a trunk and five packing-cases. They were
dispatched to Nome.

In the very last hour, it was a frenzied start. Leaving with
family and friends for the plane with plenty of time and to spare,
I saw in the window of a men's-furnishings store a boy's fleece-
lined jacket that looked like a very good thing. I went in to buy
it, slipped it on, zipped it up to my chin—and the slide fastener
stuck. The big red fist of the salesman tugged at the fastener,
with no luck. Other fists, all muscular: my chin began to feel
bruised. I was due at the airport in fifty minutes, forty minutes,
thirty-five minutes. They finally had to cut me out of the jacket,
and I went tearing away to my rendezvous with the distant Eskimos.

Which Eskimos had not yet been decided. U.S. Coast and
Geodetic Survey maps of Alaska had been tacked on my wall in
San Francisco, and there, comfortably wrapped in the sounds
of a passenger elevator, cars, and the little E trolley laboring up
Columbus Avenue, I had studied the gray lines on buff paper,
as austere as a steel engraving, that were the only picture I'd seen
of that far Northern coast. The country, I thought, appeared
rather lonely; distances between nearest villages seemed to be
more than a hundred miles. The names gave no clue as to where
the natives would be the most friendly: Barrow, the farthest-north
tip of land, Point Hope to the southwest, obviously built on a

sandspit, or Kotzebue on the end of a long peninsula but enclosed in a bay on both sides. These three settlements faced the Arctic Ocean, though Kotzebue seemed rather sheltered. At Wales on the Bering Strait the shoreline became the coast of the Bering Sea and ran north and south. At Nome, however, it made a turn east to form a great bay, Norton Sound, which looked on the map as if someone had taken a giant bite out of the land. On the inner curve of the sound was a settlement with a name like the tripping of musical brooks: Unalakleet.

Coming back out to the southern corner of the big bite, there, where the Yukon River entered the sea, was St. Michael. Every naturalist knows the name, for two early biologists, E. W. Nelson and Lucien Turner, were stationed there at a meteorological station. St. Michael I thought it should be. I would follow the lead of those scientists, gone from St. Michael seventy years and more; and the thought of the meteorological station was reassuring.

In Nome, then, my first questions were about St. Michael, and I was referred to Omie McCarthy, a woman who once had taught there. I would not want to live at St. Michael, she was sure— only about 150 inhabitants and no way to get out in the winter except by dog sled to Unalakleet, 65 miles away. The village was built on tundra so spongy I'd have to stay on the boardwalks. She never had heard of a meteorological station; that must have been long ago. And anyway there was no roadhouse, as all inns are called in Alaska towns though they may be 500 miles from the nearest road. Was it possible that a family would take me to board, I asked. Mrs. McCarthy was doubtful, but I still was not willing to give up St. Michael.

Meanwhile, as soon as I came to Nome, I had been told about a small freighter, the *Kotzebue*, which plied up and down this coast in the few, ice-free summer months. Its scheduled run took two weeks, starting at Kotzebue, the settlement on the Arctic Ocean, down through Bering Strait to Nome and thence south around Norton Sound to St. Michael. Sometimes it carried a passenger, for there was a single cabin, and several people suggested that I should make a cruise on that little boat. As supplies were unloaded at different villages, I could go ashore, inquire what animals might be seen near-by, and find out about living quarters. The *Kotzebue* would be back in Nome in two or three days, I learned. The exact date was uncertain, since Bering Sea weather disrupted schedules.

She would dock in the river, the Snake River which pours out to sea near one end of town. To be sure that I wouldn't miss her I walked down to her berthing-place several times each day. The banks of the river here were firmed up by revetments, walls of interlocking steel beams. They were very high, always high above water level but especially so at low tide. The river makes a right-angle turn just before it enters the ocean. The revetments end there, and beyond them the river is guided by two short concrete jetties. A few Eskimo skin boats and small fishing craft went in and out of the river, and a dredge worked off the end of the jetties continuously, for the swing of the sea at this point keeps building a sandbar across the channel.

The *Kotzebue* was delayed, but finally one morning was there, anchored down in the river below the revetment. A crane on the bank was lifting freight off the deck. The boat was a type designed actually for fishing, a purseiner, sixty-four feet long and built in that size so that its owner could avoid having a licensed crew. All ships of sixty-five-foot length and more are required by law to be manned by crews who can prove their competence. The *Kotzebue* did look small, but anyway it was freshly painted, white with black trim, and had nice clean lines.

The stern end was all deck with a hatch several feet square opening into the hold below. In front was the pilothouse; no doubt the cabin would be inside. A narrow railed walk surrounded the pilothouse. On the deck were some Eskimos handling the freight, which consisted chiefly of cartons of salmon. I called down and asked for the captain, was told that he was not there. I asked that he call the hotel and leave word when I could come back and see him.

Later that day my door threatened collapse under a sudden and violent banging. Indignant, I flung it open, but the young, blue-eyed giant who stood outside looked so amusingly, boyishly bold that my protest died.

"What's this about your wanting a trip on the *Kotzebue?*"

He strode in and without being invited threw himself in a chair, stretching out his enormous legs in their tan dungarees. His hair was the shade of the dungarees, and tucked into them was a blue turtle-necked sweater. He's wearing that sweater because it matches his eyes, I thought, and he probably would admit it. This is one of those men who can be stunningly frank.

"I'm the captain," he said. "Tell me about yourself."

I explained my project, my need to discover some Eskimo village where I could watch arctic wildlife and where living quarters could be arranged.

"The place where you'll see the most animals is around Norton Sound. That's south of here. We've just come from there. Now we're going up north. We'll be back down in a week and you can ship out with us."

The conversation took a new tack:

"Do you get seasick?"

"Not very."

"The *Kotzebue* really plunges around." And then, "I should tell you that I am not much of a navigator. This is the first time I've ever been handling a boat. I was working for the *Kotzebue*'s owner and he needed somebody to run her, so I took on the job." He grinned. "I have some books on navigation. I take 'em along and I read 'em too, and so far we haven't gone on any rocks."

He's having fun trying to scare me, I thought.

"The engineer is a white man, good with a boat when he's sober but that's not very often. The first mate is a native. He's a convict, paroled to me for the summer. The second mate is another native. Deaf and dumb. He acts pretty peculiar, but you don't have to worry. Then I have two native deckhands, and a native girl cooks when I can get the engineer to let her out of his cabin. That's the crew."

If he wanted the satisfaction of seeing me startled, he would not have it.

"That's quite a big crew for so tiny a ship," I said. What I thought was, This has the earmarks of something I shouldn't do. Yet the captain, although he might seem so brazen, looked like a decent fellow. I was less confident about the crew. I hoped that the captain was exaggerating. As it turned out, he wasn't. The crew were just as he said. It was true, too, that this was the first time he ever had run a boat.

I had written two books about wildlife, and to study the animals I had spent several years in one wilderness and another. Often I'd been alone and a few times had had to rescue myself from emergencies. Out of them I had become convinced that I could handle most situations as long as I thought I could. I had found that even the roughest male characters size up a woman well. If she is sincerely interested in what she is doing, if she is not out for adventure but to observe and learn, they are usually respectful. Also I had developed a personal policy: that I would not get into danger for the excitement merely, but I would not avoid it if my work stood to benefit.

"I'll be ready," I told the captain.

The *Kotzebue* left on the northern lap of its route. About a week later a morning came when the sky was heavy with more than the end of night. The gulls were all flying inland, and the rollers were breaking far out on the sea's dark expanse. The waves had not come in so fast yesterday and had not tumbled over in foam till they ran up the beach. I had gone to sleep hearing their crystal splash. And then it was day, loud with the unceasing plunge of whole series of breakers, white, as many as ten curling over behind one another. They were gnashing their way to shore with a sustained and powerful roaring.

The spray stung my face as I walked down the street to the

North Pole Bakery. While I ate breakfast at one of the long, sociable tables, the man next to me, small and weathered and with the bright, hopeful eyes of a miner, said, "This storm will bring the men in from the creeks." I mentioned that I was supposed to go out on the *Kotzebue,* which was due that day, and I said that I wasn't exactly happy about the prospect. An airplane mechanic, drinking coffee on the other side of the table, let his face break into a grin and asked in a teasing tone, "Do you want to be old some day?" It's an Alaska saying.

The miner was more reassuring.

"You won't have to go," he told me. "When the winds are as strong as this, all the ships run to cover. The *Kotzebue's* probably riding it out up in Teller Bay. The captains of the small boats have been pretty cautious ever since one of them, the *Good Hope,* was lost. She disappeared during a blow up near Bering Strait. Just vanished, the boat and the crew and two passengers, girls. Funny thing—the mail came ashore in the lifeboat, perfectly dry." In a moment he added,

"The *Kotzebue* couldn't get into the river, anyhow. The dredge doesn't go out in a storm like this, and the bar builds up at the end of the jetties. The *Kotzebue* couldn't get over it."

I returned to my hotel room and got back into bed to keep warm, since the temperature in the room was but forty-eight. I watched the waves for a while, from between the white starched lace curtains, and then, feeling so safely on shore, started reading some of my research notes on the Bering Sea.

This is the region where most of the continent's storms begin. The "prevailing westerlies," as they are called, fairly warm winds, sweep up over the Bering Sea from the Pacific Ocean and are met here by the cold "polar easterlies" from Alaska's mainland. The irregular, shifting boundary is known as the polar front, and it is along this front that the stormy lows are developed. The low-pressure areas may roar all the way across Canada and the United States or may stagnate up here near the Arctic Circle; but for every disturbance that passes, another one soon arrives.

"The weather over the Bering Sea is generally bad and very changeable," is the succinct way it is stated in the *Coast Pilot*, the mariners' guide published by the U.S. Coast and Geodetic Survey. The area is described as one of the stormiest in the world. "In the early fall the gales increase." This looked like a gale, all right. How long would it last? "A characteristic of the storm movements . . . is that the individual storms are not clearly separated from each other . . . but occur in close series." Each succeeding storm "appears to increase in force."

The *Coast Pilot* is one of the most colorful documents ever published, starkly realistic even if some of the entries seem whimsical:

"There are few aids to navigation. All of the rocky islands and rocky cliffs of the mainland are frequented by thousands of birds, whose numbers, constant cries, and flight may serve to indicate the approach to shore at some places." We'd have to depend on birds, then, rather than lighthouses. "The currents are much influenced by the winds, and are imperfectly known and difficult to predict. . . . Safety depends upon constant vigilance." Vigilance on the part of the drunken engineer, the Eskimo convict, or the boyish captain?

The Bering Sea is an ocean almost completely landlocked. It is roughly the shape of a triangle with a curving base, the Aleutian chain, about 1,800 miles long. Its apex is up at the Bering Strait. An arm of the Japanese Current flows through passes between the Aleutian Islands and races northward along the Alaska coast at velocities of up to three knots, or five feet per second. Some of this water escapes through the Bering Strait into the Arctic Ocean, but most of it turns around and flows south along the Siberian coast, back out through the Aleutian chain, and westward. It has been chilled in the Bering Sea, so that when it reaches the shores of Japan again, it is the "cold Oyashio."

The speed of the current would be considerably hastened by a storm from the south, which this was. In such storms, said the

Coast Pilot, the bar at the mouth of the Snake River at Nome might build up to within three feet of the surface. "With heavy surf, boats crossing the bar before entering the jetties will ground and are liable to overturn."

So of course the *Kotzebue* would stay somewhere else till the storm was over. I looked out through the window. There she was. She was approaching the jetties. Rolling and wallowing, but speeded by wind and waves, she was coming in fast. On the top of one of the heaviest swells she got in past the bar at the end of the jetties, chugged to the turn between the revetments, and was lost to view. In less than an hour a telephone message was brought to my room. The captain sent word that the *Kotzebue* would be leaving that night about ten o'clock.

It was dark and pouring rain when the taxi came to a skidding stop in the mud beside the revetment. The deck of the boat was at least ten feet below the bank. The captain stood down on the deck and the cab-driver tossed my bags to him. There was no ladder, no gangway. "How do I get down?" I called. "Jump," said the captain.

Someone loosened our mooring lines and we started out through the swells in the river. With all our power we rounded the bend where the river turns, sped forward—and hit the bar. The next wave lifted us off and carried us backward. We tried again and again we hit. We can't make it, I thought with relief. But we could. We finally got over.

And then we were taking the full force of the Bering Sea waves. In each trough the *Kotzebue* seemed to dive for the bottom, but the next roller heaved us aloft, to shudder across its top and plunge down again with a sickening drop. I could not believe that we would get anywhere this way—we were just fighting the sea. Nevertheless, we did progress. Back behind us, beyond the violent water, the lights of Front Street were drawing closer together; they were becoming smaller and fainter. They were all that showed in the black scene, the red and green

harbor lights on the ends of the jetties and one line of street lights
between the black sea and the black endless tundra behind the
town . . . Nome.

I was not nervous then, exactly, but it was more pleasant to
sit in the lighted galley for a while than to shut myself up alone
in a tiny cabin that was continually tipping itself on end. The
crew were moving around at their work. The engineer had made
only a very brief, reeling appearance as we were getting out of the
river. An intelligent-looking Eskimo, whom I took to be the
first mate, the convict, was up in the front of the pilothouse at
the wheel. The deaf-mute was out on deck, tightening a rope
here and there, making the freight, some oil drums and a small
dinghy, secure. The two younger Eskimo boys had disappeared
into the hold. I had not seen the girl.

The captain directed them with a combination of authority
and frontier good humor, I thought. He moved with a kind of
unlocked exuberance, as if his energy had an absolutely free
channel, and the chance to spend it in large, masculine action
was not a task but a fiery fulfillment. Even I caught a part of his
pleasure in finally taking the boat over the treacherous bar. When
he had everything under control then, he poured us both coffee
and sat down on the other side of the table against which I had
braced myself in the pitch of the galley.

"What do you do in the winter?" I asked him.

"Next winter I'm going to build a log house," he said, "in the
town where my wife and I live. It's up on the arctic coast."

"Primitive?"

"Well, we get our water by dog sled. We go out to the lakes on
the tundra behind the village and haul in big cakes of ice."

"Does that become tiresome after a while?"

"Not to me. I don't know how I could put in my time in a
better way."

"What did you do last winter?"

"Trapped, about 150 miles northeast of Fairbanks. Rugged
country—headwaters of the Salcha River. Our nearest neighbor,

another trapper, was sixty miles away. My wife was there. She stayed with me all through the trapping season."

"Did she have a trapline too?" I asked.

"No, trapping's not work for a woman," the captain said.

"Since I am a naturalist, I don't like to think about killing animals for their fur. But up here I suppose I'll be as glad as anyone else if their hides keep me warm."

"I try to kill the animals in a humane way," said the captain. "A trapped animal often freezes to death quite quickly. If I find one alive—a marten, say—I hold out my mitted left hand and he jumps for it. While he grabs it, I stop his heart with my bare right hand."

He told about the shelters he built on the trapline and about the hot biscuits his wife would make, how good they would taste after he'd walked all day in the arctic cold: "But those walks weren't unpleasant. Of course it was night most of the time, a kind of blue-white dark. Often the Northern Lights would be swinging around overhead." He talked about the dog that went with him, how that dog would try anything, tackle a grizzly alone: "He had the heart of a lion."

Another winter the captain had bought a tractor and hauled freight along the Bering Sea coast, traveling on the shorefast ice. The spring break-up came suddenly, while he was some distance out from the beach. He worked his way in, he said, by driving the Cat over the broken cakes in the leads. (Leads, pronounced "leeds," are the lanes of water between floes or pans of ice.)

He told of such incidents with great relish, saying at one point, "I wish I'd been born a hundred years ago, so I could have put my snowshoe tracks over more country." I looked from his spirited face to some volumes of Dostoevsky on the shelf with the navigation books, and wondered whether the North had molded this man, or he came here because he was born with an inclination to grapple with nature's elements—arctic animals, danger among the ice floes, and now the raging winds and waves through which he was piloting this very small boat. I understood

why he'd insisted on coming out into the height of the storm
—he couldn't resist a challenge.

I still thought of my cabin with dread, and therefore, to keep
the talk going, I asked him to tell me more about the crew.

"We may not have any crew by this time tomorrow," he said.
"Every time we put in anywhere I expect to lose one or more of
them."

"Why?"

"Eskimos just aren't able to stand sustained labor. To keep
going at some dull job, or a job they don't like, for money—it
isn't in them. Last year the captain lost crew members after
every trip. Before I took on this bunch I made every one give his
promise to stay through the season. It's a personal thing, loyalty,
not the wages, that's kept them."

"Hasn't anyone quit?"

"Not yet, but they're all ready to. They keep asking if I won't
let them go. Then I scold them like children."

"If it's so difficult for an Eskimo to stand strain," I asked,
"how do they ever support themselves anywhere?"

"They work awfully hard in spurts. They get most of their
food from the sea, and any time that the weather's nice they may
stay out in their boats forty-eight, fifty-six hours. They would
never choose to go out in a storm like this. I'd better go and
relieve the man at the wheel."

The one who had been steering our course was indeed the
convict. He came back to the galley, slid into the captain's place,
and poured himself coffee. His face was not young but not
middle-aged yet. It looked more sophisticated than most of the
Eskimo faces I'd seen at Nome, also more clearly molded. Most
of theirs had been plump or muscular rather than bony, but
this man's had definite shape in the cheekbones, chin, nose, and
brow. Perhaps he was partly white, quarter- or half-breed.

We were joined by the deaf-mute, and the two men talked in
the Eskimo gesture language, which was so comprehensible to
them that several times they both laughed. The strangeness began

to seem overwhelming. I felt lost and had difficulty in keeping my thoughts from dashing themselves around wildly.

When the convict went forward to take back the wheel, the captain returned. I was convinced that he really was trying to substitute daring and ingenuity for experience in this job. Since the engineer was not able to function, our safety lay in the skill of the first mate. I hoped he was being vigilant, and I thought that he probably was. His eyes, although sullen, had a sharp look. I asked the captain why he had been jailed and the captain said on a morals charge.

Through the open door of the galley the light struck across the deck and out over the black, heaving water. The shoreline had disappeared. The immense chop of the Bering Sea surrounded us. The captain smiled with impulsive kindliness, as if suddenly he had wondered how all this would seem to the passenger. "Let's have some music," he said, and turned on the boat's radio. He picked up Chicago, and even amid the sea's thundering and the engine's clamoring, the music was clear and lovely—a string quartet playing *Stardust*.

Norton Sound averages about 75 miles wide and extends 150 miles inland. Cape Nome is its northern portal and the Yukon delta the southern. On its shores are ten Eskimo villages with such melodious names as Golovin, Koyuk, Ungalik, Shaktolik, Egavik, Unalakleet, Golsovia—and St. Michael. If the sea had not been so high, the *Kotzebue* would have stopped at several settlements on the north shore of the sound. As it was, the captain postponed all those stops but one, at Golovin.

Golovin, near the end of a sandbar, was bleakly surrounded by vast lagoons. Most of its buildings were boarded up. Once it had been a port for gold-mining operations up the Fish River and for a reindeer industry. Now it was almost deserted. I did not go ashore. It was obvious from the ship that this was not a good wildlife habitat.

I was giving up thoughts of St. Michael too. After breakfast

the captain and I had had a long talk about my objectives. At
St. Michael, he said, I would see little but birds and muskrats.
But Unalakleet, at the inner bend of the sound, was surrounded
by more wildlife, of more different kinds, than any other Eskimo
village in all Alaska.

The town had a population then of about 400 people. It was
built on a sandspit at the mouth of the Unalakleet River, a
sizable watercourse that wound back seventy-five miles or more
into a range of mountains. Beginning three or four miles from
the coast, the captain said, the river and all of its tributaries were
bordered with spruce, birches, and alders—trees for firewood,
trees to build cabins and boats, trees here so far north: a nearly
undreamed-of luxury.

A rich animal life was found behind Unalakleet: black and
grizzly bears, marten, mink, beavers, wolverines, arctic hares, foxes.
Even more fabulous was the wildlife that swam past the shore.
The captain explained that some of the current which flowed up
the Alaska side of the Bering Sea followed the turns in the
shoreline, all the way into the farthest reaches of Norton Sound.
It swept along numerous little fish and the plankton on which
they lived. Pursuing the smaller fish came smelts, tomcod, herring,
salmon trout, silver and king salmon. Unalakleet was the northern
limit of kings; they and some of the silvers ran up the Unalakleet
River to spawn. To feed on this horde of fish came seals of
several kinds and the white beluga whales. I had not hoped to
find all the arctic animals in one place, but at Unalakleet it
appeared that I could see most of them.

"If only there will be living quarters!" I said.

"You can stay at Charlie's," the captain replied. "He has a
vacant apartment. Charlie Traeger, the white trader. He's eighty-
one and has an Eskimo wife."

The captain pronounced the name "*You*-nulla-kleet," though
the older Eskimos, I was to learn, say "Oo-nulla-klik," with the
emphasis on all syllables equally. Translated loosely it means
high-water wind, and is derived from the fact that storms like

the one we were in, from the southwest, blow such large waves against the shore that occasionally they have swept over the town. Those usually are the winds of late summer and fall. But once in the winter, when there was ice on the sea, a southwesterly wind picked up slabs of the ice and hurled them on land with such force that they cut through some cabins.

We arrived at Unalakleet about seven o'clock in the evening. There was no dock. It was necessary to anchor two or three miles out at sea, for the inshore waters were shallow. Though the waves were still very high, the wind had stopped screaming around the pilothouse and the sky looked a little brighter. Perhaps this was the end of the storm, or of course it could be its quiet center. The latter, no doubt; for the captain, who had been getting weather reports on the radio, had said, "Tomorrow the storm is really going to bite us in the face."

We dropped anchors both fore and aft, and all of us crowded around the small galley table for a wonderful dinner of beef stew with fresh airborne vegetables, and hot biscuits, and hot wild-blueberry pie. The Eskimo cook was young, with skin sleepily pink and so dreamy a look that when I first saw her I wondered if she could so much as fry an egg. But she gave me one of my unforgettable lessons in Eskimo ways, for with no bustle or clatter, with only the softest, indolent-seeming motions, she prepared the most appetizing meals, on a stove surrounded by an iron railing, within which the pots and pans never stopped sliding around and banging against the sides.

The captain had promised his crew that they could all go ashore here. The engineer still preferred to lie in his bunk, but the captain's plan was to allow the others to take the dinghy to town for an hour or two. Then they would come back and about ten o'clock the captain would take me in, with my bags, and if the trader was willing, I'd rent his apartment and stay.

The crew were not back by ten. Nor by eleven, nor twelve. The weather had worsened. The captain heard on his radio that a new storm was coming up, one of those secondaries which always "appeared to increase in force." For the present the wind was driving from off the land, against the waves. It was turning them, breaking them into a sea of wild pinnacles spurting up, to be pushed down by new peaks of rising foam-crested water. The *Kotzebue's* fairly regular motion became senseless now, pitching one way and another so violently I could not stay on my feet. I crawled from my cabin to the galley on hands and knees and sometimes sat on the floor of the passageway with my feet braced against the opposite wall. It was the only way to avoid being hurled about, which was physically very tiring.

"The crew couldn't get back in a sea like this, could they?" I asked. The captain swore and said yes, they could if they wanted to. I was glad they'd been late, for I certainly would not have wanted to go ashore. I assumed that we would lie anchored here until morning. When, at a quarter of one, the dinghy came back however, the captain said, "Hurry up, get your wraps on!" He threw my bags into the dinghy, dropped me over the *Kotzebue's* rail, and jumped into the dinghy himself. We pushed off.

It was raining again, a gale-driven downpour slashing across those black slopes of water, which for a few dozen yards glistened with the reflected lights of the ship. The motion was unbelievable. When a peak would rise under us, sometimes the whole outboard motor hung clear in the air—till we careened down into a pocket, when it would catch again. The rain did seem to be flattening the sea's heaving a little, but every time we were in a trough both the ship's riding lights and the one small light on the beach disappeared. The lights seemed important. When the boat rose again, I would look to see that they were still there, as if in the brief time of a wave's passing the lights could have got drowned in the over-all darkness.

The captain had lent me his rubber slicker and I sat huddled in it while rain dripped off the brim of my hat.

A single oar lay in the bottom of the dinghy, and in what I

hoped was a light, humorous tone, I asked, "What good would one oar be?"

"To steer with if the rudder broke," said the captain.

But a broken rudder was not to be our big problem. We had gone a third of the way to shore when the motor began to sputter. There were a few warning coughs, which caused the captain's dark hulk to bend over it more attentively, and then it was dead. If possible, the boat's motion became even dizzier. The dinghy was not of course going forward, but it rocked on the waves with a slithering rise and fall. The rain was still pelting down heavily, and on all sides the sea's voice seemed a menacing growl. I thought of our single oar and looked at the lights, almost equally far away.

"Come back here and hold the flashlight," the captain said.

I crept to the stern, took the light, and crouched close to the motor. The flashlight battery was so nearly gone that it cast only a small, dim, yellow beam. The captain discarded his gloves and started taking the motor apart, while the rain ran in streams off his hands and his wrists.

I asked if he knew what the trouble was. He did not answer, but he cursed the crew for not telling him that the motor was not working well. It seemed that he could not do what he needed to do because he did not have a wrench. I still watched the lights.

Once the captain said irritably,

"Stop wasting the battery! Keep the flashlight turned off till I tell you I want it." His annoyance means that we're really in danger, I thought. Sometimes when he wanted the light on for several minutes, it would go out entirely. I would leave it off for a while, and when it went on again, for a short time it would glow brighter.

In the back of my mind there had been a comfortable feeling that, whatever might happen, the waves would carry us in to shore. But I now had a different impression. I had to voice it:

"The light on the shore is quite faint."

"I know," said the captain angrily. "We're drifting out. The tide's on the ebb." The riding lights of the ship, too, by that time were smaller. The Bering Sea on the west became suddenly real in its vast expanse. By daylight would we have lost sight of land? Would anyone search for us? There was no Coast Guard station up here on the Bering Sea. And when the new storm reached its height, would this tiny skiff stay afloat?

The impersonal rain, the wild, lonely water that surged around us, and the cold, wet wood of the boat all became terrifying because of their lifelessness. These, as well as the clouds and the unseen stars, were a non-living universe that I could not face in those hours—not till an instant when there might be no other choice. In the meantime my thoughts turned with unbearable, tender longing to everything that was alive.

Nearest would doubtless be fish in the water beneath our dinghy. All those gracefully flashing creatures, perhaps stimulated to playfulness by the waves' massive movement: did they like it? Or had they retreated to lower depths to wait out the storm in sandy troughs they had scooped by the waving streamers of their own bodies? Did they wait with alert eyes and fins slowly pulsing? Fish were beings I'd never felt close to before, but now, I saw, they were kin. The captain and I belonged in their company. We were all of us part of the brotherhood of the living.

The security of the fish seemed to extend a little from them to us: that notion came to me anyway, and somehow it was comforting. And the Eskimos back on the *Kotzebue:* were they perhaps in the galley, drinking coffee, sharing their gloom at the prospect of having to stay on the ship for a few more weeks? Anticipating his later freedom, was a smile lightening one of the somber faces? Were the men lifting cups, crushing out cigarettes? Breathing, at least. Even the people of Unalakleet seemed my own, strange though they were, Eskimos now asleep. I began remembering those farther away whom I loved, and I thought about them until the ship's lights had disappeared, until they were only a dim arc of glow on the black horizon.

The captain had not explained what he was attempting to do. Nor did he say anything when the time came that he hoped the motor might run again. Through the darkness I could detect that he was winding his short length of rope. He pulled it; and after two or three more windings, with a few sputters the motor leapt into a strong, steady pulse.

We went back to the ship. The engine was started, the anchor chains were drawn up, and we left Unalakleet, heading out of the sound for St. Michael.

When we arrived the next day the captain would not allow me to go ashore; the waves still were too high. I could tell, however, that here, as at Golovin, there wouldn't be much to attract the animals: an exposed treeless mound of moss-covered earth with rocks at the shoreline. In the scattering of houses it was evident that some were abandoned.

The next afternoon we were back at Unalakleet. The rain had stopped but the waves were as high as ever. I would have preferred to return to Nome rather than attempt the ride in to shore, but we'd picked up two passengers at St. Michael and of course they were entitled to have the cabin. Getting into the dinghy again was just one of the things that had to be done. With, however, no further emergencies, on that windy, cold day I was put on the beach with my bags, and the dinghy pushed back out to sea.

I had come to my village of Eskimos.

A group of children, who had gathered around the boat, went along with me to the trading post. The ground-floor room that I entered was big, smoke-darkened, and dimly lit. But a cast-iron stove glowed in the center, and near it, sitting relaxed on the floor or on up-ended sticks of firewood, were a dozen pleasant-faced Eskimo men, dressed in parkis but with their hoods pushed back. A few native women stood at the counter.

The atmosphere of the room was indeed unfamiliar, with its pelts of wolves and wolverines, foxes, martens, and bears hanging from walls and rafters; and with its traps and guns, and its odors of seal oil, new rope, dried salmon, potatoes, onions, and apples, and, pervading all, the scent of the pelts.

Unfamiliar too was the stillness, not only the silence but the utter quietness of these peaceful people. There was no frown on any brow in that room, no tension lines around any eyes or mouth, no nervous movement, no sign of impatience or hurry. I seemed to have walked into some kind of waking dream, an element where time did not exist and no one took part in events, only stood apart, watching.

If the journey from San Francisco had been made without any unsettling incident, I would have entered that room too crisply and would have greeted the Eskimo postmaster, who came forward, with too brightly cordial a manner. The stylized ways of civilization, ways that have as their purpose the getting of everything done in a hurry, cannot be dropped at will, and they would not do in this world to which I had come. To these people I would have seemed busy and rude, and our mutual confidence would have been much delayed.

But I had arrived in a mood overwhelmingly humbled, because, though I hadn't expected it, I was on land again. I was alive and safe. I did not feel a stranger. Though these Eskimos did not know it, on a recent night I had thought of them as my own people.

The crew may have told them that I was coming to live among them. That knowledge would have explained their interest but not the kind impulse of the woman who said in the gentlest possible way,

"Welcome."

2

Every Day Is Saturday

OVER THE DARK LAND of sleep spread a song. It was wild and melancholy, and lonely though blended of many voices. The separate strains began high or low and would glide up and down, interweaving with others but all in the same mood of plaintive urgency—music as weird as a chorus of English horns.

The singers were dogs, but the voices were those of wolves, the wolves in the sled-dogs' throats. Wolves had been the dogs' ancestors. In feature and size the dogs were becoming modified, but they still could not bark. Their voices were still of the wilderness, and now in the fall they were singing most of the time.

It was their voices that woke me after my first night at Unalakleet.

During the evening the trader had spoken of wolves. I had asked him about the high-pole caches, the little log houses built up on stilts, that were scattered throughout the town: what were they for? To store part of the winter supply of food, the trader explained. They were elevated to keep it away from wolves.

"Do wolves come into the village?"

"A herd of reindeer is pastured over along the hills," he said. "Wolves stay around to prey on the deer, and they'd bother us here if they could get at the Eskimos' fish and meat." I asked if their howling was ever heard. "Sometimes," said the trader, "but their voices are hard to tell from the dogs'."

In my dream a regiment of the wolves had been approaching the trading post. The wolves' marching feet sounded like soldiers'; they arrived at my stairway and started up. Then I woke, and the only sound was the howling of tethered dogs.

I was cold. An inner-spring mattress, like the one on which I had slept, apparently was impractical in the North: the cold air flowed right up through the little coils. And what was the startling movement across the floor? The linoleum rug, brown painted with coral and turquoise flowers, seemed to be heaving up, quivering, and then sinking back. I watched it until I knew I was fully awake and had no indigestion. Out of bed then, on the cold linoleum, I found that it was indeed heaving. With each step my foot pushed it down. I walked off the edge and knew why. Gusty drafts of cold air whirled up through the cracks in the floor. The temperature on that day, I guessed, would be about fifty. In midwinter when, I'd been told, at times it would be a hundred degrees colder than this, what would that wind from the floor do to the temperature in the room? I sat on the edge of the bed and shivered in prospect.

This was the morning towards which I had been planning and working for a long time. For a year I had done nothing but library and laboratory research on arctic animals—and now at last I was among them: white beluga whales, spotted, ribbon, and bearded seals, walrus, polar bears, arctic foxes, wolves, hares, lemmings, and the millions of waterfowl that come to the North to breed. The birds were then, in September, flying back south, and Unalakleet, I knew, was on one of their migration routes. This very day I could watch them go over, perhaps birds as rare as snow geese and whistling swans. Before night some Eskimo might have taken me out to his whale net, or up-river, where surely we would see ptarmigan, white too early as they would be for the camouflage of the snow. This was the morning, anticipated so eagerly, when it would all begin.

And so perverse can be human nature, so disappointing one's

own desires, that all I wanted that day, sitting there on the bed, was a Stateside newspaper. With one bare foot up on the other to keep it away from the chilly floor, I counted: four days since I'd known anything about what was going on in "the world."

When I came in to breakfast, the aged trader was tending a skillet of pancakes. As soon as I'd greeted him I said,

"You sell newspapers down in the store, I hope."

"Nobody sells newspapers in Unalakleet."

"What time does your news broadcast come on?"

"Three radios in there," he said, tilting his head towards the sitting-room. "You can try them, but all you'll get is a lot of static." He piled up the cakes in the skillet and lifted the stack with a pancake-turner onto my plate. "Unalakleet's in a kind of a pocket. Radio doesn't reach us here."

"You mean you don't get any news at all, ever?"

"The rest of the world is a long way off," he murmured as he went back to the stove. He said nothing more, but something dropped out of his manner—his interest in me, in what I had come to do, I thought. I was sure I could read his mind, and he had concluded that I would not be here long. Anyone who was worrying about newspapers in Unalakleet would not stick it out.

As I helped wash the dishes, I said,

"Now I have to go down and get acquainted with my new village. What would the people be doing at this time of day—nine-thirty?"

"Sleeping," the trader said. His face relaxed in a tolerant smile. "They were probably up fishing till late last night. But we don't have alarm clocks anyway."

I descended the trader's ancient and shaky stairway into a town that seemed under a spell—not deserted, for bright-colored washings hung on several clotheslines, and fish, blubber, and whale-skin were drying on dooryard racks. But no one hurried along the lanes, late for work, no faces looked out from the windows, no babies' crying issued from open doors. One could almost hear the low, regular breathing of all the sleepers. As I started to wander around, I was feeling a little embarrassed, as one does when watching the smile on a dreamer's face.

The storm had subsided. Clouds hid the sun, making a gray day of it, but not coldly gray. This being the fruiting time, the slopes of surrounding hills looked as if they had been watered with wine, so rich-colored they were, in the rust and blue of profuse berry bushes. The clouds were low. They rested upon the hills and picked up the autumn tones of the foliage, becoming deep-tinted billows of mist. The wind came from the sea and, once I was out in it, seemed a soft wind. Though the sun was not shining, this was a pleasant day.

All the foreground was wide and spacious: water and sand, mossy tundra and yellow marsh. Nothing to interrupt the eye, nothing to fence the spirit. Off in the distance however, beyond the expanse of the marsh, a range of low mountains circled around like protective arms. They came to the sea in two headlands, I judged perhaps twelve miles apart.

A sandspit, about seventy-five yards wide, connected these cliffs like an archer's curved bow. It enclosed the marsh. On one side of the spit was the sea, on the other side a lagoon. The lagoon snaked around in the marsh. The Unalakleet River, issuing from the mountains, coiled around too in the marsh, the lagoon and the river, islands and tongues of land, all intermingled. Finally the flow of the river did reach the spit. It cut through that barrier and poured itself out to sea.

South of the cut the sandspit was wild and barren: sand, drifted in dunelike knolls, pierced with sharp beach grass and scattered with driftwood. That half of the spit was deserted except for one tent, pitched on the lagoon side with a gillnet stretched out from shore. The tent, I learned later, belonged to the family of David Paniptchuk, who said, "In summer we like that side better because there's more air over there." But air certainly wasn't lacking anywhere in that country.

Just north of the river's mouth, on a greener part of the spit, clustered the sixty or seventy village cabins. They were built in two somewhat irregular rows, one row along the sea beach, which was sandy, and one along the lagoon, above a low, grassy bank. There was no proper road or street. A wide lane ambled along near the center, with smaller paths leading off to the cabins. They were graceful paths, touching in their expressiveness. Like animal trails and brooks, they were following nature's route, widening out where the surface was flat and avoiding the elevations—the gentle, the acquiescent way. They invited one's steps.

They all drained towards the middle of town, towards the vertical group of the white-men's buildings: the trading post, the three-story schoolhouse and clapboard teachers' cottage, and the mission buildings. The upthrust walls, shouldering over the snug little native cabins here in the lonely winds, somehow seemed aggressive. Besides the trading post there was one other store, an Eskimo co-operative with a weathered sign on its unpainted wall: NATIVE STORE.

The lack of all other kinds of business was conspicuous. A town of this size in the States would be serving surrounding country and surely would have a drugstore (one with a rack of newspapers), a movie theatre, a dealer in fuel, a filling station, perhaps an agency for cars and farm machinery—chances for people to work as well as to buy supplies. There were none of these here: little reason, I saw now, for any alarm clocks to ring at Unalakleet. The only gongs to rouse anyone in the morning would be the waves' breaking, the dogs' musical voices, and the mewing of terns and gulls, sounds that would prod very gently. They would not disturb anyone's sleep as long as the sleep was needed.

The Eskimos' cabins were made of peeled spruce logs. Some were new; more were weathered and silver-bright from the polishing of the salt sea wind. They were built very much like a white-man's cabin, with windows and sloping roofs, but were lower-set, with their floors on the ground or in some cases a few feet below it. The base of the outside walls was banked up with earth or sod blocks; no wind would be coming up through the cracks in those floors. The sod blocks completely covered a few of the cabins. Some of the others had roofs of sod, bristling now with late summer flowers. The sod roofs suggested hair standing on end so unavoidably that they gave to their cabins a whimsical look of surprise.

The three most widely accepted notions concerning the Eskimos are these: they live in snow *igloos*; they put their old folks out on the ice to die; and a husband will loan his wife to a visitor. As for the first, only the Northern Canadian Eskimos, wandering as they follow the caribou, have lived in snow *igloos*. *Igloo* is simply the word for house, and the Eskimos who maintain permanent *igloos*, like most of the natives found in Alaska, have built them of whatever materials were available locally. Because most of the Eskimos of Alaska have led more or less settled lives, their aged relatives could be cared for at home. When any elderly persons became too ill to travel and therefore endangered the livelihood of an entire group—as among the nomadic Canadian Eskimos—it was generally on the old person's initiative that his life was sacrificed.

At Unalakleet there have always been logs, and the earliest white men who came to this part of the coast found the Eskimos living in cabins not greatly different from those of today. At Little Diomede Island in Bering Strait, and at Wales on the near-by mainland, the only wood to be had is a scant supply of driftwood. Houses are partly tunneled back into sod banks, with front walls that are often composed of rocks, and the roofs may be of walrus skins.

Farther north on the arctic coast even driftwood is almost unknown. Lumber is sometimes imported now, but the ribs of the giant whales have been used as support for walls and roofs of sod—very practical homes in that country of frigid winds. I went into a sod house at Barrow and found it clean and comfortably, cozily warm. The inland Eskimos make tentlike structures of willow poles, covering them with strips of sod or with caribou skins.

The cabins at Unalakleet, as elsewhere in the arctic, were small—only one or two rooms. Each had a shed, or a "storm porch," which formed the entry and also was used for storage. Most of the shed doors were open, and inside could be seen equipment that was both primitive and civilized. Fur parkis, snowshoes, and Eskimo boots hung among outboard motors, guns, and steel animal straps, saws and axes, wooden butter kegs —filled, like the trader's, with salted ducks?—and always hides, from squirrel to bear skins and especially the hides of reindeer and caribou.

The doors were invariably on the south side of the houses, due no doubt to the direction of winter winds and therefore of snowdrifts.

Each house had its dooryard garden, an import from civilization. What vegetables were left at that time grew in straight, well-weeded rows. They included cabbages of enormous size, lettuce, onions and radishes, dwarf celery plants, carrots, potatoes —plenty of vitamins. In this latitude, where the ground is frozen permanently to great depth, gardens are possible only on sandspits and river bars; there the adjacent water thaws out the ground during summer. The summer at Unalakleet had been short, but with sunshine most of the day and night the vegetables had grown well and fast.

I had heard murmurs in Nome that the Eskimos lived hand-to-mouth. A garden was thrifty—but where were the fuel supplies? Near the doors of the cabins were scant piles of sticks, not more in each case than a stove would consume in a day or two. In Wyoming the woodpile with which I began a winter was almost as large as the cabin itself, and the logs were all gone by spring. Hadn't the Eskimos started to get in their cold-weather firewood yet?

The answer, I later learned, was that gathering wood was a

dog-team operation. The occupation in summer was the securing of Nature's harvests. In most of the dooryards stood kegs of berries and tubfuls of silver salmon. Much greater quantities of the fish, beheaded and trimmed, hung like scarlet fringe from high rustic racks. Besides other meat, it takes about five thousand fish a year to feed one Eskimo family and its dogs. Some fish are available in the winter at Unalakleet: tomcod snagged under the sea ice, and trout trapped under the river ice in a few places where warm springs keep the river open. Most of the fish, however, are taken in summer months.

Also drying up on the racks were slabs of white-whale skin and strips of blubber, and nearly black meat, the innermost flesh of the whales. Bonfires of birch logs to smoke the meat and fish were smouldering under some of the racks. A few families had little smokehouses, with wisps of smoke drifting out from cracks.

The racks were versatile pieces of architecture. They were up in the air like the caches; some, in fact, were extensions of those small, elevated storehouses. The poles forming the floor of the cache would continue out at the back for ten to perhaps twenty feet, and over these hung the fish and meat. Fishnets also were drying, draped with misty grace from the ends of the poles. And then up on the racks, lying across the poles, were the family dog sled and *kayak*. Finally the racks functioned in still one more way: most of them had a superstructure built like the bare frame of a house, and high on the tilting slope of the timbers were stretchers with skins of seals and beluga whales laced onto them. The skins were taut, white-to-yellow translucent tissue, four to twelve feet in length, and nothing in town was prettier. They were so bright, with the light from the sky shining through, that they seemed to be giant overhead lanterns.

The *kayaks* were the Eskimos' small, shallow hunting canoes, entirely covered with skin or canvas except for a hole in the deck where the hunter sits. They were not the Eskimos' only boats. All along the lagoon side of the sandspit were moored larger ones of the dinghy type, apparently made by the owners. Some were powered by oars, but many were rigged for outboard motors. Most of the motors had been detached and carried up to the cabins, and if that was done every night, such care would indicate how much the Eskimos prized at least one of the white-man's inventions.

Besides motors, guns, and various metal tools, the elements of our culture most in evidence were the many galvanized-iron tubs and pails. The first washtubs the Eskimos ever saw, the first large containers they had, must have done much towards winning them to the white-man's ways. By the time I arrived, water supplies were kept in old oil drums, and I wondered what would have been used to hold water, even in drinking quantities, before tubs and barrels were brought to this coast. Animal skins, perhaps.

The water at Unalakleet came from several miles up the river —in summer by boat; in winter, as ice, by dog sled. When I learned where the trading post got its water, I worried: if the river started to freeze before snow had fallen, there might be too much ice to use boats but not enough to support the dog teams. Boats and, later, dogs were our only means of getting across the marsh. I asked Eula, the trader's Eskimo wife, about this. Her only reply was, "It will be all right"—said with a frown, because one with a quiet mind would not try to solve problems like this before they arose. And it *was* all right. One day the river was, indeed, too filled with slush to progress with a boat in it, but that night the wind and the temperature fell, and the next morning the ice on the river's surface was as smooth as glass and four inches thick. Dogs could not run on it till it was covered with snow, but the men skated up, pushing the sleds with the water barrels ahead of them.

On my first tour of the town it appeared that the civilized contributions had made the activities of the Eskimos easier but had not replaced them in any important way. The natives were hunters and fishermen still; they trapped, used animal skins for warmth, lived in houses built not of processed materials but materials of the earth. When I saw the insides of the houses I found stoves, tables, a few chairs and cots—never as many as there were people that lived in the house. In that country two or three caribou skins make a better bed than an inner-spring mattress does. Yet on one of the clotheslines, that first morning, were three sheets in the new pastel shades.

It was going to be fascinating to see where the Eskimos stood in this conflict of cultures: basically in theirs, in ours, or uncomfortably between? And what would determine the answer— the container in which they kept drinking-water, or the way that they spent their days? How they spent their days would have the most meaning, I thought, as I wandered on through the village, which still was sleeping although now the time was past ten o'clock.

As I passed one little homestead after another, it was impressive to see how much more it was than a place to eat and sleep. The Eskimos, who were classed as a Stone-Age people when white men first came to this coast, had even then rather elaborate tools. Some are used, unchanged, today, and are very ingenious and practical. It must be a great satisfaction to walk up the path to one's cabin in Unalakleet, with its tethered dog team and sled, at least two kinds of boats, the rack to smoke fish and meat and the cache for storing it, the frames for drying skins and the articles made of the skins: clothing and several kinds of boots, including snowshoes. Add a gun (formerly a harpoon) and you have a life.

In 1954 I was back in the village, and at the request of Alaska's civil-defense director I asked the Eskimos for a list of the civilized things they thought should be stockpiled in case they should ever be isolated by war. All they considered essential were ammunition and canned or powdered milk for the children. They would be glad to have fishnet twine and rope, but in a pinch they could make those from hides.

During my first autumn there, Dwight Milligrook and his family from Nome moved back to the village, where once they had lived. He had done well in Nome; at the time they returned they had a good-sized savings account in the Nome bank, Dwight told me. However he said, "I have money and I still have my house here, but I have nothing else now—no dogs, no sled, no boat, fishnets, traps, not even an ax. And I can't buy most of those things. I am a poor man."

It was easy to see why that Eskimo thought of his neighbors at Unalakleet as rich. Even a newcomer might share that view in a year when the wildlife was plentiful and the caches were full of meat.

Bering Sea Walden

THE first Eskimo that I talked to that morning was about two years old, a baby boy playing out of doors, quite naked except for a short cotton shirt. Thinking that he had escaped from his family unnoticed and surely would catch a cold, I took one of his hands. It was warmer than mine, which had been in my down-coat pocket. Finding his feet and legs also warm, I decided I had no business to try to get him to go indoors.

Shy but not frightened, his dark eyes looked out from his round, ruddy face while I knelt beside him, attempting without success to get him to say a word or two. He turned away from me, with a flicker of smile. It was a lingering smile, seeming courteous, seeming to say that he was not leaving me, it was just that this sand, here, had to be patted now. As he turned over, his Mongoloid mark came uppermost. It showed as a bruise-colored patch at the base of his spine, a mark which is found at birth on most children of Mongoloid blood and which usually disappears later.

I went down to the beach, where the waves were casting up some of the ocean's discards. Before the sea froze, I wished to collect evidence of the life in its waters, for I would be writing about the marine animals and I needed to know what food these creatures were able to find in the depths. In a few minutes I had gathered sand dollars, clamshells, the carapaces of soft-shell crabs, and the egg cases made by marine worms, though I didn't know at the time what they were: little, pocked collar-shapes apparently fashioned of mud. The gold threads of purple-black mussels had tangled pieces of some of them into their colonies, which also included small shellfish, weighted down with sharp, stony barnacles.

An Eskimo came along the beach trundling a homemade wheelbarrow. He walked with an eager step, smiled as he passed, went on, and stopped a short distance farther. He too began picking up mussels. That was a delicate kind of approach, I thought: he went beyond where I was in case I did not want to talk, but only so far that my own collecting could make it natural for me to join him if I should wish. I worked up in his direction.

When I was near, he swept an arm towards the ocean.

"Pretty soon all ice out there. Interesting, to see how ice will be. Every year different." He spoke with vitality and with only a moderate accent. In the Eskimos' language, and also in ours when they speak it, there is a curious knobby effect, with the emphases like a series of vocal bumps. This man sounded almost as if he might be a European.

I asked if the sea would be frozen as far out as we could see.

"Maybe," he said. "Sometimes only two, three miles—to the bar. Sometimes twenty, twenty-five miles."

"Beyond that will there be open water?"

"Not much open water. Out beyond shore-ice will be big floating pack. Drifts around. When big wind blows in from the ocean, that pack-ice comes toward the shore fast. It hits edge of shore-ice, and BANG!" The man's arms flew up. "Edge of ice buckles way up like wall, higher than house sometimes. Pressure ridge, white people call it. Some years shore-ice gets heaved every place, all the way in to beach. Big jagged heaps. Then we have to cut trail out through ice. Lots of work, but we have to get our boats out to water."

"Do you go out to the open water to fish?" I asked.

"To get seals. We fish through the ice, close to beach, down through holes. Upriver we catch fish in traps."

All this sounded like cold, rugged work, but it was evident that the prospect of it was filling the man with zest. "Ice come pretty soon now," he finished gaily, with one of his frequent smiles.

Starting to gather his mussels again, the man darted in and out of the water. Most of his clothes had come from the States: a sweater and cords and a hunter's cap. But he wore Eskimo boots, and I asked him if they were waterproof. "Better than rubber," he said. "My wife make them. *Oogruk* skin rubbed with seal oil. Keep out water just fine. Threads are sinew. When they get wet, threads swell up, get bigger. No water can get through the stitches." At the top of the boots were hems with draw-strings pulling them tight around the man's knees.

Continuing work, he said,

"My grandsons like clams we buy in the store in cans. I like fresh mussels better. Besides, nice, picking them up." I said,

"In California some people have died from eating mussels during the summer. They may be poisonous then. In winter they are all right."

"Same here," said the Eskimo. "We never eat mussels till fall time."

"The white men, the scientists, didn't discover the poison until a few years ago. The news got to Unalakleet pretty fast."

"Eskimos always know," he replied. "When I was a boy my mother said, 'Never eat mussels till just before freeze-up.'" His manner in telling this was not boastful. It merely implied respect for his people's experience. I felt very humbled, however. This was the first of many times that something I'd say would reveal a white-person's ingrained assumption that our ways are superior, often to find that the Eskimos were ahead of me. "The white men discovered . . . The news got to Unalakleet . . ." Before civilized research chemists found that some toxic substance exists in mussels from May to September, white people in California thought that cases of mussel poisoning were due to the eating of mussels with broken shells, which had become contaminated. The Eskimos had known better. Why not suppose they might?

I asked the man if there were other poisonous foods on this coast. He said yes, the plant called beaver poison. "People die if they eat the root, but other parts of plant only make them little bit sick."

Many small clamshells were strewn on the sand, each with its fatal hole bored by a marine worm, through which the worm had sucked out the clam. That was one of the ecological factors that I was studying, and I asked where the clam beds were. The Eskimo said,

"I don't really know, but I think maybe off Tolstoy Point. That's about forty miles from here, toward St. Michael. When we catch white beluga whales here, lots of fresh clams in their stomachs. Whales swim pretty fast, though. Maybe clam beds not so near." I began to understand why I had been told that I could trust the observations of Eskimos. This man's conclusions, careful and skeptical, were like those of a scientist.

He was slighter in build, with a narrower face and less prominent cheekbones than the Eskimos I had seen in Nome. Unlike the others too, many of whom have no facial hair, he wore a full, graying, walrus moustache. I judged him to be about sixty, though very active. As he was picking up mussels, he was bending as easily as a child, and was gesturing as he talked with free, lively movements. I asked him if he had been born in Unalakleet.

"Right here, seventy-six years ago. My father was Russian. Unalakleet was Russian trading post once. When United States bought Alaska, my father stayed. He married Eskimo woman, my mother. I married Eskimo woman, myself. Very fine wife. You will meet her.

"We had three sons, one daughter. Two of my sons have died. One drowned. You hear of the boat, the *Good Hope?*" I told him I had. "I built that boat, at Shaktolik. I build lots of boats, but the *Good Hope* was my best. Anyway, I think so. My son was captain. Next thing, that boat went down and my son was lost." As he said those words, his manner and voice remained firm, but his eyes brimmed with tears. "Fifteen years ago."

We went back to searching for mussels.

I told this man something about my project and showed him my own little hoard of shells. He identified the worms' egg cases, and then, "I can help you," he said emphatically. "I can find things for you. Maybe you would like to go out to my whale net some day, in my boat?"

I told him I'd be delighted. I asked his name.

"Russian name, Stefan Ivanof. Eskimo name, Solovelik." I asked him what I should call him. "Stefan would be just fine," he said.

What a thoroughly good little man, I thought as I said good-by to him, so enthusiastic and yet with no self-assertiveness. Soon I learned that he was the U.S. commissioner at Unalakleet, and was a fabulous hunter, the best in the village. One day later that winter during a storm, when the temperature dipped to 40° below zero, Stefan was the only one who went out to his trap-line. He was gone several hours and came home with a beautiful fox. "I am glad I went," he said. "That fox was alive. I would not want him to have to freeze to death."

By the time Stefan went home with his mussels that morning, the sound of an outboard motor was jolting the air. A boat, handmade of wooden planks, came out through the mouth of the river, turned north, and stopped at one of the several gillnets that were hung out in the sea on floats. Somewhere someone was chopping wood, and other people were moving around their dooryards. The village was starting its day.

Following one of the paths from the beach to the center lane, I came on a woman who was preparing a tubful of salmon for drying. She sat on a stool outside one of the cabins, with a low, improvised plywood table in front of her. On her right was the tub brimming with salmon, some nearly three feet long. Two buckets stood on the table across from her, one for the salmon entrails and one that held water. In a tub on her left were the finished pieces of fish, and there too was a pail for the heads, dog food possibly.

A professor of time-and-motion studies could not have arranged the equipment better.

The cutting was done with a homemade knife shaped like a chopping knife—an *ulu*, as it is called. As the woman held it, the handle was not against her palm but was under her forefinger, with her thumb gripping the side. In this position the knife was like an extension of her own hand, and that was the way she used it, slicing into the fish with circular motions that swung all the way from her shoulder.

With a quick thrust of the knife she would first cut off a salmon's head. Then she slit the fish down its belly, deep enough to expose the entrails. These were separated from their attachments, and the head and entrails went into their different buckets. The knife slid down the back, as deep as the belly cut, thus freeing the spine and its radiating bones, which were lifted out all in one piece and detached from the tail. The tail was not severed. At the end of this operation the woman had two large fillets, the two sides of the fish, joined at the tail, from which they would be suspended over a pole on her drying-rack. A dip in the water to clean them, and they were dropped into the final bucket.

It is interesting to see a good craftsman at work, and I asked the woman if I could stay and watch. She looked up with a smile and then said to a boy who stood near, "Maybe get box, eh?" From the cabin he brought a crate, and she indicated that I should sit down.

As she continued to dress the fish, she was silent and yet obviously not because she was shy or embarrassed. I had expected to talk, but the woman had dignity that was like a quieting hand, and so there we sat, without a word, and in some way that was new to me, we were becoming acquainted.

The farthest place—Nome in winter.

Off the beach at Nome: shelf-ice buckled by wind-driven floating pack.

Eskimos in bright parki-covers meet at "The Glue Pot."

The Snake River at Nome, channeled by high revetments.

Unalakleet, at the tip of its sandspit on Norton Sound.

The frozen Unalakleet River is a dog-sled trail in winter. Left, a bush plane; right, a meat cache.

Stefan Ivanof, Russian-Eskimo boat-builder, U.S. Commissioner, gardener, and champion hunter of Unalakleet.

Unalakleet Trading Post: "Charles Traeger, General Merchandise."

Eskimo islanders from Little Diomede carving walrus-tusk souvenirs.

Two of the Eskimos' ingenious tools: elements of the famous bow-drill, and root-picks for digging wild roots.

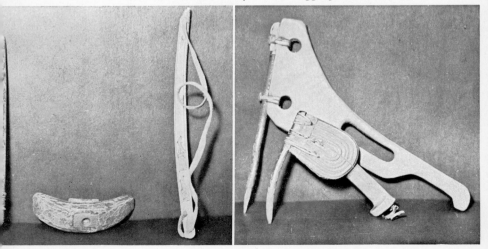

Eskimos in their kayaks.

David Paniptchuk, linguist and expert kayak-builder.

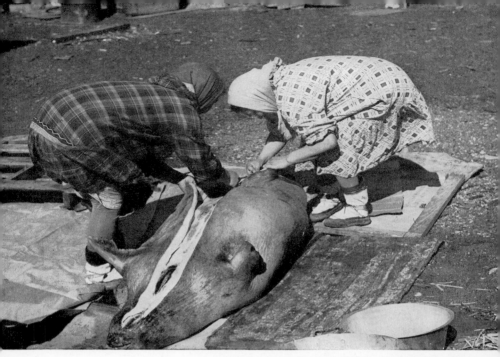

Carving the hunter's kill is a woman's work.

Moonlight at midday in the world of the Eskimo hunter.

Mrs. Abraham Lincoln with boots she has made.

Accibuk, gifted story-teller and once a famous medicine man.

She seemed about forty, was plump but no more so than any mature white woman who does not diet. She was wearing a parki with blue-printed cotton cover, the hood pushed back from her straight, black, braided hair, and a man's cotton shirt over the whole, no doubt to protect her own clothes. *Parki*, incidentally, is the way the word is pronounced in the North. It is of Russian-Siberian origin, and was introduced as the name of the shirts of bird skins worn in the Aleutian Islands.

The woman's sleeves were pushed up, and anyone new to the Eskimos would observe that her arms did not taper much; they were moderately, roundly full in all their length, like a child's. The face bending above the table was definitely adult however, handsome and clear-skinned, with hair parted above a smooth brow. Her expression was firm but not fixed. Her smile came readily, and she had no frowning lines on her forehead or at the sides of her mouth. She looked strong, the kind of person I characterize to myself as "a fine creature."

Finally we did talk a little, beginning with telling each other our names. Hers was Gertie Auliye. The trader had said that the salmon runs had held up well all summer, and I asked Gertie if the fish were more plentiful this year than usually. She was not willing to say so. "All right this year," she replied, her voice noncommittal. She added, "Maybe nobody go hungry next winter."

"Is everyone fishing?" I asked.

"Some women are picking berries now. And some people can't fish. They're too old or sick. Others will give to them." As if prompted then by the thought of a gift, she said, "Maybe you would like salmon for dinner?" She flipped over some of the finished fillets until she found one of the largest pairs. "My son will take it to trader's. I'll send some greens, we call wild celery. Very good with fish. Just eat greens without cooking."

Everywhere in the village something was happening now. Some of the women were doing what women do everywhere: taking a wash off the clothesline, getting vegetables from the garden, walking along the path to the trading post or the Native Store. Others were doing more typical Eskimo tasks.

One, who sat on her doorstep, was at work on the skin of a seal. The hair had been taken off the skin and all the openings had been sewed up tight except for a small space left at the mouth. Into this hole the woman inserted a hollow, whistle-shaped piece of bone. Tightly she tied the lips of the seal around it, using a leather thong. Through the hole in the bone she blew into the skin till the skin bellowed out like a black balloon of a body. With a peg of wood the woman stoppered the mouthpiece, looked at the skin with apparent satisfaction, and put it up on the family drying-rack. I said,

"I'm wondering what the skin would be used for."

The woman did not reply. Perhaps she did not know English, for just then she said something in Eskimo to a child who came running by, and the little girl asked, "You want something?"

"I was just wondering what will be done with that skin on the rack."

"We put seal oil in it." And she skipped away.

On the main path I met a woman walking out towards the tundra, no doubt going for berries. She carried a beautiful little pail made of a thin slab of wood whose ends had been bent around and laced together with thongs of hide. On her back, inside her parki, rode a child who looked at least two years old. He sat heavily on the strap that was suspended across, and around from, his mother's chest. But the woman walked buoy-antly. She smiled as she talked to several other children who darted and danced along with her. Each carried his empty tin can or small bucket. All the children could not have been hers, for three or four appeared to be the same age, about nine. Through most of the day I could see them, bright in their parki covers among distant bushes. Other groups like them were out at the base of the foothills, the children, including boys, busily picking berries.

Children were everywhere. Whatever an adult was doing, he

had his audience of bright eyes in pleasant small faces; or the children played their own games, but not far away. Most of their play was silent. Sometimes the boys and girls laughed, and a few times I heard a musical, drawn-out "Ooooh!" from some girl, but no yelling, no squeals or taunts, none of those wordless bellows most of us think of as being the overflow of high youthful spirits.

The men of the town were individually busy at different kinds of work. This was a Tuesday, and yet their jobs appeared chiefly to be the kind that a Stateside husband does on Saturdays or a holiday. One man was caulking the logs of his cabin with moss, another was splicing a dog harness, still another was mending a fishnet. Two or three worked on their outboard motors and guns. An older man with a sensitive, knowing face—Accibuk, who was later to tell me wonderful tales—was carving a mask. A tall, slim young fellow stood on the roof of his house for a long time, staring out over the ocean. I thought that he might be looking for signs of whales or seals.

Boats seemed the men's chief concern however, and they handled them with such skill and such evident pleasure that the comment of Robert Louis Stevenson came to my mind: "For will anyone tell me that business is more entertaining than fooling among boats? He must never have seen a boat, or seen an office, who says so." These Eskimos never had seen an office, but they certainly did enjoy fooling among their boats.

Most of them stood as they rode around. They had extended the rudder handles so that the man operating the outboard motor could reach it while he was on his feet, and anyone with him stood too, in the bow. Their balance, even out in the Bering Sea waves, which were still rather high, was remarkable. When he beached his boat, one of the men, sure-footed and light, ran the full length of it on the edge of the gunwale.

Some were bringing home water in tubs. But most of the boats were arriving with fish. Those that went up the river set out with seines; in those that came back the crew stood knee-high in salmon. I heard a man estimate that one boatload weighed half a ton.

A boy on the beach explained,

"Everybody have fish camps. When we get to our camp, one man stay on shore, other men go out in boat around fish, dropping down net, real slow." Apparently neighbors helped one another, for when they returned, the fish were divided carefully, one by one, on the beach. They were carried up to the cabins in wheelbarrows; then the wives went to work on them. No Eskimo men were engaged in cleaning the fish.

The hunter who watched from his roof left his post. He came down to the beach with his *kayak*, waded out with it into about two feet of water, stepped into his light little skiff, and seated himself in the hole in the skin-covered deck. He was wearing an Eskimo raincoat, a parki-like garment made from the guts of *oogruk*, the bearded seal. The coat had a hood. A draw-string gathered the hood close to the hunter's face; at the wrists too it was snug. He tied the hem of the coat with a rope over the wooden hoop rimming the hole in the deck: in effect the coat sealed up the opening in the *kayak*, so that the man and boat were a nearly watertight unit—a clever arrangement, for water would surely break over the deck, which was only a hand's width above the surface. The Eskimo did not delay. A dip of his paddle, and man and *kayak* sped over the waves as if they were one, fleet, sea-going bird.

Soon it appeared that he had gone out on the sea chiefly to practice his skill in handling his tiny boat. He paddled against the waves for a time, cutting through them as clean as a polished splinter of bone. He quartered across them, a feat taking somewhat more effort, and then he sped back and forth parallel to the crests, so that briefly he would be perched on the ridge of a wave and then it would cave out from below him, dropping him into its trough. If he had been chasing a seal, the hunter would not often have been able to go in the safest direction, and so, this day too, he was making himself cope with hazards.

I was using binoculars and had the *kayak* in focus, out there under the curl of a giant wave, when a sickening sight appeared in the little glass circles: the *kayak* tipped over! A new wave had begun to heave under the boat, slantwise beneath its side, the rider was tilting frightfully, and suddenly he was gone.

After the *kayak* upset, its light bottom showed briefly. The *kayak* turned onto its side. Still farther it turned . . . the hunter's drenched figure showed there at the surface and—a marvel!— rose out of the water, forced up by a mighty thrust of the paddle.

Now he was right-side up and I could begin to breathe again. But too soon! For he had gone over a second time—then once more came safely out. By that time I understood that the stunt was part of his practice. The strength he put into the push of his paddle could only be guessed, but, with pauses to rest, he capsized himself several times. The reason, of course, was that if he could do it deliberately, he would be safer in case wind or waves tipped him over when he was hunting.

It seemed a perilous chance to take, and yet courage does have rewards—at the moment exhilaration, and later, dignity. When the fellow was back on land, he walked with a kind of suppressed elation, I thought. Several men on the beach had been watching him, and when he passed them they shot frankly approving glances in his direction.

Armistice

AFTER lunch I decided that I had better begin my wildlife-observing. Almost any day snow would fall and the river would freeze. Before winter closed down, I wanted to follow the river back into the mountains, to see the trees that were filling the valley with clobbered shade, to see what the banks were like, steep or dissolving away into ponds. I would visit that country by dog sled in winter, but the wildlife could be understood better if some of their riverside trails and dens were seen without snow on them. I set about finding an Eskimo who would take me up in his boat.

Near one of the better-built cabins a man of about thirty was tending a bonfire. He was taller than most of the natives, also darker, with chalk-white teeth, some of them missing. Since his wiry black hair was cut very short on the sides and left long on top, it gave an exclamatory look to his face, and the look was intensified by his eyes. They were almost ferocious until he smiled; then his face broke into friendliness.

In what talking we did, his manner was very direct, as if he were seeing me as a human being, a woman and white only incidentally, and no artificial barriers need be set up between our minds. That matter-of-fact attitude was to be typical of the Eskimo men and was to make it easy for us to share our interest in the animals I was studying.

In his bonfire the man had six or eight knots of driftwood. When they were thoroughly charred on the surface, he drew them out and added them to a smoking pile of such knots at one side. I asked, "Are you making charcoal?" He answered that he was making floats for his whale net: "If they are black they are easy to see when the sea has white light on it. They are cheaper than cork, and better."

I introduced myself, explained why I had come to Unalakleet, said that I'd like to see the river before the freeze-up, and asked, would he take me this afternoon in his boat? Turning back to his fire, he said,

"My boy little bit sick. I think my wife need me."

A little bit sick didn't sound very convincing; probably he did not understand that I was offering him employment. I said, "I would expect to pay you. It would be worth at least five dollars for me to go."

He continued to rake at the driftwood knots, but he did not answer. When I still stood there, he went in his house and quietly closed the door.

On a tussock of grass not far away sat a neighbor who seemed to have nothing to do. He sat with his hands clasped between his knees, looking out over the marsh towards the mountains. When I told him my story, he shook his head. Now it occurred to me that perhaps five dollars was not enough. Gasoline was expensive here—I should have thought of that. Quite confidently, then, I said, "I'll be willing to raise the pay to ten dollars." The fellow again shook his head. "Maybe that man over there take you. He needs money."

That man over there was cleaning a rifle, sitting at ease on a piece of firewood. I went over to talk to him. We were both smiling; the prospect appeared to be promising, but by now it had come to seem almost essential to get up that river, and so, when I told the man what I wanted, I said, "I'll offer you fifteen dollars."

A look almost of anger flashed into the Eskimo's face.

"It's not worth fifteen dollars," he said.

"Whatever you wish," I urged. "You can name the price." But he would not go. "I have to be fixing my rifle," was all he would answer.

I felt quite abashed. Here I was, living among Eskimos for the purpose of learning about arctic animals from them. If most of them were unwilling to help me, even to run a boat for an hour or two, what were the chances of getting the much greater co-operation that would be needed—the answers to thousands of questions, and the observations I hoped they would volunteer?

I went back to the trading post and asked the trader what had been wrong in the way I'd approached the three men.

"Maybe you urged them a little too hard," he said. "They don't like to feel pushed. But that might not be it. No Eskimo likes to work for another person—especially for money, it seems. If you'd just asked them to let you go along the next time they went up-river, they probably would have been glad to take you for nothing.

"That way they could have felt independent—free. They just have to be free, they think. If they don't feel free, they are so depressed that they aren't worth much."

"How do you get them to work for you?" I asked. He had several in the store, and others were sawing up wood, getting water, and doing various chores.

"Two are half-breeds," he answered. "Half-breeds can stand routine better. On a nice day some of the others are likely not to show up. They're out fishing or hunting. I have a big enough crew so that we can keep going if some of them are not here. If they know they can come or not as they please, it isn't so hard to come." He smiled understandingly.

In the evening I went out again for a walk on the beach. Farther along a woman appeared, pulling a sled. I hoped I could talk to her, and so, following Stefan's example, I passed her but stopped a short way beyond, where I resumed my earlier search for shells.

The woman was gathering driftwood, small pieces that she could put into a gunny sack. The sack stood on her sled. Apparently she assumed that I was collecting my dinner, for soon she came to me with a handful of mussels and, as she offered them, made a delicate motion towards her mouth, as if to say, Mussels are good. I thanked her and added the mussels to those in my pocket.

She was a really old person, her face webbed with lines, but she was dressed as prettily as a girl, in a pink, bell-shaped parki, with a pink and green scarf on her snow-white hair. She did not turn away but stood smiling, so radiantly that I was astounded by her sheer beauty. Travelers to the North always mention the smiles of the Eskimos, and during the day I had thought I knew why. For everywhere I had been greeted with smiles, which had been remarkable for the genuine welcome they seemed to express, and for the ease with which they had come. The old woman's smile was surpassing them all. What it conveyed was a transcendent kindliness. I believe that she realized I was a little lonely, and the thought moved her to tenderness of the purest sort. She smiled, and the loneliness melted.

"Do you speak English?" I asked. She answered with a few words of Eskimo. Illogically, I said, "It does not matter. We understand each other. Let me help you gather your wood."

As often as I picked up a right-sized stick, she would find a mussel. Her gunny sack and my pockets filled up all too fast. She was very communicative. One of her pieces of wood resembled a fish, and she commented on it by a chuckle and rippling her hand. She showed her pleasure in the white tissue wings of a late flock of snow buntings suddenly taking flight from the beach grass. And once her serene brown eyes met mine with a message that plainly meant, *Look,* and her gaze shifted up to a patch of bright yellow willow brush on a hillside. Through a rent in the clouds the sun fell on it. I had been missing it, but the old eyes had found it.

This part of the shore was beyond the last cabins and, to go home, the woman was pulling her sled on a tundra path. I helped of course. I was admiring the nimble way that her feet in their soft-soled *mukluks* were finding their way on the lumpy surface, when she stopped suddenly with a small cry of pleasure. She pressed a foot here and there and then dropped to her knees and quickly started to tear up the moss. Below was a hoard of *masu* roots, the winter store of a tundra mouse. Eskimos eat them, I later learned.

Two little girls were near, picking wild cranberries. The woman motioned for them to come and then with a few words of Eskimo sent them scampering back to her cabin. The first girl returned with an empty sack into which she and her grandmother—for the woman seemed to be that—scooped up the roots. The other girl had brought back a fish head. When the roots were all gathered, the fish head was put in the ground and the moss on the surface was smoothed. I asked the older girl why they had left the fish head. "For mouse," she said. "When we take roots, we always leave mouse something else."

I returned to the beach. There was a lift in the air, something so fresh and light that I was not ready yet to go back to the trading post. The events of the day were weaving themselves into a thought—what? I wanted to find it.

This was it, but it was less a thought than a sensation: that all pressures had been removed. In Unalakleet there was no coercion. Strange, that this, which was the natural state, could be almost a shock!

How much pressure there was in the civilization that I had left! *Vote! . . . Slow . . . Teach your child to . . . Don't wait . . . Come in today . . . Phone . . . Scrapbook this case . . . Bring your problems . . . Write your Congressmen . . . Try this . . . Drink* (beer, Scotch, coffee, cola, milk) *. . . Smoke* (so many brands: what warfare in the realm of our minds where suggestions lodge) *. . . Listen tomorrow . . . Let us . . . See your dentist . . . Give! . . . Wear these . . . Learn how to . . . Make sure that . . . Hurry . . .*

Even headlines were compulsive, for who would not have to know why BOY, 11, MURDERS FATHER . . . 40 DEAD IN PLANE CRASH . . . FIEND RAPES, SLAYS GIRL, 9 . . . PARLEY ENDS IN DISCORD . . .

"Good morning, lady, just give me a moment of your time to show you—" "Your first payment won't be due till next month, and I'll get the machine out today—" "Just sign here—"

In Unalakleet nobody wanting to run your life, no commercials or billboards, no politicians or propaganda. No selling. At noon I had asked a clerk in the trading post for a package of raisins. He drew me aside: "I'll get them for you," he said. "We keep a lot of our goods in the basement, out of sight, because they won't last till next summer's boat anyway. You just ask me privately if you want anything you don't see."

Here no one was acting busy to make a favorable impression upon a boss, or slowing down because a union official had told him to. And no newspapers; was it only this morning that I had been disappointed not to have any news? Instead of neon signs there would be Northern Lights reflected in still tundra ponds, the phantom of a phantom. As I started back to the trading post I was thinking, A battlefield would feel like this on the day of an armistice, when the guns suddenly ceased.

On the center lane, then, I met an Eskimo that the trader had introduced at lunch: David Paniptchuk. He took care of the trader's dogs and had come to the post to report one of them sick. Now he approached me, accompanied by two native men. They stopped in my path.

"Good evening!" said David, in a fluent and hearty voice. "I'd like to ask you a personal question. May I?"

"You can ask it. I may not answer it."

"Are you interested in church work?"

"Why— Of course."

"What church do you belong to?"

"Sometimes I go to a church of all faiths."

"Oh, a federated church."

"No, it's broader than that. It's for everybody. All nationalities."

David would have it different:

"There's a federated church in Nome, too. I have been there."

Squaring back, with an even more purposeful manner, he continued:

"At our church here we have two services every Sunday. In the morning the missionary preaches in English, and in the evening I preach in Eskimo. I have been the interpreter in the church since nineteen-oh-six. Will you come?"

Once, changing buses in a Los Angeles slum, I had been the sole audience for an earnest Salvation Army troop. Now I remembered that embarrassing experience as David looked me in the eye sharply and went on:

"If you are going to be here for some time, I am sure you will want to help with our work. Will you be with us next Sunday?"

My sense of coercion had snapped into rebellion.

"Some Sunday. But don't count on me. I have come a long way and I have a big job to do."

"We'll be hoping to see you." His smile was almost a command, and I started to back away. David raised his voice:

"Your mother—is she a good Christian woman?"

"Oh, definitely!" I turned and fled down the path.

I didn't know whether to be annoyed or amused that, after all my early attendance at Sunday School, after all my donations in those days "to carry the Word to the heathen savages," I should be having Christianity pressed upon me insistently by an Eskimo up on the shore of the Bering Sea. The incongruity won. As I climbed the trading-post stairs, I was laughing.

3

Outpost

"SHE HAS ALL THIS," Charlie Traeger said, waving his hand across shelves of canned fruit from the States, "but she wants to go out and pick berries."

It was his Eskimo wife that he spoke of. She was away on a camping trip when I came. As new storms, with a high wind, hurled rain on the coast, I suggested that maybe the weather would bring back his wife before he expected her. The old man shook his head: "It was just as bad when she left." He was impatient to have her return, but his tone showed forbearance. "Every so often a native just has to stay out of doors for a while," he said.

Mr. Traeger had been the trader at Unalakleet for forty years. Although over eighty, and half sick with neuralgia and other ills, he insisted on doing the cooking himself, always refusing my help. Clad in a bathrobe over pajamas, and a fur cap, and with eyes watering with pain, he would drag his slippers from cupboard to stove. When the meal was ready, then, there would be mushrooms in the gravy and a sauce for the salmon—delicious as food only is when the cook is by nature an epicure.

The family included a boy of four, Clairon, who had been left at home because he had had a cold. He had been taught to say grace, in his own words, which changed from meal to meal but usually ended, "And help ev'body to be nice." I think that each time our amiability was raised a notch by the little prayer, but not to the point where the suffering trader wanted to talk. As we ate, the bleakly silent old man, the shy child, and I, each was listening to his own thoughts, the roar of the cookstove, and the Bering Sea gale whirling the wind battery-charger on the roof.

The trading-post building was two stories high and large for a log structure—forty by eighty feet. It had an outside, enclosed porch to house dog sleds and hunting gear, and to trap the wind before the main door was opened. Half the first floor was the room used as the store and post office. It was rather dark, all the windows being up under the ceiling; otherwise snowdrifts would have covered them in the winter. Some of the merchandise was on shelves under the windows, some hung from the rafters, and some was in showcases, but the cases didn't really display anything, only stowed it. The post office was in a small partitioned area at the back of this room.

Half the rest of the first floor was a stockroom for machinery items and dried fish. In the main line of travel stood a granite bucket filled with tarnished knives and forks; nobody moved it as long as I lived there. The end of the first floor, twenty by forty feet, was the open woodshed. Before winter closed in, it was filled to the second-story level with logs cut to stove-wood size.

My apartment was over the woodshed. It was furnished with nothing but beds and two chairs, since ordinarily it was used as a dormitory for bush pilots. (While I was there, cots were put up in the main lounge of the trading post.) The trader's nephew had once intended to live in those rooms and had fixed them up like an apartment, with a modern sink and built-in cupboards and drawers, and a bathroom painted red and black with a lavatory and tin tub and a "facility," as it is called in Alaska. There is no running water in Unalakleet, or plumbing of any kind, and so the faucets were just for looks, the sink and lavatory for holding washbasins, and the facility was a disguised ten-gallon can.

For water I had a barrel, filled periodically with ice by Ransom Bradley, the chore boy, who lived next door. He also kept me supplied with wood. There were two stoves, neither of which worked very well. One, an oil stove, would burn only at top speed, and its red-hot sides and pipe obviously were dangerous. The other, the wood stove, had the trademark of a manufacturer in the South. He should have been ashamed to have his name on it. It was new and pretty—pale green enamel; to reach Alaska it had been shipped five thousand miles, and it probably had cost plenty. The oven door wouldn't close because one of the hinges had broken almost immediately; two of the lids on the top had cracked; and after three months the lining of the firebox fell out—it had melted. When I was writing I used to sit in my sleeping-bag, with a woodpile near-by, and feed logs into that maddening stove. The draft wouldn't close, and so they burned out every twenty minutes. It was all I could do not to insert, in my descriptions of tundra and swans and whales, a few paragraphs expressing my thoughts of so shoddy a piece of merchandise. What would have happened if that stove had been sent to a Northern family who had no other heating arrangement?

Between my rooms and the trader's living quarters was the main stockroom. The stock was kept by the natives who worked for the trader, and that room told me as much as I ever have learned about the distance that has to be traveled before a primitive people can feel at home in our culture.

We, who are accustomed to having and using literally thousands of products, have learned to assort them. We have learned to organize—not only things, but our time, for we could not lead the complex lives that we do unless we kept both possessions and hours in order. An Eskimo also can organize in his own life. A native wife cleaning salmon, or a man packing his hunting gear, is as efficient as any civilized engineer. But our kinds of possessions are new to them, and new, too, is the bewildering multiplicity.

And so the stockroom was fascinating in the wackiest kind of way: shelves on which, in this sequence, would be stored crepe paper, chamber pots, calico, hinges, Christmas-tree ornaments, walnuts, washtubs—and the arrangement mattered not in the slightest because Eskimos have such good memories that the six men who worked for the trader knew the location of every article on the shelves.

The Traegers' big comfortable kitchen, larger lounge, and a bedroom were arranged more as we would, although they told something about an Eskimo's wish to keep anything that could ever be used again. As Judge Joseph W. Kehoe of Nome once remarked, "It is unfair to say that the Eskimos are not thrifty. They are only not thrifty with money, which is unfamiliar and new to them. In their own villages they save everything they might possibly need, any scrap of fur, or rope, or a brass bolt picked up on the beach. They have had so little. . . ." I remember the pleasure with which one of the men at Unalakleet showed me a few strips of flooring brought in by the tide. "That is very fine wood," he said. "Oak."

When anyone has as many possessions as civilized people do, he discards things without reluctance. The Eskimos also will do that in time. But the trader's wife, who could have almost anything that she wanted, had wanted much and had treasured it all. Therefore the lounge, which held most of it, was a little bewildering. I remember especially a typewriter that her husband had brought to Alaska before 1900, and a wicker fern stand in which real morning glories climbed strings amid crepe-paper roses. Besides the three silent radios, there were nine ageing musical instruments, one a piano whose parts had come unglued from having been stored in excessive cold. An organ that Mrs. Traeger had taught herself to play very well, so her husband told me, was useable.

I was eager to meet Mrs. Traeger. She, a daughter, and other relatives had their camp several miles up the coast. A boat was to go for them. Their return was not mentioned at breakfast or lunch on Saturday, but when I walked through the kitchen during the afternoon, kettles of water steamed on the stove, a rubber bathtub was partly filled, and a slim young girl, very pretty, was brushing her long, wet, black hair. I guessed that the native woman scrubbing the floor was not the wife, nor the one washing clothes, but that Mrs. Traeger was back at home.

When I appeared for dinner she stood in the door of the lounge. No apron, or perspiration on her smooth forehead revealed that she had prepared the meal, though in fact she had. She was cool and sedate, about thirty-eight years old, with a trim figure and wearing a smart black dress, high-heeled pumps, a string of pearl beads, and small diamond earrings. Her hair was short and well curled, and the make-up had been applied with restraint on her creamy-tan skin and full lips. But it was not the good taste of her civilized clothes that impressed me most; it was her innate poise.

I knew at once that my own appearance had disappointed her —my slacks and poplin windbreaker, and hair purposely cut so that it could be washed in pans of river water. I suspected too that she would have preferred my greeting to be more aloof. She did not know how to proceed with this woman naturalist who was not critical, only hoping to be her friend.

She had got together an excellent dinner out of those cans on the shelf: fricasseed chicken with airy dumplings, two vegetables, fruit salad, and hot apple pie. We sat down and I asked her about the camping. She said they had picked five butter-barrels of blueberries. They had slept in tents "with down comfort over us and down comfort under us, but we were c-o-l-d." Eskimos indicate a superlative by lifting their flexible voices and drawing the word out to different lengths, depending upon the degree they mean. Mrs. Traeger held "c-o-l-d" for so long, it suggested "unbearable." She told about losing some food supplies, and how far the campers had had to walk to find berries, all this in a plaintive tone, as if to say that uncivilized ways of spending one's time did not appeal to her. She was tense, guarding every word.

I said I was interested in animals and asked if she'd seen any up the beach. "I did not notice," replied Mrs. Traeger. "The rabbits, Mamma? And the fox on the shore?" her young daughter, Matilda, reminded her. The mother frowned. I told a few anecdotes about my trip from the States. The conversation became an effort. Mrs. Traeger said,

"Last night I had wonderful dream. I dreamed I lived in b-i-g house. I had so many servants I did not know their names. I was sitting in big room. My servants came in, each alone, and I said what I want them to do."

The trader put his hand on her arm, as if to show that he liked her just as she was, but then he made the mistake of introducing a subject that she could not share. Was Geraldine Farrar still singing, he asked. He told how he used to go outside to San Francisco each year for the opera season, a journey that would begin with a thirty-day trip by dog team to Fairbanks. "And finally I would ride up Market Street to the Palace Hotel. . . ." He was a cultivated man, and what an experience that must have been, to find himself in the civilized world again. As he described it, his old eyes had a youthful shine, and his wife of course felt excluded.

I changed the subject and spoke again about Unalakleet. But I think she saw through my purpose and did not like it. Her eyes became darker and her face heavier—a defensive queen.

Eula Traeger was a perfectionist. She was trying very hard to fit into her husband's culture, and in most ways, at most times, she succeeded well. Sometimes she would call us to one of her excellent meals, sit down with us for a moment, and then leave, to pace up and down the lounge, or play the organ, or disappear with a boat or dog team. She might be away for so long that the worried trader would send some of her relatives out to hunt for her, and when she reappeared, from upriver or back on the tundra, she would seem more at peace. Her husband wanted her to conform to his memories of the domestic schedule he had known in his boyhood, seventy years before, a routine so formal that it would have been a strain to almost any white woman today. For an Eskimo it was indeed difficult.

The start of my own friendship with Eula was not very promising, but I liked her, and in the end we understood each other, I think.

The Wild Harvest

"The freeze-up" was heard in all conversations now. The natives spoke of it with a quiet eagerness, but their preparations for winter were no more hurried than Nature's. For quick fires they were burning driftwood, called "squaw wood" since women and children collected it. Later their fuel would be timber, small spruce and birch poles from the riverbanks a few miles away, and coal from an outcropping twelve miles down the beach. They were not getting timber or coal in boats when dog sleds used no gasoline and when it was going to be so enjoyable to be out, snug in one's furs, in the sparkling cold. Now in the white-trader's woodshed, however, an old gasoline saw was chugging through logs all day.

For each season there were appropriate chores, and to an Eskimo it seems fretful and nervous to do in advance things that can wait till a later, more suitable time. Then, in September, was the time to be gathering in the last of the wild harvests.

Every day from the town we could see, across the vivid blue ponds and the tawny grass of the marsh, family groups stooping to strip the berries from the low tangles. Other berry-pickers were making trips up the river. Foods are slow to decay in the North, where most kinds of bacteria do not thrive, but the Eskimos tried to gather their berries as close to the onset of freezing weather as possible.

They were starting the winter with other stored vitamins besides those in berries. Such greens as willow leaves, sour dock, wild celery, and wild rhubarb had been lightly boiled and preserved in seal oil, in pokes. To find some of the hordes of roots gathered by mice, women were walking about on the tundra, probing the ground with sticks. Finally, in the small gardens culti- vated at Unalakleet, enough of the white-man's vegetables had been grown to last through several months. Even in March I was served potatoes and carrots, and blueberry shortcake made with delicious thawed berries. Root vegetables, as well as the wild roots, were stored in sand in the "timber cellars," dugouts beneath the warm cabins.

A government dietician had come to the village two years ear- lier, to teach the natives the white-man's ways of preserving foods. She persuaded the women to buy a canning machine, and they had made articles like aprons, fur socks, and knitted mittens, and sold them to raise the eighty dollars that the machine had cost. There was some village friction about the procuring of it, and when it came, therefore, one group wanted nothing to do with it. The machine had found its way into the missionary's kitchen and nobody seemed to care. During the year I was there, fish were dried, meat was frozen and dried, berries were frozen, and vegetables were stored as they always had been, quite satisfac- torily.

The men were out on the sea for the year's final hunt in the open water. The animals now most plentiful were the white be- luga whales and the large bearded *oogruks*, which were migrating south ahead of the polar ice already moving through Bering Strait, down into the Bering Sea. A beluga whale might weigh a thousand pounds and a bearded seal more than half as much. Sufficient food means survival in two ways in the North. It means an insulating layer of flesh and, if plenty of meat is eaten, a high metabolism. One does not have to be told. Before I had been in Unalakleet a month, I developed an interest in food, a sense of foreboding if, before mealtime, I became hungry, that was in- stinctive and almost irresistible.

One rainy day Stefan Ivanof climbed the stairs to my rooms with the gift of a live tundra vole and an offer to go with him to his whale net. Eula fixed up a quick lunch for me and I joined the Eskimo on the beach. His crew were two nephews, Richard and Kermit. They were stowing guns, a harpoon, extra gasoline, and a huge mound of net in the boat, which was a kind of dory with a flat bottom and flaring sides.

Stefan's net was several miles west of the village, out in the sound. As we rode along he explained that each man had his "place in the sea." I asked him how anyone could identify any "place" on the open water, and he said, "Opposite mine is a little creek come down to the shore."

All three men stood up in the speeding boat, looking intently over the surface, hoping to glimpse a seal's snout or a whale's blowhole. And all of them saw the big seal at the same instant. Their guns came up and Stefan cut back the motor and turned the boat—not towards the spot where the seal had risen and quickly vanished, but in the direction it seemed to be traveling. When ten minutes had passed with no sign of the seal, Stefan stopped the motor and the boat flopped around in the swells for a while. By then the seal must have come up to breathe, but where? With the motor at half speed, then, we putt-putted along slowly. Suddenly the three rifles cracked. The water was nicked by three bullets, all striking within a yard of the spot where a forehead of wet gray fur had, briefly again, broken the surface.

Stefan said that if the seal took the right course it would be out of rifle range by the time it came up for another breath. And now it was warned. I thought that the sea was certainly a good hiding-place. Before guns or motors came to the North, the natives paddling around on the ocean had somehow guessed where a seal or whale would rise and had managed to be at the spot, close enough to throw a harpoon, at the right instant. Securing a food supply in so chancy a way seemed incredible—even that these three men should get the seal would require the very best gamble.

A missionary at Point Hope told me that once he had asked an Eskimo, "How did you ever kill whales before you had outboard motors or guns?"

"Oh, we had songs," said the native. "Magic songs."

"Did they work?"

"Better than guns and motors."

Nothing was said about songs in our boat. After a short conference in Eskimo, Stefan said, "Now we go to the net."

The men continued to scan the ocean, trying to find Stefan's row of charred driftwood floats. It was Stefan who sighted them first. He counted aloud.

". . . three, four. Some floats are not showing! Something is in the net!" His voice was thrilled but controlled, and he quickly added, "Do not get excited."

The rain had stopped and we had a clear view across the surface. A string of floats would appear and then quickly vanish below the water. Soon a large crescent of gleaming white rolled up, out, and down.

"Whale!" cried Kermit.

"Do not get excited," his uncle reminded him.

When the boat came alongside the net we could see the twelve-foot beluga whale down below. Its head was caught through one of the net's large meshes, and it was thrashing about, trying to free itself, every few moments having to come to the surface to breathe. The only color anywhere on its body was the soft blue-gray of its eyes, and it had a curiously human look, with its smooth, naked, white skin, its fleshy lips, and prominent forehead, which Stefan said is a pad of fat "used to bump through thin sea ice when whale has to have air." Each time the whale rose, its breath made a small cloud of steam, exhaled through the blowhole on top of its head. Most times its mouth would be closed, but once it gaped, showing a glimpse of teeth and perfectly white gums and tongue.

It was very disturbing to see the creature so plainly desperate and, much as I dreaded the killing, I wished that the men would hurry and end the whale's anguish.

Richard was going to harpoon it. In turning to pick up his spear, he looked back and discovered a bearded seal, snared in the net behind us. At that Stefan did have difficulty in persuading the younger men to keep calm. Stefan shot the seal in the head, and then came the whale's turn. Richard pressed himself into the boat's narrow prow, with the poised harpoon in his uplifted hand. Since the whale was already caught, he could wait for a chance to drive the harpoon towards the base of its skull. In older times an Eskimo cast it wherever he could; after the tip of the spear had entered the flesh of a whale, the point would come out of the shaft—it was constructed to do that—and a long rope of hide, tied to the point, would trail an inflated sealskin, so that the hunters could follow the whale till their chance came for a fatal dart.

Richard's strike was a perfect one. The dead whale almost floated, and the men, working over the side of the boat, tied a rope to the flukes of its tail. Stefan said we would tow it. They put the seal into the boat. The seal's weight—about 500 pounds, the men thought—was difficult to lift over the side. I perched on the upper edge of the tossing boat, which the men tipped so that they did not have to raise the seal more than two or three inches out of the water. The seal had wrapped itself in several layers of net, shroudlike, by its attempts to escape. The men pulled all that section of net into the boat, put out the new section that we had brought, and made ready to start for home.

They were poling along the net, to be sure it was nowhere tangled, when Richard cried out in Eskimo. They had captured another whale, a younger, smaller one, therefore green-blue in color and not obvious down in the water. This one had caught its head so low, near the rocks that anchored the net, that it could not come up for air and had suffocated. Since the motor did not have enough power to pull both of the whales, Stefan decided to leave the last one where it was and come back the following morning.

Two beluga whales and a bearded seal at one haul: more than a ton of meat! Stefan was tactful enough to say I had brought them luck, and the two young men, who at first had not seemed especially pleased to be having a passenger, smiled approval.

Towing the one heavy whale, we went home at a minnow's pace. The sun did not show itself as the afternoon came to an end, but sank in a glowing rose-violet mist. The wind was down and the water was glossy, a fluid silver that on our left was licked with magenta light. On the opposite side it was tarnished by the deep dusk moving up from behind the land. The shore, backed by low mountains, showed from the sea as only a narrow band across an immensity of darkening space. There was no sight of Unalakleet as yet, our few little cabins, the only settlement on a hundred miles of the coastline—and the only settlement for nearly a hundred-mile distance back over the mountains and tundra too.

The sandbar that extends all along the shore, more than two miles from the beach, is cut in one place by the flow of the river. We missed the channel. On the ebbtide, on which we were coming in, the water over the bar was not deep enough to float our dory, weighted down now with the seal. The boys got out in what seemed midocean and dragged and pushed the boat and the whale across.

It was night when the boat finally scraped on the landing-beach of the slough behind town. I was tired and chilled, but when I came up the stairs into the kitchen, the room was deliciously warm and Eula was lifting out of the oven a sizzling pan of roast white-fronted goose.

Arctic Freeze-up

As THE fall advanced, no more shivering strangers got off the mail plane. Twice a week in that year, about noon, the plane, a DC-3, would approach from the southeast, over the mountains. When it first appeared it looked about the same size as a soaring gull. Planes were our only tie with the rest of mankind since there are no roads in or out of Unalakleet, and I thought then, and still do, that a DC-3 is one of the most beautiful machines that modern man has designed. It would come on, with its uplifted wings and two engines like searching eyes, and when it swerved to the right we knew it would land. Sometimes it didn't. The wind might be hazardous, or the airstrip slippery, or the temperature and humidity might be so combined as to produce icing conditions, the threat Northern pilots so greatly dread. There were periods in the winter when no plane stopped for several weeks, the cold being too great or the airstrip too badly drifted. But most of the time in the fall the plane made its regular calls.

It would circle the airfield beyond the town in a pattern that took it out over the ocean. With a great swoosh, then, it would slant in, just missing the stovepipes, to let down on the very first yards of the runway. That's been called an Alaska landing—as close to the end as possible. The pilots practice it because most Northern airstrips are short.

Anyone who had walked the mile to the field would watch while the pilots and steward heaved out the freight and mail pouches. The big silver door would slam shut, the motors rev up, and the plane would take off for Nome, swinging at once into the clouds above Norton Sound. We would walk back to town, to the warm and welcoming cabins.

Since Unalakleet was a transfer point for mail, some of the sacks were for other villages. Once a week two small, single-engined bush planes would arrive, from north and south, to distribute the mail to the tiny far-scattered settlements on the coast and the riverbanks. Most of the time the bush planes could carry all the mail, although there was a crisis each time the new mail-order catalogues would arrive. And one day the DC-3 disgorged twenty garbage cans. An outsider, visiting one of the villages, had decided it was unsanitary for the natives not to have garbage cans and had persuaded twenty families to send some of their meager dollars away for them. Up in that country every scrap of food is needed to feed the dog teams, and other trash is put out on the ice, which floats it away every spring. But the cans arrived, and the pilot dutifully delivered them, as he had room, over several weeks.

As well as the mail, the bush planes carried supplies ordered from Nome and Bethel and took anyone who was sick or injured to hospitals in those towns. The Bethel plane was on floats and came down on the river. The Nome plane, on wheels, made its landing out on the airstrip. The pilots of both were waiting impatiently for the change to skis, for the time when, in an emergency, they could land almost anywhere. If the river and sea off Unalakleet should congeal with a smooth surface, they would come down on that ice for the rest of the winter. The kind of surface meant even more to the natives, since the river was used as a dog-sled trail and the hunters must cross the shelf-ice with *kayaks* and sleds when they went out to the open water for seals.

On the morning of October ninth the tops of the mountains were white, snow-covered on all the slopes to precisely the same level. A stinging west wind was blowing under a slate-colored sky. During the night the river had frozen in ridges, and everyone was dismayed at the look of the sea. For the wind had deposited off our beach a limitless width of great slabs and cakes of ice, chunks, masses, and knobs heaped together in rigid slush. These had blown into the sound from the edge of the polar pack in the Bering Sea. They were dirty ice, coated with sand and gravel, meaning that somewhere they had been grounded—off one of the lonely islands north of the arctic coast, Herald or Wrangel Island perhaps, or the reefs called the Sea Horses? The scene was appalling. Cutting a trail for the sleds would have been almost impossible; even walking across would have been like a walk through Purgatory.

After a few days, however, the temperature rose and the wind swung to the east. The river ice thawed, and a combination of high tide and a stiff breeze carried away the desolation that could have lain on the sea all winter.

For a week then we had a little Indian summer. But the turn into winter had been made for the Eskimos. They could still have gone out in their boats for whales and continued their berry-picking, but instead the men worked at repairing the dog sleds, and the women at knitting mittens. The last scarlet salmon fringes were taken down from the drying-racks and put into the caches, and in the lounge of the trading post native women were starting to make fur parkis for sale. Their talk, crisply energetic and cheerful, filled the room all day. One could sense their anticipation, excitement, at the impending freeze-up.

Stateside clothes disappeared from the lanes of the village. No more rubber boots clomped along; the men's feet in their *mukluks* trod as resiliently as a fox's feet. The jackets had vanished, and movements were very free in the larger, loose parkis. The faces looked more alert in the wolverine ruffs than they had under caps.

This was the dark of the moon, and so what could be the bright cloud that lay one night like a roll of luminous cotton above the mountains? Its light was shed on the earth, showing the texture of mosses and grasses across the marsh, and silvering the lagoons. In a space of seconds the white cloud folded. Its ends rippled up and together. The cloud was no longer a roll, it was a fabric, drawn high and still higher until it was gauze. It parted, exquisitely rent. Celestial tatters of light were hanging across the North. Now they formed themselves into another roll, a roll becoming a curl, a drawn-out curl, a curve only, a wave, a curl again, shaken, shaken, worried as if by a lofty wind.

The daytime sky, even when cloudy, was always spacious, its beauty changeful and iridescent, and now the Aurora illumined each night. Meanwhile the harvest-bright marsh had faded to straw color, and the lower slopes of the mountains no longer seemed to be gushing springs of wine; they were dusky brown, merging up into the snow's sifted white. The men were still going up-river for water, but the boats moved slowly; the water was heavy and thick with ice crystals. The river, congealing, clutched at the keels of the boats.

The old trader stood on the shore of the slough, wrapped in his fur parki with lavender cotton cover, a wolf ruff surrounding his tissuelike features. He didn't want to miss any of this, although, he said, "I have seen an Alaskan freeze-up fifty-two times." It was still an event. In most parts of the world there is no single momentous occasion like the North's freeze-up and, in spring, the break-up. They are two of the many proofs that Nature rules in the arctic.

Darkness came over the earth that night as quietly as a bird's shadow. The lagoons mirrored the stars, so little stirring them that the reflected points seemed the tips of small torches held up from the depths (and I thought that on nights like this it would have been easy for primitive folk in King Arthur's country to imagine the lighted sword, Excalibur, rising out of the Lake). The temperature was thirty-three.

It had dropped to eight in the morning. The river ice was as smooth as the evening ponds, and transparent: we could see down to the mossy stones on the bottom and could watch the schools of tomcod dreamily swimming. At noon the children joined hands and ran on the ice, all jumping together, when a wide ringing would fill the air. "The ice cry!" shouted the children. It did— and it also broke. Four fell in, but were rescued. Men were skating, some pushing dog sleds ahead of them up the river for tubs of ice, this ice near the river's mouth being too salty. After dinner, in the Aurora's light I saw one of the boys, Leonard Brown, far out on one of the tundra lagoons, skating alone with lyrical skill, expressing his joy at the freeze-up perhaps.

The sea was an absolutely flat plain, a sheet of unbroken glass to the farthest horizon. No more wash of the waves now, and the silence seemed like a great listening. But village sounds became louder as the temperature continued to drop. In the next few weeks it went down to 47° below zero, and in cold like that one can hear a caribou walking two miles away. We were not hearing caribou, but the settlement seemed much more alive when all the voices and closing of doors, even dogs chewing on bones, became audible.

Now the last moisture froze out of the air. As hoarfrost it coated the sea, as it coated everything, with two-inch spicules of crystal. The sea ice appeared to be plush, white until the sun started going down, when the surface shimmered between a gold wash and the minute violet shadows cast by the frost.

Off the river's mouth one small pond remained briefly. Its pale green water was outlined trimly upon the white ice. Three immaculate glaucous-winged gulls floated on it. They did not seem to be fishing, but paddled around slowly. One rose from the water and circled the pond, with his breast gilt in the sun's light, burning dim on the distant horizon. He flew lower and, with his wings lifted, made a soft landing upon the pond again. When the sun was quite gone, as if at a signal all three birds left the water and, taking a steady course, flew away towards the southwest, over the frozen sound.

For seven months they did not come back. For them and for us a new life had begun with the freeze-up.

4

In a Man's World—Men

BECAUSE I AM A WOMAN, yet a naturalist, and have stayed at times in the wilderness, people often remark, "You live in a man's world." My reply was once that nature should be for everyone, that it's too basic and healthful to belong only to men or to women, to old or young. In Alaska, however, I found a world men may have to themselves. It's too rugged for me.

The frozen sea: I have walked out on it many times and have pushed through its broken floes in boats that were safely large and most of them safely powered. But the Eskimos hunt in that realm of glittering danger in little skin *kayaks*, vulnerable to the unpredictable ice, the weather, and animals such as killer whales, walrus, and polar bears. Seeing the hazards, I was surprised that the men even usually return to the land alive. Many times they don't—but such hunting is the supreme experience for the Eskimos. Though they never forget the risk, though they always are apprehensive when they are out on the ice or paddling along its leads, the danger apparently does not diminish their pleasure. Perhaps it enhances it.

In a man's world—men.

From the eager talk about the fall freeze-up I had supposed that the first day the ice was thick enough to support a man, the hunters would set out upon it. They did not go. I asked why and was told, "The leads are not open yet."

The sea mammals that surface for air stay in the leads—if there are any. When the ocean is solidly frozen, one vast plain of ice, as it is in the first few weeks after the freeze-up, the seals make themselves breathing-holes by scratching through from below with the claws of their foreflippers. The other animals are then down at the southern edge of the ice pack. It is after the ice becomes broken that the good hunting develops, and also the insecurity.

Seals are not vicious. They are the gentlest of animals as they swim along in the leads or throw themselves up on top of the ice pans to doze in the winter's diluted light. That is the way the Eskimos hope to find them. The seals lie with their faces close to the edge and their foreflippers braced to push them instantly into the welcome depths if they sense danger; but when a hunter can kill one instantly with a shot in the head, he has his seal where he can lower it into the hole in his *kayak* very conveniently.

In the fall when the seals are fat (they have grown thick layers of blubber which insulate them against the cold) they usually will float if they are shot in the water. In spring, when the seals are thinner, a hunter is more apt to lose them. The report may be that a man "got two seals and sank one." Before Eskimo hunters had rifles they seldom lost a seal, because even if killed in a lead it could be hauled to the top with the line attached to the harpoon head. A new weapon is needed: a rifle whose shot will carry a rope.

Broken ice opens the way for the killer whales. They travel in packs, all rising together to breathe and then diving down under the surface again in unison. It is thought that the Eskimo boats made of light-colored skins look to the whales like the white bellies of their particular prey, the smaller beluga whales. A killer whale, thirty feet long, will rise from below, grasp a beluga in its huge jaws, throw it into the air, and catch it as it is falling. In exactly that way killer whales have attacked men in *kayaks*. That the men greatly dread the animals is apparent from many legends, from the respectful way that they always speak of killers:

"fine, brave killer whales," and from the fact that they never will point a gun at one. If they did, they think, sometime the killer would take revenge. Some Eskimos have the belief that killer whales may turn into wolves and wolves into the whales.

The walrus are shrewd. With their long tusks, mainly used for scraping up clams on the ocean bottom, they can rip a skin boat to pieces. Curiously, they seem to know they can. Very frequently they have attacked in that way when shot at close quarters. Most walrus winter near the Aleutian Islands, though some of them spend all the year farther north. When the ice starts to move in the spring, the herds ride on it up past the arctic coast. As they are carried along on the ice rafts, sometimes they "sing" together, a sound I have heard described as sounding both like bells and like banjos.

A man out on the ice also may meet a polar bear any time, and if he does, he will be elated—but cautiously so. Different species of bears are a staggered menace in their relationship to men. Black bears, of course, usually can be bluffed away. Grizzlies will attack if startled or angered. The big brown Kodiak bears sometimes will kill a man without provocation and maul his body, apparently only to express their ill will. But polar bears have a taste for human flesh; at least they consume it. Perhaps in the case of Eskimos, the polar bears think they are eating seals, since the Eskimos, who eat seals themselves and whose clothes smell of seal oil, carry the scent. Yet the bears have killed white men too. More than a few Northern hunters have thought they were stalking a polar bear when they happened to look around and found he was stalking *them*.

White "sportsmen" sometimes hunt polar bears in small planes. When they find one they run him back and forth with the plane till the bear is too exhausted to be a hazard, and then the man lands and shoots him. An Eskimo hunts the bear from his *kayak*, on foot, or traveling with a dog team. Before he had guns, it is said, an Eskimo would tease a polar bear into charging. As the bear came on, the hunter would brace his harpoon on the ice, and at the instant of the attack he would hope to swing it so that its barbed head would go into the bear's open mouth. (Wolves were hunted in a similar way in some places. When a wolf with his jaws wide would fling himself towards the hunter, the man would put his hand into the wolf's mouth and clamp his lower jaw down against his neck—a position in which an animal cannot bite.)

The belugas are harmless. The other sea mammals challenge a hunter's courage, but it is still the ice that is the greater hazard, always, from the time it forms in the fall until it disintegrates in the spring. Eskimos never talk of "the sea ice," only "the ice," and there is a special tone in which they say it, of respect, of fear, and of fascination. "The ice": even the white people up on that coast speak of it with a trace of awe in their voices.

At the time the sea froze I asked a hunter how soon the leads would be open off Unalakleet. "After wind break up offshore pack," he said. "The sky tell us." I thought he meant that the weather would give a warning, but later I learned that the low Northern clouds reflect what is below them—so well that an Eskimo, glancing up at the sky map, knows exactly where lanes of water have opened and even how far away they are. And when he is out on the ice, too distant to see the land, the clouds tell where the shore is. The sky maps are watched everywhere in the arctic and they are especially clear over the Bering Sea, whose waters are dark because of black mud on the bottom. The white ice on that surface makes, therefore, a very distinct cloud picture.

While the hunters were waiting for storms to break up the ice, the tomcod fishing was getting off to an eager start. The tomcods, small fish seldom more than twelve inches long, were used largely for dog food. It was chiefly the old women who did the fishing, and most of them seemed to think of it as recreation. As soon as the ocean froze, the men chopped out holes in the ice near the shore and the women went down with sleds, on which they sat with their feet on reindeer hides or grass mats. Each of their lines was rigged with several hooks. It was not necessary to bait the hooks. The lines were attached to short sticks, and with other sticks the women kept striking the lines, a motion that jigged the hooks, and the poor stupid fish, which apparently swallow anything that moves, were thus snared—in such numbers that once when trying tomcodding I caught ninety-eight of them in an hour.

The good weather held for too long. Now for sport the men had their dog teams out on the ice, especially after a two-inch snowfall gave the dogs better footing. They said they wanted "to see how things are out there," but they already knew; they just couldn't stay off the shimmering white field beyond the beach. I couldn't stay off it myself. It was too inviting.

This is something few people experience anywhere else: to have their world expand suddenly to unlimited distances. It was astonishing, really, to be walking on top of the sea, with all that so-level, clean, sparkling surface extending in every direction; with the village and even the mountains, now also white, looking small and flat back there, and the immaculate snow recording one's tracks. The sense of freedom was exhilarating—and if it was that at Unalakleet, where we could have traveled a thousand miles up the beach if we had wanted to, what must the freeze-up have meant to the Eskimos on the offshore islands? Those on the perpendicular King Island have no horizontal area big enough for a small plane to land on—until winter, and then one day they can walk out and out.

The first day that I tried it I met Fred Paniptchuk, David's son, on the beach as I returned. He said, "I have been watching you. You must never go out there alone." With surprise I asked why. "Sometimes the ice breaks at the shore on a high tide and blows away. You would be lost." How about the hunters? "If they're going to be gone very long, they take boats." But that winter, and every succeeding winter, was to prove that anyone, even a hunter with dogs and a boat, could lose his life on the ice.

And still the wind held, and the sky map showed that the ice, far out from the land, was unbroken. Now the huskies, eager to run, howled night and day. Their baying was like a chant. More snow fell. One night there was a rift in the clouds along the horizon, and the Northern moon, which doesn't set through the whole twenty-four hours when it is full, shone through the softly descending flakes. There were other extraordinary phenomena in the arctic sky. The sunrise and sunset were one, the first blending into the other, then in early November. Soon the sun did not rise at all, though from under the mountains along the horizon it gave a pink tinge to the light of our midday moon.

I was finding how endless the evening can seem when you've already had several hours of night before dinnertime.

During the daylight period most of the men took off up the river with dog sleds. They went to get firewood and ice for water, and also to hunt. They had set their traps under the river ice for Dolly Varden and salmon trout; and set traps through the riverside trees and brush for foxes, marten, mink, ermine, muskrats, and later for beaver. They shot ptarmigan, snowshoe rabbits, and the huge arctic hares. Most of the Unalakleet Eskimos did not do their inland hunting with much enthusiasm, however. They were men of the sea, and that was where they preferred to be. The drawback was that even after the leads would open, they could not turn seals they caught into cash, whereas the trader and Native Store both would give money, or at least credit, for the furs of land animals that could be marketed in the States.

The amount of cash that an Eskimo family vitally needed was small. At one time when I was there it was estimated that less than a hundred dollars was circulating in all the village. Sometimes most of it would be in one store and then in the other, and the post office had so little change in the till that stamps had to be sold on credit. I heard it said that one of the town's better trappers made about $1,000 a year from his trapline. It would buy more of civilized goods than most families used. Every summer one of the Stateside salmon canneries, fishing in Northern waters, sent a plane and took some of the men and women away for a few weeks' work, for a guaranteed minimum of $525. Aside from the government benefits, most of the money in town was derived from the cannery, but there was a question about the wisdom of going, because the height of the fishing season came at that time and any industrious man could seine more than $525 worth of fish at home. Yet some cash was required, if only for gasoline, ammunition, and milk. Whether to go or not was therefore a subject of much discussion.

Inland trapping and hunting would seem to be the solution, at least for the people of Unalakleet (most Eskimo villages do not have that resource), and it was hard to see why the men didn't enjoy it more. Unforgettably pleasant were trips such as I made up the river one day with Henry Nashoalook. A small daughter was with us, she and I snugly tucked into reindeer robes on the sled, while Henry's beautiful huskies raced along, plumy tails waving, on ice smooth as silk.

First we crossed the wide tundra marsh behind town, all frozen and white now. On the far side the avenue of the river turned right, circled a headland, and entered a valley. The valley was steeply walled on the left with mountain cliffs, but spread out on the other side in groves of snow-frosted spruces, birch trees, and willow thickets.

The dogs' nerves were electric with their excitement. They roused a raven, which crossed ahead of us from a spruce top to a crag. In the silence its *quawk* echoed against the mountain, and the dogs speeded up a bit. Our pace was already fast—about fifteen miles an hour, which seemed more like fifty, since a sled is so low that the ground appears to be racing by.

We stopped on a small, flat area, doubtless a riverbar in summer. In less than five minutes Henry had made a fire and had coffee boiling in less than ten. The dogs lay in the snow, resting but still alert, as Henry moved around with a quiet skill, untangling a harness or adjusting the crotched pole from which the coffee pail hung. We did not talk, for an Eskimo will communicate or be silent in the same unstrained, natural way he does everything else.

For thousands of square miles around us spread uninhabited mountains and the wide flats of the Yukon delta. Every sound was hushed; every animal's footfall was blanketed by the snow. A wolf might have been up on a hilltop, motionless, watching us, but all the birds except ravens were gone to the south. Henry took up his rifle and vanished into the brush.

Henry is one of those Eskimos, a type seen fairly frequently, who look more like Spaniards than members of their own race. Slender and tall, he has a proud carriage, a high-bridged nose, and a rather sardonic smile, none of which traits is typical of an Eskimo. The explanation in most of such cases, though possibly not in his, is that the Eskimo has an Indian in his ancestry.

Henry's father had come to Unalakleet from the Kobuk River, a mountainous country close to lands claimed by the Indians. The Eskimos and the Indians are antagonistic everywhere that they come in contact; their traditional areas are not marked on the map but are well known to the races concerned, and formerly there was frequent warfare across the borders. Wife-stealing during the raids accounts for the mixture of blood. Actually the combining of the two races often produces very good people, especially when the social responsibility of the Eskimos is coupled with the Indians' sharper outlook for opportunities.

The original Nashoalook, Henry's father, was brought up on his inland hunting-grounds to kill bears and caribou. But after only a few years on the seacoast he surpassed in skill all the local hunters of whales and seals. He was able to maintain two wives and families, a practice permitted in the rare cases when a man could provide for two. Moreover, adhering to the Eskimos' traditional code, Nashoalook undertook to support most of the village needy. He became thus the head man of the town, a post that white travelers often refer to as "chief," but Eskimos had no chiefs in the sense of men with authority. A head man was called *an-yai-yu-kok*, which means simply "the one to whom everyone listens." Nashoalook was also a medicine man however, and therefore a leader of doubly powerful influence.

Henry has a brother and several sisters living, and all of them are above average in their abilities.

When Henry came back to the riverbar that snowy day up the river, he brought an arctic hare. It weighed fourteen pounds, we found when we had returned to the village. He gave me some of it for my dinner and also its hide of downy white fur for the California Museum of Sciences, for which I was collecting specimens. He was one who quite evidently did enjoy inland hunting, and as we finished the coffee I asked if his father had taught him his woodland skills.

"My father did not believe in learning from anyone. He made us go out alone. He always said, 'Don't let other people teach you how to do anything. If you teach yourself, you'll do everything better.'" I remembered that Henry's sister, Mrs. Gounangn, Nashoalook's oldest child, had told me her father named her Miowak, meaning "try to climb up."

As we were getting ready to start back home I asked Henry if the Eskimos' life had improved since the white men came.

"No," he said quietly but with conviction. "The old days were harder, but they were better."

By then it was almost dark. Even at noon I had noticed an extra sheen on the shadowed, nacreous, winter sky. As the sunshine faded completely, it became evident why: this was a day when the sky was luminous with the Aurora. During the short daylight hours it had shone as only a very soft glitter, but after the sun was gone, the full brilliance of Northern Lights spread over the sky from one horizon across to the other. When we came out on the tundra marsh, curtains of light were swinging from vast heights above our heads. The fabric was silver-green when it was hanging straight, but wherever celestial winds blew the draperies into folds, there the shimmering became iridescent, like the colors in moiré silk.

Thus we approached the village after a day of what for Henry had been normal work.

Creative Chores

As THE men continued to wait for winds to put the finishing touches on their fields of ice, they also made household and hunting equipment; and, as always, they were attending to civic affairs. The life of an Eskimo has great variety in all seasons.

Before the freeze-up, when I had walked on the beach I had noticed how often a man or boy would pick up bits of driftwood and study them; also any bones or pieces of caribou antler or scraps of metal. They would examine the new treasure thoughtfully: what could they make of it?

Now I saw them at work on these vagrant materials. I was impressed with their respect for the grain of the driftwood; however they carved it, they always adapted their design to the wood. They never would say, "This piece is big enough so I can carve it into a root pick," but instead, "The way this grain go, it will make a good root pick." All their finished articles therefore were beautiful in the most basic way: the need and material were combined without doing violence to either. Stefan Ivanof was putting a new bowsprit into the trader's tug. He could have hewed it out of a piece of timber, but he searched till he found the branch of a tree that in itself had exactly the bend he needed.

Although civilized dishes and silverware have largely replaced the wooden ones of the older days, all Eskimo women still use their native knives, *ulus*, and the men make them as well as their own hunting and carving knives. The handles are carved out of wood or bone (farther north sometimes of ivory), and are skillfully shaped for their purposes. The blades, formerly often of jade, are now cut and filed out of old saws and are kept razor-sharp.

The fishnets are made by hand, a process that requires two carved tools, a shuttle and a gauge for the size of the mesh. Berry buckets are fashioned of spruce wood, thin slices softened in hot water over a period of weeks, when they can be bent into circular shapes and laced together with thongs of hide. The Eskimos are especially subtle in carving those objects that fit the hand; a skin-scraper I bought, the handle of my berry bucket, and a throwing-board (to increase the distance a bird dart will travel) all have such a good feel that I sometimes wonder what our machines would be like—typewriters, hammers, or cooking utensils, for example—if Eskimos had designed them. In a touch as congenial as that of the Eskimo tools there seems almost a kind of friendliness.

A family will have many other objects made by the man of the *igloo,* including most of his hunting gear. In my own small collection are three different kinds of "fishing-sticks," for tomcod and grayling and sheefish; and bird darts and the throwing-board; six ivory balls connected with lengths of sinew, a bola for snaring birds on the wing; and a harpoon with its detachable barb—all marvels of ingenuity.

A man makes his *kayak* and larger skin boat (his wife sews the skins), or his timber dinghy in case he has one. He makes his dog sled. Imported oak is now used for the sleds, since it is stronger than cottonwood, birch, or spruce, the only trees found near Eskimo country. The design differs somewhat according to region, but acknowledged as the most handsome are the "basket sleds" of the Yukon area, including Unalakleet. The sides of the frame, like a slender railing, sweep up at the back to form a curving support behind a passenger's head; it is this support which a driver grasps as he rides with his feet apart on the runners. A proper sled is not nailed or screwed together; it is constructed with pegs and thongs which allow the whole structure to give as it goes over bumps or cracks in the ice. All metal or wooden sleds from the States break up quickly under the stresses of Northern travel.

Sometimes toy sleds are made for sale, beautiful little authentic models. I wanted one and was directed to Edward Kayoukluk, whose luck at hunting had been poor recently, so that he needed money. He would not make the toy, however, until he could get some oak. When I suggested that any wood could be used for this fourteen-inch model, he seemed shocked, as if I had proposed a dishonest thing. After several weeks he found a bit of oak, and the sled, complete with harnesses for a miniature dog team, was delivered. I asked Edward the price. He would not name it, and I said, "As a figure to start with, we might say ten dollars, but I know it is not enough." Edward said, "It is too much. I would not take more than seven dollars and fifty cents."

(Again as a sign of the Eskimos' integrity as workmen: I asked Mrs. Anawrok to make me a miniature seal poke, but she would not because, in her words, "A seal poke is a whole skin. It would not have all that stitching.")

Eric Accibuk, who was the most creative craftsman at Unalakleet, carved masks of wood and a few ivory objects, but ivory-carving was seldom practiced there because the men did not often get walrus. Nor did they make the resonant drums for dancing, which are one of the coveted products of native skill. No doubt they were once made, but for thirty years the Unalakleet missionaries have forbidden the people to dance. Therefore the drums, as well as the dancing, are lost arts in that village and others where that particular sect is active.

Simple toys still are made for the children. Ptarmigan stomachs, when dried and inflated, are like pretty little lavender balloons. They often contain some willow buds, and to amuse the babies a father will attach two or three of these small balloons to a stick —an Eskimo rattle. Some of the games are for grownups rather than children. The men among themselves sometimes play poker now, and, incidentally, few white men at Nome would play with them. It is too hard, they say, to win against an Eskimo.

To watch these men working at anything is to see artists, if they are allowed to proceed in their own way and at their own pace. A white man at Unalakleet, supervising repairs on the trading post, wanted an Eskimo to replace a piece of worn wood at the eaves. The native climbed up the ladder, measured off the required distance with his hands, climbed down, separated his hands on the board until he had "felt off" the same distance kinesthetically, sawed the board, and went back up to the eaves with it. It fitted so perfectly that it did not even have to be nailed in place. Obviously the Eskimo men derive a serene kind of creative pleasure from thus using their hands so cleverly; and it was no wonder, I thought, that the exciting chases out on the ice could wait. Every day was good.

The Bright Flower

FINALLY the weather had done its work. The hunting conditions were perfect. That is, the shelf-ice, the crust attached to the land like the crust around autumn puddles, was smooth and had just enough snow on it to make sledding easy. It extended two and a half miles to the offshore bar. Beyond that the deep-water pack had broken away, but it had blown back against the edge of the shelf-ice with so much force that high walls of broken slabs and blocks of ice had buckled up—pressure ridges or *eewoonucks*, as the Eskimos call them. Beyond the *eewoonucks* there was open water, the habitat of the seals. A man climbing up on the ridges could see for miles over the drifting floes.

The Eskimos have astonishing eyesight. Once in spring when I was up on an inland slope with Fred Katchatag and his family, something far down in the valley below, on a little lake, attracted the natives' attention. "Those loons make a nest," said Fred's wife. "What loons?" I asked. "Other side of that lake," she said. Through eight-power binoculars I could make out two tiny, bird-like forms at the shore. Later I asked an Alaska oculist whether Eskimos' eyes really are better than ours. No different, he said; they just use them more keenly. And so the hunters out on the *eewoonucks* could discover seals a long distance away.

I not only wanted to go out there, I needed to, inasmuch as I expected to write about seals and their habitat. I asked Fred Paniptchuk if he would come with me and he agreed. We set out on a cloudless day with a soft breeze for our walk. Fred obviously was nervous, for we did not take a boat. As we started he pointed out that the tide had broken the ice at the beach; and farther out it was necessary to step over numerous cracks. As we scuffed along through the soft snow, he said, "I have gone fifteen miles from land on the ice. When you're out there you always think the ice is moving away from the shore."

Even two miles or so from the beach, it seemed evident that fear was, in a way, intensifying Fred's pleasure. Rolfe Humphries advises, "From this nettle, safety, pluck the bright flower, danger." Fred's eyes kept sweeping over the shining white field that surrounded us. "One breathes differently out on the ice," he said. Differently: it was true. More lightly, here where one's hold on life seemed less sure than it was on land.

We found there were three pressure ridges, one beyond another, all parallel to the edge of the shelf-ice. They too had been snowed upon, although there were many vertical faces of clear green ice, and ice of a darker blue than the bluest sky. The blue ice was "polar ice" and had come from above the farthest-north arctic shore, Fred informed me. We climbed over the ridges and down through their nooks, and detoured around the long fins of drifted snow. When spring came, the mother seals would make holes through the ice from below and would have their young in unseen shelters that they would scoop out in the drifts.

Finally we stood on the last ridge and looked westward across the sea. Far out was an ice blink across the low part of the sky. The offshore pack, then, must be more or less solid out there; the light was reflected from it. Near the edge where we stood the deep-water pack was much broken. In the leads the salt water was starting to freeze again. It was covered with little spiked balls of ice like small crystal chrysanthemums.

One of the hunters was out in his *kayak*. He was paddling around through the floes at a dreamy pace, dipping his blade noiselessly to avoid startling a possible seal. Fred, up on an *eewoo-*

nuck, saw a sleeping seal on a small pan of ice. When the hunter looked towards us, Fred pointed, and, still with the same quiet movement, the hunter moved in its direction.

He manoeuvered around so that he could approach from behind the animal. The seal raised its head warily, as they do even when sleeping—about once every seven seconds for hair seals, half as often for the large, bearded seals. This was a good-sized hair seal. Its head was up again—then collapsed suddenly on the ice. The hunter's rifle had snapped and his shot was a clean one.

He climbed out on the ice pan, where he and the seal took up most of the surface. Holding his *kayak* close to the ice, he eased the seal into the hole where he had been sitting, whence it could be pushed along under the deck. But the instant the seal's weight was removed from the floe, the hunter, aside at the edge, unbalanced the ice and it tipped him into the water.

He did not sink out of sight. In the prow of each *kayak* there is a hole provided for such emergencies, and the hunter caught into it. He pulled himself up on the ice again and then got back into his boat. Now he was wet, however, and the temperature of the air was 35° below zero.

He paddled hastily to the shelf-ice, not near where we, stood, although Fred would have been glad to pull the seal home for him. Perhaps he knew that exercise would help to prevent him from getting too cold on his trek to the beach. In any case, he was not entirely soaked; his boots of oiled sealskin, for example, were waterproof.

It was true, nevertheless, that he had had a narrow escape. For one cannot remain alive in arctic waters for more than eight minutes, so say the experts. Even in summer the Northern seas are close to the freezing-point, about 28° for water with a salt content, and one dies quickly of shock. During the short time I had spent at Nome in late August, a young boy had fallen out of a boat in the tidal area of the river. It was shallow enough so that he could walk to the bank, and he started but died before he could climb out of the water.

I was very cold myself before Fred and I arrived back at the village. The ice seems to breathe up an extra chill, and my feet and legs lost all feeling. One's heart races and pounds at such a time, to keep the blood circulating in tissues which are approaching the outside temperature. It is this effort that is the immediate cause of death by freezing: heart standstill, the scientists call it, when the effort becomes too great.

Two days later the sky was scratched with high clouds. Two hunters went out however: Henry Nashoalook and Franklin Soxie. They were taking one *kayak* on a small sled, pulled by two dogs. I watched them go, following the tracks Fred and I had made, since a trail already broken made it easier for the dogs.

They were not more than halfway to the edge of the ice when an offshore breeze started to lift the snow. At first there were only a few little swirls, and the hunters could not have thought they were serious, because they did not turn back. By the time they had disappeared in the *eewoonucks*, the wind was becoming stronger. But the men were two of the town's best hunters: they would know how to handle themselves, and they had a boat.

Soon the *eewoonucks* were completely hidden, lost to our view in a full-scale blizzard. Alarm spread through the village. The air was so filled with snow that we could not see fifty feet. It was filled too with the sound which became so familiar that winter: a sustained rumble that every few seconds rose into a slapping, buffeting roar as the wind beat the walls. Even if the two men had not left the shelf-ice, how could they find their way back to land in this driving mush?

The men did return but with a harrowing tale. They had reached the edge of the shelf-ice and were standing there, trying to make up their minds whether they should continue their hunt or go home, when the *eewoonucks*, yielding to the wind's pressure, broke away. On the same ridge where Fred and I had stood looking across the leads, Henry and Franklin found themselves rapidly drifting out.

Though the water between them and the rest of the shelf-ice was widening fast, Henry wanted to save his dogs. It was agreed that he should put the dogs in the *kayak*, take them back to the shelf-ice, and then return in the tiny boat and get Franklin. A *kayak* is made for a single occupant; for two to fit themselves into the circular opening would be difficult—impossible if both of these Eskimos had not been slender. But the men had no other choice.

It was during the time Henry was taking the dogs to the shelf-ice that the full blizzard struck. Now there was wild, white, blinding chaos between him and the *eewoonucks* sailing away ever faster. He turned into the sea again and, sped by the winds, reached the floe.

Without knowing it however, he had been blown off his course. He landed a long distance from the part of the ridge where Franklin was waiting. The strip that the wind had torn loose was several miles in length, miles of tumbled ice. Hours passed while Henry searched through its peaks and its caverns. It was night now, darkness thickened by the torrents of snow. And yet the friends finally found each other and, squeezed into the opening of the *kayak*, battled their way through high waves back to the shelf-ice. They found the dogs, too, and at last arrived home— with no seals from this hunt but almost miraculously with their lives.

Many have not come back. At Unalakleet there was an aged grandmother in almost every cabin, but seldom a grandfather. The majority of the men had died in hunting-accidents. Most, perhaps, had been carried away on the ice. It is a possibility always in families' minds.

In the household a hunter leaves in the morning, work goes on, with the gentle and fine-spun cheerfulness that all sensitive people attempt in the face of danger. The children play, but not boisterously; the woman may sew. After a period of many hours, then, there is the sound of boots stomping off snow at the door, and the man of the *igloo* comes in. He will be tired and cold. He is helped off with his parki, no doubt, and served the hot food that is ready. No one would dream of asking him if he caught anything, because maybe he didn't and the Eskimos would not humiliate a man by making him tell them so. If he was successful, he has pulled the seal home. It is outside the door, but nobody looks. In good time he will let them know.

That man, relaxing there with his family, is an authentic hero. He has a maturity and a dignity that he has earned. After dinner he probably takes up his youngest child, and he talks to the others because he delights in their company. He can control them with only a gesture, authority with the lightest possible touch but real authority, which he created himself, miles away on the ice, out of his vanquished fear.

It was towards the middle of winter that one of the Nome bush pilots told us of three King Island hunters lost on the ice. They had gone out from their village, with a boat, and had caught a large bearded seal. While they were cutting it up to put into the boat, the ice parted along a crack, taking their boat away from them. An Air Force rescue plane had come over from Fairbanks and, basing at Nome, was searching through the few hours of light every day. Local planes too were out, but more than a week had passed with no sign of the hunters.

An Eskimo who was listening asked the pilot, "Their boots—do they walk?"

"Two pairs," said the pilot. "We hear on the teacher's radio that one man's boots have stopped."

After the Eskimo left I asked the pilot what he had meant. "When a hunter is lost on the ice," he said, "the family hang up a pair of his boots from something, maybe the rung of a chair, and they say that as long as the hunter's alive, the boots move a little—they 'walk.'" He went on: "Whenever the boots stop walking, they say that the pads of dried grass move up, part way out of the boots that the man never will wear again. And there is another sign they believe in. The family tie a rope made of hide across the room under the ceiling. As long as it's tight they think that the hunter lives. When it goes slack they lose hope, and then they take down the clothes they have kept hanging above the stove to be warm when the hunter comes in."

The next week when the pilot returned, he told us that the island teachers reported the second pair of boots had stopped walking. The search planes were still going out. They had covered the sea from St. Lawrence Island to Bering Strait, but the weather was worsening. The final report was that the third pair of boots never became quite still. And the third hunter did come to land: Gregory Iyac, a lad of twenty-one. When he reached the shore he had been lost on the ice for more than three weeks, and the ice had carried him north through Bering Strait and far beyond, northeast along the coast—125 miles altogether. Numb with suffering, and with frozen feet, he looked up one day and saw a mountain-peak on his right. He stumbled towards it and happened to come on a shelter cabin, one of the stops for dog teams traveling between the villages of Shishmaref and Wales. He went in and fell to the floor, too exhausted to make a fire or even to eat the food stocked in the cabin.

The next day some hunters, out with their teams, found Gregory's tracks and followed them to the cabin. They made him warm and from the Shishmaref teacher's radio summoned help. The blizzards were starting again, but the Wales weather-observer, James Brooks, who owned a small plane, risked an extremely hazardous flight to come to the cabin for Gregory and take him to the Nome hospital.

Most of his feet had to be amputated, but he recovered—to an extent. I know him, and he is a young man terribly wounded in spirit. When he first found himself safe, he could tell about his companions: how one could not go on and, falling upon his knees, urged the others to leave him, saying that he would pray for them; and how the second man lost his mind and refused to walk any farther. The great tragedy was that, day after day, the planes flew over the men but nobody saw them. The hunters waved, they ran about, they marked their position with tracks in the snow that covered the ice—but the planes would race by above, not distinguishing men or the signs from the ice pinnacles and their shadows.

Gregory is not now able to speak of his experience. One evening when Captain Morrell of the icebreaker *Northwind* was a guest at my house in Nome, Gregory came. He intended to tell the captain about his ordeal, but he could not. Later his uncle explained, "Gregory has not forgotten, but if he talked about being lost, his brain would break." The captain invited us out to the ship the next night. We were to go the several miles over the shelf-ice by dog team, and giant searchlights were blazing a path for us, but at the last moment, understandably, Gregory could not face the prospect of being again, even so short a distance from shore, on the ice.

An episode with a happier outcome occurred that year, on a sunny Sunday in March, when many of the Nome residents were out on their shelf-ice for recreation. Some fished off the edge, some were trapping crabs, some were tomcodding, some skiing, and one man was driving around with his dog team—when the ice broke at the beach and blew out to sea. With two or three bush planes and one little boat that was got from a warehouse quickly, all were rescued. One of the planes landed near the outer edge to pick up a fisherman, who looked up in surprise. Intent on his sport, he had not even realized that the ice was moving away from the land.

By late spring, May, shelf-ice everywhere is heaved over all its surface. Parts of it, yielding to pressure from the big floating pack, have crumbled, to freeze again with a grainy texture. There have been overflows through the cracks. When these remain on the top as water, they are a clear, pale blue. Drainage pools from the land, stained from the roots of plants, are brown. Cracks in the ice widen, sometimes to three or four feet, and their sides become mushy. The ice, like a honeycomb now, is a structure of thin-walled vertical tubes.

The men still go across it to reach open water, where the seals are abundant at this time of year. One of the Eskimos, Frank Degnan, took me out with his dog team. We went close to the edge and watched while three hunters in a large dinghy "beached" three seals. They had difficulty in finding ice that was solid enough to land on. Finally another man from the village, who had come out with his team to help them, untied his dogs and pushed the sled forward on more substantial ice, a tongue of it perhaps four feet wide and twenty-five feet long. The seals were lifted up onto the sled, and the driver cautiously pulled the sled back.

The spring light in the sky was delicately green-blue, and so was the water that lay two or three inches deep over much of the ice. Across the ice, across us, passed a continuous web of shadows, the shadows of waterfowl migrating by tens of thousands up to their arctic nests. I suddenly knew how much I was going to miss scenes like that, and I said to Frank, "It will be hard to leave Unalakleet." He smiled.

"What pleases the eye pleases the heart," he said.

But we were two miles from shore, and while we were standing there, our feet kept sinking deeper and deeper into the rotting ice. Frank said, "My wife thought it was dangerous for me to bring you out here." I had been thinking the same thing myself, and I said, "Let's go back."

Safe on shore again, I was filled with a buoyant happiness and a sense of such sweetness, it was as if honey flowed in my veins. This is the way the Eskimos feel every day, I thought. At least, so they act. Is it because of the danger, present in all their lives but most in the lives of the hunters? Danger, if not overwhelmingly great, makes the small events of the day become precious, and kindness rules in relationships. Men in battle know this. It is proved by their published memoirs and the way they speak of their wartime companions.

Danger makes one aware. It gives every moment significance.

5

The Proud Eskimo Igloo-Wife

THE FAMILIAR CARTOONS in which Stone-Age men drag their women around by the hair might be revised if the artists would visit Alaska. Except for a few routine customs the Eskimo women are truly emancipated. In proportion to numbers more of them vote than white women do; they have clubs; they hold auctions to buy new clocks for their churches, to get funds to help elderly people in need, and such purposes. They think for themselves, and all these abilities are not new. Eskimos are well out of the Stone Age by now, but not long out. They were still in it when "Sinuk Mary, the Reindeer Queen," was born. She died at Unalakleet in 1949, while I was there.

Sixty years earlier, about 1890, the Eskimos of Alaska were facing starvation. The hunger was largely due to the fact that the whaling ships, which came into the Northern waters each summer, had depleted the whales. In Siberia, less than a hundred miles away, reindeer had been domesticated and were being herded successfully, almost like cattle, by Eskimos. In Alaska the climate and forage were practically the same, and therefore the officers of our revenue cutter, the *Corwin*, suggested that we should import some of those deer and teach our Eskimos how to herd them. Urged by a missionary, Dr. Sheldon Jackson, our federal Bureau of Education set up the project.

In order to buy the reindeer it was necessary to have an interpreter. At Sinuk, a village just north of the present city of Nome, was a young Eskimo woman, Mary Ana-chah-look, who knew the Siberian dialect. Perhaps her family had come from Siberia. She boarded the cutter and went to Siberia with the officers, and the deal was arranged. When the ship returned to Alaska she was asked whether she would rather be paid in money or with a few deer. She chose the deer.

Her ability with the animals was uncanny; none of the other herders was so successful. Increasing numbers of deer were brought in, some from Europe too, and Siberian and Lapp herders were employed to teach the Alaskan Eskimos. The Siberians went back home before long, and the Laplanders did only middling well in this alien land; many reindeer ran off and joined the wild caribou herds, and wolves brought down others. Commercial interests took over the deer, with the intention of selling reindeer meat in the States. But that had not been the purpose of bringing the deer to Alaska: they were to furnish the Eskimos with a stable food supply, and the government therefore took back the herds. Some of the deer still remain and still are a disappointment and subject of controversy.

Meanwhile, as the other herds waxed and waned, Mary's prospered. I have seen a picture of Mary; she had the straightforward glance of a clear thinker and doer. She set about breeding and herding her reindeer, and they multiplied until at one time, according to estimate, she had 85,000 of these Northern cattle. She could not manage so many personally and she was not able to find assistants who had her ability. Dividing her animals, sending small herds farther away to avoid exhausting the forage, she lost many. Her wealth declined. At the time she died she had less than 1,000 deer.

Meanwhile she led a respected and useful life. She and her husband, Charlie Ana-chah-look, were childless, but they adopted twenty-two children. One of them, Eunice, was the daughter of a girl that Mary had adopted a generation earlier. Eunice is now married to Frank Ryan, the postmaster at Unalakleet. When I came, Sinuk Mary, helpless in her last illness, lived with the Ryans. In what seemed a typical selfless gesture of an Eskimo woman, Frank's mother persuaded the family to move Sinuk Mary into her cabin. "You are young," she said, "but I am old, and so it is proper that I have the burden."

Sinuk Mary died and was buried during a blizzard. The grave was hewed out with picks in the solidly frozen ground, and the coffin was made by the Dorcas Society, a volunteer group of men who take responsibility for the funerals. In the blowing snow Mary's coffin was pushed on a sled to the cemetery a mile away, with the Eskimos following in their parkis and bright parki covers. Due to three weeks of bad weather we were cut off from the rest of the world at that time. When communications again were restored, most newspapers in the States carried the story that Sinuk Mary, the Reindeer Queen, had died.

There have been other famous Eskimo women. Some have been shamans, or witch doctors, able to foretell the future, so it was believed, and work magic and cure sick people. It is said of a "medicine woman" still living in the mountains east of Kotzebue that in her younger days she performed operations on eyes and restored sight to more than a few blind persons. She is supposed to have used a jade knife.

If the Eskimos had a matriarchal society, this high status accorded their women would not seem unusual. But they don't have; the husband is the accepted head of the family. He is not the head in any overpowering degree, however. In most ways the marriages seem like partnerships, and that state of affairs may be due to the attitude that the Eskimo women have in regard to work.

I first noticed it in Matilda, the eleven-year-old daughter of Charlie Traeger and Eula. Matilda loved to work. Every day she would press her own clothes and even the slacks of her small brother, Clairon. She could cook, and she helped her mother in many other ways. Yet she never seemed like a little busybody

—it was just that the work was enjoyable. She reminded me of what Margaret Mozee, the wife of the U.S. marshal, had told me in Nome. An Eskimo girl was scrubbing her stairs one day, and she looked down with a flashing smile and said, "Isn't this *fun*, Mrs. Mozee!"

Matilda's father, born in Ohio, had had a good education before he came to Alaska during the gold rush. Her mother had more pride, of race and of station, than any other Eskimo woman that I have met. In Matilda the best of both strains were combined. She was a sensitive little aristocrat. In school, when marching lines passed, some of the smaller girls would reach out and touch Matilda's coat. In the second grade, when the teacher asked the pupils how many knew their birthdays, few could tell their own but they all knew Matilda's—March 11.

She often came in to see me late in the afternoon, and it was our custom that one day she would tell me a story and the next day I would tell one. Hers included many incongruous details from the two cultures she had in her life, and from things she had read. Her father had sent away, for example, for books of fairy tales.

One story, especially, showed the ideal that she had absorbed from her mother and the Eskimo women who were their neighbors. As Matilda told it, a prince came riding into the village on his horse. Two girls competed for his love, and most of the story concerned the girl he chose and their life after he took her away to his kingdom. He spent every day out of doors, riding around with other princes, and while he was gone his bride "stayed in the palace and made him the most beautiful parkis and *mukluks*." But on some days "she went out on the tundra and hunted for wild celery and *masu* roots, and she picked barrels and barrels of blueberries for the prince, and she cut up and dried his fish and his seal and whale meat just right." Even though he was gone from home almost all the time, "she did not mind—because she was doing her work."

As I was hearing this little tale I was thinking that if it were told by a child in the States, the princess probably would have been sitting all day on a velvet cushion, or playing a harp, or embroidering on silk with gold thread and pearls. At least, that would have been my imagining when I was small. But Matilda's princess not only was doing productive labor; there was something in the child's telling that made the work sound like a privilege. It was evident that the princess was proud to be picking those berries and drying those fish. "She was doing her work." As Matilda said it, "work" sounded as if it were an honor and a fulfillment.

Soon after Matilda had told her story, I was in one of the Eskimo cabins one afternoon and I picked up, to examine with admiration, a girl's parki made of ground-squirrel skins. How many skins were there in it, I asked the girl's mother, who of course made the parki. Eighty, she said. The skins were sewn together with the most minute, even stitches, sinew being the thread. I knew by then that preparing the sinew was in itself a task. By sinew the Eskimos mean the shredded muscle fibres from along the spine or legs of a reindeer or caribou, or along the spine of a seal. After the muscles are pulled from the carcass, they are hung up to dry, and in this process they become tangled and bunched. The women patiently separate them into fine, silklike strands, and they make their sewing thread by winding together two of these with a skillful rolling motion, one palm down across the other.

The squirrels had had to be caught, in the first place—in the spring, out in the "squirrel camps" to which all the families go with the most contagious joy as soon as the snow melts from the hillsides and the squirrels wake up from their hibernation. The squirrels are taken with snares at the holes of their dens, and even small children help. But the animals have to be skinned and the hides prepared, and those are a woman's tasks. The parki I held was trimmed around hood, wrists, and hem with wolverine fur, and therefore the mother had skinned out a wolverine too and had tanned the pelt. Every member in that large family had one of these parkis, and I said of the one in my hands, "A lot of effort went into this."

"Not too much," said the Eskimo housewife. "Anyway, that's my work."

My work: her tone was the same as Matilda's, the same that a serious painter would use when he spoke of his pictures, or a composer his music. Work: there is no way to convey in print the self-respect, the head-high pride.

I thought at the start that the Eskimo women led easy lives— they could relax so completely and quickly. Whenever they came to see me, they dropped immediately into a mood of contented leisure. So comfortably they would sit in my room, their hands never restless, capable hands but quiet in the wide laps, hardly a muscle in all their bodies that was not taking a chance to rest. Though their faces were animated, their bright talk and merry eyes seemed the flowering of a sense of peace.

As the winter wore on and I spent more and more time in their cabins, they continued to work when I was there, as they did with their other neighbors, and I was impressed with the sheer volume of their accomplishments.

An Eskimo woman makes all of her family's outside clothing and footwear. Since the parkis are worn hair side in, with cloth covers, the covers must also be made. The housewife does not have a pattern. Either she measures her subject with her eye or she measures, the length of an arm perhaps, with the repeated span of her hand. Then she lays out her cloth and, working very fast, cuts it by guess, we would say, including the elaborately fitted hood. The garment is not simple. It has a ruffle around the bottom, a double pocket across the front, the hood, which can turn with the head, and intricate bands of trimming. The man's cover is made of drill; the women's and girls' are usually of percale or Indianhead, though the trader's wife, who was conscious of her prestige, had a wine-colored velveteen parki cover embroidered with sequins. Most people have several. I know one

man who has five. And the *igloo*-wife makes them all, besides the
fur parkis beneath.

Boots are a famous product of Eskimo women's skill, and some
women make them to sell. Tourists buy them readily. White people, and Eskimos when they talk to us, call them *mukluks*. That
is a Russian word, introduced at the time the Russians had trading
posts in Alaska. The Eskimo word for boot, differing somewhat
according to tribe, is pronounced something like *kommick*. The
plural is *kommahk*.

In one version, Lapp boots, the soles as well as the legs are of
fur. I tried a pair but gave up; they slip so much on the snow
that half the time I was coasting—and not on my feet. The soles
of the typical Eskimo boots are of sealskin, the hair having been
removed. The uppers are fur of seals, reindeer fawn, or caribou
legs. Removing the hair from sealskin for the soles is done by
rotting it off with warm oil. If the skin is to be bleached, it is
soaked for three days in fresh snow water, frequently being wrung
out. "If our men will help with the wringing, we appreciate that,"
said one Eskimo housewife. Then the skin is stretched on a rack
and hung out of doors to freeze and thaw, after which it is
scraped, and finally it is put back on the rack to bleach in the
winter weather. In Alaska extreme cold is considered a good
bleaching agent for anything, sealskin to sheets. Preparing the
sealskin is thus a laborious process, but the skin at the end is
almost as fine as white parchment.

The soles of the boots are cut large enough so the edges can
bend up around the foot, and the edges are finely crimped where
they will be sewed to the uppers. The crimping was formerly always done with the teeth, wherefore many old women have worn
their teeth to the gums. Most of the younger women are using
pliers. In making the boots, the small measurements are com-
puted by the joints of a woman's thumb, and the fur for the
uppers is cut, as the women do with all fur, by laying it hair-side
down and slicing just through the skin with an *ulu*. Most *mukluks*
are about eight inches high, topped with trimming composed of

fine mosaics of different-colored fur, or bands of the skin of wolf fish, or beading on felt, beads having come in with the Russians and felt with the Laplanders. The Siberian Eskimos do embroidery, but this art has never caught on with Alaskan Eskimos. As a finish the *mukluks* may have draw-strings of wool ending in bright yarn tassels. The fanciest *mukluks* often are seen on young men, made by devoted brides or fond mothers.

During the summer a woman will gather quantities of fine grass and dry it for pads in the *mukluks*. These pads are not only warm; they absorb the perspiration from a man's feet when he is hunting out on the sea ice. Moist feet freeze most quickly, and frosted feet probably are the North's greatest hazard. Only last winter a trapper was found dead on his trail, where he had lain down and crossed his hands on his chest, probably because frozen feet would not carry him the two last miles to his cabin. Sometimes when an Eskimo hunter knows that he will be out on the ice for many hours, he takes extra pads of grass to replace those in his boots.

In addition to parkis, parki covers, and boots, most *igloo*-wives knit the mittens and gloves and sometimes the sweaters their families wear. They also knit these to sell, and their skill baffled me. One could say to them, "I'd like a sweater with a dog team" —or man in his kayak, or a bear, seal, beaver, anything that they know—"in a different color across the front and back," and the woman picks up her needles and starts to knit with no design, nothing to follow. When she has finished the sweater, the picture in wool will be the right size, perfectly centered, and often with some attractive extra detail, like a bear's tracks behind him.

Tradition rigidly regulates the separate duties of men and women. In the government boarding school to which native high-school children are sometimes sent, it was thought logically that tanning would be a good trade to teach Eskimo boys. They were not willing to learn because, they said, "tanning is women's work."

In the securing of food, however, the work of the men and

women is complementary. A woman will gather the berries and herbs; she *may* hunt with her husband, though rarely if ever out on the sea ice; she *may* have a trapline, though she seldom does; she probably does do a share of the fishing; and assuredly she will butcher the meat that her husband kills, short of walrus and whales. In even the case of those monstrously large animals, occasionally she will help. If the seal killed on the ice is one of the bearded species, up to ten feet long, a man usually finds it necessary to cut it up partly, in order to get it home. In any event, he has probably walked several miles over hummocky ice, at perhaps 30° below zero or colder; he has dragged home possibly three hundred pounds of meat, and he arrives much too tired to carve up and hang the seal. Therefore the wife takes over.

Sometimes the women will work at this job in pairs—a mother and daughter, or sisters, or friends. The one helping will be rewarded with part of the meat.

First they sharpen their *ulus*.

If the skin will be wanted all in one piece, for a poke to hold oil or a float to be used in whale-hunting, the skin is deftly slipped off the animal over its head. Otherwise the seal is laid on its back and a median slit is made from its chin to tail. The blubber adheres to the skin, and this layer is spread out in a sheet at the sides of the animal. The viscera are removed and, while the rest of the carving goes on, some elderly woman (the older ones frequently offer to do tasks like this) cleans the intestines. She does this by pouring water into the upper end and working it down, again and again repeating the process until the casing is sanitary, as it would be for our sausage.

The intestines of seals formerly had picturesque use. Before canned milk was brought to the North, it was a crucial time when a child was being weaned and could hardly digest the heavy meat diet of older Eskimos. Sometimes a mother would chew the meat for her child, her saliva thereby starting the digestive process, as some birds and perhaps wolves do for their young. She also would make a broth of fish or meat, fill a short length of cleaned intestine with it, and hang it around her neck to keep it warm for the child's next feeding: the Eskimos' baby bottle.

The rest of the seal's carcass is cut up in pieces, much as a butcher would do with our meat. At the end there is a very dexterous separating of blubber from skin with the *ulu*.

On one of my earliest days at Unalakleet I watched an elderly woman, Mrs. Shafter, flensing the excess fat from a white-whale stomach. The stomach, bright red, was perhaps five feet long. It was hung from an overhead pole, and Mrs. Shafter had put a stovepipe into the upper opening to hold it in shape. With her *ulu* she was flecking off any tissues that stuck to the membrane, and her skill was so interesting to watch that I wished I could try what she was doing. I asked what the stomach was used for, and she said that when it was dry, slabs of the white-whale skin would be stored in it. The skin, like all whale skin, is called *muktuk*. It is eaten, and many civilized people like it.

When we think of carving a seal, whale, or caribou, our minds don't go far beyond the picture of slicing meat. But this is the way one of the older generation of Eskimos uses a caribou: meat for food; hide for parki, trousers, or mattress; leg skins for *mukluks*; head for soup and butter; sinew for thread; leg bones and meat for stew; bone marrow for butter; hoofs and bones boiled to eat as soup, or with lye for soap, or glue, or as a source of grease; eyes for pudding; fat from viscera for food; stomach eaten, including contents; intestines washed and dried for storage of food, or split and sewn into raincoats and windows; heart, liver, lungs, and kidneys eaten on the spot.

Up on the farthest-north coast, where the really enormous whales are secured, and also walrus, each of which may provide more than a ton of meat, the problem of keeping these vast supplies would be complicated if it were not for the fact that in many locations along the shore there are ice caves. The meat stored in those caves quickly freezes and keeps for a year or more. Thus, after a season when several whales are caught, a village looks forward to many months of security.

As a special treat when the whale meat is fresh, some is covered with blubber and allowed to sour behind the stove for a
week or so. The resulting strong flavor is much enjoyed.

Incidentally, the Eskimos are very sensitive about the fact that
most of their white neighbors do not like native foods. I think
that the Eskimos could have taken this difference in taste philo-
sophically, as they have taken the difference in dress, if so many
white people had not expressed frankly their feelings of queasi-
ness: "How can you eat that *revolting* blubber?" The Eskimos in
Alaska are quite well informed about the way that the Russians
treat their kinsmen on the other side of the Bering Sea, and they
dislike many things that the communists do; but our Eskimos say
rather wistfully, "The Russians do eat our kind of food."

One time Colonel M. R. Marsten, who formerly commanded
the Eskimo Scout Battalion of the Alaska National Guard, asked
if I'd like to meet with some of these men who are guarding our
most remote shores. For this gathering, which would include the
wives, Colonel Marsten had provided a large slab of raw *muktuk*,
the black skin of one of the giant whales, and he said to me, "If
you go, you must promise to eat the *muktuk* and promise to
keep it down. If you refused their delicacy, my Eskimo friends
would be hurt."

By then I had tried beaver, seal, arctic hare, reindeer, owl,
ptarmigan, and the skin of the white beluga whale, and the only
three that I liked, the only three that my not very robust stomach
could even hold on to, were the hare, reindeer, and ptarmigan.
It was therefore a precarious promise I made, but Colonel Marsten accepted it, and we set out for the Eskimo home where the
meeting was held.

The Eskimos feel at ease with the Colonel, and since I was
sponsored by him, they accepted me, even though I was strange
to that particular group. I was a little tense, thinking about the
muktuk to come, but I enjoyed the evening.

When the talking was over, several plates were brought in with
neatly cut one-inch squares of black rubbery-looking meat with

about an equal amount of what appeared to be suet adhering. I
took one of the squares, chewed it, swallowed it—and quickly
reached for another. And then another, and another. When all
the Eskimos were through, I was still eating *muktuk*. They were
much pleased, of course. I actually had enjoyed the meat, which
tasted rather like fine-grained beef. The blubber in that case was
more like gristle than grease, and it did take some chewing. The
muktuk probably came from one of the baleen whales, which
nourish their mammoth bodies on plankton, the most minute
plants and animals of the sea. The whales that eat fish, I found
later, have skin and flesh that taste fishy, and I cannot eat them.

Among Eskimos, cooking is almost never a very elaborate
process. Some of the women at Unalakleet baked bread (delicious!), and they made pies and cakes too, but not often. To
prepare a meal usually meant little more than putting some meat
on the stove to boil—perhaps not even that. The meat, boiled or
raw, may be placed on a single dish and the family gather around
and dip into it. The smoked salmon strips never are cooked.
Many a white Alaskan carries a strip in his parki pocket, from
which he takes a bite or two any time he feels hungry, and Eskimo
children always do. Salmon strips are known as Eskimo candy.

Cooking and dish-washing are therefore no burden for most
Eskimo housewives. But one dish does take time: their famous
"ice cream." The recipe can be found in a little cookbook prepared by the schoolchildren of Shishmaref, who allow it to be
sold for the benefit of the Alaska Crippled Children's Association (sixty cents at Box 912, Anchorage—it is a favorite souvenir
of tourists). Along with some rather startling recipes, such as
that for boiled bears' feet, is this for the "ice cream":

> *Grate reindeer tallow into small pieces. Add seal oil slowly*
> *while beating with hand. After some seal oil has been used,*
> *then add a little water while whipping. Continue adding seal*
> *oil and water until white and fluffy. Any berries can be added*
> *to it.*

·   ·   ·

Due to the heat of the beating hand, the tallow does become white and fluffy, and when a quantity of wild berries are added, the "ice cream" at least looks like ours. Sometimes in winter it is put outside to freeze, but in summer is eaten warm. Any white newcomer is a *cheechako* (tenderfoot) until he has tried it.

Many Eskimos keep their homes simple—by preference, it seems. When they don't, they feel smothered. The white husband of one native woman I know allowed her to send to the mail-order companies for an overstuffed living-room set, tables, lamps, extra chairs: what would be the complete furnishings of a civilized house. When they came and had been installed, she pushed everything back against the walls "so there would be some space." The family of an Eskimo CAA operator, who were given furnished government housing, put most of the furniture in their storage locker. They did not want the clutter.

The average Eskimo woman therefore seldom has knickknacks to dust or carpets to sweep, few lamps, draperies, coffee or end tables, pictures, books, fine cooking utensils that add up to housekeeping as most Stateside women know it. Considering also that her meals are no burden, she largely escapes a routine, and that is the way she wants it. The production of something new is the kind of work that lifts the morale of an Eskimo *igloo*-wife. She would rather be making clothes than mending them, rather pick berries than cook them, rather bleach sealskins for *mukluks* than scrub a floor. When these women are doing a washing, they don't speak of "my work" with the same bright voices as when they are helping to fill the caches with winter food.

It seems to me they have hold here of something basic to human happiness: the need not to be bored. There are signs that life for the civilized woman, too, trends in the same direction. Modern interiors are less crowded, family meals are becoming more simple. We still make a fetish of cleanliness, beyond what is needed aesthetically or for health, but if we can cultivate a little indifference, all our household machinery will free women from grinding monotony.

In deciding what we shall do with that leisure, again there are
hints from the Eskimo *igloo*-wife. For she uses her mind, as well
as her hands, creatively.

An eight-year-old boy told me: "Last year we find a dead crane
in the marsh. When my mamma cut open its stomach, she see
many seeds, not the kind here. She plant them, because she want
us to know what kind of weeds grow in the white-man's country."

"Did they grow?"

"Yes, but we did not know the names of the weeds."

I asked him to describe them, and one sounded like clover, a
different kind from the arctic plant.

"Not clover, my mamma said, because no bees come to it."
He added hopefully, "Maybe next year we find another crane
and you will tell us the names."

"If I know them."

He looked at me with surprise.

"You will know them. Because they are white-man's weeds."

But would I? I was only a naturalist, not an Eskimo mother.
Even the five-year-olds had an amazing knowledge of nature.
A group of small children were with me one day on the bank of
the slough behind town, watching a flock of terns diving into the
water. I asked, "What are they diving for?"

"Needlefish," said one of the little girls. "Have points sticking
out of their backs. The papa fish make the nest in a ditch, away
from the sea. The mamma come there and all she do, she lay
eggs. Then she go away. The papa bring food to his baby fish,
he take them out for a swim, he teach them everything." Sticklebacks, of course, whose habits are exactly as the child had described them. How did she have all that information, which I had
acquired in biological laboratories?

"I see them. My mamma show them to me."

In other ways too the women's minds strike new paths—in
courtesy, for example. A public-health nurse arrived, one who
would be staying at Unalakleet. On her first Sunday afternoon

some of the Eskimos came to call. Mrs. Oliver Anawrok, greeted her:

"We would not want to have to ask your help before we had welcomed you to our village."

The women, as well as the men, were trying to think out the problems that arise in adjusting their culture to ours. Mrs. Miles Gounangn, daughter of Nashoalook, the last head man of the village, said this:

"Eskimos always used to be generous, always giving, always helping. When a man catch a seal, his wife cook a big meal, and they send the children to every family, say, 'Kah-kheim! Come! Come and eat!' Now—no! We do not share very much now. That is because of money. We always owe to the store. We know debts are not right, and if we give our seals to our neighbors, we have to buy food and our debts will get bigger. When we cook a meal now, we call our children inside and we eat alone."

But it still is true that all who need it are given help.

I had heard before I went to Alaska that there have been few societies in which a woman has had as much independence as among Eskimos. And from the beginning I enjoyed seeing these husbands and wives together, talking and seeming so unrestrainedly to be sharing anything that was in their minds. Few women had even a trace of coyness. They often were shy with outsiders; some who were far from young appeared shy in the trading post. But with their own men their manner could be summed up by saying that they were just natural—feminine, always concerned to look pretty at every age, up to the oldest, and yet with a dignity that was akin to the men's.

All that is true, although from our standpoint the traditional life of an Eskimo woman has been a strange mixture of freedom and subservience. Not too long ago a husband might offer his wife to a visiting stranger—merely a gesture of hospitality, and in some cases a wife could refuse. And in the old culture a wife did not eat until after her husband was served; a very old woman in

Nome always walked a few steps behind her husband when they came downtown together; and I have heard that some women on St. Lawrence Island do not wear gloves—they pull their hands up into their parki sleeves to keep them warm, because "gloves are a luxury reserved for men."

Formerly—less today—Eskimo women assumed an inferior position in these outward ways. And yet one could become a Reindeer Queen, not because she had blond hair but because she had built up a herd of eighty-five thousand deer. These women do not, as Francis Fergusson phrases it, "define their actions and their beings only with reference to their men."

The Eskimo men don't admire incompetence in a woman. They assume that their wives and daughters will want to do most of the things that men do, such as to shoot well. Many Eskimo women have their own rifles. They drive dog teams. I have seen little girls of ten and twelve driving in sled-dog races, although Northern dogs, most of which have some wolf blood, often are dangerous. When outboard motors came into the country, women as well as men learned to repair them. A woman can set a net and bring in a boatload of fish, and now when the summer freighters arrive, the Eskimo wives sometimes do more of the long-shoring than husbands do, and no one thinks they have sacrificed their femininity because they have strong arms and backs. The lovely Matilda, who has recently finished high school, said a few months ago, "Sometimes I think the greatest happiness is the knowledge that one has done something well."

We hear often of vicious circles. There are benign circles too. Because an Eskimo wife has so many valuable skills, her husband treats her in most ways as an intelligent human being. Thus encouraged, she has self-respect and the wish to develop more skills. Wherefore her husband treats her as an intelligent human being. . . .

When the weather is too bad for hunting, the men spend most of their days together, usually in the trading post. In the post at Unalakleet a stairway rose from the store to the living quarters above. Although I could not see the men, I could hear them. They often were silent, but occasionally they would laugh. Eskimos' laughter grows out of small, immediate happenings—they see the humor in a situation and chuckle. I did hear that, but not once in a year the particular laughing tone which, in many men elsewhere, means that the subject is women.

Little Isaac Sing Too Much

THE FIRST TIME I went through Nome, on my way to Unalakleet, I was not there long enough to get well acquainted. But I was included in two or three social gatherings, and was interested to find that a topic of lively discussion was the recent combining of the white and Eskimo schools.

The Alaska law does not permit segregation of any kind, anywhere, for reasons of race. But in practice most of the Eskimo children at Nome were taught separately until shortly after the end of the Second World War. Their school was a tottering structure with vast windy rooms, while the white children, fewer in number, were scattered around in a new modern building, more than large enough for all pupils of both the races. The Indian Bureau, which had been educating the little Eskimos, therefore closed its school.

A year later I heard that the change was recognized as a great success. Would the white parents have anticipated anything different if they had read, as I'd had to do, the journals of arctic explorers? None of these men, it seemed, whatever his interest, could resist speaking with pleasure about the well-behaved Eskimo children. The scientists who were based at Barrow in 1880 with the International Polar Expedition had said, for example, "We never saw a child struck or punished, and a more obedient or better lot of children cannot be found in all Christendom." When John Muir came to Alaska, he wrote, "Lads from eight to twelve years were well-behaved, bashful, and usually laughed and turned away their faces when looked at. But there was a response in their eyes which made you feel that they are your very brothers." At Nome however, when it came to welcoming the small Eskimos into the Territorial school, the civilized parents had been a little concerned. For few of the Eskimo children spoke English well and the smaller ones did not speak it at all; they were "aborigines," and would they not hold the white pupils back? Their standards of living too, many in shacks that would make slums in the States seem luxurious: what values or lack of them would the white children pick up?

In Nome the children of the two races had not often played together. In even the coldest weather the Eskimo youngsters had been in sight out in the snowy street, having contagious fun with their sleds, pulled by malemute dogs; some of the white children hitched up their cockers and bird dogs; they had watched the Eskimo children, but seldom joined them. Native children could always be seen in the post office too, scrambling up and down the long stairway—the "*up*-stairs," they called it—for a stairway fascinates Eskimo children, whose cabin homes are built all on one floor. The white parents admitted the little natives were cute, with their merry eyes and their busy ways, busy but never boisterous—but nobody knew them really.

In September of 1947, then, the parki-clad mites with the bright brown eyes climbed the steps of the newer school beside children whose skin was white, by birth and abnormally white because most of them play indoors for much of the Northern year. (Eskimos' skin is as light as that of Caucasian brunettes but is very tannable. In the sunless winter it bleaches out—becoming dark in the brilliance of the spring sunshine on snow.)

The teachers were able to estimate some of their problems immediately. First was the language difficulty. It had not been exaggerated. Most native families speak Eskimo in their homes, and the smaller children did not know the English words for even the things the two races share: words like "skin," "house," "day," "teacher." The teachers did not know the Eskimo words for these: *amek, inni, obluk,* and *ayokutookti.* And so the lessons were meaningless sounds to the younger pupils. Mysterious too were things they began to hear about: trains, plows, chickens, haystacks. These are not known in northwest Alaska, but the little Eskimos had to learn words for them, because the books used in Alaska's schools are the same as those used in the States.

The older ones spoke fair English. But now they were sharing the classrooms with children who had been born, it must have seemed, knowing about the American Revolution, the invention of steam engines, Napoleon's conquests, the plays of Shakespeare, the fall of Rome—all the white-man's civilization. It was hard to catch up with so much information familiar to their white schoolmates, and to drop their own culture entirely. The Eskimos too have their legends, but these were not studied. (And couldn't they be? Some of these tales are fascinating, and to enjoy them as told by their Eskimo classmates might give the white pupils a head start in racial tolerance.)

When the results of the merger were known, they amazed everybody, with the exception perhaps of the Eskimos. For the small natives, tossed into that great confusion, had adapted themselves very well. They excelled in art and in sports requiring co-ordination, and in their academic work many could keep right along with the children of civilized backgrounds. Some were up with the best in carrying off the honors. One teacher's comment was that the Eskimo children differ as much among themselves as white children do, and roughly divide into the same two groups —those who like mathematics and science, and those who prefer the humanistic subjects such as literature and history.

Most of the ones who failed did so because they were finding it hard to adjust to the routine. Since it is typical of their race to become depressed if they have to do the same thing at the same time every day, the trait showed itself in the children as a feeling that they could go to school or not as they wished, and arrive any time they pleased. If a teacher asked why they were late, they smiled adorably and without embarrassment said, "I sleep long." The children were not defiant in this, any more than a captured wild bird would be if it tried to get out of its cage. An Eskimo simply has to feel free, it appeared—as many of us have learned in regard to the grown ones.

In spite of the interruptions, the days missed, the Eskimo pupils had proved themselves very smart. Something else had caused even more surprise: the way peace descended on all the school with their coming. As one teacher said, "Our discipline problems dissolved." Looking back, they could realize that the Eskimo children playing out in the street never fought. They did not yell, or sass their mothers—they had been very good children, a fact that became conspicuous in the classroom. They were terribly eager to learn; every small bit of information the teacher gave them seemed precious. The Eskimo race never had had their own written language; yet the small brown hands worked their pencils as carefully, as precisely, as they would bait a fishhook.

They liked the teachers. They were not apple-polishers; it was simply that they were for a teacher instead of against her. Most of them had a quick sense of humor, and during the lessons they would make funny little asides. They always included the teacher in these; they thought she should share in the fun, apparently. She was one of them. They were comfortable with adults. Before the two schools were consolidated, the teachers of the white children had had the usual difficulties, the squirming inattention of younger ones, and the assertiveness of the adolescents. But after the Eskimos entered the school, their mood of co-operation prevailed. Their pleasant behavior challenged the white children, just as these, with all their vast lore of civilization, challenged the natives.

It should also be said that William Angell, superintendent of the Nome school, has an enlightened outlook, almost an anthropologist's sense of justice, and most of these Territorial teachers

who find their way out to Nome have a pioneer's open-minded-
ness. These attitudes did of course help to make the combining
of the two schools a success.

In Nome, then, my previous curiosity about Eskimo children
became even keener. Was their good behavior due to their temperament, I wondered, or their environment, or their training?
What kind of guidance did parents give them? Since I was going
to spend a year in one of their own native settlements, I hoped
that I might be able to find the answers.

On that cold autumn day when I came ashore at Unalakleet, I
turned from the departing dinghy and found at least twenty Eskimo youngsters surrounding me. Every one smiled. When a
smile goes with a stare, I decided, it is a stare no longer. I said,
"Hello. I've come to live at Unalakleet for a while. I want to
learn all about your animals." Nobody answered, but the smiles
widened and dimples puckered in most of the russet-red cheeks.
Some of the bigger boys picked up my bags. At the top of the
beach was the trading post. We all climbed the lane together,
the children pouring ahead with a kind of harmonious grace.

A few of them wore the same outdoor clothes from the mail-
order catalogues that country children wear everywhere, but most
of them had on parkis. Some had their hoods up, with ruffs of
wolf or wolverine framing their faces. They were handsome children, their features invariably symmetrical.

A day or two later, as I was unpacking, there was a modest
knock. When I opened the door, eight little girls filed in, all of
them smiling. In age they were possibly seven to ten. "I have only
two chairs," I said. "Will some of you sit on the bed?" Five lined
up on the edge, five little maidens, all with a look so innocent,
so demurely expectant, they seemed mediaeval. They pushed
back their hoods, showing smoothly braided black hair.

I asked if they'd like to take off their parkis, and other ques-
tions. They continued to smile, but none of them said a word.
Perhaps they did not know English. I pantomimed the fact that
I'd come a long way, that I would write a book about animals,

and that I hoped the children would help me find them, especially the small ones like lemmings. The little girls laughed politely but heartily as my imaginary lemming scurried around the floor. I offered them candy, and daintily, reticently, each took a single piece. Finally an older girl led to the door and the others followed her. "Please come again," I said. From the foot of the stairs they waved, smiling still, but they did not answer.

Two groups of boys came the same afternoon. With them I was more successful: I could get one of the boys to say "yes." He pronounced it "yuss," as all Eskimo children do. I thought that if anybody were limited to a one-word vocabulary, "yes" would be a good choice. But whether the children spoke English or not, they did understand it. I learned that by telling them things instead of acting them out, and the smiles broke in all the right places. A day or two later, as I was walking along a lane, I heard "Hi, Sollee!" and turned to see the small legs of six-year-old Walter Anagick carry him, fast, behind one of the cabins. Soon all the children would talk. They saved up stories about the animals for me.

Much later I was told something that might explain why they were so silent at first. I had asked an Eskimo woman what is their word for "hello." "We do not say hello," she answered. "When two people meet, we smile to show we are friendly, and then for a while we let our thoughts speak to each other. Later we start to talk." While I was new at Unalakleet, perhaps the children were speaking to me in ways that I didn't recognize.

I know now, too, that the Eskimos' smiles are almost a supplementary language. They smile to say something—different smiles with different and conscious meanings. At Barrow the native school children prepare a mimeographed yearbook, and in a recent copy Laura Kanayurak wrote: "When I saw my mother standing by the table she was carrying a cake with 13 candles. I was very surprised. I don't know how to thank her, so I just smile. When I smile I thought I say thank you to her."

About forty children dropped into my rooms at Unalakleet

every day. I told one of the teachers, a part-Eskimo woman, that I hoped the youngsters did not feel unwelcome when I went on with my work. She said, "They expect you to. The native people visit around a lot, and if we are busy when somebody comes, we never stop." One day, in fact, when I was telling something to one of the little boys, he said, "You don't have to talk. I just like to be here." I would continue to write up my notes, and my visitors watched, always meeting my eyes, when I looked up, with a smile. The children weren't restless, they did not giggle or whisper, and no one ever touched anything. Yet they were not timid; they were relaxed. I was always glad when I heard their light knock on the door.

I was learning to know them also by watching their games. They played one called *munna munnah* in which there were teams—something like prisoners' base. White teachers had taught them football, and the trader had introduced marbles. They must have been told the elementary rules of football, but they didn't form sides, they just kicked the ball around. Apparently it was fun enough merely to see how high or far they could send it. When they played marbles, they did not try to win from another boy, only to roll the glass ball into a little hole. As for their native games, I never saw one except *munna munnah* in which there was any suggestion of combat. The white teacher told me that once when two boys were grappling—clumsily, as if they didn't know what to do next—other boys tried to separate them, saying almost in horror, "Don't *fight!* Oh, don't *fight!*"

Most of the children's play was the practicing of some skill. In one game, *ayuluk*, a pointed stick was tied with a length of sinew onto the thigh bone of a seal. The bone was thrown into the air, and the player attempted to catch it by jabbing the stick through a tiny hole in the bone. The leader devised more and more elaborate ways of throwing the bone, and anyone who could not imitate him successfully had to drop out. Two pretty, small balls were used in another game. They were made of decorated sealskin and stuffed with dried grass, and were attached by long strings of sinew to a carved piece of ivory. A child, holding the ivory in his hand, tried to make the balls rotate, one ball to the left, the other to right. When both balls were whirling, the child was seen through two fan-shaped blurs.

The little girls juggled pebbles, almost as well as professionals; all of them could keep three stones in the air at once, and some four. The boys skipped stones on the water. (In villages where the beach is smoother, they skip lids of coffee cans on the sand.) And the boys, and to a lesser extent the girls, practiced marksmanship. A few boys of seven and eight had their own rifles. Leonard Brown, then fourteen, told me that by the time he was ten he could throw a gun up in the air and shoot, hitting a target, the instant he caught it. In the Denver Museum there is a habitat group of Alaska polar bears, all huge, but the prize male, an enormous animal, was killed by a fifteen-year-old Eskimo girl.

Both boys and girls jumped on the ends of teeter-totters. That probably was their favorite pastime. As they rode up and down, standing, they tried to bounce one another off, and the one on the up end always leapt high in the air, hoping to land on the board again without losing his balance. The children were almost as light as birds. They also were light in heart. Their laughter was often heard, but their games never were noisy, excited. Their happiness seemed like the joy in creativeness which, as all artists know, buoys up the spirits like a breeze under a feather.

Much of the children's play was in fact creative. Crossing the schoolyard late one Sunday afternoon after a new snowfall, I found that the whole area had been trampled by children's feet into a beautiful and precise design. To finish the picture, it had been necessary to carry it up to the top of a lofty snowbank, and the youngsters had done that. That was the way they had occupied themselves, obviously for hours.

Some of their play could more properly be called work. The training of puppies to pull in a team was left to the boys of about twelve years. In the process the boys would be learning to handle dogs. I still have a jolly memory of one of Henry Nashaolook's sons coming up over the ridge of a snowdrift, skidding along after his father's big sled, which was drawn by six nearly grown malemutes, all frolicsome and all trying to pull in different directions.

The children liked mental skills too. On St. Lawrence Island a teacher had drilled the pupils in the Morse code, and they whistled their playtime talk in it. Those at Unalakleet explored, endlessly. All over the tundra and beach one could see little knots of them, picking berries, catching minnows, which they ate alive, hunting among the driftwood, searching for treasures and also for knowledge about their world. Any child could identify every bird's egg and tell me about the bird, and it was interesting to me that they described the birds as a scientist does—not by color, which in most species changes from season to season, but by the bird's structure and posture and habits. I would say to some tiny youngster, "What is that bird we are hearing?" And he, or she just as likely, would answer, "It have little sharp mouth. When it sing, it stand up on some bunch of grass. It put its head back and open its mouth and always never make any sound. Then it open its mouth again and we hear it." That would be a savannah sparrow, whose first two notes are usually not audible.

The play of most children, everywhere, is related to what will be their grown-up activities. Perhaps it is even true that the fierce competition in sports of Stateside school and college teams helps to prepare the members for loyalty to a corporation, for teamwork there as the firm tries to outsell its rivals. What the Eskimos need in their hunting and fishing is something more individual—sharpness of eye and hand, and their children's play helps to develop it. For example, the balancing on the teeter-totters gives them coordination, essential when they will be out on the turbulent Northern seas in their little skin boats.

And meanwhile the play of the Eskimo children helps to promote that good emotional climate which is important, psychologists say, if a child is to have a constructive and wholesome outlook. Watching their games, in which battling had almost no part, I thought I had found the first reason why they are so amiable.

Another hint was apparent every time I looked out of the window: the happy, easy association between the adults and young.

A week or so after I came, several native men began getting the trader's two barges and tugboat up on the beach for the winter. There was never a time when a dozen small youngsters were not underfoot, very much in the way I'd have said, but the Eskimo men did not think so. They would pick up the little ones, tumble them playfully once or twice, and set them down off at the side —all day that went on. And whenever the men stopped work to sit on a log for a cigarette, each would pick up a child. They talked to the youngsters, they wanted them there, and none of the children could doubt it.

The last runs of fish were being cleaned and put up to dry. They were not all hung over the poles of the caches; sometimes a braid of grass was made, with single strands pulled through the gills of the fish. The women were doing this, and they too were surrounded by children. The teen-age girls helped; babies were bounced about under the hoods of the women's parkis; and the in-between-year-olds played near-by. The women, as well as men, unmistakably were enjoying these young ones. There was never the attitude, even unexpressed, of "run along with you now."

Later, as I got family groups straightened out, I found that the children wanting to play near the grownups were many times not their own. The toddlers around the men beaching the boats were not. A grown-up at work was someone to stop and watch, then to hold one there, in a neighborhood sure to be comforting with affection. For that is an attitude that distinguishes Eskimos: *all* of them love *all* children.

Commercial recreation has not yet arrived in the typical Eskimo village, and the natives themselves say that their chief source of pleasure is watching small children—these perfectly natural children, who are as unselfconscious, as full of spontaneous charm, as puppies or kittens are. Older brothers and sisters enjoy them too. At the Holy Cross orphanage on the Yukon River both Indians and Eskimo children were cared for. A priest formerly

stationed there told me that even the larger Eskimo boys preferred play with a baby to most other kinds of fun.

It frequently happens that Eskimo families trade children
around; a couple who have none, or only one or two, may take
some of those from a more numerous family. In Unalakleet there
were cases, too, in which a strong bond had grown up between
some adult and a neighbor's child, and its parents showed no
sign of jealousy. The child was perfectly free to have this rich supporting relationship, and from time to time he slept and ate some
of his meals at his second home. A few prosperous Eskimos have
reared numerous orphans.

In civilized countries we have been talking as though emotional security depends almost entirely upon one's parents: are
they affectionate, do they always make a child feel he is wanted?
It may not be necessary for all of that reassurance to come from
a mother and father. It should come first from them, but for an
Eskimo child neighbors, too, are like a devoted family. Everywhere that a child went in Unalakleet, he was welcomed with
pleasure. Everywhere love opened out to him—proof that, small
though he was, he was recognized as a valuable human being. It
appeared to me that this wide acceptance was one of the reasons
why the children were so relaxed, also perhaps why they were
never aggressive. Neither at home or anywhere else were they ever
on the defensive.

It must not be thought, however, that Eskimo parents are not
fond of their own. They love them so much that they generally
refuse to take all the family out in a boat at one time. If the
boat should capsize and its riders be drowned, the parents want
to be sure that at least one or two would be left alive.

I had what appeared to be good opportunities, and yet I was
not able to learn very much about the home training—not in
Unalakleet, at least. Since my rooms in the trading post were
not heated well, when the native women stopped in, they often
would say, "You are c-o-l-d. Come to our house."

With fuel always a paramount problem, the houses were small.

I am thinking of one where the parents and ten children lived in two little rooms. Blizzards at times forced the children to stay indoors for days at a time, and isn't the picture one of staggering pandemonium? There was none. The boys kept themselves busy making snares or toy boats or airplanes, the girls helped with the housework or endlessly fixed their hair and in other ways made themselves pretty. Older ones played with the babies. And often they just sat still, watching the rest of us. Sometimes they went to sleep for a while.

Once when one of the boys was telling about a rabbit he'd killed, his voice rose with excitement. His father lifted his hand, and the young voice dropped lower. There were a few other signs of a careful control. The mother would not let the babies cry, not even the smallest. She cuddled them all the time, but when they cried she would say, "No more, no more," in a tone that was perfectly kind but firm. None of the Eskimo parents would tolerate crying. I was out on the tundra one day with a family whose two-year-old, struggling through brambles as high as his head, finally started to howl. "Enough, Sonny," his mother said. "Be tough boy. Be tough." I could sense in these incidents that some toughening process was going on, but I got only hints of it. Most of the discipline seemed to have taken place before I had come to town.

When my field work was done, I returned to Nome and began writing the animal book. Writing and housekeeping don't combine very well for me, and when the disorder became chaotic, I sent for an Eskimo friend, Bertha Aukon. She would always go first to the kitchen, tear off the last outdated sheet from the calendar, put clothes to soak, and, while she was washing dishes, would bake a cake. Before she would leave, the house would be spotless and food enough would have been prepared to last several days—all without any instructions. She could thaw out the complicated plumbing when need be, and she repaired my oil stoves as skilfully as a mechanic. Besides helping other distraught housekeepers, she took care of her children, her parents, and a sick sister and brother-in-law and three of their young ones. I used to think that Eskimos of her quality were the good fruit of the frozen North, of the arctic earth which is so unproductive in other ways.

Watching her one day, I asked impulsively, "Bertha, who made you the woman you are?"

"My mother," she answered. "When I was a child, my mother was always telling us how we should be."

I said that the parents in Unalakleet did not do that, they never corrected their children. She laughed.

"I think they do," she said. "All Eskimo parents talk to their children about being good. They only do it when they are alone, though. The children would be embarrassed if anyone heard them." That, then, was the reason that there had not seemed to be any particular training in the homes at Unalakleet—only no training when I was present.

Bertha had other comments on bringing up children: "Eskimos never let a child know when we think it is cute. We never laugh. We just can't stand it to see a child showing off."

She said further: "An Eskimo father never tries to act young. He doesn't pretend that he is another boy with his son. If he did, when he had to correct the child, he would not have—" She sought for the word. Authority? Bertha nodded. "A child doesn't know what to think if his father acts like a boy one day and the next day he demands respect." That remark made me realize that among the Eskimos I had known there was always dignity in an adult's relationship with a child. However, the dignity might be combined with a whimsical tenderness.

After a while Bertha's family took all of her time, and then Alma Pauwok came in to help me. Slender and shy, Alma seemed like a girl, but she was the mother of four, two of them old enough to be going to school. With her too I brought up the subject of rearing children. I asked how she made hers behave. "Like everybody. We talk to them." Just talk? "Yes, every day we talk to them about being nice." I asked her if she explained "nice-ness"—if she tried to give to her children a picture of what was expected of them. She said, "Children know. Nobody has to tell them." I asked, "Do you mean they watch you, and you give them a good example?" "We try to do that," she answered, "but they just know what goodness is. When they are born, they know." Then what did she tell them? "We keep reminding them when they forget."

I understand from my conversations with other natives that some of them do define good behavior. Lela Oman, a thoughtful Eskimo woman from Noorvik said, "My mother used to tell us, 'In summer you can just be yourselves, but in winter you must be kinder than you really are. Many people will be cold and hungry then, and they will need special help.' "

I discussed with two intelligent young Eskimo men the way that they had been reared. One, Robert Mayokok, is an expert ivory-carver from Wales. I asked him if he was punished when he was a child, and he said, "Eskimo parents do not approve of striking a child, because then the child will feel ugly. He will want to strike someone himself. In our family we were encouraged to be good—always encouraged, not scolded. We could feel we were being loved all the time, and that made us love right back."

I asked him if it were true, as I'd heard, that Eskimo parents think the soul of a dead relative enters a newborn child. He replied, "That is a superstition, but some believe it." Would a thought like that stop a parent from spanking a child, since one would not wish to punish a grandfather, for example, whose spirit might be in that child? Robert said, "Yes, that does stop a parent, not necessarily because he would feel he was striking the older person, but if you have given a baby the name of a dear relative—and we often do that, a relative who has recently died —then we have some of the same feeling for the child that we had for the older one." Even the name would not be required, I thought, if one always remembered that the beloved grandfather of a child is, in the realest sense, in him. A belief that the spirit of a dead ancestor enters a newborn baby is not very different from our scientific knowledge about inherited traits.

Wilbur Wallach is twenty-six, an artist from Shishmaref who makes beautiful etchings on sealskin. Born in one of the more remote hamlets, he has already won recognition beyond Alaska. He has a most pleasing manner, at ease with white people and very articulate. He too pinned down the effectiveness of this training by means of talk: "My parents talked to us all the time, at most of our meals and in the evening, about being good people. As soon as the babies could understand, they were hearing these things, and so they were trained to be good before they were old enough to be bad."

I asked if the children in his family helped with the work.

"All of us did. The older boys chopped the wood, and the younger ones brought it in. We helped with the dogs and the hunting and trapping; the girls helped our mother. Everyone did what he could in the work of keeping the family going. My parents were always telling the small ones that they must mind their older brothers and sisters, but they told the older ones not to expect too much of the little ones."

Wilbur then looked at me with some mischief in his eyes, as if he knew that I would react to what he was going to say next. "They told us: 'Do everything well, but don't get too tired.' They reminded the older children to be careful not to work the small ones too hard."

I did react. I said, "Wouldn't that tend to make a child lazy?"

"No," Wilbur answered. "As my parents said, 'If you don't get too tired the first time, then you won't rebel at doing the same work again.' "

Knowing Eskimos rather well, I believe there was also the thought that a very tired child may become an overwrought, keyed-up child, and the natives are cautious about getting out of emotional balance. In the Barrow school yearbook there is this little "Poem about Sleep" by Dorcas Ahvakana:

> *Some people don't have much sleep.*
> *When they wake up they are weak.*
> *They stumble and are tired.*
> *Sometimes a mouse squeaks and makes them jump.*

Until white people came, with their nine-o'clock school bells and jobs that begin on time, Eskimos used to sleep until they were rested completely. Their poise, their relaxed attitude, must have been partly due to that fact. They know that fatigue can cause nerves to be frayed, and in teaching a child to stay well inside the limits of his energy, they are helping him to have self-control.

Such advice could be part of a toughening program, and it is evident to me now that they do consciously toughen their children. To love them and toughen them: apparently that is the way that an Eskimo parent forms, molds, his child into a good adult.

As civilization penetrates further into their lives, the children will need to be toughened against new temptations, liquor and gambling and promiscuity. And since the children may some day compete with white workers, their training will have to include a real rightabout-face—they will have to learn how to drive themselves.

And then will they lose the poise which comes of natural living, of stopping when one is tired and not beginning again until one is rested? An Eskimo girl at Unalakleet, who was scrubbing a floor at the mission, got up off her knees with the job half done and went home, saying, "I feel lazy about scrubbing floors today." Giving in to that impulse, good in its way, will of course have to end.

When it does end, the Eskimo will lose something more than the equilibrium of his nerves. He will have to abandon some of the sensitive and creative approach that is now a source of his joy. My favorite portrait of an Eskimo child is this from the Barrow yearbook, about Isaac in the third grade:

> *Isaac sing too much. Isaac like to make noise in school.*
> *Isaac and I like to play outside. Isaac is slow when he is write.*

Isaac write with his left hand. Isaac is good boy in the whole world. Isaac mother is Edna. Isaac have four brother. Two of him brother were little and other were two big brother. Isaac always funny in school.

Some of the teen-age natives already are more ambitious than most of their white schoolmates. Challenged perhaps by their handicaps, they have made themselves accept routine, they dream of going to Fairbanks or Anchorage or the States; they make good grades now and later will make good wages. They are not the ones who are funny in school. I am glad that I have known some of the others. Little Isaac: unrealistically I hope that for a while longer he will continue to sing too much.

7

Eskimo Love Song

WHEN ALASKANS GO DOWN to the States, many people they meet work around before long to the question: "Is it true that the Eskimos have no morals?"

My own reply is, "They're perhaps the most moral people I ever have known," and in honesty have to add, "by their standards."

Some very respectable white men and women would be immoral according to Eskimo values, whereas many Eskimos could be called saints if we meant their conscientiousness about doing what they would consider right.

Turning the mirror around, one must say that the Eskimos who, with their standards, come into the white communities create problems that fairly stagger the welfare and law-enforcement agencies. It is not that the Eskimos do not want to co-operate. They do; it is typical of them that they think "goodness" is not only important but interesting. Their ideals and those of the white people are, however, so far apart that sometimes it seems there is no communication whatever between the groups.

The president of the native council at Unalakleet told me, "When the missionary came, he wanted to see our laws. I told him we didn't have any. 'But you must have laws,' he said. 'You must get together and make some laws and write them down.'

Now, wasn't that silly," the Eskimo commented, "when everybody knows what is right and wrong?"

If I'd asked him, he would have explained that "right and wrong" do not apply to his personal, emotional relationships. The Alaskan Eskimos, as Diamond Jenness wrote of the Copper Eskimos, feel that "goodness means social goodness, that and no more." Their own, native religion has consisted chiefly in rituals and taboos for the purpose of pleasing the spirits of animals they have killed—so that the animals will allow themselves to be killed again in their next incarnation. If a taboo were broken, the animals might stay away and the whole village starve. It was the welfare of neighbors that was important, even in the religion.

But I realize that few people who ask about Eskimos' morals are thinking of the appeasement of seals and walrus.

As far as sex is concerned, the Eskimos never have thought it immoral—no more immoral than eating when hungry is, or sleeping when one is tired. Yet they recognize sex as a powerful force, usually beneficent but able to arouse dangerous jealousy. Sex is considered very much like a loaded gun—not "bad" in itself, but the gun either can furnish a cache full of meat or it can destroy the hunter. Most Eskimo murders are due to fights over women. Because they realize that such killings are possible, Eskimos seldom gossip. Children are taught that if they should see a man and woman talking together some place alone, they must never tell anyone, no other child nor even their parents. Rumors can build into tragedies and therefore must not be started. But children aren't told that sex in itself is wrong.

In the Christian code, one's relation to God, and duty to fellow men, and one's free or restrained sexual expression are all interrelated. It is hard to separate these in our minds, to put ourselves in the Eskimo's place. His conscience is usually a very finely developed instrument—only it is directed at targets different from ours. If an Eskimo caught a seal and failed to share it with someone who had been having bad luck in hunting, that selfishness would, in his eyes, be immoral. There aren't many wealthy or even comfortable Stateside families who feel guilty because they have more than somebody else.

These differences are the cause of endless misunderstandings, and misjudgments of Eskimos such as the general impression that "Eskimos have no morals." They are distressing both for the natives and for the white settlers who are trying to establish stable communities. Some of the white-man's laws go exactly counter to the old Eskimo code of good conduct. To which code shall an Eskimo try to conform? And by which shall he be judged? I once asked those questions of Mr. Ben Mozee, who had been the United States marshal at Nome for a long time, and he said, "I've been trying to solve that problem for twenty years but I still haven't found the answer."

One year I was a member of the petit jury at Nome and saw at first hand how confused is this conflict in standards. More than three-fourths of the cases we tried concerned Eskimos, and Eskimos outnumbered the whites on the jury. Eskimos make good jurors, good voters too, for these are social responsibilities. A former judge said of them, "As jurors they take very seriously their understanding and weighing of evidence. They do not play angles, and they bring in a logical verdict." In clashes between their own code and the white-man's law, the ones who were serving with me tried to decide by the law.

One of the cases involved a primitive man and woman who lived in the Yukon delta. They were in their late thirties, and both looked as if they had been beaten down by life until they had no reason for going on except this attachment between them. No one in Nome could speak their dialect except a nineteen-year-old girl from their area who was another prisoner. She could talk to them, but her English was sketchy, and the entire proceedings were carried on with her as interpreter.

When the woman was very young her father had given her to an older man whom she did not like. There was no marriage be-

cause in their own culture Eskimos did not have the equivalent
of a wedding. A man and woman simply accepted each other as
partners, with the understanding that the arrangement probably,
but not certainly, was for life.

By the time of the trial the couple had had seven children; two
of the girls were almost grown. The man in the case was a friend
of the husband. He had become sick a few months earlier, and
the wife often went to his cabin to take him food. Her dislike of
her husband had become something like hatred by then, and the
attraction between her and the friend must have been recognized
before the time of the illness. The pair even looked alike, the
same slight, weary figures and humble turn of the head, and their
movements were synchronized in the way more often seen in couples who have spent a long and congenial lifetime together.

Knowing her older girls could take care of the other children,
the wife had moved in with the husband's friend. Somehow, perhaps through a game warden, the husband got word to the marshal, and a deputy flew down by plane. He took the testimony of
several local witnesses and the plaintiff, but only the wife
and friend were brought back to the court at Nome.

They waived jury trial, surely without having the slightest idea
of what the procedure meant. The judge therefore had to render
a verdict. There was no denial of the cohabitation, but since the
woman had taken no marriage vows, in strict legal terms she was
not a wife and had not committed the felony of adultery. The
Eskimos' code turned the situation exactly around. She was a wife
in their eyes, but if her husband was not good to her, going to
live with another man was not wrong.

Judge Walter Hodge is humane in his handling of prisoners,
but he tries to maintain the dignity of his office. When the three
stood before him, the man, the woman, and girl interpreter, he
began as usual:

"It is the judgment and decision of the court— Translate that,
please."

The interpreter's face went blank. The judge's own face was a study in perplexity, for this was the first time he had held court in Eskimo country, and how in sedate, formal terms could he get his meaning across to these people?

He couldn't. Finally he told them without any legal embroidery that he sentenced them to one year in prison with ten months suspended. No one knows what the interpreter did with "one year with ten months suspended." Looking completely dazed, the three were led back to their cells.

Sometimes in cases of minor importance the Eskimo village councils are allowed to pass judgment, although, strictly speaking, they have no legal authority. Soon after I came to Alaska there was a case in one of the smaller settlements, decided by the five men of the local council, and interesting because it illustrated another aspect of the natives' sense of justice that is foreign to ours: that is, the practice of attaching the penalty to the first act in a chain of events that may lead to a bad ending. The first act may have been innocent in its intention, but if the final result is serious, the whole disaster is pinned on the original, perhaps slight, offense.

In the following simple example a native storekeeper had made some blueberry wine and had given enough of it to a young neighbor to make him drunk. The young man went out in that irresponsible state and raped one of the village girls. Nothing was done to him, but the council decided that the trader who gave him the wine had to pay a fine.

One of the older men at Unalakleet, Accibuk, told me about a melodramatic incident in his youth. It illustrates not only this remote-cause type of justice but also the Eskimos' former attitude towards the custom of exchanging wives. What would a wife-exchange be in our courts—double adultery? With the Eskimos in the older days, such an exchange was sometimes required of them as a penance. If at any time the game animals became scarce, the shaman, the witch doctor, might suspect that one or more of the wildlife taboos had been broken. Then he might decree a twenty-four-hour wife-exchange as atonement, in the hope that the animals might come back.

Lending one's wife was part of the rather elaborate tradition concerning hospitality. Usually the guest was a hunter, a traveler away from his home. Or two couples might temporarily exchange partners, a practice that might at times please the Sea Goddess, as Edward Moffat Weyer has explained of the Baffin Island Eskimos.

A more matter-of-fact reason for wife-exchange was the effect on the birth rate. Although some Eskimo families were very large, a surprising number were childless. With a high death rate, due to infant mortality and to hunting accidents, a village might have had difficulty in keeping its population up to a stable level. Wife-exchange was believed to result in more births, and no doubt it did, since one sterile partner would not then necessarily mean a childless couple.

Of the custom as practiced at Point Hope, Froelich G. Rainey has written:

> The immediate families of men who exchanged wives were considered to be blood relatives, and thus their children could expect mutual support. Moreover, when one man exchanged wives with another, he might expect to borrow his boat or hunting gear when a critical need arose. . . . The custom was undoubtedly misinterpreted by the first white men at Point Hope who did not make their property available to their Eskimo host, as was expected.

And not only the *first* white men, one might add. Civilized visitors who have enjoyed this arrangement never seem to have understood it. Incidentally, a young daughter never was "loaned."

Since wife-exchange was practiced for practical as well as emotional reasons, Accibuk's story has several meanings besides showing the chain-of-events type of justice. It is a savage tale. It was told in the antiseptic white-porcelain atmosphere of the nurse's laboratory, because that was the only place in Unalakleet where there was enough electric current to run my tape recorder. To us who listened—the nurse, Iris Jette, the photographer, Ivan Dmitri, and I—it seemed as if we were hearing about something that had happened twenty or perhaps fifty thousand years ago, except for one detail: the guns. And yet there sat Accibuk, who had gone through that Stone-Age ordeal, and for this occasion, important to him, he had put on a blue suit and a shirt and tie.

With him he brought a family friend to verify his story—Mrs. Martha Nanouk, an intelligent Eskimo, mother of a large family and with a capable and devoted husband. She is a granddaughter of Nashoalook, the early head man of Unalakleet, and she has the quiet self-assurance of most of Nashoalook's family.

She explained the background of the story before Accibuk started his narrative.

He was seventeen at the time of the happening (about sixty when he was describing it to us), and he then lived with his parents at Sinuk, a coastal village northwest of Nome. Part of the year he was a herder for "Sinuk Mary, the Reindeer Queen." Mary's husband, Charlie Ana-chah-look, was a trapper, accumulating fox, otter, beaver, and seal pelts while his wife managed her reindeer herds. It was their custom to go to Wales near the end of each winter, so that Charlie could trade the skins.

Wales, up on Bering Strait, was one of the largest Eskimo towns at that time. It was a trading center where the Siberian Eskimos, rowing across the strait, came to meet the Alaskan Eskimos from the surrounding country. There were four clans in Wales, each with its clubhouse, or *kazhim*, presided over by one of the whale-boat captains. The four leaders were something like village chiefs, with no authority but with immense prestige, part of which was due to the fact that their boats furnished a livelihood to a number of men, and part to the fact that if a boat succeeded in catching whales, meat was given to more than the families immediately concerned.

One of the leaders was named Kah-kah-dook. He was a special

friend of Charlie and Mary from Sinuk. On their annual trip to Wales they always stayed with Kah-kah-dook, whose family, then in the winter, lived in a two-room *igloo* built partly underground. It had bunks around the walls and a tunnel connecting with the *igloo* next door of Kah-kah-dook's brother.

While the couple from Sinuk were there, Kah-kah-dook and Charlie always exchanged their wives. This arrangement may have pleased Kah-kah-dook particularly, since Mary was a dynamic woman, well known and respected through all the Eskimo territory. Boasting is frowned on by Eskimos, but after those visits it is possible that Kah-kah-dook strutted a little.

After filling in those details, Martha Nanouk turned the story over to Accibuk. But first she said, "The customs were different in those times. Exchanging wives—they thought of that as a very simple thing." Her own modesty and yet lack of embarrassment, her completely natural, unaffected manner as much as her words, made it clear that in the old days the wife-exchange was no breach of morals—"infidelity" of a kind but acceptable if the husband arranged it.

Accibuk started by saying that one year Mary decided not to make the trip up to Wales. Charlie asked Accibuk if he would like to go. Accibuk was delighted. Herding the deer, out on the snow-lashed tundra, was lonely work. The journey would be exciting. They packed Charlie's furs onto a sled, hitched up the dogs, and set out. Recent storms had piled drifts along their route, but Accibuk ran ahead to break trail: "I leader to dogs."

After two days they reached Teller and pushed on, camping out at night. "*Ala-pah!*" Cold! "But we had lots of clothes." Above Teller they entered the York Mountains, and, since it was winter, "All around, can't see sun." They came out on the shore then and camped at a small village, Boulevik. The next night they reached Wales.

Kah-kah-dook was very glad to see Charlie. Accibuk impersonated the eager host: "Charlie, you come! All right, Charlie, all right! *Quoi-ana!*" *Quoi-ana* means "thank you," but is also an exclamation, a burst of joy. Accibuk paused to suggest Kah-kah-dook's wait of a moment before he asked: "Your wife? She come? Mary come with you?"

No, said Charlie. "Too cold. And snowdrifts too heavy."

Kah-kah-dook gave no sign of his disappointment. Through the tunnel he went to his brother's house, leaving his wife to Charlie. Accibuk slept on one of the bunks.

Even the next day Kah-kah-dook did not go outdoors. Was he humiliated, dreading to see his neighbors because Mary did not come this year? He was at work on some home brew: *tong-nuck*. Charlie was anxious to get back home. He wanted to start his trading. But Kah-kah-dook, no doubt somewhat drunk by then, would not hear of it. "Now now," he said. "Lots of time."

"I want to go back right away," Charlie told him.

"Stay right here," said Kah-kah-dook. "I want to see you little bit longer. I don't want to trade yet."

Two days passed. Both men were drinking the *tong-nuck*. That evening Kah-kah-dook went out. His wife was nursing her baby; Charlie had fallen asleep. Accibuk in his bunk was wakeful. He saw Kah-kah-dook come in. "It look to me like that man was mad. Some way, it seem, he was getting ready." He put a long knife in his boot, and from over his bed he took down a rifle.

Kah-kah-dook's wife asked him where he was going. He did not answer. She got up and put her arms around Kah-kah-dook. She begged him to stay at home. "Kah-kah-dook jerk her hands off." Shivering with fear, Accibuk lay in his bunk. Kah-kah-dook went out.

Soon Accibuk heard five shots. Kah-kah-dook's brother rushed in, crying: "Kah-kah-dook is dead!" When Kah-kah-dook went out the first time, he had words with a man named Star-duck. Perhaps Star-duck teased him about Mary's failure to come. Drunk as he was, and with his pride already hurt, Kah-kah-dook determined to kill Star-duck. But Star-duck, defending himself, had killed Kah-kah-dook instead. Star-duck had not been injured.

To Accibuk the thought came at once that the murder had put

him and Charlie in danger. "I scared. Maybe some people come and kill Charlie. I shake him. Charlie say, 'Don't wake me up,' but I tell him, 'Kah-kah-dook is killed.' " At that Charlie too saw the threat.

Two rifles still hung on the wall. He took them down; neither was loaded. Charlie's own rifle, as well as his fur parki, was on his sled, which had been put on the roof of Kah-kah-dook's summer house. Charlie went outside. So did the dead-man's wife. Accibuk was alone in the house with the baby and one other child.

To make sure that we who were listening to the story had understood, Martha Nanouk interrupted Accibuk. She said that the danger to Charlie, and to a less extent Accibuk, was due to the fact that Charlie did not bring his wife. Kah-kah-dook was left out of the celebration that he had expected. While his own wife was with Charlie he therefore got drunk, and in the fracas that followed, Kah-kah-dook, an important man, one of the village leaders, was killed. Charlie and Accibuk had understood at once that they would be blamed for the death of Kah-kah-dook, and that the penalty would be the usual one among Eskimos: a life for a life. In many cases it would have been up to the family of the murdered man to take revenge, but, due perhaps to Kah-kah-dook's position as whale-boat captain and head of a *kazhim*, the whole village took the question of punishment into its hands.

Accibuk heard footsteps coming and hid under the steps of the entrance. Kah-kah-dook's father entered and, following him, the brother. The brother had come for a gun, but the old man "tried to hold him with talk." They started making a torch out of wood soaked in seal oil, and while they were doing this, Accibuk fled outside.

He wanted to find Charlie desperately, but in spite of himself was drawn to Kah-kah-dook's summer house. The torch had been brought and now burned there for a light. Kah-kah-dook's body lay on his sled, in the house. "His wife cry over him." Another woman, Kah-kah-dook's sister, came in. She took hold of the wife's hair: " 'What kind of woman are you? When you see him start to go out, why didn't you tell his brother or his father? You could have screamed that somebody was going out to kill.' "

The old father arrived with three cross-fox skins to put in Kah-kah-dook's burial box. He left and returned with a fine new rifle, to put that in too. And, "That Kah-kah-dook, he had mother." Accibuk pronounced it "mudder." He held out his own hand: "Old lady—hands like that, crinkled. She standing, that woman. She push her son's hair back off his forehead. His blood came onto her hand. 'My own boy. Even I told him, be nice boy, even I talk to him—look at that. My hand, colored, black. Look at my hand, the blood of my son. I told him, be good, but he disobeyed. Now his blood on my hand.' "

The mourning chorus were there, women moaning in the haunting way Eskimo women do at the time of a death.

" 'Well,' his sister say, 'better clean him, my brother.' She go out to get water. I follow. She talk to me: 'I got boy too. You come to my house. You stay with him.' " Accibuk's voice was very light and tender as he repeated the kind words. "*Quoi-ana!* She put water in dish, *atahwuk*, and she go out. I stay. Night come, but I can't sleep. I choke when I think of my mudder.

"Now, morning. Men walk around, come to that house. One man say, 'Every place we look for Charlie Ana-chah-look. We want to kill him. Young men, old men, everyone try to find him. After we kill him we let the dogs have him.' He point to me and he say, 'If we find him, we will feed you alive to the dogs' "— to the Northern dogs, some of which are as wild as wolves. "Men go, but little while they come back." They had found the tracks of one man and two dogs on the beach, but they had lost the trail in the blowing snow.

"I think Charlie run away. Maybe I try to run away too." But when Accibuk went outside, he met Star-duck. Star-duck took him home. "He say, 'You stay here little bit. Don't be scared. I, a man, I watch out for you.' He kind to me, Star-duck."

At Wales there was another visitor, one from Teller. He had

been on the trail ahead of Charlie and Accibuk when they were coming up. Accibuk didn't know where he might be, but after two days he went out and found the man, making his sled and dog team ready for his return journey. Accibuk asked if the traveler would take him along, and the man agreed. He said that Accibuk wasn't dressed warmly enough, and he wanted Accibuk to get his other clothes from Charlie's sled, but Accibuk was afraid that the driver would leave without him. An old man stood watching the preparations, and he went and got Accibuk's parki and boots and then sent his own boy to guide the pair out of town. They went on a roundabout route so they would not meet the men who were still looking for Charlie.

When they had gone some distance, and the boy had turned back, the driver and Accibuk saw a man who seemed to be hiding behind a hummock. They both had the same thought: he could be one of the searchers. Maybe he had a gun. The driver told Accibuk, "If that man shoot me, you try to keep going. Don't look to me if he shoot me. You run." The trail took them closer: "It was just old man working on some wood with his little ax, to make dish." *Quoi-ana!* He was from Boulevik, the village where Charlie and Accibuk stayed the night before they reached Wales. The travelers asked, "How are the people at Wales?" The old man said, "Bad time at Wales. Star-duck kill Kah-kah-dook." Accibuk risked inquiring if he had seen Charlie, and the old man said, "Three nights ago, pretty near morning, dogs barking. I think maybe Ana-chah-look go by."

Accibuk and the man from Teller went on. "Now! Right here! Ana-chah-look's tracks! Tracks of man and two dogs. Those are tracks of Charlie. I know." They started into the mountains. "*Alapah*—I think we will find Charlie frozen. He had only house parki and short boots. Maybe today we see him, Charlie lie dead in the snow. I worry." But when they reached Teller they found Charlie there, well except that he had badly frosted feet. Accibuk stayed there with him several days, and then Charlie rented a

sled and some dogs and, with Charlie on the sled, Accibuk drove
to Sinuk.

In the evening, as they approached their village, Accibuk saw
someone coming in from the sea ice where he had been hunting.
"Look like my fadder—he is my fadder! He hold me: 'My son
—*quoi-ana* you come! My son. *Quoi-ana!*' My mudder cry. 'Finally you come.'" They were joined by Mary, who was the one
to blame for the tragedy if one went back to the *most* remote
cause. Mary told two of her herders, "Ana-chah-look, my husband, and Accibuk come! In the morning get us fat reindeer.
Everybody will eat!"

"Morning, boys go out, get fat reindeer, and everybody had
feast, everybody at Sinuk."

It would be interesting to know the real reason why Mary had
wanted to stay at home, and first to know why she ever had gone
to Wales. Eskimo friends have told me that most of the women
did not like these wife-exchanges. Froelich G. Rainey says that
many women describe such experiences as "unpleasant and unde-
sired." Mary was childless, and she must have been fond of children since she eventually adopted twenty-two. Did she start going
to Wales each year because she hoped thus to have a child of her
own, and did she stop going because in that hope she was disappointed?

The custom of wife-exchange is not now practiced by Eskimos
except possibly the most primitive. A year ago, when an Eskimo
from the North coast was flown to New York for a publicity
stunt, he was interviewed by Saul Pett, a newspaper reporter.
Pett asked him about the custom of sharing a wife with a visitor
—was it still done? The Eskimo said it was, but Dr. E. S. Rabeau
from Kotzebue, a physician who has been treating Eskimos for
about fifteen years, qualified the statement: "In the more advanced Eskimo families it is not done. . . . But it's not considered immoral."

In a primitive country the whole subject of sex is treated more freely, by white people too, than it is in more civilized areas. The frontier attitude does not imply license, for people who are self-disciplined in their relationships will have the discipline wherever they go. But in conversation some of the barriers are lost sight of, and large issues, as large as sex is everywhere, are discussed with some honesty and with lessened embarrassment.

None of the white newcomers can, however, really put himself into the primitive state of mind. Some try to do that, but they have too much mental baggage. While the long pageant of history was passing, the Eskimos up on their arctic ice floes knew nothing about it; while events as crucial as our own Revolution were happening, the Eskimos did not even know we existed. They escaped knowing some things that are only encumbrances. Sex, for the rest of us, is by now weighted with thousands of complex associations. Many of them are contradictory: St. Paul and Scheherazade and King Saud's ninety women; flagellants, homosexuals, sadists; the Brownings, *Die Meistersinger*, and Héloïse and Abélard; "I would not love thee dear so much . . ."; the Puritans, Faulkner, Tennessee Williams, *Guys and Dolls*; Freud, teen-age dating, the divorce rate, "virginal feminists"; integration, *Rock Around the Clock*, Peter Arno, Miss Universe. . . .

We have assimilated so many attitudes in regard to sex that it's a wonder any civilized man and woman ever find their way to each other directly, naturally. Perhaps none ever do in the way that Martha Nanouk, irreproachable wife and mother, meant when she said so quietly that her people had thought of sex "as a very simple thing."

The simplicity and the lack of possessive feeling about a wife may partly be due to the Eskimos' indifference to the concept of property. In the white patriarchal system a man's pride in his name and his goods are thought to be largely the basis for his insistence on his exclusive rights to his family. He will not risk handing down either to another man's son.

Till the white people came to the North, Eskimos did not even hand down a name. Each person had only one, his "given" name, and the names had no gender. Accibuk, for example, was named for a girl in Sinuk who was captured by raiding Siberians but escaped and made her way back alone over the fifty-three miles of ice in the Bering Strait. She returned just before Accibuk was born, and his mother, admiring the girl, gave her name to the baby. A child might be given the name of a friend or relative who had recently died. The relative's name-soul was believed to enter him, but the line was not often direct; it was not a father-to-son succession. The white-man's system prevails now, although it is still somewhat flexible. Accibuk's son is called Paul Accibuk. Sometimes his wife will be called Mrs. Paul, and if he has children, they may become known as John Paul and Susie Paul.

Missionaries and teachers, finding the Eskimo names hard to pronouce, have arbitrarily given many natives such names as Robert Martin and Simon Smith, and especially Biblical names; in all the villages there are Isaacs, Isaiahs, Moseses. Someone in Unalakleet has been responsible for a flock of romantic names: Kermit, Roland, Wilfred, Lowell, and Isabelle, Sophia, Thora, and Stella. The Eskimo children who had white fathers sometimes have taken their names, whether the parents were married or not. There are some whimical names, legalized now: Cabin-boy, Billikin, Mouse, and Walkingstick. One George Washington and until recently two Abraham Lincolns have lived on Alaska's north coast. Each native has his own, private Eskimo name too, but there still is no talk or thought about "handing down the family name."

The concept of property is only now taking hold in the Eskimos' minds. Each village has had its recognized hunting territory, owned by all of its members, but no one possessed for himself more than the barest minimum of personal belongings. If someone died in a house, the house often would be abandoned. At present some of the villages are in the process of being surveyed, and natives are being given title to the land that they have so long occupied. It will be interesting to see if a sense of possessiveness grows in them with these new acquisitions: patrilineal names and real-estate deeds that they can pass on to their children. If it does, perhaps even their sex mores will be affected.

The present sex attitudes start, of course, with the children. In the small arctic homes the Eskimo children see adult love-making from the time they are born. They see other things too: deaths and births. There are none of the thundering, inaccessible mysteries with which most civilized children have to grow up. The Eskimo child is not moving forward, helplessly, to a series of shocks. The pattern of what he will be throughout his life, even including his death, is there from the beginning in all its completeness.

Sex play among Eskimo children is not usually frowned on— gently laughed at sometimes, but the children aren't often made to feel guilty. Such play has therefore none of the fascination of what is forbidden. I doubt that there is very much of it; the children are all so eagerly interested in what is around them, outside of them, from sticklebacks and birds' eggs to the maps on the schoolroom walls, that they'd hardly have time to be absorbed in more personal experiments. When they become conscious of themselves at all, they are likely to be trying to perfect some skill, such as juggling pebbles or making rabbit snares.

A teacher at Nome discovered the basically wholesome attitude of the Eskimo youngsters. Expecting her own first child, she began wearing maternity clothes with dread; she was afraid there would be snickering or other signs of embarrassment. Nothing like that occurred. She said that these well-behaved children seemed to become even a little more sweet and considerate, obviously understanding why she wore the smocks. They were drawing names to see who would give whom a Christmas present, and one little girl said, "I hope I get your name so I can give you a rattle for the baby." When one boy asked, "Mrs. Atkinson, why don't you have any children?" another boy said, "She does have one. It's floating around here somewhere."

In being permissive about children's sex play when it does occur, perhaps the Eskimo parents instinctively are adopting the attitude of Yale's professor of philosophy Paul Weiss: "The child's sex acts have not the same urgency that an adult's have. They are prompted on different occasions and by different stimuli; they end in different ways and with different results. . . . One man reads a book, another uses it instead to stop a draught. Only one is interested in literature. Similarly the fact that a child and an adult may both occupy themselves with sexual matters does not mean that they are dominated by a common sexual interest. . . . Radically different are the effects and intents of the two. . . ."

As the Eskimo boys and girls approach adolescence, however, the parents recognize that what has been harmless, in their view, may still be harmless or on the other hand it may mold the young person, especially the girl, in directions that will not bring her happiness. Some Eskimo parents think it is all right for the young people to experiment in their love-making, but only enough to help assure a congenial marriage—never so much that the girl may acquire a preference for changes of partners. It is a fine line that they try to draw, and in even the older, simpler days the parents worried about it.

They have a phrase, *kah-zung-nah-zhook,* which means "loose woman." I asked one of my Eskimo friends if they would use the same adjective for a loose rope or loose tie on their boots. The very same, she said. Their thought has not been that promiscuity is immoral, but that it is unwise; it does not often lead to a happy life. Parents therefore have hoped to arrange a permanent union when a girl is still very young.

In the standard civilized approach, all sorts of sexual stimulations are present. Sex appeal is used to sell almost every kind of product, even business machines and trucks; it is the staple of most entertainment, of course; it is the idea behind women's fashions. But anyone who allows himself to be swept outside the legal limits of conduct by the avalanche of sexual propaganda is, at least officially, ostracized.

The Eskimos believe that the stimulations should be carefully avoided, but then, if the powerful, instinctive impulse is overwhelming, most of them do not condemn. When I was at Unalakleet movies were being shown, in the school, for the first time in the village. They were opposed not only by the mission, a fundamentalist sect, but by many non-churchgoing parents who saw dangers in films that most of us would consider quite harmless. "We don't want our children to learn to think like that," as one father told the teacher. They did not want the young people to see some of our picture magazines, those that "everybody reads." As for the Eskimo women's clothes, no garment could be less revealing than the long, loose woman's parki, extending down to the boots, which are made wide in the ankles, exactly like men's. Formerly and to some extent today Eskimos undressed to the waist when they were indoors (till the white man came they had only fur clothing, which was too warm in a house), but their attitude is like that of some civilized nationalities where nude mixed bathing is popular: that the unclad body is not as alluring as one dressed provocatively. In the lagoon behind Unalakleet the water became warm enough for swimming in summer, but the parents did not want their daughters to go swimming there. They considered that the bathing suits offered for sale in the mail-order catalogues were too suggestive.

Meanwhile the young people were being taught that in love, even more than most relationships, there should be delicacy, a sensitive courtesy.

The girls were coquettish but not in a sharp or bold way. As one mother said to her daughter, "There is nothing better to give anybody than a nice smile," and the nice smiles were much in evidence. They seemed only the fresh and youthful version of a kind of courtesy that prevailed everywhere in the village: *politesse du cœur*, manners prompted by the heart.

A young white boy from Anchorage, who stayed out on that coast for a while, found the Eskimo girls enchanting. He said,

"They are just so natural and sweet! After I've spent an evening at my little friend's house, when I am ready to go she gets my jacket and she shows by the very way she holds it that she loves it because it is mine."

The family of that boy have adoped Zen Buddhism, and I know from the way he talked about his friend that he was treating her with restraint. What happens when these Eskimo girls encounter the military personnel is a holocaust. That is another story, but to understand it we need to know what the Eskimo attitudes are in their own environment.

An Eskimo boy, for his part, does not pursue a girl very aggressively. It is not in his nature to try to force his will upon someone else. He can tease, he can promote a frolic and hope it will lead to something more, but ordinarily he does not try to overwhelm a girl; he does not try to beat her down. He does not want her to come that way. And he has no line.

Formerly, in the rare cases where a man or boy seemed to be the philandering type and would not stay away from some reluctant girl, her mother made her a chastity belt of sealskin, "with strong buckle, so she would have time to scream anyway," as one of the Eskimo women told me.

At Unalakleet there were about twenty young people of courting age. A boy would go out in his *kayak* and paddle along near the shore, not seeming to notice the girls on the beach but all the time demonstrating the strength and skill needed to make any man a capable hunter.

Next door to the trading post lived a young man of eighteen, energetic and handsome. "He will make a good husband," said eleven-year-old Matilda, watching from behind the window as the boy hitched up his team of dogs, stepped on the sled runners, and gave the command that sent the dogs racing away up the frozen river. He often chopped wood outside his father's cabin late in the afternoon, and a bevy of teen-age girls would stand around talking to him, pooling their shyness but each looking her sweet-

est and prettiest, shiny black hair braided sleekly, parki cover
span-clean, and little wool tassels bouncing at the top of her
boots.

The Unalakleet airstrip is a mile from the village. It runs for
five thousand feet along the sandspit to the base of the foothills.
A plane lands only twice a week, in the morning, and on summer nights the pavement belongs to the pairs of young people
who walk up and down slowly, hand in hand.

By midnight the sky has gone into that stage of glossy yet
shadowed light which is composed of the arctic sun's oblique rays
and of starshine. The airstrip is narrowly bordered with tundra:
moss, wild flowers, and Hudson's Bay tea, pungently fragrant. Beyond, on one side, is a quiet lagoon; on the other, the sound,
which in that windless season is apt to be smooth. The sea ice
has drifted away by then, but over the surface float tall masses of
river ice, carved into fantastic shapes by the river's spring currents.
The sun burns their edges: small ships of gold moored on the
violet sea. Among them the pairs of loons rest and splash and
summon each other with haunting calls.

Some of the young Eskimo couples stroll all the way to the end
of the airstrip and farther, up into the hills, and after those summer wanderings occasionally there is urgent cause for a marriage.
It usually takes place.

Whether the marriage is triggered on hillsides or snowbanks or
neither, almost invariably it is a good marriage, because survival
in the Eskimos' close and interdependent little groups develops
the same qualities, generosity and tolerance, that make family living successful. It seems that the opposite qualities, selfishness and
meanness, have largely been bred out of these people over the uncounted centuries. A man who was not helpful and considerate
could not often have found a wife, nor a girl of that kind a husband.

It is true, of course, that every society tries to surround the sex
instinct with guards. An impulse so strong would wreck a people

if no restraints whatever were placed upon it. I am not an anthropologist and could not list all the systems of taboos by which various peoples keep this emotional dynamite under control. For some, I know, continence is required in certain seasons, or under certain conditions, often having to do with the planting of crops. Among the Eskimos themselves association with women was forbidden formerly in the most crucial hunting periods.

In most cases it has been the religion of an aboriginal tribe that prescribed the rules governing sensual pleasures, just as Christian ethics have done by promoting sanctified marriages. With the Eskimos, it seems to me, the main limiting factor on destructive excesses has been their great sense of social responsibility. Eskimos do not cheat or exploit or harm one another—not in any relationship and therefore not in the relationship between men and women. In a human society so aware of others' needs, where all share what they have and are quick to note signs of distress, a trifler of either sex would not be tolerated. Many Eskimos do not have strong restrictions that prevent single incidents, but they recognize marriage and fidelity as their goals, and almost irresistible community pressure would fall upon anyone who consistently acted in such a way as to endanger social stability.

Where it occurs, alcoholism alters the whole picture. Any system of morality based on such subtle restraints requires clear thinking and fine self-discipline. When liquor destroys the clarity and the control, a people may suddenly seem to fall very fast and far.

Several of the men at Unalakleet had lost their wives from illness, usually tuberculosis, and were still single. Of one they said, "He lost all his hunting luck when his wife die, because he feel so sad for her." Some of the women whose husbands had died or been carried away on the ice were feeding their children by diligent fishing, aided by government grants; some had remarried and the new husbands supported their families. I heard of no divorces in Unalakleet and only one separation. Two families, out of the population of about 400 people, were obviously not very happy. In both cases the husband had worked at Nome and had developed bad habits.

In going into the other cabins I found a warm serenity that seemed only a distillation of the attitude between neighbors. One of the Eskimos named it. On the day when I finally was to leave, the trader's wife had a breakfast party. As I looked at the circle of faces, honest and all so dependably kind, I said,

"In this village there is something that I have been looking for all my life. I don't even know what it is, but I know I have found it here."

Thora Katchatag, who was sitting next to me, said with a modest manner,

"Maybe that something you found here was love."

8

Men of Magic

FOR ALMOST TEN YEARS I have talked to Eskimos here and there about their medicine men or, as the anthropologists call them, shamans. Most of the natives say that the medicine men had magic powers once, but "those powers would not work now." When I've asked why, they have looked puzzled and miserable. "Everything's different these days." Or, "You can't have magic at the same time you have this—" with a gesture perhaps towards Front Street in Nome. Or, "Most people don't have quiet minds any more." White people certainly don't; and most of us would be skeptical about any spiritual power that hadn't been labeled by some widely accepted religion.

Even drawing out stories of medicine men in the past has been difficult. For the missionaries have tabbed the shamans as Devil's agents. In discussing the question with one ardent Eskimo Christian, I asked if the medicine men never did any good: "They healed the sick sometimes, didn't they? And helped the hunters to find their whales and the housewives to find their lost needles?" The convert replied, "The Devil allowed them a few good acts because otherwise they would not have agreed to follow him. The good was a kind of bribe." No one speaks easily of the Devil, and very hesitant therefore are any references to the witch doctors.

Ahn-gok-kok is the Eskimo word for witch doctor, with slightly differing versions in various tribes. "Medicine doctor" is the natives' preferred translation. Since white people too have their "medicine doctors," the term leaves out anything that the missionaries could label as superstition, though the natives themselves use "medicine" to mean magic. Jim Sirloak at Nome, in telling me of a shaman who was arrested for drunkenness, said, "He made medicine and escaped from jail."

When I went to the North I knew only a little about the *ahn-gok-koks.* I understood that they used sleight-of-hand tricks, and many of them were ventriloquists, but that skills like those were no more than trappings. The shamans were said to be masterful in the art of suggestion; some were hypnotists. Authentic cases are known in which Eskimos have died due to a medicine man's suggestion; at least one *ahn-gok-kok* secured another man's wife in that way. Henry Nashoalook may have had something like that in mind when he said of ability like his father's, "There could be evil in it." Or his statement may simply have been an echo from mission sermons.

Most of the medicine men have been sincere; they have really believed they communicated with spirits—so, anyway, say the anthropologists. One of the most respected authorities on the Eskimos and their ways, Dr. Edward Moffat Weyer, Jr., has written: "Skill and knowledge in everyday matters may come to the assistance of the medicine man, but the strength of his reputation rests upon nothing so obvious. . . . A mysterious power is felt, indeed, by the civilized onlooker when present at certain of the protracted ceremonies."

By now I have known two *ahn-gok-koks* personally. I have tape recordings of some of their stories and one of their healing songs. In the beginning I only hoped to hear about some of the things they did, but such stories were hard to come by until one spring day when a boy of eighteen walked with me over the marshy tundra to a still wetter marsh called Grassy Lake, so that I could watch grebes. The birds were too far out for a close view of them, but apparently they could throw their voices, as some birds do, for the calls came from everywhere, close behind us and up in the empty sky. The voices were musical but disturbing, and the boy became restless. "I wish I had brought my gun," he said. "Those voices make me so mad. I just have to kill something that sounds like that."

As both of us knew, this was a land too that could trick you. The warm sun was lying upon an earth frozen to bedrock; it was lying on curious primitive plants whose roots embraced ice, or whose roots were suspended in unseen ponds of meltwater. Those ponds had thawed down where something dark had once fallen upon the surface and, by attracting the sun's heat, had melted a well of water to bedrock. Such wells never freeze up again except on top during winter. Most of the smaller ponds were covered by innocent-looking grasses, and as we were walking back to the village I stepped into one of these dangerous traps. By throwing myself ahead, I escaped onto drier ground. Then my guide, as a kind of teasing, let himself down in the pool and proved it was "bottomless." We laughed, but I think that we both were uneasy, then, to remember that other such traps, menacing, unsuspected, surrounded us.

As we sat resting a bit on some hillocks of moss, two sandhill cranes soared out from behind a fine, high pencilling of cloud. They sailed slowly above the marsh, and their voices, warbling and rich, seemed to make the very air pulse around us. After they passed, the boy still looked up at the sky, and he said,

"When Nashoalook died, he cried out like a crane, and people heard him up the coast, twelve miles away. That was on Good Friday, and it was not spring yet. It was a long time before the real birds came back."

I waited. The boy, meeting my eyes now and half smiling, continued,

"The old people say that he could make sick people well. He cured them by taking their sickness into himself. Some people claim that a medicine man can't heal that way, but it's true.

They can do magic things. The old people say so, and they have seen them."

The boy began walking back and forth, whipping the grass with a willow switch. It was evident that the thought of magic was stimulating, exciting to him. I thought I could risk a question:

"Did Nashoalook perform other miracles?"

"All the time. But not when he was old. He became a Christian, and after that he did not do very much magic. The day he confessed Christ, the church rose up eighteen inches off its foundations. Everybody knows that. They felt it."

"I suppose it sank back to its old level," I said, and felt ashamed of myself for the literal-minded suggestion.

"It came up and sank back like a wave," said the boy.

I thought of the little white chapel, now old and weather-beaten, with its small, pretty bell tower. Nashoalook had seen it built more than fifty years ago, among the log cabins of his own primitive village. He had gone into the church and had heard the missionary speak of miracles that had happened almost two thousand years before, in a land halfway around the world. And what did Nashoalook think, he who had convinced his people that he was performing miracles every day? Christ healed the sick; well, so also, Nashoalook would say, had he. But finally there came a day when he entered the church with a purpose. By this time he knew that the other medicine man had fed multitudes with a few loaves and fishes; he had been raised from the dead. Were those superior powers, inspiring respect? After the hymns were sung and the missionary had preached his stern words, Nashoalook walked forward and bent his head and was baptized, and gave up his magic, and the congregation felt the floor under their feet rise like a wave.

"Henry and one of his brothers-in-law took care of Nashoalook's body the day he died. After they had him dressed and put in the coffin, they folded his hands on his chest and laid a Bible on his hands. That was on Friday. He was buried on Easter.

During the funeral his arms moved down to his sides, away from the Bible. By that time he was stiff and cold—and he moved. I was thirteen years old then, and I know that."

The boy was so deeply stirred that I didn't say anything for a few moments. Then I asked,

"When Nashoalook's hands moved away from the Bible, do you think that meant he was turning away from the Christian religion, back to his old Eskimo beliefs, at the very end?"

"I don't know," said the boy, and his voice drifted away. I wished I knew more, but one avoids any insistent questioning with the Eskimos. They have a delicacy that restrains it.

During those weeks in the spring my time was spent in observing the birds, whales, and seals—the advance of the migrating wildlife. But thoughts of Nashoalook kept teasing my mind, and when I had a chance I would inquire about his talents. The Eskimos were evasive: "I didn't notice whether the church rose up." "I don't remember much about how Nashoalook died." Several told me, "The old people say those things happened, but I wouldn't care to talk about them." It seemed interesting that no one really denied the guide's stories.

Everybody was willing—eager, in fact—to describe Nashoalook's achievements in practical matters. He was one of five brothers, tall dark young men who came to Unalakleet from the Malemute country. To most people "Malemute" now means a breed of sled dogs, but it once referred to a tribe of Eskimos, larger and stronger than most, who lived east of Kotzebue. No one remembers exactly when the five brothers arrived at Unalakleet. By 1887 they were there, for that was the year when the first white missionary, Mr. A. E. Karlson of the Evangelical Mission Covenant Church, appeared. The Malemutes saved his life. In some settlements at that time Eskimos were resentful of missionaries, strangers who came uninvited and scolded them, tried to make them feel guilty about ways that they thought were good. There was a plot to kill Karlson, but the Malemute brothers persuaded the village to give up the plan.

In their very names the five sounded like leaders: Teleluk, Paniptchuk (David's father), Toctoo, Moktlok, and Nashoalook, and from the start they were dominant in their adopted tribe. It was the youngest however, Nashoalook, who became "the one to whom everyone listens." He rose to that honor through intelligence, hunting skill, and great generosity, Now and then a few supernatural details were allowed to slip into the stories told to me: Nashoalook could always find anything that was lost; he could cure anyone who was sick. And there was one longer story, about a happening that was said to have taken place early one night—and the light would be bright at that time in the summer, about as it is at midafternoon in the temperate zone.

The village was nearly deserted, for most of the families were staying up-river at fish camps. A few of the older boys were playing sandball outside the school, and the story is that one of them, Frank Ryan, happened to glance towards the tundra. The boy, or a young man he was, saw a large brown bear ambling into the village lane. Frank said nothing except to his closest friend, to whom he whispered, "What do you see out there?"

The boys, agreeing to meet at the lane, went to their separate homes for their weapons. The bear was still shuffling among the cabins. The boys did meet and shoot at the bear, but they did not hit him, for the bear turned and fled back to the tundra, that flat, narrow part of the sandspit, all of which can be clearly seen except a small hollow, five or six feet deep, where a spring seeps up.

The bear went into the hollow and did not come out of it, and the boys rushed ahead, sure that they had him now. But when they came to the little basin, they found only Nashoalook in it. He was dipping water out of the spring. They asked if he had seen a bear, and he said he hadn't.

Nashoalook, like most other *ahn-gok-koks*, did not limit his doctoring to the use of magic. He would knead aching joints, lance boils, and prescribe diets. *Ahn-gok-koks* on St. Lawrence performed appendectomies, using ice locally as an anesthetic, a

practice which of course is one of the techniques of modern surgeons. David Paniptchuk remembered that once Nashoalook required of a woman whose knee was ulcerated that she walk in
the sea every day. The knee healed. But a man died who had
pain in his stomach and ate fish when Nashoalook had told him
to go for three days without food. David said that Nashoalook's
instructions were not always meant as an aid to the cure, but
as proof of the patient's faith in him. "Sick people would not
get well without faith," David said.

Apparently all medicine men knew that the mental attitude
of a patient was an important factor in his improvement. It
seems to have been true everywhere that after an *ahn-gok-kok's*
treatment he required the patient to carry out some instructions,
and the program might or might not be allied to the illness.
What medical arts they did have, the *ahn-gok-koks* could have
learned partly from their extensive dissecting of slain animals;
and no doubt they experimented with cures when their dogs,
which were valuable, became sick. They were paid for their doctoring, usually with the gift of some small useful object.

It was after these tales that I started the search for a living
medicine man—one or more who, at some time at least, had
practiced the magic arts. I wanted to know if one could sense in
the personality of the shamans anything extraordinary. How
would they prove to be—would they talk like a priest or a next-
door neighbor? Be aloof or companionable? Would their minds
be poetic? Would they be charmers? Intelligent? I wished that
I knew, but was not very hopeful. Who would admit that he
once had worked for the Devil?

The Little Gold Man

SOMEONE had told me that one of the hunters at Unalakleet,
one who had come from St. Michael, was the son of a medicine
man. If his father was living, I wondered, would this hunter go
back with me to his birthplace? Would he vouch for me with

his father, assure him of the sincerity of my interest? I explained
to this fellow that I thought the medicine men should be understood better, that information about them should be preserved.
But before I had reached my request that he take me to see his
father, he turned his eyes to my face with a long and meaningful
gaze and said:

"You know Accibuk."

Accibuk, one of the older natives at Unalakleet and one of the
finest story-tellers—why, Accibuk was my friend! It never had
entered my mind that he might be a medicine man; yet the
thought was convincing. I asked two or three of the other Eskimos—point-blank, which was the wrong way—if Accibuk ever
had been a witch doctor. No one denied that he had. They all
said they did not know. Later a public-health nurse told me that
she had heard from a white physician in Anchorage that Accibuk
had been one of the most famous medicine men in Alaska.

Now—how to get him to talk to me frankly? It would have
been simple if I could have said, "I've just found out that once
you were an *ahn-gok-kok*. Come and have dinner with me and
please tell me all about it." But if he had wanted to tell me,
Accibuk would have done so. It would be quite all right, however, to let him know indirectly what I was hoping that he would
reveal. I said as much to Martha Nanouk, the pleasant woman
who had been given the Eskimo name Ahya-kana in memory of
Accibuk's former wife. She carried my message to him and
brought back his answer: "He is not willing to say that he was a
medicine man, but he will tell you some stories about them."

They were to come and see me together, and in the meantime
I rearranged what I remembered about Accibuk. The picture
was different now; the old facts had to go in another frame. I
thought of the first time that I ever saw him, how proud and
how generous he had been. It was a cold afternoon. Accibuk
came to my door and, as is usual in the North, walked in without knocking.

"I—Accibuk," he said, pronouncing it *Ott-see-buck*, and he paused dramatically, his head high but the sensitivity in his face contradicting the boldness. "I hear you ask about bears. I kill— my life—twenty-two bears. I tell you?"

I welcomed him and made coffee, but he took only two or three swallows. He had come to talk about bears and my interest was all the stimulant that he wanted. His English was better than that of most older Eskimos. When he was a boy, there had been no school for him to attend. Later, when white men came, he had picked up their words. He still omitted the articles, "a," "an," and "the," and he often used English words in the Eskimo sentence order, with the subject left till the end, but his meaning was always clear.

To give him a start, I said, "Twenty-two bears! Were some of them big ones?"

"One, brown bear, this big between ears," and Accibuk indicated a distance from his elbow to knuckles. But he wanted to talk about polar bears, which live out on the sea ice. "White bear—*Nanook*, my language. *Nanook* . . ." Accibuk's voice lingered over the word—I had thought even then with some special significance. The familiar spirit that every sorcerer is supposed to possess, that stays with him and helps him in his performance, was thought usually to be an animal or a bird. Nashoalook's spirit was said to have been an eagle. Later I wondered if Accibuk's was not a polar bear.

"One day King Island people go out to hunt. Spring—ice break up—lots of walrus come by. People go out in boat, *umiak*, maybe catch 'em walrus, see. Walrus sleep top of ice. People look, but, too—something—bear! *Nanook!* King Island people go closer.

" 'What he do, *Nanook?*' " Accibuk had a whole vocabulary of little sounds for emotions; now they expressed the hunters' surprise, curiosity, and excitement. "*Nanook* watching one walrus, maybe try kill 'im. But that walrus now, something he smell. He want to go down in water, want to go right away. Any animal, something smell, want to run some place, hide. Walrus swim down to bottom.

"*Nanook* wait. People wait. Walrus come back top of ice. He sleep on ice again. Now *Nanook*: 'I try get 'im.' Just like men, just like hunter, that bear—because he want to eat, too, see? He hungry. Even nice bear, he want to get walrus, kill 'im.

"*Nanook* swim down to bottom, pick up rock. He come up, he climb out on ice. People watch 'im. 'Look at that! Look at bear! He got something in his hand.' Rock, weigh it, that bear. 'Maybe just right. I kill walrus. I wake 'im up!'

"He go where that walrus is, very slow. Now he standing by walrus. Just like man he stand. He raise hand with rock. Eee! King Island people: 'Oh! Look! White bear, he hit walrus! He hit 'im side his head, break his head. White bear no more hungry now.' That's what people say.

"Wait awhile, King Island people do. Let *Nanook* eat. Then they kill 'im. Bear kill walrus, and King Island people kill bear. Right there. Kill 'im, *Nanook*.

"That's all."

That was all of the story, but pity remained in Accibuk's manner and voice. I believe he had told me the incident to explain that killing is necessary to live, necessary for *Nanook* and for men. I am well aware of that ancient tragedy, being a naturalist, but never have heard it described more movingly, and I came out of the tale as out of a spell. For Accibuk's story-telling was art. He would be the bear vividly; then with a quick switch would be the hunters peering across the ice, and the whole scene came to life, the wide, white expanse of the broken floes, the dark sleeping walrus, the silence, the cold, the solitude. Because he so keenly imagined it, I saw it: acting of the most subtle sort, enchantment that happens, even on the stage, rarely.

All Eskimos, if they want to, communicate very well with their gestures, but most of the time they don't. They move with a blunt simplicity, like a man shouldering into a blizzard. Their faces, pleasant, courteous, most often hide what they think. Accibuk, on the other hand, seemed to be one of those people, born in all races, who are eloquently expressive in every way. His moods dissolved quickly into other moods, and as they did, his posture would change and his face would seem like the face of a different man. His voice too was remarkably flexible, storming and gruff and then instantly light and soft as a mother's. It had a strange, disembodied tone, as if it existed free of his throat. The voices of *bel canto* singers are like that, and also some metal bells, those with a very pure pitch. Such voices throw us off guard, they are so affecting—surely an asset if one were a medicine man.

Accibuk came other times, and before long he asked me to visit his wife, May, who was not well. She had broken her arm and, with no doctor or nurse in Unalakleet at that time, it had not been set. They had a son, fourteen, and an adopted daughter, and lived in a two-room cabin of spruce logs at the far end of town.

When I entered, the wife, a tent of a woman, got up to remove some caribou skins from a chair. Then she sat down again and, as long as I stayed, did not stir. Her eyes, dark as the ages, watched from under the epicanthic folds of her lids, seeming not friendly nor unfriendly or, in fact, really interested. Though I talked to her, she did not reply, and I thought that she might have been isolated by pain in her arm, but, "Ears gone," said Accibuk. "She hear nothing."

It was not warm in the house, which should have been desolate, what with the chill and the ailing wife, but it wasn't, for some artistic hand had arranged animal skins and photographs on the walls and had placed the chairs so they faced towards the center sociably. Whose hand it was I guessed when I saw the table in front of a window, covered with tools, pieces of walrus tusk, and carved ivory figures. They were excellent carvings, not tourist bait but products of Accibuk's own creative impulses. Two or three wooden masks, the kind used by medicine men, also lay on the table.

Even then, when I did not know that Accibuk was an *ahn-gok-kok*, he differed in so many ways from the hearty Eskimo hunters that I asked him to tell me something about himself. He said he was born at Sinuk, herded reindeer when he was a boy, and had two other wives before May but no children from those marriages.

"Was May born here?" I asked.

"Golovin. Wife for another man first. Had eighteen children, all die. One time, I little boy, my mudder say, 'Sometime maybe you find woman, all her children die. You want her your wife— that's all right. Take her to different village and she will have child.' I marry May and we come to Unalakleet. Here she have Paul. He live. Only one, Paul, my son." Accibuk did not seem to think that his mother's prophecy was extraordinary, but his son's name brought a marveling happiness into his voice.

No dog team was tethered outside the cabin, and there was no cache for stored food, no frame to dry nets, no rack for a boat—no boat. Only the house, and no sign of anything to sustain the life there but the carvings. They would not do it. I rather suspect that Accibuk had some clients, older Eskimos who asked him to perform magic healing arts, but any such practice would have had to be very secret. The missionaries at Unalakleet were vehement when their disapproval was roused. Obviously in any case Accibuk was not earning much money, and yet he gave me a silky black bear skin, and when I asked him to make me a little camp stove, like one he had made for himself, he insisted on loaning me his.

That was the Accibuk I had known—generous too with his stories, and also generous now with the different kind that I wanted to hear, about medicine men.

He did not at once start to tell me about the *ahn-gok-koks*, but from the time Martha took him my message his stories all had some supernatural elements. From then on it was assumed that our mutual interest was magic.

First there were incidents showing the power of amulets. These were charms like the lucky coins and the rabbits' feet that civilized people carry. The power of charms is worked out in the Eskimos' minds in detail. Eskimos think of everything in the world as having a soul; a tree does, a mountain, a pebble, a *kayak*, a coat, and the soul of some intimate little thing, worn through life, is believed to be helpful in an emergency. Accibuk said that charms were secured for a child by its mother, shortly before it was born. The charm might be almost anything, for example a flower. The woman would bring it home, give it water, and then make a small sack in which her child would wear the dried blossom. Any time in his life that he might be thirsty, "Talk to flower: 'I got no water. One time she give you water, my mudder. Now you help me.' After that talk, look some place. Oh! I find water!"

Accibuk's father wore a small ivory flounder that saved his life several times, he said—once when some Indians shot at him with their "quick" rifles and Accibuk's father had only an old muzzle-loader "that never shoot right away"; and another time when he was chased by a polar bear.

One of the new tales concerned an emergency in which Accibuk himself was caught. We, today, might say that it illustrates premonition and perhaps thought-transference.

Paul, his beloved boy, soon was to have his first birthday. On such occasions of great joy an Eskimo tries to provide a feast for all of his village. That is an ambitious effort, hardly possible in the winter unless one can catch an *oogruk*, and Paul's birthday was March 10. Sometimes the year's coldest weather comes at that time, but, "I want to feed 'em, all people, because birthday, Paul, my son. I feel nice. I want to go out. Maybe I catch 'im *oogruk. Quoi-ana!*"

The shelf-ice had broken along the beach and an offshore wind had blown it far out into Norton Sound. Accibuk had a *kayak*, but those little boats are not made for voyaging such a long distance from land. Nevertheless: "I say my wife, 'You got little bread?' 'Yes, I got 'im.' 'Put some in dry bag. I catch 'im *oogruk* maybe.'"

Accibuk, starting out for his *oogruk*, had lashed himself into his *kayak*. Fastened in easy reach on the deck was a knife, so he quickly could cut the rope binding his coat to the hole if he needed to free himself. His rifle and an old telescope that he owned, in waterproof bags, were with him, and so was his bite of bread.

It was early morning when he left home. After hours of steady paddling he reached the ice. By the time that he came to it he was so far from shore that when he looked back through his telescope, all he could see of the town was the bell tower on top of the three-story school. He was already a little tired.

Along the edge of the ice Accibuk soon had found two of the small hair seals—nothing to make a feast, but he killed them and put them into his *kayak*, under the deck. He continued his search for his *oogruk*, and just before noon he saw one. "He sleep. I know I got 'im. But maybe something wrong. I feel some way, see—if I wait, kill that *oogruk*, some danger maybe. Some danger to me, my body. I know. I scared to stop any longer now. I start home."

It would be typical of Accibuk's sensitivity, of any medicine man's perhaps, that in spite of his wish to have the great bearded seal, he would heed premonition. He lived like that, it appeared, very aware of his intuition.

An amazing thing happened, however: the *oogruk* woke up, dived into the water, and followed the *kayak*. It would be easy to shoot it, but Accibuk still had his curious foreboding. He swung around so he was chasing the seal, and it did not flee. Accibuk shot it.

He pulled it on top of the ice and skinned it and cut it in pieces so it could be stowed away in his *kayak*. An *oogruk* of the size he described would be nine feet long or more, and carving it up is a heavy job for a man alone. But he rushed the work, left the two small seals on the ice, and set out for home.

After about an hour the sea began to get rough. As so often happens in Norton Sound, a wind of gale force had come up within minutes. The sea, which had been nearly calm, quickly was thrashed into giant waves. When the waves broke over Accibuk, he and his boat were completely submerged. "*Ir-re-ghee!*" It is a cry of alarm. "I say to my raincoat, 'You better help me. Don't break. Because I want my bones to get home.' "

If his "raincoat," lashed to the boat's circular opening, broke, water would flow into the decked-over *kayak* and it would sink. But the coat, made of *oogruk* gut, did not split; the boat did not swamp.

At this point Accibuk thought of something that was an inspiration through all the terrible hours ahead. He told himself this was the Fourth of July and he had entered a *kayak* race. When the waves covered him, he imagined that he was purposely somersaulting his boat to win. "One time, when I young, I good in races, good turning my boat upside-down. Now I press hard on my paddle, same way. If I win, my prize will be to get home. Get my body on land, dry, warm. 'I make you prize, get home.' I talk like that to my body."

The storm increased and the day grew even colder. And a discouraging memory came to Accibuk. Once his brother-in-law, Obloogalook, had said to him, "Whatever way I go, you will follow. You will walk in my tracks." And that brother-in-law had drowned. He had gone out on the ice to hunt and never returned. "Obloogalook say, 'We'll go same trail.' I remember that." But Accibuk did not give up. Quickly, between paddle strokes, he took the bread out of its waterproof wrapping. He talked to it: "Help me, bread. I want my body get home to my wife and Paul. If I lost, she look, my wife: 'Where Accibuk? Paul, your papa no come.' Bread, you help. Make me strong." And then, Accibuk told me, "Pretty soon I feel little bit better, little bit stronger."

Hours had passed and he was still many miles from shore. The *kayak* was heavy with its big load of *oogruk*. Also, by now, ice covered Accibuk and the boat, greatly increasing the weight. His hands started to freeze. As he paddled, he let the low hand go down in the water, and when one hand had thus become "warm," he would reverse the paddle. So many waves had broken entirely over him that he had swallowed too much of the salt water and was becoming sick. "Wave cover me, I stay long time in water, I remember first time I upset myself. I choke, upside-down. When water cover me now, I talk to myself: 'Try to win! Push hard on paddle, don't be scared. Get home—that's your prize.' "

He was to have new help in his battle. "Waves so big, I am in valley of water, and I hear voice coming down from air to me." It was the voice of one of the village women, Mrs. Moktlok. She seemed to be talking to some of the young men and Accibuk thought that he heard her say, "Come on, boys, try to help Accibuk. Accibuk is trapped out there on the sea. Chant for him, help him get home." Accibuk says that he heard her voice clearly: "Boys, chant for Accibuk! Pull him home!" And immediately, "I feel better. I shout!"

His struggle had lasted for ten hours by then. Night had fallen, darkness across the cold and tumultuous sea. The meat of the *oogruk* had frozen, and ice was an inch thick over the *kayak*. But Accibuk could see lights on shore. He held the prow of the *kayak* towards one near the mouth of the river. When the *kayak* approached the beach, he could not untie the rope that fastened him in because of the heavy ice that encased it. But he got his knife with his half-frozen fingers, cut the rope, and stepped out into water up to his waist. "I fall down, because my legs so cold they feel nothing."

He saw a young man, a relative, and called to him: "Help me! I had hard time, but I got *oogruk*. Now I want to drink coffee." He did not have to walk far. "I come to my house. Oh, my—

feel my wife! See my boy, Paul, my son! *Quoi-ana!* My body get prize, get him home."

Later his neighbors told him, and they told me, that Mrs. Moktlok had in fact sensed that Accibuk was in trouble and called to some passing boys and urged them to "chant for Accibuk, help pull him home."

By the time Accibuk was ready to talk about witch doctors, he had told me so many tales in which intuition plausibly had resulted in marvels, that perhaps he thought I was ready for stronger fare. He brought Martha one night, and I knew (was my own intuition becoming trained?) that this was the time for the great revelations.

I had become convinced by then that Accibuk really had been an *ahn-gok-kok*. As I explained to Martha, though, it was important for me to *know*. If I was hoping to analyze the personality of a man of magic, it was essential to know that he really was one, and not just an observer. The intelligent and perceptive Martha could understand that. She would try to get Accibuk to admit his magical powers and practices: that she had promised me.

The atmosphere in the cabin that I was living in then was just right for story-telling. It was a little sod-covered hut. Only one lamp was lighted. Its dim yellow kerosene flame flickered over the smoke-stained logs of the inside walls. The burning wood in the stove settled. Briefly it would blaze up again, die down, and be replenished. Outside the walls the Bering Sea wind moaned and whined, and the sled dogs intoned their long woes.

One other, the sympathetic Ivan Dmitri, was there as an audience. That afternoon, as he had told me, while he and Accibuk walked along one of the lanes Accibuk stopped and faced him. "You like Eskimos," he said. "Oh, very much," replied Ivan, meaning it. "Lots of white people don't," Accibuk had said with tears in his eyes and then started up, vigorously, to walk down the lane again. And so I had invited Ivan.

Accibuk began:

"I, boy. Maybe five, six. Long time sick, had pains right here," and he put his hand on his abdomen. "People talk my mudder: 'Good Eskimo doctor at Golovin. You send, maybe come, make Accibuk well.' Yes, he go, somebody. Bring doctor. He talk: 'Bad spirit take 'im away, this boy's soul. But I get 'im back. I trade for 'im.' "

The cure was to take place in the *kazhim*, the community building where gatherings of many kinds were held. When a witch doctor ministered to a patient, friends of the family and other observers came, for such a performance was always exciting, with drummers and chants and often with dancing.

The sick boy was there, of course. For the "bargain" the doctor had brought "little hard stone, very good stone, very nice," and from the way Accibuk held the imaginary stone in his fingers, it was of pebble size, quartz perhaps. For this he would buy Accibuk's soul back again; as Accibuk told it he stretched out one hand, then the other, indicating a trade.

Still impersonating the doctor, he made the motion of taking out of his mouth a small object:

"My soul! He have my soul, there, his hand! It is little—" as tall as the first joint of his thumb, and "all gold! He shine just like sun! Set little man down on drum, that Eskimo doctor. Show to all people, everybody in *kazhim*. They see him, they talk: 'That Accibuk, that little gold man! Look 'im! Look how he shine!' " Accibuk held out his hand to us.

The man was a hypnotist! Ivan and I agreed later that we too saw the little gold man and "he shine like the sun."

"Now—Eskimo doctor lift up little man, stand 'im top of my head. Press 'im hard. 'Go in! Go in Accibuk!' " Accibuk pushed with his fingers against his now-thinning gray hair. "I feel 'im. I feel his little sharp legs work down through bones in my head. Inside me then. Nobody see any more."

After a moment I asked,

"Were you well right away?"

"Not right away. Next morning, yes. Then all well."

Martha said to me quietly, "You have not got what you wanted. Shall I ask him again?" I nodded, and she leaned closer to Accibuk and talked to him in their language. It was obvious that she was urging him. He listened silently, with his lips in a stubborn twist. Then he answered her with a short phrase, and she turned to me, smiling helplessly: "He says he can't remember if he was ever a medicine man."

He was beginning a final story:

"You know *romay*?" *Romay* is a thong, many feet long, made from the hide of a seal or walrus by cutting a narrowing spiral. It serves as a rope and may be any width, depending upon the strength required. The Eskimo hunters once made their nets of *romay*, string size for herring, almost half an inch wide for whales. That morning I had watched Accibuk and a neighbor stripping the hair from an odorous seal *romay*.

"One day Eskimo doctor take *romay*, thick kind, put *romay* around his neck. Two *romay*." Martha prompted him: "Double." "Stand one side of doctor, two big men, take hold ends of *romay*. Stand other side, two big men, hold other ends. Four men—" He wished to be sure that we understood the impressiveness of this arrangement: the medicine man with the double thong circling his neck, the ends of one strand held by two men, and the ends of the other strand held in hands equally strong on the opposite side. "Choke 'im, those men."

Accibuk got on his feet to impersonate the men pulling, how they leaned all their weight on the cords. Then again he was the doctor, veins standing out on his temples, his face puffed and red as he cried in a high, strained voice: "Tighter! Pull tighter!"

He relaxed suddenly and, with a quizzical smile, looked back over his shoulder. "Head cut off. Fall down on floor, head that Eskimo doctor."

Ivan and I must have seemed suitably startled, for Accibuk's smile turned to one of triumph.

"Doctor on floor now. Lay seal-gut coat over him, over his

head, somebody. Four lamps, that *kazhim.* One each corner. Voice yell: 'Put 'em out, lamps.' Almost dark. But people see something move under seal-gut coat. I talk. I say, 'I put my head on again. Maybe I get 'im on crooked. Maybe little bit not straight, but I try.' " Accibuk laughed.

" 'Fire 'em, lamps!' I stand up. Pull off seal-gut coat. 'See—my head on!' Yes, sir! Everybody say: 'Look! Accibuk head on all right. Straight, too!' "

Martha and Ivan and I applauded and laughed and congratulated Accibuk. No one remarked about his switch to "I" in the story. Occasionally I still wonder if he intended it, if he was even aware of what he had revealed. Most of the time I believe that he was, that that is the way an Eskimo would be likely to grant an unwelcome request—grant it, but indirectly.

Was Accibuk only a charlatan, then? I do not think so. Undoubtedly he was able to throw himself into a trance state, as all *ahn-gok-koks* could, and what happened after that he would not know. After a séance it was the custom for the Eskimo audience to tell the witch doctor what he had done, what had happened, and since the audience were completely or partially hypnotized, some very remarkable narratives have grown up.

As for Accibuk's personality, it was that of an artist, sympathetic and sensitive, buoyant (one of the other Eskimos said, "For Accibuk the sun shines on both sides of the fence"), not very thrifty but rich in sentiment and imagination. Nashoalook apparently was a contrasting type, successful, efficient—in our civilization he probably would have been an executive. Accibuk and Nashoalook were almost as different as men can be, and yet both were gifted in intuition. In both of their lives were what could be called psychic factors. That being the case, one could guess that a psychic talent might show up in anyone, and exactly that claim has been made.

Every year more and more scientists in related fields are supporting the men who are experimenting with psychic phenomena and believe that before long they will have undeniable proof that the human race has some non-material faculty, or capacity, that we can utilize. If they succeed, people should be allowed to picture it in whatever way makes it real to them individually—as a mental ability, or as one of the symbols in present religions, or as a little gold man that shines like the sun. And if that proof ever comes, so positive none can doubt it, and we are trying to cultivate a new skill of the spirit, it may happen that we shall go back for some hints to the legends of races like Eskimos. For it may be found that their medicine men did know something about the power we hope to develop. It may be; at this stage we only can speculate.

9

The Missing Spirit

AFTER THE TEMPERATURE at Unalakleet dropped below minus forty, I could no longer spend the days in my rooms at the trading post. To spread over the chilly mattress, Eula had given me seven bed pillows; I slept between those and down comforters and was warm at night. But even when a thermometer held in the hand would register sixty degrees, in the daytime, a pan of water set on a shelf would freeze, so cold had all the materials of the room become. A frigid wind blew up out of cracks in the floor, also out of the built-in drawers every time they were opened. Spikes of frost an inch long protruded from all the nailheads in woodwork and walls, and ice coated the inside doorknobs. This was what I had come to experience, arctic winter, in order to share in the country's exuberance when the migrating birds and animals would arrive in the spring. And the winter was good in itself, for it sent me out to spend most of my time with the Eskimos in their snug, warm cabins. There we had long days of talk. I learned much of value about Northern animals—and what was of value to me personally, much about Eskimos themselves.

We shifted the conversations around until we discovered what things we had in common, and then we branched out from those. The Eskimos wanted to hear anything I would tell them about the States, and it is interesting to try to describe a civilized scene

Movies promote cowboy hats and toy guns in the arctic.

Popsie, 5, takes care of small sister Vera.

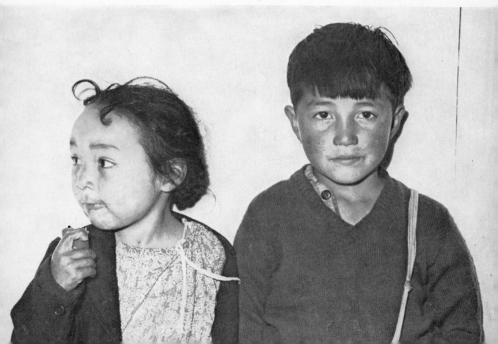

Matilda, child of poetic visions.

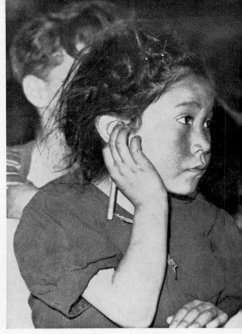

Ann Jack ponders the word "haystack."

Offshore from the beach where young lovers stroll.

A natural manner is one of the charms of Eskimo girls.

At Kotzebue there is dancing every night.

Chester Seveck, stellar
Eskimo dancer.

Anchorage, with a climate tempere
by the Gulf of Alaska, is Alaska
largest, most modern city.

Segevan, Eskimo reindeer-herder of Barrow.

Peaks of the Alaska Range divide Gulf Coast from Arctic Alaska.

Near the north magnetic pole, the Aurora displays are stupendous.

This apparent splash of ponds is the Yukon River at Fort Yukon.

Second Avenue in Fairbanks: here the men from the bush find a tie with civilization.

Juneau, capital of Alaska, is a port of call for ships on the Inside Passage.

Front Street, Nome. Federal Building, right, tipped in permafrost and is condemned.

in terms of a native village. Skyscraper, zoo, theatre, symphony orchestra could be defined fairly easily, though I probably would have been surprised if I could have seen the pictures my words created in the listeners' minds. I failed on "elevator," but I later heard Chester Seveck, Kotzebue Eskimo who had been to the States, tell about it: "You walk into little room, shut door, feel floor go up, up, up fast. I tell my wife we will land in heaven!"

The questions were sometimes startling—they revealed such great gaps in the Eskimos' experience. I was asked, "Could people read and write before the United States was discovered?" What was a tourist? And what was a scientist?

In the summer the town had been visited by mysterious teams of two or three men. The Eskimos said that most of them had beards, they wore army surplus clothes, and brought headnets, gloves, and medicine to keep away the mosquitoes. One team drilled holes in the ground. Another "dug, just dug every day" at the end of the airstrip where, yes, the natives remembered, there had been an old village. One man took pictures of flowers, and one hunted for spiders. "Everybody say they are all scientists, but they do different things," commented Mrs. Anawrok, "so we don't know what scientists are."

"Maybe teachers," her daughter, Helen, suggested.

"No," I said, starting to grope for an understandable explanation. "Some scientists teach, but not all of them."

"A teacher that doesn't tell other people what he knows?" asked one of the women, frowning at such a thought.

I had to correct that impression. "Some scientists teach in a different way, by writing books. Then other people can read them."

The family had a Bible and also a copy of Rex Beach's novel *The Spoilers*. The husband proudly took down the novel and, pointing to the author's name, said, "A scientist."

I could not leave him with that misconception and staggered on, trying to come to grips with the scientific point of view in terms that my Eskimo audience would understand. At the end

Mrs. Anawrok produced a definition that was better than any I had suggested. In her sage way she summed up the subject, meanwhile drawing a faultless stitch of sinew through the toe of a sealskin boot: "A scientist is somebody who wants to know how things *really* are." I agreed with enthusiasm, and all the rest smiled and nodded. They approved of that attitude.

Much of our talk in the cabins concerned animals, but the Eskimos also were telling me legends and ghost stories, and in nine years I have not been able to decide whether they distinguish in their own minds between facts and fantasies. I know they do believe some of the legends, and yet their description of wildlife behavior, even of species not used as food, such as grebes and phalaropes, was minutely accurate. It soon became easy for me, as it has been for other naturalists in the North, to separate out superstitions, and as for the Eskimos, perhaps moods may determine the way they think. In deciding where he should put a rabbit snare, a man would be sharply realistic; at night after dinner, if he were feeling poetic, he would be likely to say, as one hunter did, "I got lost in the mountains last year and a bird showed me how to get home. He fly around and around till I see that he want me to follow. Then he lead to a place in the river I know."

The myths that intrigued me most were those about Little Men. Everyone says they aren't often seen any more—their footprints sometimes and the wide tracks of their sleds, but the Little People are not coming down from the clouds to visit, as once they did. Almost all the Eskimos still believe in them, and when I asked why they stay away, the answer was sorrowful as in the case of the medicine men: "Everything is so different now."

The last "authentic" appearance of Little People that I have heard about was in 1946. It was winter and the people at Noorvik, a settlement on the Kobuk River, were hungry. They set out with their sleds, hoping to find one of the bands of caribou. After some time, with their food all gone, they became discouraged. But then on a moonlight night one of the men, looking out of the door of his tent, saw hundreds of Little People running along the slope and beckoning. There were so many "they looked like tall grass when the wind bends it down." Quickly hitching their teams up, the Eskimos followed and came to a huge herd of caribou. They killed hundreds and took the meat and hides home on their sleds. Back at Noorvik when one woman unpacked her skins, "a Little Man who had been hiding in them jumped out and ran away."

It's a curious thing that "the Little People fall through hard snow, but they can walk on the top of soft snow." Something else that is strange: "They have b-i-g sleds, bigger than Eskimos', always lots of furs on them, but Little People can push them easily. But if one of us touches their sleds, then nobody ever can move them again, not even the Little People."

How should white people respond to these stories? I think the way Colonel Marston did. When he was in command of the Second Scout Battalion of the National Guard, which is composed of Eskimos, the manoeuvers were somewhat disorganized when the Guards reported to him that they kept running into Little Men. Colonel Marston said, "Then, for this short time, we'll just have to consider that they are enemies and you'll have to drive them out of the hills." He sent his troops on that mission. When they reported that they had accomplished it, the regular military exercises went forward.

If one is an anthropologist, it is important to be able to make a chart of the Eskimos' hierarchy of spirits. As a novice, an amateur in meeting a primitive people, I was just interested in knowing the way they thought. Here came a boy of sixteen, one sunny day, starting down the lane to his father's boat—did he have the same emotions as a boy anywhere else who was going fishing? He was one of my friends, and he stopped as we met. In a voice filled with wonder he asked,

"Did you see the river ghost last night?"

"No—did you?"

"I did. Real plain." The wonder for me was the boy's smile, so thrilled and so sensitive.

The Eskimos are like people with dignity anywhere—they will not display the things that move them most deeply unless they know we are sympathetic. At Unalakleet I was helped by a lucky remark that I happened to make. I told one of the Eskimos that I thought I had seen a ghost once. Within a day, I would guess, the word had reached everyone in the village. Now I was one of them. I could be trusted.

The complex spirit world that surrounds the imagination of Eskimos has been dispersed only slightly by the Christian teachings of missionaries. Many natives still believe that each person has a number of souls. One soul in particular has a personal afterlife. It returns to the earth again and again—only infrequently, however, in human form. Since its appearances as a human being are rare, it is thought a great privilege to be here as we are, with human companions who also, in this reincarnation, are privileged and therefore are greatly to be respected.

Various parts of the body may have their minor souls, but it is the soul which corresponds to the little gold man that leaves when a person dies and may leave temporarily when he is sick. Weyer reports that sometimes when an Eskimo sneezes he exhorts his soul to "come back," and it may be a relic of a similar belief, that one has expelled his soul, which prompts the rest of us to say "God bless you" when children sneeze.

Eskimos have believed that inanimate objects have souls, especially such objects as have significance, like the bread that sustained Accibuk on his ordeal in the icy sea. But it is the souls of animals that concern them primarily, since the Eskimos live by hunting and they have believed that survival depended on the willingness of the animal spirits to be killed repeatedly in *their* reincarnations. In the past they were courteous to their victims in such ways as giving a slain seal a drink of fresh water. Among many Eskimo hunters, even today, there is respect for the animal spirits. When Dr. Maxwell Kennedy, dentist of Nome, shot a wolverine a few years ago, he dropped the carcass out of his plane at the village of Mary's Igloo because he knew that wolverine fur is valued highly for ruffs on parkis. He expected that he would be thanked the next time he stopped, but instead he found that the Eskimos were indignant. They reproved him: "You don't treat a dead wolverine like that."

These were complicated relationships between men and the ghosts of their prey, and it was easy to make mistakes. When bad luck, especially starvation, threatened a village, it was suspected that someone had broken taboos and offended the animals. As one of the ways to try to appease them, a medicine man, at a séance staged in the *kazhim*, might "leave his body and travel away to the ruler of animal spirits" to ask forgiveness. In the eastern area of the Eskimo country, the animal deity was believed to be Sedna, a sea goddess, but in Alaska it was the Moon.

Little Men, wandering souls of the dead, spirits of things and spirits of animals: these would seem to make a dense population in the Eskimos' supernatural world. There also are "spirits of strangers," which Weyer thinks are uneasy memories of an extinct tribe of tall Northern men, and some spirits he lists as simply "fantastic creatures," and finally the quite significant deity Sila.

Some of the fantastic creatures made appearances during my time at Unalakleet. One day when two young girls, Rachel and Lena, had come in to visit me, Lena said,

"Last winter there was a black man here. He stole axes and he left great big footprints. They were as long as my arm."

"Where did he stay?" I asked.

"At the school. In the basement. The door down there's always locked, so he was a ghost. The National Guard hunted all over, out on the tundra too, but they couldn't find him. They found his footprints, though."

Looking at Lena's round, bright, inquisitive face, I thought it would take more than a black man who left thirty-inch footprints to scare her. But Rachel, a shy, wistful girl, said,

"Stories like that make my back prickle." She added, "I don't believe them." And then went on: "But this really happened. When my brother Roger came home on furlough, we thought we'd go camping. The first day, after we put up the tent, Roger went outside. When he came in he said, 'Oomaloosook is out there.' Oomaloosook was an old man that had died while Roger was away. Roger didn't know he was dead, and he saw him."

The ghost of an old man is not exactly "fantastic," but I wouldn't know how else to classify the menace that I was warned of by one of the hunters: "If you camp in the mountains and you sleep under a tree, take a knife before you go to bed and stand off and strike the tree with it. Drive it in as far as you can and leave it there, because if you don't, the tree will wrap itself all around you and imprison you in the night."

Matilda spoke often of George, a playmate. When I asked why I hadn't seen him, she said he was "in the cemetery," and this was the reason:

"George and another boy went back in the woods to hunt. At night they saw an old woman coming towards them. She told them to go home right away. They wanted to stay, so they said that's what they were going to do. The old woman touched George in the middle of the back, she just touched him, but it hurt so much that he cried and cried. The boys came home, and afterwards, one day, George was in a boat. His gun was there and it got near the motor and went off and shot George in the forehead. His scalp flew right off."

I often heard of the "black ghost with green eyes that comes in off the tundra," and once I thought that I almost saw it myself. I had been walking a long way and was tired and lay down on the moss. The time was early summer when the marsh grass was bright and silky, and as the breeze blew over it there were dark shadows rippling the grass, coming my way, and of course all that green . . .

One morning in winter after a night when the Northern Lights were especially bright, a lad of fourteen asked me, "Did you hear us whistling at the lights last night? You can make them move fast by whistling at them." When I brought up the subject with one of the mothers, she said, "All Eskimo children believe that.

When the lights come down low and are red and the snow is red from the reflection, you can hear the lights." Some scientists say that they have confirmed a slight sound. She finished, "I don't like to go out alone at those times. I shiver. The old people think that the lights capture people and then play ball with their heads. 'Head balls,' we call those red lights."

In that woman's face as she talked about lights that might capture people, there was a fire, a vitality that I never have seen in the face of a scientist speaking of sunspots and the magnetic pole. Their subject would be the same, the Aurora Borealis, but the woman, who no longer *quite* believes in the head balls, was stimulated by even the thought that the old people have this supernatural faith.

It had been so with each of the Eskimos who revealed his sense of such marvels. Eyes brightened and voices strengthened. Some fears were involved, but any depressing effect that they might have had seemed to be more than offset by the electrifying idea that at any moment, right there outside the door, one might encounter a miracle.

I don't know what we are going to offer a primitive people that will replace the lost wonder. Julian Huxley has said that, for all of us in the future, "The religious impulse, itself one of the social forces to be more fully comprehended and controlled, will increasingly find its outlet in the promotion of the ideals of the Socialized State." That is one view of religion. To me it leaves something out. And it seems that Christianity, as I have heard it interpreted by the missionaries, leans too much on events that happened long ago; it does not offer enough surprise, surprise today, tomorrow, at the revelation of more-than-human powers.

> *From wonder into wonder*
> *Existence opens.*[1]

The religion of some Eskimo groups gives them, however, more than excitement, more than a sense of marvels. For it includes

[1] Laotzu.

Sila, a god that would have been interesting to pantheists such as Spinoza and Goethe, and possibly even to Einstein.

Sila (pronounced *Seelah*) is the only one of their spirits that the Eskimos think of as making requirements of man in his general conduct. One can win favor from other spirits by observing rites and taboos, but that's all very personal; one offends or pleases a being whose interests are selfish in the same way that men's are. But anger, morose, violent feelings, are believed to disturb the finely poised Spirit of the Air, or of the Universe, which the Eskimos have named Sila. If the bad feelings become extreme, it is thought that Sila takes action. This is a moral concept that must often have checked aggressiveness. It must have helped to promote the Eskimos' peaceful and tolerant attitudes.

The Eskimos' own description of Sila seems very close to pure spirituality, inasmuch as Sila is "air, weather, all outdoors" and at the same time is thought itself. A Moravian Eskimo dictionary defines the word (there spelled Sla and Tla) as "the world; out of doors" and also as "common sense." Perhaps sanity would be a synonym. The Eskimo word for acquiring understanding, *tlangok*, is from the same root.

The *ahn-gok-kok* Najagneq said these things to Knud Rasmussen about Sila:

"The ancients devoted their lives to maintaining the balance of the universe; to great things, immense, unfathomable things . . . a power we call Sila, which is not to be explained in simple words. When all is well Sila sends no message to mankind but withdraws into his own endless nothingness, apart. So he remains as long as men do not abuse life. . . . No one has seen Sila; his place of being is a mystery, in that he is at once amongst us and unspeakably far away."

My own clearest conception of Sila came from Dwight Milligrook. He had been explaining what morality means to the Eskimos and had said:

"Maybe the evil action, the deed, is not most important. The wicked motive preceeds the act, but we should go further back, even beyond the wish to do harm. A mood comes first, and so it may be the mood that is good or evil. If the mood is controlled, if it is kind and generous, there will be no wickedness."

And then Dwight spoke of Sila, the Spirit of the Air, and said that Sila, when angered, would touch men and they would no longer exist in any form, human or spirit. It was not a deed that would warrant that punishment, Dwight said, but the mood out of which the deed grows—"the mood that comes even before any wish to do wrong." He finished by telling me: "If you ever see a man going out over the ice in winter without his dogs, without any sled or hunting gear, don't go after him, don't speak to him. He is walking away alone because he is fighting a morose mood, and he needs solitude."

What he seeks, what is pleasing to Sila, is apparently what the Eskimos mean when they speak of a quiet mind.

Sila is abstract, unknowable, and represents the harmonious natural forces in the universe. Compare the words in which Einstein expressed his faith:

"That deeply emotional conviction of the presence of a superior reasoning power which is revealed in the incomprehensible universe, forms my idea of God."

With so many angry, aggressive minds in the world today, morose minds, it is almost with fear that one thinks of Sila, who has a new tool now for making us, all of us at the same time, vanish.

Pioneers in a Religious Wilderness

IT WOULD be hard to imagine a more demanding task than that of the missionaries who come to the arctic. First they have to adjust to the Northern living conditions. The able young Reverend Rowland J. Cox at Point Hope writes in a newsletter: "To a white man trying to master arctic life, the Point Hopers' favorite comment is, 'You'll learn.' If the white man's education progresses he is then told with measured approval, 'You learning something.' This white man has learned that arctic weather can be exasperating and monotonous and dangerous, and you have to wait for it. This is one reason why the Eskimo says 'maybe' more often than 'yes,' and answers nothing more definite than 'sometime' when asked 'when.' "

With his team of ten dogs the Reverend Mr. Cox traveled more than 600 miles in his first two years at Point Hope. The Episcopal mission there, St. Thomas', has two outstations: Kivalina, 75 miles away, and Point Lay, which is twice as far. He has had some harrowing near-disasters when he was caught on the trails in blizzards. More often he travels by plane.

Dog teams are used extensively too by the Roman Catholic priests of the lower Yukon. Typical of them is Father Harold Greif, now stationed at Dillingham. He arrived in Alaska on the same ship that first brought me North. Once a pianist in Paul Whiteman's orchestra, he was tireless in entertaining the other passengers, a man with such social grace that it was hard to think of him in the arctic solitudes. During the next four years I would hear about him occasionally—how he traveled from one little settlement to another many miles away, in what is perhaps the world's bitterest weather. And then one Christmastime he came to preach at Nome for two weeks.

I would not have known him, so spare, so ascetic he had become, but also with luminous kindness in face and manner. I attended his Christmas Eve mass, and never anywhere have I heard the Christmas story more movingly told, and yet it was told primarily for the Eskimo listeners and in their idiom.

As in preaching to all native peoples, the language barrier is a problem for the Alaska missionaries. Most of the younger Eskimos can speak English, and those who are middle-aged in the larger towns. Few of the elderly can. The missionaries must use interpreters—and are more or less at their mercy! A friend of mine, visiting in one village, went to church and noticed that the interpreter seemed to be repeating the same words every time he spoke. He asked him later what the words were, and the interpreter admitted that he kept telling the congregation: "The missionary has not said anything yet." An Eskimo woman in Nome told me that one native interpreter there preaches a sermon, but it is not the missionary's sermon. He lets the missionary say a few words and then he continues with what he himself wants to say. I am sure these are isolated instances, but, at best, preaching through an interpreter must be difficult.

I never have heard a missionary say this, but I should think their greatest problem would be the adapting of the Christian message to a race who already surpass many white people in the practice of Christian virtues. The missionaries take the great step of moving up to the arctic—and what could be more disconcerting than to find that the savages are more courteous and courageous, more honest and generous, than the civilized population one left behind? In the words of one of Alaska's highest officials, "The Eskimos have all the virtues we profess to admire." How embarrassing, if one has come up to their country to show them a better way! What can be said to them? How make a start?

Bessie Moses, an Eskimo, said that the first time she took her aunt to a mission church, a sermon was preached on the Ten Commandments. Bessie's aunt said to her: "But we've always known those things." Actually the Eskimos need leadership desperately in their adjustment to civilization, and some of the missionaries are giving it. Those who are most successful are building on the constructive elements in the Eskimos' old philosophy, but at least as many, perhaps more, of the missionaries begin by condemning everything in the native culture. One would not even let the native children spin their beautiful little Eskimo tops of ivory; he insisted that the parents make them new tops out of empty thread spools. These missionaries demand that the Eskimos now always speak of their spirits as "evil spirits." "Can the spirit of a flower be evil?" one of the Eskimo women asked me. She continued, "When the missionaries say that everything in our old religion was sinful, I think that is a sin."

Some Christian sects do bring one idea that is new to Eskimos: this idea of sin and the related concepts of hell and damnation.

To many white Northerners it seems that sometimes their missionaries lay undue stress on sin, that they are promoting all the unhappy results of guilt complexes by talking too negatively about right and wrong.

I have heard a missionary evangelist shout at his Eskimo audience: "I want you to learn every verse in the Bible that has the word 'hell' in it, because you take hell out of the Bible, you don't have much left."

Several of the Eskimos in that village said to me, "Maybe you'll tell us what sin is? We ask the missionary and he talks about things we don't do. But we have to have sins. If we don't stand up in church and tell people about our sins, the missionary says we will burn in the fires of hell forever."

I told them that some Christians don't even believe there is a hell, but the natives weren't too reassured. Other missionaries before this one had emphasized hell. One old Eskimo woman, in the delirium of her last illness, thought that she saw the fires of hell through the cracks in the floor. She cried out to her son to hold her, that she was falling into those fires. He put his arms around her, but she still thought she was slipping down into hell. He got a rope and tied her onto the bed, and then she felt safer.

One woman, ordinarily well balanced, became so alarmed about going to hell that she sent a dollar to a teacher she had done housework for seventeen years earlier, because she had eaten some chocolates out of a box one day. A child, sobbing that he was afraid of burning forever, confessed in church that when he was hungry once he took a cookie out of the trader's barrel. A woman who had had ten children and had lost seven sons by death confessed that she had not had any of them baptized. "They've all gone to hell!" cried the preacher. A wife confessed that, many years previously, she had made one indiscretion. Her husband, a pious convert, was so distressed that he was preparing to take his life when he was found and other Eskimos convinced him that he was giving too much importance to the incident.

Two women in that village have been so disturbed by the emotionalism of the preaching that they have lost their minds and had to be institutionalized. One never recovered.

The Eskimos as a people are touchingly open to any religious message. Any thought of the supernatural stirs them, and without being sanctimonious, they think goodness important. Where moving pictures are shown, they prefer religious pictures to any others. But a few are critical. An Eskimo man said to one of the missionaries, "If I did not know about standing up and confessing sins, would I burn in hell?" "No, not if you didn't know," said the missionary. "Then why did you tell me?" the Eskimo asked him.

In handling the matter of sex, one great difficulty appears to be that some of the missionaries are not well adjusted themselves. They think that they are encountering total license, whereas the problem is really one of convincing the Eskimos that they must adapt themselves to a world that is less pure, less responsible, than their own has been.

Some of the things that the more extreme missionaries say from the pulpit are characterized by the Eskimo men as "dirty talk," and they forbid their children to hear them. A missionary in Nome used to tie his female dog outside his house when she was in heat and then shoot the male dogs when they came around. One of the dogs he killed was a registered Labrador retriever, whose owner sued the missionary and got a judgment of a thousand dollars. The missionary left town, but he has opened his church in another village.

When the Eskimos ask their white friends about missionaries like these, we can only say that perhaps they are sick, as some of them in fact may be. We also wish that they could have wider training in the psychological and sociological subjects that would help them to understand a primitive people. Distressed by some of the things I was hearing a young missionary say to his troubled flock, I asked a friend of his, another missionary, what his training had been. The answer was that he had not gone beyond a year or two of high school "because he was eager to get into the mission field." He lacked judgment, however eager his motives were, and his preaching was of the type that causes the mental breakdowns and attempted suicides.

The National Council of Churches is beginning to sponsor training conferences, lasting two weeks, for missionaries who will be preaching to natives like Eskimos. The Episcopal Church has a similar program, except that they see two months as a better period of study. The fundamentalist sects do not belong to the National Council of Churches, and therefore their missionaries will not benefit from the training courses. Missionaries can have immense influence, and a question to ponder is: should they not be expected to meet some fitness requirements, just as teachers, doctors, nurses, and welfare workers are? Such requirements should not limit the freedom of worship. The law should not state what doctrines a man must or must not preach—any more than it tells a physician what medicine he must prescribe. But there should be some means of assuring that missionaries have some understanding of natives' psychological problems, and a normally healthy outlook themselves.

By 1903 there were about eighty missions and churches in Alaska. They had been duplicating one another's work, and so there had been an informal agreement to divide up Alaska among them. The Roman Catholics were to concentrate on the lower Yukon, the Moravians on the lower Kuskokwim, the Episcopalians on the upper Yukon and part of the arctic coast. The Norton Sound area was assigned to the Evangelical Mission Covenant Church, which was established by then at Unalakleet and soon opened more missions in the surrounding territory, including Nome. The agreed boundaries of influence are somewhat ignored now, especially by the many new sects that have come to Alaska. Since China was closed to the spread of American missions, Alaska seems an increasingly tempting field for new efforts.

I am not a Catholic nor an Episcopalian, but I've had many occasions to admire the work of these two groups of missionaries particularly. It is constructive, not alone because of the caliber of the men who are sent to the North, but also because of their thorough training. The Roman Catholic priests in Alaska are Jesuits, and most of the nuns are Ursulines, an order founded four hundred years ago with the main objective of training girls to be good wives and mothers. Even in the remote and bleak Yukon delta, where the Eskimos are more primitive than they are anywhere else in Alaska, the girls taught by these nuns learn almost as much about the fine points of child care as Stateside mothers who attend well-baby clinics.

The Episcopal missionaries are hand-picked by a young and very intelligent bishop, the Right Reverend William J. Gordon. They, like the Jesuits, bring a thorough grounding in sociology, psychology, and other secular fields of knowledge that help them in analyzing the natives' whole problem. And these aren't the only missionaries who visualize their work in the same broad terms. Miss Esther McCoy, for example, a sociologist with the Methodist mission at Nome, spreads around in her friendly and rather dry way a lot of good wholesome sense.

The Eskimos' problems are many, but three of them are most pressing. These are the change from their hunting economy to a competitive way of life, and the problems of alcoholism and, in the girls, promiscuity. Ideally there would be agreement among all the white people who try to guide them—teachers, missionaries, welfare workers, public-health nurses—as to the kind of help to be given the Eskimos in their great adjustment. Such co-operation does not exist, but any one group can be a helpful influence.

It's a long way from telling the Christian story to persuading a native to have more respect for clocks, but that is a sample of the sidelines that some of the missionaries undertake. The Eskimos have little conception of time as we know it. In their own culture they did not measure time. They ate when they were hungry, went to sleep when they were tired, and stayed in bed until they were rested. But a white man regulates all his life by these little ticking devices, and an Eskimo who wants some of civilization's benefits has to learn to do the same thing.

A generation ago there was a fine missionary named Replogle

at Noorvik who recognized that the Eskimos must begin to be conscious of time. He got a very large, weatherproof clock and hung it out in the village lane and urged the people to do their tasks by it. He also imported a sawmill and taught the people how to make better, more permanent houses. And he persuaded some Eskimos from the town of Deering, who had worked for white miners, to come to Noorvik and tell his congregation how they could best adapt themselves to the white-man's customs. In such additional ways, which may seem far from preaching eloquent sermons, a missionary can make himself indispensable.

It is essential for the Eskimos to become more realistic about money, but in that branch of teaching a church may be at a disadvantage. One missionary was persistent in his preaching of thrift. A few of the natives began to save—and became unpopular. The others thought they were stingy.

Stateside churchgoers are accustomed to appeals for financial support. To the Eskimos all talk of money seems to introduce a hard and materialistic thought. In their culture the one who has more always gives to those who have less; and shall the church, so apparently rich in their eyes, demand some of their few and much needed nickels?

Some of the missionaries sell the contents of mission boxes. In the natives' minds that is a practice which puts their pastor in the clothing business, and as a spiritual leader he loses influence. One of those missionaries said to me, "The natives have the nerve to ask me what I do with the money." I asked, "Would you mind telling me what you do with it?" He replied, "It's an expensive proposition to run a mission like this." Looking around the large, warm, comfortable rooms of the parsonage, I could believe him. The Eskimos, who see that house too, naturally compare it with their pitiful little cabins. In the missionary's place they probably would have given away most of the fine furniture. The pastor could not be expected to do that, of course, but if he lives rather luxuriously, as some of the missionaries do, he is going to have a hard time getting the collection plates filled at the Sunday services. He needs to make some explanation that will square with the Eskimos' ideas of unselfishness. I feel very sympathetic with a missionary in that position who is trying to figure out what to say.

Alcoholism among the Eskimos is so great a problem that it threatens their race. In Alaska a native has as much right to buy liquor as white men have. Individual communities can prohibit the sale of it, and many do, but it is bootlegged and anybody can have it shipped in from another town for his personal use. One or two of the airlines have refused to carry liquor to dry native villages, but some of it gets in everywhere through the white residents. The native men who come to the cities for work, and the students who come to school, often become alcoholics in a tragically short time.

Instead of calling the problem of native-girl sex relationships prostitution, as some missionaries do, it could be described more accurately as too gullible or too hopeful loving. The problem seldom comes up as such between Eskimo boys and girls, because those affairs are usually a prelude to marriage, as they always have been. An Eskimo married to an Eskimo takes the responsibilities of home life so seriously that even those who have seemed to be confirmed alcoholics usually become stable. But an Eskimo girl who has gone to one of the cities, or who has been thrown into contact with servicemen in her own village, assumes that the white boys also mean what they say. By the time she has learned differently, through a number of disillusionments, she is almost always an alcoholic, lost from her own people and lost in the white-man's world, as are also the boys who drink to excess.

The Roman Catholics and the Episcopalians share the opinion that the best way to prevent the native boys and girls from drifting out of control is to make their lives rich in wholesome recreation of many kinds—this in addition, of course, to the religious teaching. Dancing, especially folk dancing, is encouraged. Bands are organized. Little dramas are written and produced. At the least excuse of a holiday, gifts are made and exchanged. Movies, storytelling, singing in groups, ping-pong, parties, sports and games, including Eskimo games and dog-racing, are promoted in order to so fill up the young people's time and interest that they have no desire to wander into the dismal bars or out in the alleys.

Meanwhile, tastes are being formed. The boys and girls are discovering a new kind of companionship, less charged emotionally perhaps than their primitive pleasures were, but better suited to living in a civilized world. The atmosphere in which the work of this kind is carried on is one of the utmost friendliness and good nature. Young Father James Poole, S.J., writes of the children that he is shepherding: "Do say a little prayer now and then that His work and His plan for them may become dear to them and that I may win many children to God. . . . If we love them so much, how He must love them!"

The fundamentalist groups forbid all kinds of dancing, including the Eskimo dances that are simply pantomimes of hunting, fishing, dog-sledding, pastimes the Eskimos like to relive in rhythm. During the Christmas program at the Unalakleet school, one of the older Eskimo men impersonated Santa Claus. No dancing had been allowed there for a whole generation, but the happiness of the season must have been overwhelming, because Santa Claus broke into a few steps of a native dance. There was a gasp of delight from the audience. The elderly Eskimo woman next to me turned with tears in her eyes and said: "That is Eskimo dance! That is true dance! I remember it." The girl missionary beyond her gathered her wraps together with an indignant frown and left the room. I said to the Eskimo grandmother, "Do you think dancing is wicked?" She answered, "No, I do not think so. But if we dance and go to church too, they call us hypocrite or some word like that."

Some white parents at Nome, wanting more recreation for their young people, tried to organize a folk-dancing club, to be well chaperoned and to meet at the USO. More than half of the local missionaries opposed the plan. Children in some of the congregations are not even allowed to go to the parties at school.

No one doubts the zeal of the fundamentalist missionaries.

And no one doubts the sincerity of their belief that there is sin in such simple pleasures as folk dancing. But the rest of us have a right to our beliefs too, a right to say that we think the Eskimos, in this time of their anguished transition, will become stable more quickly if, instead of a sense of personal wickedness, they are encouraged to find outlets for wholesome, creative joy.

For most Eskimos, Sila is now out of reach, withdrawn to that "place of being . . . unspeakably far away." With what are we going to replace the discipline of the belief in Sila? With more, it must be, than threats of hell, demands for money, and scoldings for giving in to the temptations the white men have brought. To furnish the best kind of leadership, the Christian missionaries will be men of true spirituality, for Eskimos' ears are tuned to the voice of the spirit.

It also should be remembered that the Eskimos have something to give to us too, especially their sensitivity. Even an Eskimo child may have. Little Matilda Traeger at Unalakleet told me one day, "There was a man here who could always see another man just like himself, far away. Nobody else could see the other man, but he could. He and the other man didn't like each other."

She described a dream that she'd had. "In my dream I came walking along and I saw you scratching in the ashes of a fire. I said, 'What are you hunting for?' And you said, 'I am hunting for my spirit.' "

Through Matilda was a primitive race speaking to one that considers itself civilized?

10

Even Though
Ukfakineritarpitsia

ON MY FIRST DAY at Unalakleet I would not have supposed that David Paniptchuk could become one of my favorite Eskimos. When he interrupted my new sense of freedom by insisting, really demanding, that I promise to attend church regularly, his coercion had seemed so out of place in the peaceful atmosphere of the village that I resolved to avoid David. He must have sensed how I felt, for after that one almost violent missionary effort, he allowed the white woman to act like a heathen if so she wished, and our acquaintance proceeded normally.

Actually I was sorry that I could not have understood the sermons he preached in Eskimo to the old people. He was intelligent, and his talk was always full of interesting details. For example, I had admired the translucent green bands of trimming on some of the Eskimos' boots and had been told, simply, that they were skin of the wolf fish. It was David who added that wolf fish are hard to kill, that they have long, sharp, backward-curving teeth "like a killer whale's," so strong that after a wolf fish is caught and apparently dead it may bite through the bottom of a boat. Most fishermen therefore put a stick through its mouth to bite on.

For conversations like that I often invited David to tea with me. One day I'd made a cake, propping the broken oven door shut with a board braced against nails in the floor. It was a memorable day, because out of a chance remark David made, I began to study the Eskimo language with him; and the Eskimos' language opens a wide new door to their complex and fascinating minds.

Responding to something unimportant I'd said, David had commented in a wondering tone,

"You use the words 'the rest' and 'the others' as if they meant the same thing."

I put down my cup carefully. Words were my fetish, but, "David," I said, "I don't know the difference between 'the rest' and 'the others.' "

He explained:

" 'The rest' means 'the remainder.' If we were unloading the barge and had brought most of the cartons up to the warehouse, the trader might say, 'Go down and get the rest.' If he said, 'Put all the broken cartons in the store but put the others in the warehouse,' then 'the others' would have the meaning of 'not the same,' a contrast. Last night we were talking about how we'd vote, if we could. I said I would vote for Dewey, but *the others* said they would vote for Truman."

My first feelings of embarrassment, that I had been caught using words carelessly by this Eskimo, soon gave way to a doubt: was that distinction between 'the rest' and 'the others' really made in the English language? Among the books I had brought to Unalakleet was a Webster dictionary. Under "other" David and I found, "A different or additional one"—no distinction in meaning. In Webster's *Dictionary of Synonyms* was an illustration of the use of "rest": "Two stories in this book are interesting but the rest are uniformly dull." According to David, the sentence should have read, "but the others are uniformly dull," since the thought of contrast was obvious. *The American Oxford Dictionary* de-

fined "rest" as "the remainder" but also as "the others." There
could be only one conclusion—that the Eskimos gave these English words finer meanings than even we found in them.

David was finishing his piece of cake. He said,

"We have one word, *mick-shrok*, meaning 'little but satisfac-
tory.' Another word, *oo-too-koo*, means 'small and I wish it were
bigger.'" David was gesturing with his last bite of cake in his fingers, and then, popping it into his mouth, he laughed. I gave
him another piece, or, as I guess David would say, an additional
piece.

Seeing that I was interested, he went on with our language lesson:

"We have many more words for some things than you have.
If you wanted to know the Eskimo word for 'snow,' I would have
to ask, 'What kind of snow do you mean?' We have several
words for various kinds of snow. You have one word for 'walrus.'
We have nine, referring to walrus of the two sexes at different
ages.

"But sometimes we use the same word with several meanings.
You know the village Shaktolik, thirty-five miles north of here? It
is on a sandbar. *Shaktolik* is our word for 'sandbar.' It also means
'stretched-out,' and further it means the feeling you have when
you have been going towards a place for so long that it seems you
will never get there.

"Our words for 'green' and 'gall' and 'anger' all have the same
root, *tshunga*. 'Anger' seems more angry and more unpleasant
when the word reminds you of that nasty green liquid, gall—
don't you agree?" I did agree, and I remembered what one of the
Eskimo women had told me—that the people of her race not only
smile when they meet an enemy, but they try even "to feel the
smile in our hearts."

David spoke English like any American, with no accent, no
omission of articles, and no reversing of the parts of his sentences.
Most of the Eskimos of his age—he was well into his sixties—
knew very few English words, but the first missionaries at Unalak-

leet had trained David to be an interpreter from the time he was
very small. In his young manhood he had had additional contact
with white people in summer work on the Yukon River boats. He
was a full-blooded Eskimo; his father was one of the five famous
brothers who came from the northern, Malemute country and settled in Unalakleet. Having northern relatives would have been an
advantage to David in his work as interpreter. There are numerous
Eskimo dialects in Alaska. All of those south of Unalakleet are
grouped as "the southern language" and those to the north as
"the northern language." Unalakleet, combining them, has a dialect of its own.

One can get an idea of the different pronunciations in various
dialects from these different spellings, originating in different
parts of Alaska, that I have found for the name of a root that
the Eskimos translate as "wild sweet potato":

> *masu*
> *mashu*
> *muhzut*
> *mazué*
> *mahzee*

The linguists are trying to stabilize the spelling of Eskimo
words, and to publish an adequate dictionary that can be used all
the way from Alaska to Greenland. As is well known, an Eskimo
from anywhere in that vast span of territory can make himself understood anywhere else, even though his dialect may be unfamiliar
—a uniformity of language that is very significant to anthropologists in trying to trace the origin of the race. Lacking the dictionary, anyone like myself, who journeys into Eskimo country and
wants to keep a record of some Eskimo words, must conjure up
his own spelling. I first noted the Eskimo word for "thank you" as
koy-anna. Later I thought I could hear a *w* sound in it, and I began writing it *quoi-ana*. Then I found that a partial Eskimo dictionary published by the Moravian Church [1] spells the word

[1] See Bibliography.

kuyana. In Greenland there apparently is an *r* in it, since visitors there sometimes spell the word *kroyanna.*

If you ask an Eskimo how one of his words is spelled, he is of little help. Before white men came to his country, his language was not written down. The Eskimos did make drawings, wonderfully expressive little pictographs, in which, with a few lines, they could represent a man doing various things and could even indicate something of his feelings. They also had a gesture language and a "language" of different kinds of smiles and of facial expressions.

The gesture language was quite extensive both as to meanings and to area; a traveler going into a region where the dialect was strange could say with motions almost anything he might want to communicate—more easily sometimes than to try to reconcile dialects. These were some of the gesture words:

> "Man" —*pretend to pull outward the ends of a mustache*
>
> "Woman" —*a stroke down the side of the head and along the shoulder, meaning long hair*
>
> "Young woman" —*to the sign for "woman" add a touch on the lobe of the ear, meaning earring*
>
> "Mother" —*the sign for "woman" plus the sign for "to be born," which is a motion of both hands over the pelvis suggesting the curve a child's head follows in birth*
>
> "I," "Me," "My," "Mine"—*place the tips of the fingers lightly on the middle of the chest and incline the head forward*

There were signs for all the important nouns and also such useful verbs as "to eat," "to kill," "to fight," "to give," "to hunt," "to sleep," and "to die."

Even now a mother often says "no" or "be quiet" to her child by wrinkling her nose three times; and she says "yes" by raising her eyebrows.

It is not well known, but the Eskimos have, finally, a humor or laughter language: untranslatable sounds by which, it is said, very subtle humorous meanings can be expressed. The white husband of an Eskimo woman told me he often felt envious when a group of Eskimos shared the "jokes in sound" that they could not explain to him.

Some of the white-men's words have been taken into the Eskimos' own spoken language. Thus, "teacher" is *tookti*. In the Yukon area where the early Russians had trading posts, the general word for "white man" is *kazzak*, plural *kazzat*; the word came originally, of course, from "Cossack." In many parts of the Eskimo country the word they use for themselves is *Inuit*, but from Unalakleet south it is *Yut*. Usually a white man translates both words simply as "the people," but an Eskimo puts an extra sense of self-respect into it—as one might say *"the* people" or "the fine, complete people."

To mean "language" the Eskimos use a suffix, *stun*. *Kazzatstun* is the English language; *Yutstun*, the Eskimo language.

Many, perhaps most, Eskimo words are extremely complicated combinations of modifiers. A simple example is *pak*, in some places *puk* or *buk*. Affixed to a word, it increases the size. *Sik-sik* is "squirrel"; therefore *sik-sik-puk* is "big squirrel" and refers to marmots. An interesting suffix is *pik*, which means "right," and by "right" the Eskimos think of the right hand and also, curiously, "right" as we think of it, in the sense of "good" or "correct." They often speak of Eskimos as *Yupik*, the "right people."

The most significant thing about their language, and it is fairly staggering, is the number of endings a word will have to conform to its place in the sentence and intricate changes of meaning within the word itself. In their very simplest forms a noun will have thirty-six endings and a verb more than 600. These numbers, great as they are, are enormously extended by suffixes with such meanings as "new," "bad," "dear," "mutual," "feels cold in," "something that may be used for," "is in the habit of," and such complex modifications as "has come farther in that direction" and "without hesitation or hindrance." These modifiers are not always at the end of the word; sometimes they are added between other syllables, and the modifiers are spelled different ways according to rules of their own. There is one, for example, which means "goes or comes in order to," and it has all these forms: *-iartortok*, *-giartortok*, *-tshartortok*, and *-iartora*. The Moravian dictionary gives this example of its use: *kaneruta* means "said to him"; therefore *kanerutshartora* means "has gone in order to tell him."

The dictionary gives various samples of sentences that would thus be constructed, such as *imeramiutartinginakoratlerkamignun ayagtut*. It means: "They went to the places where they usually try to catch mink." Actually our sentence contains eight more letters and is not nearly so carefully put together, inasmuch as its elements are not very much modified to conform to one another. "Places" would be "places" whether the subject or object of the verb. But in Eskimo the noun would change in thirty-six different ways according to whether it was subject or object, single or plural, my place, your place, their place, or places, etc.

Verbs have suffixes that make them agree with either single or plural subjects and others agreeing with "two"; with subjects, for example, such as "I," "we two," or "we" (more than two). The verbs change to agree with single, dual, and plural objects as well as subjects. The subjunctive tense, which is increasingly ignored in our language as we speak it, is used meticulously by Eskimos when they speak either their language or ours. Thus they say: "If it *be* true," and "if I *were* the one." The endings by which these fine distinctions in meaning are made in the Eskimo language are complicated beyond anything even a Latin student has dreamed of. If the object of a verb in one of the subjunctive uses is a personal pronoun, the verb ends in these different ways:

Object of the Verb	Suffix to the Verb
me	*kuninginga*
us two	*kunigtkuk*
us (more than two)	*kunigtkut*
you (singular)	*kuniginitin*
you two	*kuniginikik*
you (more than two)	*kuniginigtse*
him	*kunigto*
them (two)	*kunigtkik*
them (more than two)	*kunigtke*

Those are samples of some of the more than 600 endings.

There is, surprisingly, one way in which Eskimo grammar is simpler than ours: there is no gender. Eskimos who speak only brokenly in our language sometimes have difficulty in straightening out "his" and "hers." Last year in Fairbanks when a young Eskimo girl was riding with me in a car, she said, "When the French people first make a new thing like an automobile, I wonder how they decide whether it's masculine or feminine. And they have to decide too about all its parts, whether windshields and speedometers and clutches are male or female." She was studying French at college, and it was typical of the Eskimo in her to have that humorous little turn of thought.

Unfortunately for those who would like to know from reading about them how Eskimo words are pronounced, there is no way to reproduce some of the sounds with our letters. During the second language lesson I had with David Paniptchuk he said:

"Did you ever realize that *k* can be pronounced all the way from the front of your mouth to deep in your throat?" He made me say *k* with different parts of my tongue till I had it so far back that I nearly swallowed it. The Eskimos use at least two *k*'s, one pronounced where we do ordinarily and one against the soft palate, bringing the uvula into play. Experience with French *r*'s had prepared me for that exercise but not for an Eskimo sound I can make only by keeping my tongue pressed tight against the roof of my mouth and then trying to say *tl*. It comes out at the sides and is apt to be rather juicy.

The Eskimo language as spoken is strong and vigorous, with fine distinctions in sound that our ears do not catch until we ourselves try to reproduce them. David would drill me in saying various words, and when I thought I was doing quite well, sometimes he would say: "Oh, no, nothing like that!" An Eskimo girl in Nome once told me: "When I change from speaking Eskimo to English, in English my tongue feels stiff." The tone that an Eskimo uses in speaking English is usually much softer than that in which he speaks his own language. The reason might be his uncertainty.

It is said that most Eskimos, in their ordinary talk, use about 10,000 words a day, while the average educated white man uses only about 3,500. And even so, some of their single words express what we would with a sentence:

> kayumigtok: *said if a person intends to go away but gives up*
> *the trip; however afterwards wishes to go*
> naktligiaguta: *is kindly disposed to him after having not loved*
> *him*
> paktok: *is not sure about something and goes to see how it is*

One could give endless examples of interesting and meaningful Eskimo words. Incidentally, they use one word, as we do, for "meaning" and "point." It is *ekok*, which would refer to a point of land and also to understanding, as we would say, "You get the point." Some words express almost a whole philosophy, as *navugutut*, "quarrel," which literally is, "They break one another." Many personal names and names of places have descriptive meanings. One of my favorites is a settlement on the Kuskokwim River, Ugavik: "the place where someone cried 'Oh!' "

Perhaps the most interesting word in the Eskimo language, however, is *Sila*; for is it coincidence, only, that the Eskimos chose this name for their deity, when they have no present way of knowing that the same word is found in most Oriental languages, also there meaning the concepts of self-discipline, avoidance of anger, cultivation of a calm, quiet mind, and at the same time, command, or rule? *Sīla* was the original Sanskrit word, used for virtues almost identical with those that the Eskimos have objectified.

Many white neighbors of Eskimos never have taken the trouble to learn how their minds are working behind those courteous and misleading smiles: how the Eskimos are poetic enough to have one word for "the feeling you have when you have been going towards a place for so long that it seems you will never get there"; and how they have combined in the name of a god the complexly related ideas of sanity, good will, natural laws, and the infinite sky.

"Eskimos are like children": I have heard that said often. Sometimes I have thought, then, Even though *ukfakineritarpitsia*,[2] the Eskimos aren't the children.

[2] "You do not believe me."

11

A Race Adrift

A NOME ESKIMO, Jim Sirloak, had been telling me how his nephew, Gregory Iyac, was lost on the Bering Sea ice for three weeks after the currents had carried away his boat. At the end of the story Jim paused, and smiled sadly, and with a look of patient hopelessness said,

"All Eskimo people are like drifting away on the ice. We don't know if we ever will come to land again."

It was a very good figure of speech. For the Eskimos are indeed lost at the present time, without a firm footing in either their own life or ours. Some of them in the more remote settlements still feel fairly secure in their old, immemorial ways, but for most of them contact with civilization has swept aside everything they have always believed to be right and safe. They are adrift and, through no fault of their own, almost helpless.

Almost—but in comparing his people's condition to Gregory's, Jim Sirloak was suggesting even more than he may have meant. For his nephew did come to land. Gregory reached the shore for two reasons. One was his own harrowing effort, the way he kept moving through all those weeks, jumping across the leads from one pan of ice to another, always trying to find some beach that he could not see . . . and a few Eskimos do work out civilized lives, by making very great, almost superhuman demands on themselves.

With the utmost exertion Gregory could not have saved himself, however, if the ice floes had not also been pushed towards the land by the winds and tides—if fate had not come to his aid . . . and the Eskimos will not reach their new cultural shore unless the intelligent help of white men gives them the right direction.

When we expect an Eskimo to adjust to our way of life solely through his own efforts, we do not recognize the vast distance he has to cover. We see him, perhaps dressed in cords and a leather jacket, running a tractor at one of the military construction sites. Although his face is more deeply tanned than ours, and its contours seem Oriental, we think that he's "civilized" now, that most of his problems are solved. But this job is temporary, and a look at his whole situation shows it to be one of all but crushing discouragements.

Ill health is the most immediate threat. In the past, entire villages have been wiped out by epidemics of measles, and even this year many Eskimo babies may die from it. For Eskimos as a race have not had time yet to build up immunity to the white-man's infectious diseases. Of these, tuberculosis is much the most prevalent. In some villages between Unalakleet and the Aleutian Islands eighty per cent of the natives now have it or did in the past. When I was at Unalakleet only one person in four was tubercular there, but that proportion—so shocking itself—was low for the Eskimos as a whole. For decades the Indian Bureau made rather ineffectual efforts to bring the disease under control, with so little success that the United States Public Health Service has taken over the care of Alaska natives. This agency's more decisive policies, aided by recent discoveries in chemotherapy, are resulting in fewer new cases, fewer deaths, and more cures. Tuberculosis still is a menace of terrifying dimensions to individual Eskimos; however it probably will not destroy the whole race, as for a long time it threatened to do.

At Seattle's Firland Sanitorium, where many Alaska natives are treated, a seven-year study has shown that emotional stress seems to have made Eskimos more susceptible to the disease. As reported by Dr. Thomas H. Holmes, Associate Professor of Psychiatry at the University of Washington, typical patients had been facing emotional crises a short time before they were hospitalized for tuberculosis. For Eskimos, as for all of us, health is related to other than purely physical problems.

Living on an uncertain supply of wildlife, Eskimos were accustomed in former times to actual danger that they might starve. Malnutrition does sometimes occur now, but the U.S. government does not knowingly allow anyone under its flag to die of hunger. Insecurity for the Eskimo today is the more subtle but powerful complex of fears that results from the loss of his ancient culture.

A culture is something too deeply ingrained to be laid aside as a parki is. It includes the kinds of houses, furniture, clothing, food, tools, utensils that we have known since birth and which give us support emotionally if only because of their being familiar. Sociologists find that slum-clearance projects, which provide better housing for underprivileged families, may create a psychological strain by taking away the comfort of older associations. The Eskimos, changing to civilized clothing, food, housing, weapons and other gear, are making a transition which is much larger than that of the former slum-dwellers.

A culture is also something far more significant: an approach to life, the combined habits, attitudes, and religion that have seemed to work best in assuring a given people's survival. It is in such intangibles that the Eskimos are most perilously adrift.

In their own way of life, for example, all relationships have been based on co-operation. Now, they learn, they must compete with one another. In place of trust, they must develop wariness. Instead of being alert at all times to help any neighbor secure his food, an Eskimo of today must ask himself whether the neighbor may not be seeking the same job that he is, and, if so, try to beat him to it. Most white Americans have acquired the ability to feel good will towards others while attempting to get ahead of them—a difficult feat and not always achieved to perfection. Such juggling of one's emotions does not come easily, even to some who think of themselves as sophisticated. It certainly can't be developed from scratch in a day or a year, and no one should expect that an Eskimo would have mastered the skill simply by climbing onto the seat of a tractor. He may be able to drive the tractor a whole generation earlier than he can drive himself into some of the civilized ways of thinking.

Related, too, to Caucasian aggressiveness are such mental habits as working according to plans, and accepting a grind, and adjusting to a fast pace. If a white worker walked off a job in the middle of the afternoon because he was bored with its irritations, we would consider that he was lacking in self-discipline, since dogged endurance has been bred into him through generations. A very different kind of adaptability has been required of an Eskimo. As a hunter he had to wait, to watch and listen, to grope for his hunches—to be passive yet vigilant, ready to act instantly if a whale should swim by or a fox appear on the beach. He has had to keep himself sensitive, as a wild bird is sensitive, always receptive to nature's cues. His consciousness has been as different from that of a civilized worker's as it could be and still have the qualities of an intelligent human mind.

Many of those who ought to know better have said,

"Let the Eskimos move to the white-man's cities. As a race they are famous for their mechanical skill. Let them put on overalls and go into factories. They would be better off living like the rest of us anyway."

It is a question how well one of us could adapt to a totally contrasting culture. Here is a young white American, brought up in Detroit and employed for a time in an automotive plant. Some quirks of circumstance, perhaps a few enemy missiles, have put him up in the North and out of touch with others of his own race, and have made it necessary, for the foreseeable future, for him to live like an Eskimo.

The mechanic was once a good deer-hunter, and so he should

be able to fit into the Eskimos' life, just as an Eskimo should be able to use his clever hands on an assembly line. Of course this is a different kind of hunting, out on the arctic sea—no stalking of prey along game trails, just paddling around among ice pans, slowly and silently, and keen-eyed to discover the wet silvery fur of a seal's forehead among the wet silvery waves. Meanwhile it is very cold (the confusion and noise of a factory would be quite as disturbing to Eskimos).

The only companionship the American has now are people of a strange race. All their traditions and habits and ways of thinking are foreign to him. How do they find their animals? Largely by intuition and also, they say, by using their magic songs. They do not eat breakfast before they go out, because no prey would allow itself to be caught by a hunter who wasn't hungry. The mystic discipline goes even further. Two or three years ago there was agitation among the Unalakleet Eskimos on the question of voting to incorporate as a second-class city. The discussions soon turned into murmurs that "We have to settle this city thing right away because it is causing bad feelings, and bad feelings will drive off the seals."

Could anybody expect our white boy to make the transition happily to that life just by putting on Eskimo clothes and utilizing his skill with a rifle? Could he quickly come to believe in the magic songs, and learn to like whale meat, and forget modern plumbing, and never again long to watch television or see a baseball game? Could he abandon his old religion and by one act of faith become a disciple of the Eskimos' Sila?

If an Eskimo went to Detroit, his companions there would be talking about union elections, this year's models compared with last year's, tonight's prize fight, and perhaps the gang war in a mixed neighborhood. Even if the Eskimo could speak English well, every word of that talk would be unfamiliar. Not one thing in his past would be related to any of this, and here he stands in this alien atmosphere, not creatively using his mechanical talents, just pushing one piece of metal into a groove in another and

sending them on their way, and picking up two more, thousands
exactly alike, day after day, and going home to the strangeness of
an American apartment, to hear how his children were taunted at
school because they are Eskimos.

Bureaucracy in Action

No one can lay his culture completely aside any more than he
can discard his bones. But the Bureau of Indian Affairs is proposing just this: that the Eskimos be removed from the Northern
hunting grounds that they love and sent to factories in Los
Angeles, Chicago, and Detroit. A team of officials, headed by Mr.
William H. Olson, Alaska director of the Indian Bureau, are going
out to the villages and holding meetings at which they offer to send
native families to an industrial Stateside city. They not only offer
to send them—they urge them to go. A few of the Eskimos,
having no slightest idea of what they are getting into, accept.

This is a really amazing policy on the part of the bureau given
responsibility for our native people, because they know from extensive experience that many Eskimos cannot even adjust to
Nome, in the natives' own arctic, a town of 1,800 where they
constitute half the population. Those who find summer work
there on the gold dredges usually are the half-breeds, who do
better at fitting themselves to the white-man's ways. Even for them
a summer seems endless, tied as they are to a routine and doing
work that is only drudgery. By autumn the strain can become
overwhelming, and then the direction in which their feet auto-
matically move is towards the bars.

If our American, lost from his racial background, could escape
into alcoholic oblivion for a while, does anyone think that he
wouldn't be likely to do it? Of course he would. Alcoholism is
only slightly less a menace to Eskimos than tuberculosis is, and
no one is better aware of that fact than the Indian Bureau officials.
Yet they are taking the native families from dry Eskimo settlements to cities where they pass bars in block after block, and with

new reasons then for needing that kind of solace. What is called for, it seems obvious, is an interim program, some means of permitting the Eskimos to hold on to familiar values while they are becoming stiffened for a competitive life, and a life in which they will meet many new kinds of temptations.

The Eskimos all do want money now. The old hunting economy does not satisfy them because they are becoming acquainted with civilization's comforts and safeguards and naturally they desire these benefits for themselves. Some Eskimos work on road gangs, at longshoring, in mines, construction, etc., during the summer months and return to their coastal villages for winters of hunting and trapping. In many cases that arrangement is not at all bad. It has the great advantage of not being a total change from their aboriginal life, and of being carried out on the Eskimos' own initiative. With more help, more sympathetic interest on the part of the Indian Bureau, a seasonal kind of life could furnish an educational transition period of great value. But the Indian Bureau, with their determination to empty the native towns—in the States as well as Alaska—do not supply that encouragement.

There is no doubt that most Eskimos do want to remain in their own arctic country. It may look bleak and forbidding to sophisticated officials from Washington who fly up for typical three-day tours of inspection. Many white settlers, including myself, think the North an inspiring and wholesome place. At any rate, that's where the Eskimos want to stay. One of the reasons was explained by a girl from Unalakleet, Ida Degnan, who was taken down to Seattle by a family of Stateside friends. "It was exciting at first," she said, "but pretty soon it just seemed too busy."

The question is, what can the inhabitants of small arctic towns produce that people elsewhere will buy and thus furnish the Eskimos with cash income? They of course should have better houses, food, recreation, and a few of the luxuries, but for the present they would be content with much less than people whose civilized background is older. In the last few years military installations have been built in several Eskimo towns. The contractors have paid Eskimo laborers union wages, with huge bonuses because the jobs were classified as "remote site," although most of the natives were living in the same cabins where they were born. Some have earned $1,500 a month—and they didn't know what to do with the money. No means were provided for banking it, and no one urged them to save it. They spent it for knickknacks (one man bought six expensive watches), and by now it is mostly gone. One has to learn gradually how to be a consumer as well as a producer, and until the lesson has been absorbed, the Eskimos will get along better on modest incomes.

The problem of fitting the remote Eskimos into the over-all American economic picture is not an easy one. On the other hand it is not hopeless. If local resources are utilized, there will be no one solution. All Eskimos, everywhere, cannot be put to doing the same kind of job, but the following are some suggestions.

Eskimos can collect eiderdown. Many eiderducks nest in Alaska. The mother duck pulls some down from her breast to cradle the eggs. If the down is removed from the nest, she will pull more, and three batches can be secured without injury to the bird or its young, for the duck has an ample supply of down and it grows again. Eskimos in both Greenland and Canada gather and sell eiderdown.

Eskimos could, and do in Canada, raise geese, which thrive in cold climates. The market for goose feathers is even greater than that for eiderdown, and the geese, without too much difficulty, can be domesticated. Besides sales of feathers, the birds themselves and their eggs could be used as a source of food for Eskimo families.

Eskimos could sell specimens of many kinds to museums and scientists. Included would be fossils, skins and skulls of arctic birds and animals, insects, plants, shells, mineral specimens. Every scientist who goes up to the North is weighted down with requests from other scientists that he send such-and-such a wild-bird skin, or plant, or butterfly. Eskimos could assemble these very well, once they were given simple instructions. Perhaps organized

in school science classes, such a project might develop into the
kind of part-time source of revenue that is needed to supplement
the food and clothing that the Eskimos take for themselves from
nature. Scientists probably would be glad to publicize such a
service.

The present raising of vegetables could be much expanded.
Gardens cannot be grown on permafrost, but they do surprisingly
well on river bars, sandspits, and around hot springs, where the
ground thaws in summer. Some produce is now sold half-heartedly,
sent to such towns as Nome. There is never enough of it in the
markets. For some reason, perhaps the quick growth under the
continuous summer sun, the vegetables are unusually delicious
and tender. Most vegetables sold in Fairbanks and Anchorage are
flown up from the States, while those grown at Unalakleet, only
a fourth as far away, are more tasty and would be cheaper. With
encouragement—always the need is encouragement—Eskimo
families at one of the garden locations could add substantially to
their incomes.

Considered so far are occupations that would require little
training or capital. The list could be much expanded if those
forms of help were supplied.

For example, it seems a grotesque situation that no commercial
tanning of furs is done in Alaska. Skins tanned by the native
methods will not sell to white customers because the skins have
an odor. Tanning plants could be built in the North however,
and the tanning techniques certainly could be taught to Eskimos.
They catch and dry the skins, and why not send them to market
ready to be made up into garments? Why not, indeed, establish
Alaska fur factories? The services of good stylists would be required, but the actual handwork of Eskimo women, even if they
were using machines, would at least equal that of any skin-sewers
in the States. Eskimos have a wonderfully adept touch with
hides.

In my house at Nome I used only bear skins for floor coverings—

white, black, grizzly, and a blond glacier-bear skin. All had been caught in Alaska but had had to be sent to the States to be tanned. Not only bear rugs, but those of wolves, wolverines, and bearded seals almost certainly would sell well if tourists could buy them. Besides skins like these there are furs supplied by Alaska trappers: fox, marten, mink, ermine. Why are they not tanned here? More valuable than all these together are the fur seals of Alaska's Pribilof Islands. It seems both unjust and unreasonable that one of the Territory's chief natural resources, the fur seals, should be processed in St. Louis, Missouri. Nome is close to the islands; and if the factory were transferred there, it would support many Eskimo families.

And then coal: there are surface deposits of coal in many places throughout the Eskimo country, one of the best being twelve miles from Unalakleet. They are not being worked, except one at Meade River, and for the Franklin stove that I used in a bedroom at Nome I paid $67.50 a ton for coal brought from Utah. If cheap coal were available, it is likely that many people who live in northwest Alaska would switch from the use of expensive imported oil to heat their homes, or from driftwood or the uncertain supply of whale blubber still used by some natives.

Such mining is practical. Japanese interests plan to develop one or more of the local mines and ship the coal to their country. Is there less initiative on the part of Americans? Some equipment of course would be needed, and a few technicians, but both native and white Northerners would profit from an opening of these mines.

Even those forms of employment that would require supervision should be owned by the Eskimos themselves wherever possible. The projects should not be thought of, at present, solely in terms of profits but as means of helping a primitive people to gain experience in a civilized craft. In the beginning, therefore, the enterprises might warrant some government subsidies. From the billions in aid to the people of foreign countries, might not some small proportion be expended upon our own Eskimos? If our foreign-aid program can be described realistically as an effort to hold back Communism, that argument too might apply in Alaska.

The project would best succeed, perhaps only possibly succeed, if the Eskimos were given a chance to keep some feeling of independence, and to use skills. Almost all Eskimos have something like an artist's approach to work: they want to do it creatively, in tasks that call for imagination and judgment, at the very least to make some important decisions themselves. It is irrelevant to say that we'd all like to work that way. Most of us would, but long ago we accepted a different system. The Eskimos haven't, and as yet probably can't. In planning means for them to make money, it should be kept in mind that, at this stage of their development, their morale simply collapses under the strain of too much monotony. Hours and working conditions should be tempered to what they can stand.

The philosophical Dwight Milligrook at Unalakleet said this:

"When you work for wages, your thoughts turn towards yourself. You look down when you walk. You no longer love simple things like little animals and the sky and beautiful country. You are self-centered and feel sober and thin. If you are locked up in jail, you do not feel like yourself, and having to work for somebody else is only like being locked up with a longer string."

It should be remembered too that Eskimos still like to help one another, and for that reason co-operatives may do better than individually owned businesses. Admiral Byrd employed a number of Eskimo women at Nome to make the men's clothing for one of the antarctic expeditions. He was so pleased with their work that he sent the women a bonus of $5,000. Under the leadership of the able Eskimo, Emma Willoya, they used the money to start a co-operative to make ski parkis, fur mittens, boots, and coats, Eskimo dolls, sealskin footstools, and other such articles that civilized people will buy. Called the Nome Skin-Sewers Cooperative Association, the women have assets now of more than

$40,000 and fill orders from many parts of the States. A few years ago they were called on to outfit an Argentine expedition into the polar regions.

The legal machinery for giving Eskimos some financial assistance already has been established. Congress has appropriated funds, under the Wheeler-Howard Act, to make loans to natives to set themselves up in business or to have individual training. Logically, the Bureau of Indian Affairs is the agency to disperse those funds. A few loans have been made to finance fishing boats, and a few co-operative canneries in Southeastern Alaska got their start in that way. The Indian Bureau is now trying to have those canneries transferred into private hands, and their policy regarding the training of special talents is illustrated by a project conceived by Ernest Gruening when he was Alaska's governor.

With great difficulty Dr. Gruening persuaded the reluctant bureau to send a few gifted young Eskimo men to Mexico to work under William Spratling, the artist who has trained Mexicans in the field of silvercraft. Later the Eskimos' work went on display in Washington. As described by Alaska's Delegate, E. L. Bartlett, "It was novel. It was striking. It could have been the basis for a notable stimulation in the sale of ivory and related handiwork. But nothing at all was ever done with it. The bureau's opposition, apparently, had never diminished."

The 1957 Alaska Senate requested that Congress investigate Indian Bureau policies in Alaska. The Committee on Government Operations made the study, and in their partial report stated:

> The attitudes of Bureau personnel have not aided the carrying out of the objectives of the Wheeler-Howard Act. These attitudes reflect complacency and a skepticism of the natives' capacity to aid themselves. . . . The Washington office of the Bureau seems to . . . put little emphasis on the basic objectives of the act: To help provide . . . economic enterprises for the [natives'] self-help and self-support, and thus to assist them in attaining a wholesome American life.

One project, however, the Indian Bureau has always supported enthusiastically: ANICA, or the Alaska Native Industries Cooperative Association, mainly a group of village stores. The organization was the idea of Indian Bureau personnel who, in 1946, secured Wheeler-Howard Act government loans to finance the stores. The announced plan was that the village stores would pool their buying orders through a Seattle office and thus lower the wholesale cost of goods. Store profits were supposed to be turned in to liquidate the loans, after which time the profits—the promise was—could be retained by the village people, either as dividends, or lower prices, or financing for community improvements such as water and electric systems.

Wholesale prices did not come down. Inferior, off-standard brands arrived at the stores, and also goods that the Eskimos cannot use, such as oversized work pants. In many cases the merchandise was billed at prices as high as, or higher than, those charged by regular wholesalers. The natives, not experienced but not stupid either, assumed that Indian Bureau officials had bought shoddy goods cheaply and had pocketed the difference in cost.

The original loan to the Unalakleet store was $40,000. The store had been operating for three years when I was there and never had been able to get a statement of its financial condition. A traveling Indian Bureau supervisor told the store-manager, however, that the indebtedness had increased, not decreased. At one time it reached $70,000. Where had the profits gone?

The revamping of orders in the Seattle office, the sending of unwanted goods while essential supplies are cut down in quantity, have been constant causes of irritation. There are others. The native store-managers have so little to say about the way things are run that the project is not, as it could be, an education in merchandising. As I heard one of the managers say to a bureau supervisor, "You don't ask us, you just tell us, and so you never know how things really are." The local Indian Bureau teachers are given, as one of their chief responsibilities, the directing of all the store functions. Few of these teachers have had previous merchandising experience, and their insistence that they must authorize every decision made by the native managers can be galling.

The Eskimos are not pleased, either, that the teachers spend so much time in other than school activities. Besides regulating the stores, a teacher may supervise the nearest reindeer herd; he acts as law-enforcement officer and also health officer, holding regular clinics and rendering aid when needed at other times. He has a daily radio schedule to broadcast a report to the district Indian Bureau director; he runs the school plant and is expected to be a good enough mechanic so that he can repair the heating and lighting systems except in cases of major breakdowns. If there is a hot-lunch program for the children, he directs that too, and often he is the village welfare agent. Does he also teach? Yes, but obviously not in a very effective way.

It is relevant to ask what kind of teachers would consider work that so scatters their energies. They fall rather generally into two classes. Some are among the most intelligent and dedicated people in the profession, teachers drawn to the North by the challenge of helping a primitive race adjust to civilization.

Others are of a type found on all frontiers—neurotics, escapists who have had difficulty in getting along anywhere else. Some of these simply let their responsibilities slide, but too many have dictatorial tendencies and seem to enjoy their authority over so many aspects of natives' lives. They have even the power of life and death, since they can issue free travel orders to hospitals. I have seen the transportation withheld in cases of personal animosity, race prejudice being an evident factor. (I once asked the Alaska director of the Indian Bureau how the agency screens its teachers for race prejudice. He replied, "We don't. That would be against the law." The Territorial teachers are so screened very carefully, but the Indian Bureau, in Alaska, at least, appears to be permeated with that kind of bias.)

Two slightly redeeming factors should be remembered concerning the poor quality of the teaching in most native schools. One is an attitude of the Eskimos themselves. Both parents and children would prefer to have stiffer instruction. They want longer hours and harder studying. But they sometimes defeat this wish by their traditional way of reacting when any white man adopts a superior attitude towards them. If an Eskimo senses that he is being patronized, he puts on a clever act of being even more stupid than the outsider has assumed he is. The civilized way to respond to patronizing treatment is to hand back a subtle insult, and I am not sure the Eskimo's trick is not also an insult, except that it does not wound. It's a habit that should be recognized however, and as soon as possible broken down, for when a teacher with ingrained race prejudice goes to the North and finds Eskimos acting moronic, they only confirm his feeling that serious teaching efforts are useless.

Secondly, when the classroom work is done superficially, the teachers are backed up by Indian Bureau policies formed in Washington. I have one of the bureau's information bulletins sent to applicants. Under "Objectives of Indian Schools," which include Eskimo schools, nothing is said about the material to be taught from books, nothing about the best ways to present the vast storehouse of civilized knowledge to primitive minds. The objectives are such as these: "to teach students . . . to become constructive citizens of their communities; . . . to give students first-hand experience in . . . the use of native materials in housing and clothing; . . . to aid students in achieving some mastery over their environment." No Stateside man or woman, especially one of the misfit types, can teach any member of the Eskimo race very much about constructive community attitudes, or the use of arctic materials in housing and clothing, or can aid them in achieving mastery over their environment. The Eskimos are the world's supreme example of co-operation and skill in mastering a difficult environment.

From what Eskimo children and parents have told me, it has appeared that at least half the hours in school are spent in handicrafts, singing, making valentines, pasting cutouts on curtains, and like activities. More than a few of the parents said, "If the law did not make us send our children to school, we would keep them at home. We could teach them more, ourselves." The feeling is almost universal among the natives that the Indian Bureau is trying to keep their race ignorant because, as the intelligent Eskimo bush pilot, Art Johnson, phrased it, "When we are well educated, we are self-sufficient—and if we have been taught enough to be able to manage our own lives, there is no need for an Indian Bureau. Those officials are only trying to hold onto their jobs."

Art Johnson is one of several Eskimo pilots. Their success and that of a few other Eskimos in the professions—a physician, an airline executive, and a number of native teachers—suggest that it's not entirely their so-different culture which makes it difficult for some Eskimos to adapt to our civilization. The four native pilots that I have known all had better schooling than is available in most Indian Bureau settlements. Many more of these bright young people no doubt would make the great effort necessary to progress in civilized fields if they had teachers who really drilled them, hard, in the conditions that they would meet in the white-man's world, such as competitive business methods, the law, the wise handling of money, and the requirements for good health, especially the dangers of alcoholism. Lacking that foundation on which to build, most young native adults soon become too discouraged to keep on trying.

The teachers must be alert to do more than impart facts however. They should watch for individual talents, as do the inspiring pair Mr. and Mrs. Herbert Bingham at Kivalina. The Binghams have helped to create careers for several of their pupils, such as one who has set up a workshop to produce fine handmade furniture, and others who are making quite-fashionable jewelry out of gold and polished caribou hoofs, which are as pretty as tortoise shell.

Such skills are not deeply hidden. I have had Eskimos do carpentry work on my house that surpassed the work of some cabinet-makers. They are good plumbers, even better if the mechanical job is complicated. If you ask one to fix a piece of machinery, however, you must allow him time to take it all apart and have the fun of discovering why and how it operates. The machine will be put together again—and it will run. I was told of a military tractor abandoned as beyond salvage up on the arctic coast. An inland Eskimo, who never had seen a tractor before, asked if he could have it. He was told (humorously), sure, go ahead, take it. And take it he did, after he had dismantled it, studied it, and repaired it. When an Eskimo has a watch that stops running, he doesn't send it away to a jeweler—usually he mends it himself, even splicing a broken mainspring.

Until the change of administration at Washington in 1950 there may have been truth in Art Johnson's analysis of the reason for Indian Bureau inefficiency. Since then the gradually evolving plan is for the bureau "to get out of the Indian business," to abolish the Stateside Indian reservations as soon as possible and send the Indians to industrial cities. To be consistent, of course, the policy must be carried out in Alaska too. That policy, called "the relocation program," is the excuse for sending Eskimos to Detroit and also for a new plan, to remove the brighter Eskimo children from their families after the second year of high school and put them in a boarding-home at Fairbanks, where they will go to the same schools as the local white pupils.

The idea was vehemently condemned by fifty-seven out of sixty delegates to a conference on the health, welfare, and education of natives, held in Fairbanks in 1955. The delegates came from many parts of the North at their own expense. They were nurses, doctors, missionaries, welfare workers, traders, and some of the better teachers, all people who knew the natives through close association with them and cared deeply about their welfare. Unanimously, except for three Fairbanks Chamber of Commerce delegates, these people felt that to bring the Eskimo boys and girls into the city's far-from-Victorian atmosphere would be a slaughter of the innocents. Even at a boarding high school operated by the Indian Bureau in the isolated small town of Sitka, a retiring bureau official told me, "Many of the boys become alcoholics and the girls promiscuous." At Anchorage, where a number of Eskimo girls are nurse's aides in a former Indian Bureau hospital, streams of servicemen pass, like a parade, waiting for these children to come out of the building. What will it be like at Fairbanks, where twenty-five thousand GI's are stationed near-by, and where the Eskimo boys have access to seventy-six liquor establishments? The Indian Bureau says the pupils will be "supervised," but no one who knows the town or these youngsters believes that adequate controls can be devised.

Eskimo parents as well as the conference delegates oppose the program, which is nevertheless to be carried out. In the President's budget for 1957, $9,310,564 was allocated to the Indian Bureau, of which only $30,683 was to be spent on the development of native arts and crafts, but $1,248,000 on the unwanted children's boarding home. Not only are the youngsters to finish their schooling in Fairbanks; Mr. Olson, the Alaska bureau director, stated in an interview in the Juneau *Empire* of April 29, 1955, that the bureau is "seeking a method to make the traffic a one-way street out of the villages and into the white-man's world." After the children have been graduated, the plan, he said, is to include "an intensive effort to keep them from returning to their homes."

Indian children in the States are similarly being removed from their families, and some of the Indian parents have an explanation. They say that a group of southwest bankers are behind the effort to take the Indians off the reservations in order to get control of rich mineral deposits that the white men cannot secure while the Indians own the land. But does the Bureau of Indian Affairs really contemplate getting out of the Indian and Eskimo business by destroying the Indian and Eskimo races? That will be the result of the present policies if continued.

A People to Cherish

This crash project to integrate our natives into civilized communities this year, this month, is in startling contrast to the long-range, scientifically planned acculturation programs in Greenland and Canada. For more than 200 years, indeed, Denmark has been preparing the Greenland Eskimos for contact with civilization. By now all are literate, speaking both Eskimo and Danish. They have a weekly newspaper (a printing-plant has been in operation for 100 years) and radio programs, some of which are educational, including fine music among the broadcasts. There are fifteen night schools; and in 1951, 244 natives were in Denmark for advanced schooling. Some of the Eskimos sit in the Danish Parliament. Stores in Greenland are government-owned, and by controlling the kinds of merchandise offered in more and less primitive districts, the Danes are trying to hold back the Eskimos' eagerness for modern products until they are qualified, as people and as workers, to live in a modern society. There is an excellent banking system, with branches in even small towns. Old-age pensions begin at the age of fifty, but do not provide complete sustenance. The Danes feel that the Eskimo sense of responsibility for neighbors should still be encouraged. All native villages are out of bounds to all military.

The Canadian Eskimos are more scattered than those in Alaska —single families wandering over the tundra in search of caribou, and education therefore has been an especially difficult problem. The Canadians are providing itinerant teachers, instruction by radio, and summer schools on rivers where, in those months, the natives stay in one place and fish. Teachers in the Canadian North have none of the community responsibilities that weigh down our Indian Bureau teachers, for the Royal Canadian Mounted Police take over most of them. Besides the Mounties, the Canadian government maintains a corps of men called Northern Service Officers, whose work it is to help the Eskimos in all situations where their primitive background makes their adjustment to civilization difficult. The Canadian program is guided at every step by trained anthropologists.

The Canadians see the Eskimos' future employment as of three kinds: the traditional ways of hunting, the development of local enterprises, and civilized jobs in both skilled and semi-skilled capacities. Under the local ways to make money, the one most encouraged is the creation of really good carvings. The Eskimos are urged in the strongest way not to commercialize their talent. As a result, they are producing an abundance of beautiful little figures in ivory and soapstone. Through exhibits planned by the Canadian Handicrafts Guild, individual pieces have sold for as much as $1,000. Most prices are in the range from 50 cents to $200, and although 30,000 of the pieces already have been disposed of, the demand is greater than the supply. For Eskimos who want to work at white-men's occupations, the Canadian government does not see the answer as unskilled labor. After the natives are trained, as radio-operators, weather-observers, etc., an on-the-job program is conducted, in which the government pays the native's wages until he becomes worth those wages to the employer.

The Canadian Department of Northern Affairs and National Resources expresses its high sense of responsibility in these words:

> To fail to protect the native during this period of change from contacts and influences which might be injurious to him would be to invite chaos.

and

> A carefully developed program can transform the future of these people from that of a financial liability to an asset. The value in human terms cannot be so simply expressed, but it is a value of highest importance and one which Canadians are clearly determined shall be achieved.

With their Eskimos chiefly nomadic, the Canadians have escaped, to a large extent, the problems that grow out of the impact of the military on native life. Eight of the larger villages in arctic Alaska now have military installations either in them or on the outskirts, with the GI's stationed there numbering from a few to several hundred men. Bishop William J. Gordon, foreseeing unhappy results, has been one of many Alaskans who have asked: "Why do you have to put your installation on *this* hill—

why not the hill fifty miles down the coast?" There has been no credible reply except perhaps the one expressed by an air-force captain who said, "I think the military are afraid of the country. We feel safer if we are close to a native village."

Work on military construction projects has fluctuated from none at all in some years to intensive programs, with local labor being paid at the most extravagant rates. In the busy seasons the Eskimos have been encouraged to build themselves houses that have cost in some cases as much as $300 a month to heat—and the next year had no income whatever, for fuel or anything else. In older times the settlements were very small, no more people at any one place than the wildlife there would support. But families from wide areas have moved, for the spasmodic work, to the villages where the military have established themselves, and what bird and animal life was there originally has been frightened away by the noisy activity. In even the slack years, therefore, the Eskimos gain little food from hunting.

Hardship and suffering have occurred. These were not irrevocable, but the same cannot be said of the contact between the GI's and the Eskimo girls. Here the men are, in the "lonely" arctic, surrounded by attractive young native women who are anxious to marry white men and believe that marriage is the direction in which all love-making leads. "But it's the same everywhere there are soldiers—Japan . . ." said the wife of a civilian who works for the military. It is not the same. There are over 80,000,000 Japanese but only 15,000 Alaskan Eskimos. The 1950 Census counted but 2,127 Eskimo women between the ages of sixteen and twenty-nine, including wives. Mothers of some of the girls have told me that all of them expect marriage as the outcome of the affairs. Many of the men promise it, and then it is often discovered that they have wives in the States. They hold up such tempting inducements: "We'll have everything to make your life easy and fun—a washing-machine, dish-washing machine, sewing-machine, a big, new car, and we'll go out every night, to the movies and dances. Here, have another drink—" After the man is gone, the bewildered girl has one more half-breed baby to care for. Some have had four and five, and still they let the soldiers make love to them, because they are still Eskimo enough that they simply cannot comprehend insincerity.

And what of the young native men, deprived of sweethearts and of all hope of a married life? There is not the equivalent possibility of marrying white girls for them. How bleak can one's outlook become, and what can happen to minds put under that stress? They could become Communist spies, couldn't they? They could further the plans of the Russians.

At this point we have reached a situation that could endanger us all—not only all Alaskans but all Americans. For wouldn't it be amazing if the destruction of Seattle, or Chicago, or Washington related all the way back to one of those loving little Eskimo girls whose Eskimo sweetheart had lost her to some GI? When General Kepner was head of the Alaska Command, he was quoted in the *Christian Science Monitor* as saying that he would consider it very serious if any Eskimos turned to Communism.

So far they all appear to be loyal to the United States. But soon after I came to Alaska one of the white officers of the Eskimo Scout Battalion in the National Guard said this: "The Eskimos would be pushovers for Communism. Their own system is one of sharing, and although it is a system very different from Communism in many ways, they might fall for the Communist theory if it were presented to them as idealistic. They are a very idealistic people." Strange Russians have been seen in Alaska several times since I came to the North.

It was the Eskimos' tragedy that white people entered their lives during a time when the conquerors thought of materialistic success as the greatest good. We can hope that a future approaches when we, in our own civilization, will have more respect for the thoughtfulness of a quiet mind, for the belief that moroseness offends nature's laws, and for the principle that communities should be governed by love.

If the Eskimos had been found in such a happier period, we

would have cherished their culture. We wish they would cherish it more themselves, and hold out for a chance to maintain it. And they might do that if we had not pulled up most of their anchors and set them adrift in bewildered confusion.

"The old life was harder but it was better": I first heard that comment from Henry Nashoalook and later from many more of his race. None seemed resentful, but all were clear-headed about what is happening to the Eskimos. Yet they do not accuse us—not directly, at least.

At Barrow I met a fine old man, Segevan, who had had an extensive reindeer herd at one time. He had been the first Eskimo child to enter school in that village, and he had kept a diary in English for sixty years. I saw it, and it was an uncomplaining record of losses—not only of reindeer. Impelled perhaps by a sense of racial or national guilt, I heard myself say to him one day, rather fatuously, I'm afraid,

"What do you think are the most valuable things the white men have brought to the North? Rifles and planes?"

He looked at me long, without smiling, and answered:

"The best things are coffee and cigarettes. There are sorrows too great for consolation, but the small pleasures help us to bear them."

12

Bush Flight

AFTER EIGHT MONTHS of my stay with the Unalakleet Eskimos, it happened suddenly that I found myself in the Nome hospital with pneumonia. I was brought in on a mercy flight but went back on a regular "bush run."

This particular run, the transportation of one passenger and a planeload of freight along the northwest Alaska coast, began with a call at the laundry. A renovated sleeping-bag was thrown in the back of the airline truck, and we stopped next at the Nome general store for a yard of red flannel and ten pounds of hamburger. The meat had come many months earlier on the previous summer's boat, but at Unalakleet there would be no meat except seal, whale, and fish, and so I too decided to buy some beef. The mechanic and I climbed into the cab of the truck again, and he headed north towards the Nome city field.

The freight on the truck included some things that one "backward area" considers the finest fruits of civilization: an outboard motor, a portable phonograph, a gun, a fifty-pound sack of flour, a sack of onions, twenty-five pounds of rock salt, and a spool of fishnet twine. Besides several air-express packages and my own sleeping-bag, there were a broom, a collection of coat-hangers, and a string of hides from eight caribou legs. One more item: a pop bottle, to which had been tied a note and a streamer composed of a bandana and a red and yellow wool sock.

Bob Murphy, the pilot, rode on the back of the truck.

The month was May but the day was cold, below zero, and was one of those "white days," as Alaskans call them, on which no one ever would choose to fly. The sky looked as if the last snow had fallen up, the ground also was white, and a white mist completed the blurring. Shadows were lacking so totally that anyone stepping off a path literally did not know whether to put his foot up or down. That is familiar weather in northern Alaska, and bush pilots say that flying in it is like sitting in the middle of a bottle of milk. Landing is partly a matter of intuition, for they only can feel for the ground with the skis of the plane.

I had waited through four days of sunshine, too, for this. Early in the week I had stopped at the airline office and said I was ready to go to Unalakleet. That is all a passenger ever is in the North— ready, not impatient unless he has just arrived. At first, delayed in everything that he wants to do, he composes a slogan: "In Alaska you wait," and grinds it between his teeth in whatever small road-house or teacher's sitting-room he happens to pace the floor. By the end of a year he may have revised it: "In Alaska nobody forces a situation." I wanted to go to Unalakleet. Murphy was the pilot the airline most often sent there, and Murphy may not have been available. Or the plane may have needed working on. Or freight, flown from the States, may have been expected. Or weather that looked ideal at Nome may have been thick on the other side of the hills. I would be taken to Unalakleet when all the conditions fell into the proper pattern. In Alaska a customer is no more important, no more right, than anyone else is.

The men worked together to load the freight. Meanwhile I studied the plane, marveling that it really would fly. It was a Stinson Gullwing obsolete even then, and this particular number was marked for retirement. It had been painted black once, but the many parts which had been replaced still were naked metal. The plane certainly had, as the men might have said, a beat-up look. But paint does not help a strut to support a wing, and there is in the North a deliberate disregard of the look of things—of a machine or a man—and an almost fanatical respect for performance.

That is the method of scoring which puts Murphy's reputation high, for he goes out of his way to avoid any swagger. His coloring might attract attention, black hair and intensely blue eyes, but he is not overpowering in build. Between flights he sits in the airline office, turning the pages of a magazine so casually, one would guess that he was a passenger waiting for his ticket. Up in the plane now, he was stowing away the freight with an air of doing this just to help out the pilot, who would be along presently. Most pilots who fly in the arctic sensibly wear fur garments, including fur hoods. Murphy was not impersonating any heroic type, not even himself. That day he was hatless and had on ordinary boots, cords, a wool shirt, and a leather jacket. From the moment we fastened the seat belts, however, and he adjusted the headphones and began throwing switches and working the throttle, his concentration allowed his skill and his cool self-confidence to break through the modesty.

At two o'clock in the afternoon we flew into the bottle of milk. Mountains circle the town on the north and east; southward the shore curves back into the land to contain Norton Sound. Most of the villages where we would stop were along the sound.

As we took off, some fence posts, guides to the runway, were visible briefly. Beyond that was white vacancy. It was marred by no trees below, no highways, no farm buildings—none is down there. And the 2,500-foot hills ahead are so smoothly rounded that the snow covered them like a camouflage. Occasionally we could see a ledge or bluff, a dark line sketched in the sky like the mountains suggested in Japanese prints, but where were the summits? One could fly into these slopes. The altimeter needle, however, still climbed.

We passed Hazel, Lillian, and Buster Creeks, tributaries of the same river and commemorating what family of gold-rush children? So Murphy told me. He had fished in them. I saw nothing but whiteness.

On the other side of the hills we came to the shore of the sound and found that we still had a world under us. The shelf-ice could be distinguished, snow-covered, looking like land but unnaturally, exquisitely smooth. It extended out into the sea for about three miles. Beyond it was open water, slate-blue. We flew along what would be the shore when the ice went out, where a line of cliffs rose from the midst of the present white plain. Beside one of them, like a handful of dice thrown down in the snow, was the Eskimo hamlet of Bluff.

Out of the freight that bulged over our necks Murphy extracted the bottle. He would drop it here. The note was addressed to an Eskimo woman and said that the plane would pick her up on the way back to Nome the next day. She was sick; her husband had driven his dog team to Nome and arranged to have her go into the hospital.

We started to circle above the village. Murphy is careful, but all bush pilots like to scare passengers, and so now, with no doubt a safe margin of speed, he was banking at such an angle that we seemed to pirouette on the tip of one wing. Mysteriously, we could not arouse anyone. Eskimos, being dressed in furs most of the time, are ready to run outdoors and usually are gathered along the lanes of a town by the time that a plane gets over. This afternoon no one appeared, no human or dog. Perhaps most of the villagers were away at their squirrel camps, for this was the season, when the sun reaches down into burrows, that the squirrels come out from their hibernation. The last time around, Murphy wound down the window and flung the note, trailing its sock, earthward.

Beyond Bluff the coast pushes out in a headland called Baldy. We cut in behind it towards a river that enters the sound on the far side of the promontory. Fifteen miles up that river is White Mountain, a settlement where we would land. At that time it was a boarding high school for Eskimo children, run by the Indian Bureau.

Murphy said that we would come down on the river. The mist

was thinner here, back from the Bering Sea, yet the snow-covered surface would have been hard to judge if willows had not been lining the banks. Bush pilots love willows. We hit the ice smoothly, but the river had frozen in ripples, skis have no bounce, and so the final run rattled our freight and us.

Our coming was noticed here. Out of the white frame school buildings, which resembled a New England textile mill, scrambled a crowd of young Eskimos, colorful on the snowy hill in their parki covers. They tumbled along towards us.

From a distance the children appeared vivacious and cheerful. When they crowded under the wings of the plane, looking up to see who had come, they showed clearly something I never had seen in Eskimo children before: emotional hunger. I realized that homesickness must be a problem here, among children surrounded till now with unfailing love, not only by their own families but by everyone in their villages. They did not droop with self-pity. I doubt if they shed any tears in the night. They just were enduring a pain in the way that their people endure physical pain, so fatalistically that often a sick one will fail to take any remedial steps and die when he need not.

Murphy began a search for the White Mountain freight. The broom, the caribou legs, the flour, the phonograph came out on the ice. The children stood in a circle around them with sober, observant eyes. But when the phonograph appeared, last, one of the boys nudged another, and the face of the second boy broke in a beaming smile.

"That for you?" Murphy asked.

"His brother sent it to him from Fairbanks. For his birthday."

Murphy handed the phonograph to the boy and let him have his great moment before he said,

"There's a charge on it—two-forty. Do you want to pay it? Oh, don't worry. We'll send the bill to your brother." The two little Eskimos walked away off the river, with the phonograph bumping along between them.

On the outer rim of the circle was one of the teachers, a native woman dressed like the children and wearing glasses. Murphy passed the broom to her over the children's heads and, without trying to promote any boy-scout spirit, only to get the flour out of the way, he asked,

"Who's going to carry this?"

One of the bigger boys picked up the sack. The teacher came nearer. Murphy said,

"I told Mrs. Fraser you'd like to borrow a fifth-grade arithmetic. She says she doesn't think she can get along without hers. Do you want me to see if I can find you one some place else?"

"I'd better put in a requisition," the teacher said. "Only it takes so long—"

"I'll see what I can do," Murphy said.

She picked up the caribou legs and, squatting under the wing, laid one after another on her knee and rubbed it to see if the hairs came out. Murphy sat on his heels beside her and watched. Some of the hides did shed.

"He killed them too late," said the teacher.

"He had other skins," Murphy said. "Don't take these if you don't want them."

"Where did he get them?"

"Up the Unalakleet River. Way back, about twenty miles from the Yukon."

The teacher untied the twine on which they were strung and removed four.

"I keep these. But I will not start to make the boots until he send other good ones. If he do not have more good ones, I give these back."

"I'll see him tonight," Murphy said. "If he has any better, I'll bring them tomorrow."

He tossed the remaining stiff hairy legs into the plane, and told me he had to see an Eskimo on the hill, and asked if I wanted to come. We did not have to go far before we met Murphy's man. He was a native entering one of the school buildings with a hammer in his hand.

"I heard you're sorry you got that tent I brought down last summer," Murphy said. "I think I know where you can sell it."

"That tent waste my money. My mother too sick to go to fish camp any more."

"Fellow over at Koyuk wants a tent. What would you take for yours?"

"What he pay?"

"It's up to you."

"I want five dollar."

"He'll give you that. How about me taking it now? I'm on my way to Koyuk."

"He send five dollar, then I give tent."

"He'll pay you, all right. He wants to go squirrel-hunting. It's getting late—"

"He send five dollar first."

Murphy turned away. As we walked back to the plane, he said, "That fellow's been around white people too long."

The children had left when we did, and we were able to sneak back into the plane without their returning. Eskimo children are not conditioned to be afraid of fast vehicles. As a plane gains speed on the ground, urchins go dashing back and forth in its path—a terror to every pilot. But this time they stayed on the hill.

Near the mouth of the river is a village where we were to pick up a passenger. Murphy began to circle over the shelf-ice, where apparently we would land. We could see that the ice was level enough, but was checkered with tide cracks. The problem Murphy had now was to find a space where he could hit all the cracks crosswise, for many were wide and could swallow a ski.

The survey was exciting. For the close view of the ground he required, it was necessary to bank the plane steeply. Around and around we went, with Murphy entirely matter-of-fact, talking half to himself, half to me: "That one's probably wider than it looks. . . . Maybe this way . . . We'd have to take those on a slant. . . ." He was having to think of the wind, too, of course. "This ought to do it." He roared away towards the hills behind town, made a sharp rightabout turn, lowered the plane, and struck the ice close to shore, streaking out towards the sea. We skimmed over all the cracks safely. As we slowed to a taxi speed, swung around, and retraced our three tracks to the village, I asked,

"Can you tell what direction the wind is blowing when you are in the air?"

"No," said Murphy, "but there's always a clue on the ground. I watch the way the trees bend, if there are trees, and the water in summer, or maybe some dust whirling along—in the winter it would be snow. A line of washing will tell you."

"What did you see today?"

"Clouds—they're low and they're moving. An onshore wind, from the southwest—see?"

As we approached the settlement, I had noticed immense soft shadows advancing over the shelf-ice and, looking up, had found that the clouds were dissolving. "We're due to be out in a clear sky pretty soon," Murphy had said, tapping one of his headphones. Now I saw that the billows of mist were chasing us towards the beach.

A tall elderly white man with a salt-and-red-pepper beard came to greet us. He was the only one who did, for this hamlet is almost a ghost town. Murphy got out and talked to him. I could not hear the man's words, but his voice droned along in a tone of complaint, and all his gestures were downward, rejecting everything. When his dispirited gait had carried him back towards his cabin, Murphy got into the plane again. I asked where our passenger was.

"Oh, he's already left by dog team." Murphy did not sound annoyed. And then, as he started to rearrange the freight: "Notice that old trader? You find them all over. They came to Alaska fifty, sixty years ago. The life wasn't easy then, they had to be rugged characters, but most of them made a pile of money. They could go hunting and fishing whenever they liked, and I guess they were expert mushers—in the winter when things were slow, they'd travel around with their dog teams and visit each other.

Some had two or three native wives in their time. But their time's past. They're feeble. The country's too big for some of them now. They won't admit that, so they complain about everything else. Sometimes I stay overnight with one of them. It probably makes them feel better to talk."

An Eskimo girl wearing a scarlet parki cover came running down nimbly from one of the cabins. She was possibly sixteen years old. When she reached the plane, she pushed the fur circlet away from her bright, pretty face and looked up and smiled with the dimples characteristic of Eskimo women.

"You go Koyuk some time?"

"I'm going there right now."

"You ask my mamma, papa if I can come home. I stay here with my grandma because she sick. She well now."

"What's your father's name?"

She told him.

"I'll either stop here tomorrow, or I'll drop you a note when I go over."

Her teeth flashed in a smile of gratitude, and she backed away to watch us take off.

Murphy handled the plane flexibly, ready to dip a wing to see something below, or to swerve right or left for a better view of a hillside. For a while we followed a wolf trail that went approximately our way and finally we saw the fluff of gray fur that was making it. At the foot of the slopes was a grove of spruces, and I was surprised to see from the air with what precision nature had spaced them, each tree surrounded with its inverted cone of light, all it would need. As the Darby Mountains reared up ahead then, we turned out over the ice and flew parallel to the coast.

The sun spread the shadow of shoreline cliffs on the white expanse, but beyond the shadow the shelf-ice sparkled brilliantly, with a higher gleam on the little ridges that marked earlier limits, where waves had dashed spray on the edge. Now that the sun had come out, the sea off the present edge was blue-silver, and the large floating ice pack had come into view near the eastern end of the sound. It was five miles or so off the shelf-ice and was rough, its surface, many times broken, heaped up in glistening hummocks. There—there over the rim of the shelf-ice, a gull—the first returning bird after the long Northern winter! An immature glaucous gull, it was immaculate white, in this world of blue sea and sky and glittering crystal. It was beating a straight westward course.

We too were flying steadily now, pushing the plane's shadow along the snowy flat surface below. Our next stop would be Koyuk. On the way Murphy pointed out a second headland called Baldy and told me undramatically that one winter day he had been forced down on this coast near the eastern Baldy, but his radio message was misunderstood, and the rescue team went to the other one. All through the following night, in a temperature of forty degrees below zero, with a thirty-five-mile-an-hour wind, Murphy and his passenger, an Eskimo boy, kept themselves alive by digging driftwood out from under the snow to feed their fire. At that they came close to freezing, and the next day, when they were found, they had to ride ten miles on a dog sled without any fur robes or blankets. That was hardest of all, said Murphy.

The east end of Norton Sound receives the waters of two rather large rivers, the Koyuk at the northern corner, the Unalakleet farther south. The settlement near the mouth of the Koyuk, too, is named for its river.

I had heard about Koyuk: it was a "lovely village," a groping phrase with which Alaskans try to describe the courteous and healing sort of friendliness in most Eskimo towns. At a previous time there had been a school and a store in Koyuk, but no more. Koyuk was returning to its old, primitive ways. Part-breeds with white blood were considered inferior here, though the village was cordial to pure whites, and had acquired some *Kazzak* tastes and *Kazzak* words.

The settlement was below us now, on a rounded hillside with its log cabins placed among spruces of Christmas-tree size.

Smoke from the chimneys gave us the wind direction. Small figures moved about, chopping wood and feeding the dogs at their stakes and, now that the plane had come, waiting, looking up with hands shading their eyes. A trail wavered out from the shore to the edge of the shelf-ice. Approaching along it was a team of dogs, pulling a seal-hunter.

But where could we come down? Near the shore the shelf-ice was heaved and broken, and so was the lower part of the river, up which the tide had flowed. Murphy flew back and forth, tilting the plane for a view of the ice. He was relaxed but thoughtful. His life was made up of decisions like this, for most of a bush pilot's landings are improvisations. More airstrips are being built all the time, but it still is true that in summer the pilots use gravel bars in the rivers, when the bars are long and appear to be firm; and sandy sea beaches, if the sand is packed hard and no driftwood lies in the way; and hilltops, where the vegetation usually is smooth but in some cases is strewn with boulders. Lowland tundra is out of the question because of the tundra plants, growing in clumps that would capture the wheels of a plane. In winter most rivers can serve as landing-fields, also the shelf-ice, but a blizzard may blow all the snow off the surface, leaving it skiddy. The bush pilots never know what they will find at the end of a trip. The practice is to come down on whatever space "looks all right" at the moment.

The month when all pilots wish they could take their vacations, however, is the month we were flying in—May, for then, while they're still on skis, the ice is becoming unsafe, the snow is too deep for landing on wheels, and floats are not practical because rivers are full of ice cakes.

At Koyuk Murphy surveyed the possibilities. He seemed to consider the snowy beach best, for he flew up and down just above it. But two sleds were lying there in our way. The Eskimos understood. They ran to them and pulled them higher. The pitch of the shore was steep and I was afraid that would be a hazard;

our upper wing might get snagged on the slope. We went farther off and turned. Murphy was going to try it. We dropped lower and lower at what seemed a tearing speed. At exactly the right instant he tipped the plane so that we touched on the same slant as that of the slope. The Gullwing ran along smoothly and just in front of the cabins stopped.

The villagers had surrounded the plane while the propeller blades were still turning. They did not pull open the door; they waited under the wing, silent but smiling an unrepressed welcome. As Murphy started to lift out the freight, a dozen hands offered help.

The outboard motor belonged here. When Murphy read off the name, the natives pointed away to the hunter. Murphy sat on the crate, getting signatures or some kind of marks on receipts, and taking money and making change. Here would be left the rock salt, the spool of fishnet twine, the gun, and one of the air-express cartons; also the package of flannel. The woman who received it tore it open and walked higher up the beach to show the flannel to two other women who stood there. I wandered their way and, when they all smiled, asked, "You sew it?" meanwhile making the motion of running a needle through cloth. The women laughed, but kindly, as if at a child, and the one who held the flannel frayed out a thread and, turning one of the others around, showed me the red French knots with which her parki hood was embroidered. I was mystified for a moment but then had the right explanation, I think. When the miners of Klondike days left the Yukon River and cut across country to Nome, they used a route that would have taken them through Koyuk. The Eskimo women here probably mended their red flannels for them, learned to use the ravelings as embroidery wool, and now bought their flannel by the yard for the same purpose.

Murphy, back at the plane, was saying,

"I couldn't get any—there haven't been any potatoes in Nome for weeks." He was writing down what the villagers wished him to bring next time: a carton of cigarettes, a dozen cans of milk, yeast, and some shotgun shells. He was taking a pair of glasses to Nome to have the frames mended. One of the men had a grievance:

"Other pilot take too much money for sugar."

"He charged you too much? What did you pay him?"

"One dollar thirty-five."

"How much sugar did you get?"

"Five pound."

"How much is sugar—does anybody know what's the price of sugar?" Nobody did. Murphy asked which pilot it was. "Tall fella, black eyes." Murphy said that he would find out about it. His promise was not a brush-off, as the Eskimo understood and was satisfied. Murphy found the man who wanted the tent: "I tried to bring it, but I guess you'll have to send the money first." The native laughed. "You tell that guy he keep that tent." A woman gave Murphy a dollar and asked him to get her some stamps. "Air mail or regular?" The woman and her husband conferred in their own tongue about what kind of stamps. This was a serious question with people who have so little chance to earn money, and Murphy treated it so. He worked out that a dollar would buy eleven air-mail stamps and eleven threes with a penny left over. They thanked him effusively.

He was entitled to thanks, for this airline carried mail to the Norton Sound villages gratis. Indeed, none of the purchasing, none of the numerous missions that a bush pilot customarily undertakes, is paid for. There is no profit on any of them except for the air express charged on freight delivered. And if Murphy was doing shopping and post-office chores, he was also the village newspaper:

"You find my sister, Shishmaref, she well now?"

"Yes, she's fine. She walked down to the plane. She said to tell you your other sister's had a baby—a boy." *Ah-ree-gah!* "That pleases me!" The woman ran up the beach to tell the three I had been talking to.

"You go Kotzebue, you tell my father I get four *oogruk*."

Murphy wrote down the name of the father. He asked for the father of the girl we had talked to at the last settlement. A gray-haired native stepped forward. He spoke so little English that Murphy had difficulty in giving him the message from his daughter, but another native translated. When Murphy asked whether he should bring the girl to Koyuk, a well-built young Eskimo spoke up: "I go. I go with my dogs tomorrow." A boy told Murphy excitedly that three cranes had flown over that morning. "You'll all be eating duck eggs pretty soon," Murphy said. *Ahk-gah!* ("Isn't that something!" Literally, "That's immense!")

Finally the pilot's pockets were full of notes and of change, some of it short, but it all would be paid when the Eskimos had the money. The hunter had come and dragged his crate out of the way. He had gone to a fish cannery the previous summer and earned enough to buy this marvelous machine, with which he could set his whale nets far out in the sound. With great yearning the others watched as he started to rip the boards off the crate. When we were ready to go, however, they pulled their attention away from the outboard motor and waved good-by. More than a business transaction had ended.

If our plane had brought help to the villagers on a lonely coast, at our final stop we were the ones to receive it. My recovery from the pneumonia was not quite complete, and as we approached the gold-mining camp at Ungalik, I knew that I wanted to lie down immediately. That landing was one of the most spectacular Murphy made—on a frozen *curving* river—but I did not observe the details. When we stopped near a log cabin under some spruces, within less than a minute I was in a warm room on a couch, surrounded by solicitous strangers.

All but one, a young Eskimo helper, were white. There were Mrs. Cook and Mr. Shaw, who had lived here and operated this gold mine for thirty-one years. And two men had come up from San Francisco to work, with Eskimo labor, a vein of the mine they had leased from the owners. The men had been at Ungalik for several weeks when we stopped. They were growing white beards.

The cabin was pleasing, being furnished with only the things that the owners found really useful. In the center was that big bellyful of comfort, a "tank-stove"—an oil drum turned on its side with a door cut in one end, the standard stove in north-western Alaska. What I needed, Mrs. Cook saw, was strong coffee. She went to the kitchen to get it. Murphy followed. When they returned, it had been arranged that we would stay for dinner.

Mrs. Cook had not seen another white woman for months, and her lips were compressed in a smile that seemed literally to be containing her eagerness for some talk. As soon as our conversa-tion could start, I learned that the feverish obsession in this house was not gold, as one might expect, but pets—wild birds and animals. In the two Californians I could see signs of so-phistication; it was easy to picture them leaving the Mining Exchange and joining the sharp-looking noonday crowds in San Francisco's financial district. But here they were before dinner, luring a couple of wary snowshoe rabbits to some bread on a woodpile, and as proud of themselves as five-year-old boys. A tree squirrel was Mrs. Cook's favorite. Mr. Shaw's had been a robin. The most civilized thing about the cabin was a small sun porch, built for a crippled robin that lived in it for nineteen years. He had died the year before we were there, and the little porch was an emptiness, stacked with logs for the stove.

For dinner Mrs. Cook gave us some reindeer steaks and onions the plane had brought, also sausages, mashed potatoes, Lima beans, stewed canned tomatoes, and blueberry pie made of wild huckleberries picked the preceding fall and kept frozen all winter. After coffee the setting was just right for a long evening of stories, but the sun soon would set, and although the nights did not be-come entirely dark at that season, it might be too dark for a landing within an hour. And so Murphy and I took off again. By now we had only two express packages left in the plane. The renovated sleeping-bag had been one of the miners', and the coat-hangers had been a gift from Mrs. Murphy to Mrs. Cook. They had never met, but coat-hangers are an ever scarce article in the North.

We flew in the curiously shining dusk of the Northern spring, as if the plane moved in some airy liquid. Murphy was silent, I thought perhaps tired, but then I began to wonder if he was worried about the condition of the ice at Unalakleet. We were flying south, and with every mile we were visibly closer to summer. There was less and less snow on the land, and the shelf-ice was gone from the shore under a wall of cliffs. Anyway, it was too late to turn back. We had to come down on whatever we found.

Unalakleet on the end of its sandspit looked secure and inviting, a village anybody would like to call home. Though the land was dark, the silvered driftwood logs of the cabins caught the rosy light in the west, at the edge of the ocean. Here the shelf-ice was still in. A mauve bloom lay over its snow—what snow was showing. The ice was covered widely with meltwater now. Whether the seepage hid holes and breaks, and where the cracks might be, no one could know.

The snow was all gone from the beach and the airstrip. Murphy flew past the village and over the river. A channel of flowing water had opened, bordered with tumbled ice. We could only land on the shelf-ice, then, and because of the wind we must approach towards the coast. Just inside the *eewoonucks* water spread over the surface everywhere. We would come down in it.

Murphy circled the village two or three times and then abruptly swung out across the ice, past the edge, and above the crinkled shine of the sea. He turned back towards the land, dropped lower, just cleared the white ridges—and now we were in the water, which splashed away from the skis. The ice underneath was very smooth, so that we made a quick run to the beach, jolting over a few bumps and cracks, none of which was serious.

Although landings like that are everyday happenings to a bush pilot, they are not for that reason perfunctory. Late in the evening, when we had joined friends at the airfield and were trying to eat a second dinner, Murphy told one story after another, talking with a volubility which might suggest that a strain had been removed.

The flight had been interesting, but I did not realize what it symbolized until later that summer. By then I was in Kotzebue, having flown about trying unsuccessfully to find lemmings, the small migrating rodents, which I needed to study. Red Kline, the airline-manager at Kotzebue, said in a teasing tone, "So the lemmings are hiding from you," and in the same tone I replied, "Yes, because your pilots don't hunt for them." After a year in Alaska I still would have thought it purest fantasy to expect an airline to furnish wild rodents on order, but Red's smile dropped away; he looked as offended as if I had accused the company of sloppy upkeep on its engines. It seemed that the pilots, knowing I wanted lemmings, actually had tried to find some of them for me.

And then, as I packed my bags to leave for a while, the way of the North became clear. Here nobody's work is finished when he has done what he is paid to do. Only literally by undertaking to solve one another's problems can people live on this splendid and sometimes terrifying coast. In the States it is a satisfaction to lend someone a cup of sugar, or to receive help in changing a tire. Many needs are more desperate in the arctic. When a neighbor's baby comes prematurely, it may not be saved unless you, with a layman's ignorance, keep it warm and fed; and when you have an infection that is out of control, you are pulled back from the edge only because a ham radio-operator gets busy, and a bush pilot comes for you, maybe in hardly flyable weather.

Emotionally, too, Northerners depend upon one another, on the sense of an ancient, instinctive humanity, common to all of us but often obscured in the rush of civilized living. To discover that close web of life, and over the months to learn to fit into it, is the most moving experience to be found in the North.

What I am saying is only that those who go to the Eskimo country find that they have to submit to the discipline arctic nature enforces, and in the end they become, in some ways, like the Eskimos.

PART
II

Modern Pioneering

13

A Choice of Challenges

IT IS HARD for Alaskans to understand why so many people commiserate with the young because "there are no more frontiers." The world is a patchwork of frontiers, on every continent and including all of Alaska, which is nearly a fifth as large as the total area of the forty-eight states. What there is less of today perhaps is the wish to put one's own strength to the test, but even that urge is not lacking. No state today is attracting new settlers as fast as Alaska is in proportion to population.

Of the most recent pioneers, many first saw the North when they came with the military, or to do summer work at Alaska's high wages. They were tourists or sportsmen, or as an adventure drove up the Alaska Highway. They found a land with a grandeur and sweep that touched off some deep, unsuspected emotion, exhilarating and unforgettable, and the visitors, often impulsively, decided they wanted to be a part of this new frontier.

The nation's wealth and its present powerful status are based on development of our former frontiers. It may be that Alaska will contribute the most of all. But many settlers will tell you that they did not move to the North because of its promising future; nor do they stay for it. Alaska's attraction is more intangible. It is, however, permanent. After they've been in the North for a while, some of these pioneers try to move back to the States.

Most of them find that once they have lived on a frontier, they cannot be happy anywhere else. That experience is so common that it has inspired a familiar saying: "If you live in Alaska two years, your feet will be frozen in."

Plane travel makes pioneering today much easier in some ways than it was for the families that journeyed in covered wagons. The Northern climate, however, is tougher than that where the wagons went. The punishments and rewards of the new frontier, although somewhat different, balance those of the frontiers remembered with so much nostalgia.

All frontiers provide challenges and Alaska, happily, offers a choice of them. Many parts are as untamed, as natural, wild, and free, as any place on the earth, but all of the Territory is not austere, not even weatherwise. It has several distinct types of climate, from moist and mild to dry and extremely cold. The remoteness, too, varies widely. Ketchikan is but 600 miles from Seattle, while Nome, in the same latitude as Finland, is farther west than the Hawaiian Islands—in the last time zone before tomorrow. New settlers therefore can make their pioneering quite easy or really rigorous.

Alaska is shaped like a giant kite, soaring northward. The kite has two tails. One, the string of Aleutian Islands, streams out over the upper end of the Pacific Ocean. The other, a narrow strip at the side of British Columbia, seems to have lost its breeze and hangs down in a southern direction.

Most Alaskans refer to this ribbon of coastline as simply "Southeastern." Southeasterners call the rest of Alaska "The Westward"; it also is called the mainland. Although geographically the mainland may be a unit, it sharply divides into arctic and temperate areas. The lower part—that is, the coast washed by the Gulf of Alaska—is sheltered, cut off from the North by two of the most stupendous mountain ranges anywhere in the world: the Alaska Range, anchored by 20,320-foot Mount McKinley, and the St. Elias Range with an 18,008-foot summit. (Mount St. Elias, a white, lofty peak revealed suddenly in a shaft of sunlight above drizzling clouds, was the first glimpse of the mainland seen by Alaska's discoverer, Vitus Bering, in 1741.) The climate below this barrier could be called moderate. Above it, arctic conditions prevail. The arctic would seem to be an unpromising kind of frontier, but no settlers anywhere in Alaska are more enthusiastic about their new homeland.

The region north of the mountains is largest, with sixty-nine per cent of Alaska's entire area. It is the part I know best and shall describe in the most detail. But I do want to include a few admiring comments about the Gulf Coast and Southeastern. The census of 1950 showed that sixty-eight per cent of Alaska's people live in this warmer thirty-one per cent of the territory. They still were not crowded, averaging 2.01 square miles per person. Northern Alaskans could spread out over 9.64 square miles apiece. (In the United States as a whole, an average of 50.7 people shared every square mile.)

Under the boundary agreement with Canada, Southeastern Alaska extends inland as far as the crest of the mountains along the coast. In places that strip is less than fifty miles wide. But the hundreds of offshore islands, really the peaks of other, nearly submerged mountains, belong to Alaska, and most of the Southeastern towns are on them—seaports and fishing villages at the mouths of streams backed by timbered or snowy slopes.

Almost every coastal mile will suggest a pictorial calendar—waterfalls tumbling down into placid bays, fishing fleets lying at anchor in sheltered harbors, porpoises frolicking in the water, eagles perched on the shoreline crags. The famed Inside Passage is a channel between the islands and the continental coast, a channel so quiet that ships glide along with hardly a ripple to rock them.

Near the north end of the passage are Juneau, the capital of Alaska, and Sitka, which was the Russians' capital. Both cities are interesting historically as well as for present activities. It is often supposed that the Klondike gold rush in 1896 and the Nome stampede two years later were responsible for opening up the

Alaska frontier. To a great extent they were, but Southeastern had had its own mining boom earlier. It was set off in 1880 when Joseph Juneau and a companion made a spectacular strike. Other miners rushed in, and several claims were combined to form the Alaska-Juneau Mine, a quartz deposit which was worked profitably for the next sixty years. Its wealth has not yet been exhausted, but with the price paid for gold pegged at $35 an ounce, and miners' wages in line with the wages in other industries, the mine cannot be worked except at a loss and has been closed down.

Any Alaskan can give you the names of other mines with gold still available but abandoned because it would cost too much to recover it. That impasse is one of the pivots in Alaska's development, although certain kinds of deposits, chiefly near Nome and Fairbanks, are being dug up with dredges and the gold extracted by a process that depends more on machinery than on human labor.

Mining, then, is not at present one of the promising opportunities in Southeastern Alaska. Salmon fishing and canning, under way as early as mining was, have followed an almost parallel decline, not because of high labor costs but because Stateside commercial packers have done their fishing with methods that have depleted the salmon. The fish are taken in traps set across their migration routes to the streams where they would spawn— traps so constructed that it is virtually impossible for the fish to escape them. No spawning, no new crop of salmon coming along: the packers' policy seems as insane to Alaskans as if the Irish should eat up all of their seed potatoes. In a referendum 88.7 per cent of Alaskan voters condemned the use of fish traps, but under the Territorial status the wildlife resources are controlled by the federal government, and pressure from Stateside packers has prevented any legal action to enforce sound conservation practices. The salmon runs have so far declined that parts of Southeastern have been declared a disaster area, meaning that local fishermen have had to be supported with Stateside taxpayers' money. The vicious traps, incidentally, have been banned by law in the states where the Alaska salmon canneries have their headquarters.

Lumbering is now opening up as a new bonanza. A mill at Ketchikan is turning out 400 tons a day of fine wood pulp, a mill of similar size is being constructed at Sitka by Japanese interests, and others are being planned. All of Alaska, with its wonderful wild scenery, its sports fishing and hunting, and its picturesque natives, will increasingly attract tourists. Southeastern, being nearest the States, has the greatest chance to benefit from this trade. As long as seventy-five years ago the freighters that plied the Inside Passage were carrying sight-seeing passengers, who were buying the Indians' curios and debarking for hunting and fishing trips and vacations spent at the seaside hotels. No doubt some of these tourists returned to become settlers, even as many tourists do at the present time.

The Gulf Coast is the busiest part of the Alaska, the fastest-growing in population and already supplied with so many of the amenities that the pioneers of that region must smile when they hear themselves so described. They *are* pioneers if one means that they are developing a new country far from the older centers of civilization, and that it is largely because of their own initiative that they now can have fairly luxurious living.

The towns concentrate on the coast near Cook Inlet. At the eastern end of the gulf the mainland is overlaid with too many glaciers to attract homesteaders, although oil companies keep on drilling hopefully among ice fields.

The other end of the Gulf Coast tapers off in the Aleutian Islands. The grasses on some of them are good fodder, and a little cattle-raising is being done, but the climate, here where the warm Japanese Current meets the cold Bering Sea in a storm kettle known as the Aleutian Low, is an ordeal for humans. The winds called the williwaws can come up so fast and can be so devastating that a dory going ashore from the mail boat has set out in calm, sunny weather and before it had made the short run to the beach has capsized in gigantic waves. Island natives, the Aleuts, similar in racial stock to the Eskimos, gave Alaska its name. Their word *Ala-aska*, meaning "the great land," was adopted by the first Russian explorers.

The real hustlers among Alaskans seem to have been drawn to the area near Cook Inlet. The fishing is good. Garden produce is raised near such towns as Homer. Seward, Valdez, and Whittier have year-round employment in transshipping supplies from freighters to trucks and the railroad that serve the interior; Kodiak is an active naval station. The Matanuska and Susitna valleys have a stabilized farming industry. Matanuska was the valley to which the government moved midwest farmers in the depression years. The settlers' accomplishments did not come all at once. They had to discover what breeds of cattle would thrive in Alaska (Angus and, to some extent, Holsteins); and some crops were lost before frost-resistant strains were adopted, strains like Gasser wheat. By now most of the farms are prospering but the young generation, like young farm people everywhere, want to leave them and go to the cities, especially Anchorage.

Anchorage is Alaska's largest and most energetic town—or city: its population is estimated as 30,000. It has a beautiful setting, at the head of the inlet and surrounded by towering mountains. In the same latitude as the northern reaches of Hudson Bay, yet its climate averages only seven degrees colder than Juneau's and is much drier. Its mean temperature is well above zero in even the coldest months.

Starting late, about thirty-five years ago, as a construction camp on the railroad, it has boomed ahead with a speed more typical of the western states. Its dreams are big and are realized, and its tempo, unlike that of the rest of the North, is fast. With a fairly cheap source of hydroelectric power and an atomic-power plant under construction, Anchorage can attract manufacturing industries. It is headquarters for Alaska labor unions. Many government contracts, including those of the military, are negotiated there; more than a billion dollars have been spent in Alaska on military installations, and a large share of this money has changed hands in Anchorage. More permanently, it is a transportation center—for example, a way station for Orient-bound planes.

Cultural interests thrive. With a branch of the University of Alaska in operation, another college is planned and is largely financed. The high school is modern; I have heard that its auditorium has a stage as well equipped as that of any theatre in New York. An annual music festival, held in August, brings artists of first rank up from the States.

Anchorage is exciting to visit. Other Alaskans are proud of it— but to many of them it is not the North. They miss there the wide, luminous sky over a land of lovely and haunting quiet: the arctic frontier, found on the upper side of the mountain barrier.

Geographers and explorers argue about the exact boundaries of the area called the arctic. The definition that I like best is the ancient one: the lands under the Northern constellation, the Great Bear. (In Greek "bear" = *arktos*.) Granted, that definition is vague, and of course arctic conditions do not begin, abruptly, at the Arctic Circle, Lat. 66° 33′ N., which theoretically divides the Temperate Zone from the Frigid. Some scientists call everything above the limit of trees the arctic, but trees are found north of the Arctic Circle, where the winters are certainly cold, often well below −50° F. Other scientists have defined the arctic as the region of permafrost, the ground frozen to very great depths, of which only a shallow layer on top ever thaws. The permafrost region is spotty, however. Patches of permafrost can be found in some of the northern states. Finally, and logically, it has been suggested that the arctic should include all those areas where the average annual temperature is below freezing.

If that rule is adopted, most of the land north of the Alaska-St. Elias mountain ranges qualifies as the arctic. Nome and Fairbanks are in it. They have the same average for the year, 26° F., Fairbanks being colder in winter and warmer in summer than Nome, however. At Barrow, the farthest-north point in Alaska, the annual average is only 10°, although Barrow does not experience the minimum temperatures—even the North Pole does not—of some of the inland towns. It has been −66° at Fairbanks, −74° at Copper Center, −75° at Eagle, and −76° at Tanana. All are south of the Arctic Circle.

Children throughout this region often are asked in school what is their favorite season. The answer is always "winter." Among adults, too, those I know say that summer is welcome but they like winter better. I do, myself. Why? The answer, if it could be found, might furnish a clue to the well-known spell of the North.

No one has made a thorough analysis of the influence of the arctic climate on health. Accidents lead all causes of death in Alaska—19.3 per cent, which is three times the ratio in the States. The figure is sometimes interpreted as reflecting the number of unstable personalities on a frontier, since the rate of suicides and homicides also is high. However, the rate of accidental deaths among the Alaska natives is twice that of all races in the States, the greatest number being due to drowning, freezing, and fire.

Those who have been in the North a long time seem to retain their youthful outlook on life to the end. When I first went to Nome, I asked, "Where are the old people?" and was told, "They are all around you." The ages of some I had met, I learned, were seventy-two, eighty-five, eighty-nine, seventy-eight. They were busy and active people. I have known of numbers of men and women above ninety years of age who were still supporting themselves in Alaska. One, Alexander Malcolm Smith, is ninety-eight. He reads without glasses, writes a better hand than most people half his age, and has all his teeth. Much more important, he would think, he still goes out prospecting every summer alone, on an uninhabited part of the arctic coast, where his food is dropped to him periodically from planes.

"Sandy," as he is called, married for the first time at eighty and has a son. At our initial meeting Eva McGown, the hostess at the Nordale Hotel, had telephoned my apartment in Fairbanks that Mr. Smith, whose reputation I knew, was in her office and wondered if we could not have a talk. I said that I would come over. Out of respect for his extreme age and gallant efforts "to keep going," I dressed up a little. When I got to the office I was glad that I had—not because Mr. Smith was so old but because he was charming. He had just arrived from the States, having made the trip up the Alaska Highway in three days with some college boys, and he did not seem tired.

When the sourdoughs fail in health, they can go to the Pioneer Home maintained by the Territory at Sitka. There in a mild, pleasant climate, they can reminisce with their fellow sourdoughs. But large numbers of these rugged old Northerners cannot bear to leave the tough arctic scenes that have meant so much to them. Many stay in the far North, in their remote cabins where they may be out of contact with other people for months at a time. There they die, alone and surprisingly often out of doors—after what suffering no one ever knows, but they chose to have it that way.

There can be regrets. In 1957 one sourdough who lived near the Yukon River built and launched a small raft with a white flag flying from it and a message that he had had a heart attack and wished someone would come. A month later the raft drifted onto the riverbank many miles away and was found, and people did go to his cabin, but they had come too late. One of the diminishing number of sourdoughs had gone out past the farthest place. Alaskans miss all of them, strong, good men that they've been; but today too Alaska is nurturing strong, good people.

Some statistics suggest that the degenerative diseases are less often the cause of death in Northerners than in the populations of Stateside communities, but the figures are not yet considered reliable. Too many Alaskans die alone, or at least without having their last illnesses diagnosed. If climate and latitude do prove to be influential, there are various factors that might be considered. The polar atmosphere, for example, is highly electrified and very free of dust, since most of the dust particles have been carried down by the descending showers of positive ions; and obviously there is little air pollution from human sources.

However a human body might be affected by these and other far-Northern conditions, it is universally agreed that people *feel* better up in the arctic. Most of them seem to have more energy than they do farther south. A physiologist who made a Northern field trip and himself experienced the Alaskans' sense of well-being suggests that it may be due to the way our physical mechanism responds to hazards—with heightened efficiency. (As for the older Northerners and their vigor, he also suggests the explanation that the more vigorous types of people have tended to settle on the arctic frontier, and that the weaker pioneers have been "killed off" before they reached old age!)

At any rate, all Northerners speak of a sense of lightness and ease. I myself almost never have felt fatigue in the arctic. We step off a pressurized plane from the States, draw in a few breaths of the Fairbanks air, and have an immediate lift—a new sense of resilience. After a trip in the other direction I always am conscious of effort in moving around; and many times I have heard other Northerners say, "I can't breathe in the States," and, "There isn't any air down there." It does seem that way, in contrast to the arctic's effect of physical buoyancy.

The effect seems greater in winter, due perhaps to the dryness. By late autumn all but a trace of moisture has frozen out of the air as hoarfrost. Days of the most extreme cold, fifty degrees below zero or lower, produce an exhilaration that may turn into nervousness, but in moderate winter temperatures, minus thirty or so, many people let go in a kind of facile relaxation. One is inclined to loaf a little, to smile, to take life as it comes. I have wondered if nature is tricking us into saving energy for combating the cold. Only a real emergency seems important enough for worry.

The mood will be broken, but pleasantly, when the arctic blizzards begin to strike. Almost everybody enjoys them unless they turn into a siege. They wake us up; now we are busy chinking the hairline cracks through which surprisingly big snow-drifts can pile up inside. We already have checked our food, fuel, and water supplies, for even in towns we may become isolated. It is very interesting to be concerned with survival, and survival, no less, is a problem faced at times by many arctic Alaskans.

The stoves glow; the dog, drowsy in front of one, lifts an eyelid questioningly when we speak to him. We thaw out a moose steak and brew some fresh coffee. Friends draw together.

These are the times when the best stories are told, and Northerners' tales can be more exciting than any constructed dramas, for they are true and their heroes are people we know.

Often the stories themselves are of storms:

"When he came to, he was taking the teeth out of his shattered jaw, one by one. He never knew when he hit the mountain. He was flying along in the snow, trying to make it to Kotzebue, and the next thing he cleared out of a daze and discovered that he was tangled up in the panel. Later he found a piece of his jaw-bone in his pocket, but he doesn't remember putting it there."

The pilot was Frank Williams, an airplane mechanic who crashed when he was flying his own plane and ran into a snow-blow.

"He had a bottle of Scotch along. Miraculously it wasn't broken, and he decided to have a drink. He didn't taste anything, and he thought that was funny. He took another, and still he didn't feel anything warm going down his throat. Then he happened to notice that the front of his jacket was wet. He had a hole under his tongue that he didn't know about yet, and the liquor was pouring through onto his chest.

"He was there for three days before he was found. Tommy Richards rescued him. Tommy landed his plane on a clearing so short, none of the other pilots know how he did it. Frank was a mile higher up the slope. Some Eskimos brought him down on a dog sled. They got him into the plane, and Tommy shook loose from that tiny clearing." By the next winter Frank, with a reconstructed jaw, was as good as new.

Volleys of snow shake the windowpanes. The wind swoops and attacks. The weather is hurling the worst that it has on the earth, and inside the warm, sheltering walls the companionship is a natural, irresistible feeling of comfort that we are together.

These are some of the reasons why Northerners love the winter. It does outstay its welcome; no one loves February. March is a sunny promise, and in April the snowdrifts start settling down. May is a muddy miracle, and in June and July we drink up the summer weather and twenty-four-hour sunlight until we are almost intoxicated. For the arctic earth it is a time of furious blossoming; some plants grow from the bursting seed to the forming of new seeds in a period of two weeks. The air pulses with wingbeats as hordes of parent birds feed their young. The seas and rivers are shimmering with the fins of migrating fish.

By mid-August we realize that the summer is over. The fall is a striking but rapidly fading display of color . . . until the first sifting of snow comes silently, gently down, or wildly down— in either case bringing with it a curious, maybe irrational sense of quiet elation.

The climate, then, is one reason why arctic settlers find in the North their particular Promised Land.

The land itself is a second reason.

A man of seventy-three that I once met in Jackson Hole was selling the homestead he had established there to start over, up in the North. He said, "Wyoming's too crowded now. I want to live out where a man can get lost."

He could get lost in Alaska. Last December ten planes searched in vain every day over 90,000 square miles for a missing bush pilot. The newspapers described the area as "uninhabited." Arctic Alaska is more than four times that size, with its settlements few and scattered. One early September day a geologist temporarily in Fairbanks borrowed a car and drove up the Steese Highway 150 miles. That night back in town he told a sourdough, "It was amazing—I didn't meet one other car all day." The old miner's face lighted up: "I know!" he said. "It's a great country— great country!"

Most Northerners know how he felt. The land, wide, unpeopled, and elemental, does not appeal to the very gregarious or sophisticated, but to those who like elbowroom it is almost hypnotic. A part of the pull is the sense that one's own stature is lengthening. For the vastness and silence force us to face ourselves as we are, and interestingly, as one Alaska physician said, "In accepting our smallness, we grow."

"The bush," a term borrowed from Africa and Australia, is used in the North to apply to the arctic tundra and thinly forested river valleys. It describes the uncluttered distances—nothing rabbity, as suggested by a radio announcer, new in Alaska, who ad libs to "you people out in the bushes." The bush is a world all space and light and the lift of a clean wind blowing in from the ice-flecked blue of the arctic sea. It is immensity over the low, pungently sweet-smelling tundra cover, mostly of moss, lichens, Hudson's Bay tea, and a tapestry of small brilliant flowers. On the farthest north coast even the willows don't grow ankle-high; they cling to the ground like vines, and a man standing on land can see as far as one can on a ship.

For some temperaments such a landscape has the same kind of refreshment that dunes and deserts have, and you either respond to it or you don't. It is admittedly different. No tree grows within ninety miles of Nome. When children born in Nome are taken outside to the States, some of them plead, "Walk in the middle of the street, Mamma! The trees will fall on us!"

Lacking any disguise of shrubbery, the half-circle of plain behind Nome shows the ancient beachlines. Beyond them the lofty hills, heading up to real mountains, prove that the earth is not static; it moves, however slowly—it folds, it breaks up through

crusts. In these nakedly beautiful slopes anyone, not only geologists, reads the story. Clarity and the far view: these are two of the
charms of the arctic land.

The living conditions, the same problems that can become so
desperate, are a third reason why most of the settlers enjoy the
North. It is do-it-yourself applied to *everything*—at least everywhere in the arctic but Fairbanks.

That gallant small city exists for its ties with the smaller communities in the bush, which it serves. Anchorage looks to the
States; Fairbanks looks in the other direction. To those in the
outposts it sends mail and supplies; it receives their sick. It dis-
patches the planes to search for anyone lost on the tundra or sea
ice. Welfare aid is provided through Fairbanks; and it is the
gathering-place for the teachers, doctors and public-health nurses,
missionaries and others when they meet to confer about natives'
problems.

Rural Northerners stop in Fairbanks when they are en route
outside. It looks very good to them then; it looks even better when
they return.

Many miners, traders, and trappers make Fairbanks a second
home. They are known here and are welcomed with special
warmth: "Good to see you again, Sandy!" or Bert, Frank, John,
Pete. It *is* good to see them. Fairbanks would not have the
character that it does if some of the bush-dwellers were not always
in town. They are the true pioneers, and the sight of their grizzled
faces and self-assurance helps to keep the North real to the people
of Fairbanks, some of whom live in un-arctic comfort.

Fairbanks was named because of the wish of its early settlers
to honor Senator Charles Warren Fairbanks of Indiana, later Vice
President; he was pleading the cause of Alaska in a neglectful
Congress. The town, first a trading center for miners on near-by
creeks, had taken root in a curve of the Chena River—which
flows into the Tanana, which flows into the Yukon, which flows
into the Bering Sea. Most supplies came all the way from the
States by boat, although some were brought overland on a trail

from the Gulf of Alaska, 365 miles by dog team or packhorse, at a rate of $5.00 a ton-mile in summer. Alaska was needing money for roads, as well as much other assistance that only could come from Washington, and Washington was indifferent, then as now —so indifferent that David Starr Jordan called the Congressional treatment of Alaska "governmental pathology."

Nevertheless, Fairbanks thrived. Its site is a little more than a hundred miles south of the Arctic Circle, on the wide Tanana flats, which are lightly wooded. Once cleared, it is fair farming country, although in some places permafrost is a problem.

From any south-facing window in Fairbanks one can see the Alaska Range, which extends the entire length of the southern horizon. At its far end is Mount McKinley—Denali, as the original Indians called it: "the Great One." When the sun has gone down, when it no longer polishes the white, west-facing slopes, and the summits are disappearing, blue-gray, into the twilight mist, Denali stands out for a long time, still burnished with rosy light. On most winter nights the sky is a pageant of the Aurora's unfolding and folding color.

The town itself is a scene of intriguing contrasts. On the banks of the Chena, beneath spruce and birch trees, are attractive small modern homes—none really pretentious but inviting be-cause individually planned by the owners. There are two or three housing developments too, but their units have not sold well. Northerners do not like to have someone else telling them what they want. An urban redevelopment program is under way and is meeting with some resistance for the same reason: Alaskans' spirit of independence.

Probably half of the residents live in log cabins, some now disguised with clapboard. The log walls stand close beside two new apartment buildings eight and ten stories high, apartments with cocktail lounges, beauty shops, luggage shops, florists, and laundromats off the lobbies, and with elevators of course. Only one other building in Fairbanks has an elevator, and they are such a novelty to the Indian and Eskimo children that the

youngsters come in and ride up and down, giggling and bright-
eyed, till dispersed by the management.

In a cabin only a block from one of the modern apartments lives
an Eskimo woman eighty years old who supports herself with a
trapline beginning a few more blocks away. The police, here as
in New York, are concerned with parking violations, but they
also have to be on the lookout for lynx and moose, which come
into town—lynx on the grounds of the newest hotel, so luxurious
that no cold can enter the rooms through even an opened
window: the pressure inside is adjusted to make the air always
flow out, never in.

Second Avenue, especially the long block between Cushman
and Lacey streets, helps to bring back Alaskans when they have
gone away. At a speed limit of fifteen miles an hour, cars share
the pavement with people and dogs—many dogs; they sniff at
the boots of the sourdoughs, most of whom have left teams at
their cabins out in the bush, in a neighbor's care.

The sourdoughs stride along with the sure step of those who can
manoeuver on snowshoes well. They wear cords, jackets, bright
wool shirts, and in winter stocking caps or fur caps, like gro-
tesquely large bonnets when they are made of fox skins. The
men's eyes, gentle and slightly humorous, seem to see everything
and to see it with pleasure and freshness. "Staying long, Pete?
At the Nordale?" Of course at the Nordale, the hotel that has
been headquarters for men from the bush almost as long as they
have been going out and coming back to this settlement on the
Chena. In most cities there is one hotel lobby that is the favorite
of girls and their dates—in San Francisco the lobby of the St.
Francis, where they meet "under the clock." Romance persists, as
well, in the Nordale lobby, with its cherry-red furniture and walls
covered with paintings of Northern scenes, and with a fireplace
always glowing on winter days. It is not the romance of young
love here, but the romance of lifelong adventure.

The Nordale is one of the landmarks on Second Avenue. In

the same block are Fairbanks's two movie theatres, two hardware stores (without their merchandise no one could live in the North), a bowling alley and "Sportland," an arcade, the big, bewildering Coop Drug Store and the more sedate Fenton's Drug Store across the street, men's and women's clothing stores and two jewelry stores, one modern and carpeted and the other, simpler, patronized by the many friends of Harry Avakoff, who adjusts his eyepiece and says, "Why should I write my Alaska experiences? In gold-rush times there were good and bad men, and there are good and bad men today, and that's all there is to the story."

He is one of the good men. Some of the other kind are in the bars of this block—how many bars? You count them. It's easy to know where they are by the limp, swaying figures of natives outside most of them. In Fairbanks there is a liquor establishment for every 132 residents, but the city "has a much higher caliber of alcoholics than one finds in a typical Stateside community," says Dr. Paul O'Hollaren, a specialist. In the doctor's opinion, "Only about ten per cent of the Fairbanks alcoholics would be psychopaths—half the usual average." It's nice to know that our alcoholics have class, but Fairbanks is making an organized effort to rehabilitate them. For their treatment the local banks will even loan money.

In summer the tourists arrive, on planes, buses, the railroad, and in cars they have driven up the Alaska Highway. Looking far-away-from-home, some will walk hesitantly along Second Avenue among the Indians and Eskimos, the sourdoughs, and the big, thick-furred huskies. Often the women are clutching their handbags tight, probably with a subconscious sense of insecurity in this unfamiliar, so distant city—which is delighted to see them after the isolation of winter. Some of the traveling husbands, too, seem a bit ill at ease, trying to meet the new circumstances with a business manner and instinctively feeling it not quite right here.

Of course home-town residents are a part of the Second Avenue crowd. It is their favorite street, with the Chena River gliding by only a block away and the rumble of traffic always audible on the ancient bridge. Fairbanks women tend to be very feminine, in an instinctive more than a self-conscious way. They dress with a certain dash and independence, in pretty colors. There aren't many hats or gloves. The men too are bareheaded. Some may wear suits, possibly with wool shirts, although probably more will have on openly swinging jackets. In cold weather men, women, and children all have Teddy-bear silhouettes, in parkis made usually by the Eskimos.

In winter the lights of log cabins shine out through the snow-laden birch trees, and lights from the store windows catch on snowflakes powdering Second Avenue. There won't be anyone on the street then but Alaskans themselves and the servicemen, lonely boys from the near-by bases. Some of the GI's are bored, huddling back in their parki hoods, hating the cold, just enduring the months until they can leave the North. Others mix with the local people, feeling stimulated to be in Alaska and planning now for the time when they can come back as settlers.

At present the military do change the Fairbanks atmosphere, to a certain extent. They represent a cross-section of the Stateside population, and there are many who bring new ideas and enthusiasms to people up in the arctic. There are also the usual civilian percentage with criminal tendencies, and some of the incidents have inspired a caution in Fairbanks residents that was not necessary in former times. In the three bases to whose personnel Fairbanks is "the town," are 25,000 men—two and a half times the local population. The problems can be visualized if one imagines New York City trying to absorb the energies of more than eighteen million homesick soldiers.

With its really efficient police force, however, Fairbanks is relatively peaceful, and the town's own spirit is the one most conspicuous. A friend of mine from Chicago, one who has traveled in Europe and Asia, came to Fairbanks on her return trip from Tokyo. While we were walking on Second Avenue she said, "I've never seen people who looked like this, anywhere else in the world." Who looked like what? "So free. Their feeling of freedom shows in the way they stand and walk and wear their clothes—everything that they do."

That would be Fairbanks: lusty, a little lawless, friendly in the most genuine way, growing but not impatiently, ambitious but without losing its natural, easy pace, a city that looks ahead, although somewhat obliquely, already realizing that after Fairbanks has become thoroughly modern, some of the ways valued here will have been lost.

Fairbanks has 10,000 residents; Nome, 2,000. At the height of its gold-rush boom 20,000 people crowded the boardwalks of Nome and spilled over onto the streets. The town today is like Fairbanks, a center that serves even more remote mining camps and native villages. Nome itself is so distant that its supplies can come only on three summer boats and all the rest of the year by air. Therefore some of the settlements in Nome's district turn rather to Fairbanks for contact with civilization. Fairbanks can keep in touch with Seattle throughout the winter, not only with planes but with the Alaskan Highway trucks, and freighters that feed to other trucks and the railroad at Gulf Coast ports.

When the people of Nome were taking gold by the handful out of the hills behind town, summer ships came in streams, and all kinds of goods, though expensive, were stocked. The gold-bearing ground is rich also in other minerals, and Nome could have more prosperity if there were easier ways to bring in machinery and send out ore. A highway has been started across the 500 miles from Fairbanks, and when it is finished it may create a bright future for Nome.

At present Nome has the sourdoughs, Eskimos, husky dogs baying, and other frontier details that make Fairbanks colorful— but no ten-story apartments. It does have a general store, super-market, drugstore, and two hardware stores. The movie theatre was a bar formerly. The ceiling is not very high, and the lower part of the picture lies on the floor. The proportion of liquor establishments to population is almost exactly the same in Nome as in Fairbanks.

Nome's two small hotels face each other at one end of Front Street. At the other end of the street are the bank and Federal Building. In between are three blocks of stores, airline offices, bars, and restaurants, most of which have the false fronts associated with western towns. Even the new, rather luxurious café has its non-functioning square wall extending above the roof— non-functioning, but the false fronts are justified here for the same reason they are on a western prairie. This main street is wide and the distances on all sides of it seem to be endless. A row of flat little one-story buildings would look depressingly insignificant in so horizontal a scene.

About half the people in Nome are Eskimos. Small groups of them always are standing outside the drugstore, an ice-cream parlor, The Glue Pot, or the Federal Building, which houses the post office. Most of the women seem to be "packing" babies, as they would say—that is, carrying them in the back of their parkis. Each woman, whenever she stops, will put one foot in front of the other and tilt her weight back and forth, a rocking motion the children must like, since many of them sleep contentedly.

There on Front Street where much of the time the scene is half-buried in snow, it is cheerful to see the Eskimos' bright parki covers. In the airline office the first day I came to Nome a tourist was staring out through the window. "Look at those Eskimo women," he said to his wife with a glittering smile. "They are wearing their nightgowns out on the street!" One of those women was in the room, a small, bright-eyed grandmother. She went up to the man and, "Pardon me," she said gently, "but those are not nightgowns. They are parki covers, and we wear them to keep snow off the inside parkis. Snow would rot the hides."

Most of the houses in Nome are small. The permafrost has tipped some of them; others sag at the point where warmth from a stove inside has melted the ice in the soil beneath. Log cabins predominate. Among them stand tar-paper shacks, small frame cottages, and a few gold-rush "castles," as Eskimo children call them—homes miniature in size but with once-rich ornamentation. The luckier miners built them and, very decrepit as most of them are now, they still have stained-glass windows in halls, elaborately carved doors, and cupolas, towers, and scrollwork, or what is left of them after fifty winters of arctic storms. It was one of those houses I later bought.

The summers in Nome don't warm up enough to permit growing flowers like those that border the lawns in Fairbanks. But greenhouses and glassed-in porches are vivid splashes in every block, and these tiny gardens make Nome appear gay, with that infallible charm—lightheartedness in the face of hardships.

It is a very moving experience to see Nome from a plane. After flying for several hours over the arctic wilderness, which is the only way one can come, even in summer, there on this coast of the Bering Sea is a brave little cluster of houses. It is a town as a child might plan it, with modest homes, a post office, hospital, and a few stores; not many buildings related to industry, and no railroads leading out to connect with the rest of the world. One freighter may lie offshore, but probably not even one, and through the long winter, of course, the sea will be frozen. The something in us that always responds to valor is touched by the sight of Nome.

Kotzebue, on the arctic coast, is about half as large. For centuries it has been a site where coastal Eskimos from as far away as Little Diomede Island met to trade with Eskimos from the inland rivers. Each summer the natives still gather there, now among a fair number of white residents. These include Archie Ferguson, fabulous character, promoter, and bush pilot until he had crash-landed ten times, when the officials grounded him; and a husband and wife pair, Edith and Jack Bullock, who distribute oil and operate barge lines in several parts of the arctic; and Gene Joiner, bush pilot who sells raw jade and jade jewelry from Jade Mountain, historic landmark up the Kobuk

River. Kotzebue is a take-off point for polar-bear hunting, shee-fishing, and for scientific expeditions into the arctic. Some of the best Eskimo dancing is seen there, making small Kotzebue one of the favorite objectives of tourists. It is a gay town, sometimes to the point of dizziness. Alaskans themselves always speak of it with affection.

Barrow, a little larger than Kotzebue and Alaska's most north-ern settlement, is composed almost entirely of Eskimos, drawn there to work on the Navy oil-research program, later on DEWline installations. Its wildly veering economy is the extreme example of what the military projects have brought to the North.

In the region are about 150 other villages, a fair number with less than 50 people, and with such lonely-sounding names as Tikikluk, Takshak, and Chukfaktoolik. Even in these, predomi-nantly native, often are found a few white men—the trader, miners, trappers, most of them waiting out their late years. When the occasion is right, they will tell what is in their minds to a visitor: if they had it to do over again, would they come to Alaska? Some say they wouldn't, but then the old, fierce independence that brought them here will spring up in their eyes and answer the question differently.

Most of the pioneers who are young do not ask the question. Few were born in the North. They found it and chose it, and every day they are aware that, of all places on earth, this is where they would wish to be.

There is a look that far-Northerners recognize on the faces of people they meet in their towns. They can recognize it be-cause they have worn it themselves: a look of joy, quiet but so intense it is almost giddy. It is the look of finding oneself in the arctic again after being away for too long a time.

Alaskans are travelers. In one year seven families from Nome went to New York on vacation and twelve to the Hawaiian Islands. Frequent trips to the States are thought of by many as a necessity, as much for the pleasure of coming back as of seeing one's friends and relatives and of being a part of the Stateside

scene for a while. I am familiar with homesickness, in myself
and in others, but I never have known it to reach quite the pitch
that it does in an exiled Alaskan. Northerners can feel exiled in
two hours, two months, or two years—more often in two hours
than two years. The wish to return starts to build, and by the time
one sets foot on this frozen soil again, it can become an obsession.
One day then, finally, a plane starts its let-down above the home
landing-field, touches, rolls to a stop, and there is the welcoming
group, probably zipped up against the wind.

I was in one of those crowds when Mike and Louise Walsh
returned to Nome after trying a winter of Stateside living to see
whether they wanted to stay away permanently. They have reared
ten children here on the shore of the Bering Sea, and some of
them live in the States with their own children now.

The Walshes are dignified; even Alaskans can see what a suitable setting Boston, from which they came during the gold rush,
would be for them. But we hoped not to lose them. "How about
it?" someone asked tiny, sedate Louise. "You aren't going to
move to the States, are you?" "No," Louise answered. "There are
just too many bushes."

Bushes: we all knew what she meant—lush foliage and also
the bushes of too many people, cars, walls, telephone poles, billboards, signs, slogans, diversions, tugs and pulls on one's time,
just too much of everything, good as much of it might be in less
quantities. On the day Mike and Louise returned, one of their
sons drove them home to their pleasant white clapboard house,
where the stove was already burning. They took off their wraps,
and when the family had left, they sat down at the kitchen
window and looked out at the smooth, treeless, and restful hills,
and were satisfied.

>>>->>>->>> 14 <<<-<<<-<<<

Outwitting the Arctic

IT'S NOT FAIR to describe the satisfactions of Northern living without telling what some of the problems are. For there are, of course, problems. Three stand out: housing, securing supplies, and the making and stretching of money. Houses do very peculiar and unpredictable things at fifty degrees below zero. One must study them, learn their tactics, and outwit them if that is possible. And supplies, many of which come direct from the States— doesn't one simply order them and then wait? No, the process is not that logical. Nor is it true, as so widely thought, that Alaska wages and prices can be depended upon to balance. In finding the answers to these elementary questions, people who choose the arctic lead strenuous lives. But was any frontier, anywhere else, ever different?

Even after a year at Unalakleet I did not have all the information about arctic animals that was needed to finish a book about them. I had not seen the big humpback whales, walrus, or lemmings, three of the key species. I was telling the facts in fiction form, but I wanted the picture of Northern wildlife to be accurate, as it only could be if the author had seen the main characters at first hand. Therefore I went down to San Francisco, closed my apartment, and came back to Nome, supposedly in the interest of science but I already thought that probably I would stay in the North permanently.

The final transition from naturalist into "pioneer" came when I bought a house. One week all the questions of food, heat, electricity, water, and plumbing were taken care of by paying a hotel bill; the next week I was making a list of staple groceries for a year, to be radioed to Seattle so they could come on the last summer boat; and frayed wiring, smoking stoves, cracks under doors, and the faucet through which water would cease to flow with the freeze-up—these had become pressing problems, with an arctic winter approaching fast. The time was late August.

I rented the house at first, but after three months of preliminary expense and labor, on a very cold night, as a bush pilot broke a bottle of champagne over the front door, I became its owner. About that time the late Senator Howard Lyng, meeting me on the street, said, "I hear you are buying the Berger house. There isn't a house in Nome that will give you more trouble." "I am sure by now that you're right, Senator Lyng," I said, "but it makes me a little envious when I see how comfortable other Nome houses are, and I know the reason is that you've all outsmarted the North. You've worked out your own ways to live like civilized people up here in the arctic, and I want the fun of doing that too." "Well, if that is the kind of fun you want, you will have it," the Senator answered, and added, "But go ahead. You won't regret it."

The house was built during the gold rush by Jacob Berger, a miner who had made three lucky strikes. He and his bride planned the house with taste, at least taste in a period that did not excel in its appreciation of simple design. I was not delighted with the exterior, but the rooms were large and light, and there were good floors, exquisite moldings, and many attractive details, like white pillars supporting a beam in the living-room.

The trouble was that the house was old, about fifty years old— adolescence as houses are judged in New England but tottering senility in the weather of northwest Alaska. Not tottering really;

the house stood firm on its mammoth timbers, with 2″ x 10″ joists, many-layered walls to keep out the cold, and floors of solid wood four inches thick. The skeleton was sound. Fifty years of heaving and dropping by permafrost had opened a thousand cracks, however, and recent owners had not taken care of the house. It needed new plumbing and wiring, a new heating system, new insulation, and decorating throughout.

I owned it for five years, till I moved to Fairbanks. By then the house was completely practical and inside rather beautiful. During the time I lived in it there were some very chaotic hours, but not one when I ever was sorry that I had bought it. I did have more than the average difficulties. In that Senator Lyng had been right: the maximum difficulties. They gave me a chance however to claim that I'm an authority on arctic housing.

An Alaska house is what a home is anywhere, a center that helps to cement a family together, a place where a woman expresses her talents, and a setting for friendly gatherings. In the far North it is also, in the most elementary, cave-man sense, a life-giving shelter. These walls, only wood and some tar paper, and this roof from which shingles fly off like birds in each arctic gale, these hold off a whole skyful of lethal cold. Sometimes in winter they separate temperatures that are more than 100° apart. When all our utilities function well, the electric lights on the inside of the house glow and the thermometer registers above 70. Less than a foot away, if there is any wind, exposed human flesh freezes in less than a minute. This protective house is, then, home as it is idealized, and our interest in it is almost, if not quite, an obsession.

The utilities do break down, with results so alarming that friends greeting each other in stores or the post office are less likely to ask, "How are you?" than, "How is your house holding up these days?" In this climate a house can become uninhabitable in a dozen ways, but the emergencies we dread most are those that deprive us of heat. Within a few hours the temperature in the house will be well below 33° and the plumbing will freeze, including the pressure pump and the water tanks; also the canned goods and crates of potatoes and fruit. The food will be lost, perhaps several hundred dollars' worth if it is near the beginning of winter. A pair of newcomers had been so well warned of the dangers that when a Nome hostess asked them to dinner, they said: "Oh, we wouldn't dare leave the food that long!"

Our troubles arise because we, the white settlers, want mechanized homes in a climate for which they were not designed. Few of the Eskimos have tanks and pumps and oil lines to freeze. We fight the country; Eskimos go along with it. On trips to the States I have been asked if I live in an ice *igloo*. I always think then of a white man in Kotzebue who, remembering old geography lessons, showed his young daughter how a snow house was built. Eskimos stood around photographing the curious project. But, though they don't live in houses of snow or ice, some of those they do have can be built in a day.

We who grew up with mechanical comforts, however, still want them, and so, in Nome, there is a lively competitive effort to see how close we can come to the life in Stateside communities. Ever since the first miners arrived with the gold rush, the techniques have been worked on, and some have not been improved in the last fifty years. Others are still evolving; and every house has its adaptations.

A home-owner's principal problems are cold and the permafrost. Of the two, permafrost may not be the greater, but coping with it requires the more ingenuity. In some places permafrost is true soil, frozen as much as a thousand feet down, even into the bedrock; rocks will freeze, one learns in the arctic. Or the permafrost may be clear blue ice; or often the upper layer is frozen plant fibers, dead but not much decayed, for bacteria have as hard a time to survive in the North as most other organisms. Whenever I open a package of quick-frozen spinach, I think of the way the permafrost looks where it is composed of plants. The plants would be different from spinach, however.

In summer the surface crust of the permafrost thaws down a

bit. Then the top is about as limp and spongy as spinach when it is cooking. Or if it's composed of silt, the permafrost acts like quicksand. One sinks into it almost as fast, to the welcome spot where one's foot finds the ice. The lower layers remain frozen solidly, at near zero Fahrenheit, although that temperature fluctuates, even as far as fifty feet down, with the season. At all times the permafrost heaves and subsides, never predictably and sometimes quite fast. The house resting upon it tilts, first one way, then another way, to such an extent that, for example, the feedlines that carry the oil to the stoves sometimes loosen or break. Or during the night a stovepipe will disconnect at a joint. One may wake in the morning to find a layer of oil all over the carpet, or oily soot deposited upon everything in the room, including upholstered furniture.

Floors always are tipped, but we get used to that. One man says that his kitchen floor banks just enough to make it easy for him to hurry through on his way to another room.

About doors, on the other hand, frequently we become desperate. Doors have to fit snugly to keep out the cold. But as a house shifts, doors get so far out of plumb that wide cracks open under them or at the top or side; or they jam shut perhaps during a single night. When the doors then have been adjusted, the house may shift back again in the same length of time. We have long narrow wedges which can be put on or taken off the tops and bottoms of doors, and also another solution such as I had on my own front door. The ends of the door were sawed off so they didn't meet either the sill or the top of the casing. The spaces were closed up with two stainless steel plates screwed onto the ends of the door, outside. The screws went through slots in the plates, so that the plates could be loosened and pushed up or down, at an angle perhaps, to make the door tight.

In a house constantly on the move, walls can't be plastered or papered. In the old days the walls often were covered with tongue-and-groove paneling, which would give. Now we use one of the wallboards or plywood. The panels will shift as units, but the seams where they join, of course, open and close. All the seams in the house, in fact, spread. Wind gets into the walls then and, unless we keep the cracks well filled up, into the rooms.

One time, in a program to eliminate wind in my house, I found breezes that almost would wave a flag pouring out of the unused sockets in baseboard electric plugs. Wind blew in through the cracks at the top and bottom of baseboards, at the edges of door and window casings where they line up against walls, and through cracks under sills. Finally, for the temporary present, all the cracks and seams were closed up with moldings and with expansible fillers like caulking cotton, plastic putty, and a clay that comes in long rolls the width of an earthworm. When the work was completed, the temperature in the house went up fifteen degrees.

Besides rolling a house about, the permafrost creates other difficulties. Thawing because of the weight and warmth, the permafrost under the house will cave down. Anything placed on the frozen ground, in fact, from a tin can to a building or road, tends to sink. The natives at Barrow put much of their trash into empty oil drums left out on the tundra, and in a surprisingly short time the drums disappear. Houses subside in the same way, fairly fast since the heat from the stoves within hastens the thawing.

This, then, one tries to do: make a house firm and stationary on ground that moves and in summer is spongy. One way is with piling. At considerable expense piles can be driven into the frozen ground. They have to go very deep and, even so, will not remain where they are indefinitely. For a while they will hold a structure in place. Nome's Federal Building, a block square and three stories high, was set on piling as recently as 1937 and by now has shifted so much that it has been declared unsafe and is being replaced. At still greater cost the permafrost can be thawed artificially and a basement constructed. But the basement will crack, and so will the building on top of it.

These problems do not apply to the beach, where the sand does not deeply freeze. Nome of the gold-rush days was several miles long but only as wide as the beach, since the miners had no solution to putting up homes in the summer swamps. It was the mining itself that made such homes possible for the later settlers. Nome is ringed with gold-dredges, all digging the permafrost up with bucket lines, crushing the rock in the process, and spewing it out after the gold is extracted. The tailing piles formed in this way soon were the size of natural hills, of crushed rock in effect all made ready to firm up the tundra. Uncounted thousands of truckloads have been brought tō town through the years, so that Nome stands on tailings now. All of the houses do.

The tailings sink into the permafrost also. They sink faster if warmth from the houses thaws the permafrost. Therefore, to keep a cold space beneath the floor, most houses rest on huge timbers or skids. Nevertheless, within a few years the crushed rock under a house will have disappeared; then the structure is raised and tipped and a crew of workmen sling many cubic yards of new tailings into the basin of muck beneath. My own house stood upon fourteen inches of frozen soil. Under the soil was clear glacial ice, I was told, and along through the ice, through its layers, a flowing stream ran. Other such strata of moving water occur in the permafrost. They are due, one suspects, to springs that don't reach the surface. If the heat from the stove in a house should thaw down the permafrost far enough so that one of the streams could seep up to the top, the stream never could be contained again. There have been cases where water released in this way has come into a house and, freezing as it was rising, became an ice skeleton around which the walls were shells. Those houses were not in Nome, but we knew of them and were cautious.

Some of the streams and springs do reach the surface. On the outskirts of Nome are several—water heavily laden with minerals but delicious and fresh to taste. They are warm springs that happily do not freeze in winter, and they are the city's water supply.

Neither water nor sewage pipes can be laid in the permafrost, where they would freeze, but there is a system of mains, running along on the surface, which transport the spring water to homes in the summer. Every street has a main on one side, in the gutter, and householders, doing their own plumbing, connect pipes and for about two months have an almost conventional water supply. The mains are owned by the U.S. Smelting, Refining and Mining Company, the organization that operates the big dredges. They sell water at one standard rate, $4.50 a month—$7.50 for a household that has a bathtub. By September 15 all these pipes are frozen. Then our water is brought to us, also from springs at the edge of town, in the tank trucks owned by two "water men," Pete Reader and Lester Bronson.

For storage a simple household gets by with a barrel. The water man fills it by carrying bucketfuls into the house at 2½ cents a gallon. Other houses have storage tanks holding up to 500 gallons, with intake and overflow pipes to the tanks through the outside walls. The procedure is this: First, the water man comes with a snowplow and dozes the driveway. Then he brings his truck, fastens his hose to the intake pipe, and connects a cord from the pump on his truck to an electric plug we provide on the outside wall of the house. The water starts pouring in—when delivered that way, at 1½ cents a gallon.

In the beginning, however, the water man blows into both the pipes. If he finds either blocked with ice, he goes away and we start to wrestle with one of the more desperate problems. My own storage tank was up on the second floor, and in the original plumbing arrangement the intake and overflow pipes looped around the eaves with several elbows before they came down to the water man's level. At the point where they broke through the roof, cores of frost, which became ice, would build up. A blow torch would loosen the cores from the pipes, but the cores would not pass the elbows. Whenever the pipes were blocked, as they always were at temperatures lower than −30°, they all had to be taken down. I revised the system, with two new, plastic pipes which were contained for most of their length in the heated house.

We have one dread that rises at times nearly into hysteria: that the intake pipe will be clear but the overflow pipe will be clogged. Then the tank will run over and, if it is on the second floor, ruin the walls. Most houses in Nome have had one or more holes drilled in the first-story floor, as an easier way than sweeping to drain off an interior lake.

After the water gets into the tank it flows to the faucets by means of gravity or a pressure pump. En route it passes through coils in a stove and perhaps then through coils with a fan behind them, to heat a room. The whole arrangement is so connected with summer lines out in the street that a valve can be turned one way to have water flow from the tank; turned the other way, the supply comes from the mains. Since I was having *all* the housekeeping problems, they included one that bothers some residents but not everyone: electricity from the ground wire of a telephone pole got into my outdoor lines and through them into the interior plumbing system. I didn't know what caused the trouble, only that every time I touched the water coming out of a faucet it all but threw me across the room. An electrician found that there was enough current in the water to light a 15-watt bulb. It was eliminated by simply disconnecting the outside pipes. Ordinarily the electricity would disperse itself in the soil, but solidly frozen ground does not conduct well, and the electricity gets diverted into some surface pipes.

Most of the plumbing in Nome is planned and installed by the owners. It is one of our favorite topics of conversation. When new acquaintances call, there is soon, inevitably, a leading question like, "Where do you have your water tank?" With it goes an expectant look, and it is only courteous then to ask, "Would you perhaps like to see the plumbing?" The callers are up on their feet in an instant.

After a house has had several owners, the plumbing is apt to be rather marvelous—more elaborate than necessary, no doubt, but they've all had the satisfaction of adding pipe. I had little to do with mine except to complain and then listen to other people's experience. But it seemed an amazing, ingenious system that various functioning non-plumbers had suggested: hot water that rose and cold water that sank where it should; wonderful tangles of pipes that began at the driveway and ended in conventional faucets. The entire tangle was visible, for water pipes never are hidden inside the walls. If they were, they would probably freeze. Mine, like everyone else's, were silvered.

It is not as hard to get waste water out of a house in Nome as to get fresh water in. An official brought a young bride to town. On her second morning she happened to look out the window as she was emptying water into the sink. She cried out to her husband: "The plumbing's been disconnected! The drain is just pouring the water out into the yard!" The young husband explained, tactfully, that the drain was not broken. Bathwater and dishwater simply are cast outside onto the tailings. Formerly most of the lots were bordered with wooden sluice boxes. Drainage went into them and was carried to larger ditches beneath the boardwalks. Now the boxes have fallen into disuse. The water just disappears in the crushed rock, where it evaporates rather fast, since the air in the North is dry.

The equipment is elementary—only pipes through the wall from a shower or bathtub, lavatory, and sink. The problem is to prevent ice from clogging these pipes. We say in this climate that it is not a cold day unless boiling water poured out the window has frozen before it can reach the ground. I never have seen that experiment tried, but in some of the temperatures only a full, fast flow will get through the pipes. In all but the summer months a drip or a trickle will quickly stop them up. It is customary to pour salt into the drains at the end of day, but mine often froze until, as a friend advised, I had new ones constructed of six-inch galvanized stovepipe. So much wind entered the house through the drains that when they weren't stoppered my kitchen drain always hummed, in the key of D.

Other waste is disposed of through what is called the facility, or the honey bucket. This is a chemical toilet, a pail of heavy-gauge steel enclosed in a large metal box. The box extends through the wall in such a way that the bucket can be removed from the outside by the "sanitary man," who empties and steam-cleans it. For this purpose there is a small door of familiar design. A subsidiary problem is the fact that the little door can be opened, the bucket lifted out, and a child, or a man with some effort, can enter the house through the interior metal box. When Nome people leave town, most of them block any chance of intruders by standing a pole tightly braced between the top of the toilet seat and the bathroom ceiling. The total arrangement fills many newcomers with dismay. To some of them I have quoted what was told to me when I arrived: "As time passes, this will recede in importance."

With these various improvisations, from the adjustable plates on the entrance door to the bathwater draining out of a stove-pipe, it is possible to outwit the permafrost. In combating the cold, Northerners are a longer way from success. In some states the thermometers drop as low as ours, but they do not stay down as long; the sea off Nome has been frozen as late as the first of July. And when, week after week, the temperature never rises as high as −30°, as happens occasionally, the very materials of which a house is made become frozen. Before I came North I did not know that an ancient, dried-out piece of wood could freeze, but it will. One evidence is that when struck, it will chime. The boardwalks of Nome clang under one's footsteps, and when the wind hurls a piece of ice onto the wall of a house, the whole house seems to ring.

My neighbors across the street woke one morning to find that their blankets had frozen to an adjacent wall. Inside walls do not always freeze, but they become so cold that one's body loses its heat to them by radiation. The discomfort is lessened by using electric fans. A fan mounted close to the ceiling blows down the warm air that rises, and a fan set high in a wall sends excessive heat from a room like the kitchen into another room that is cool. Fans blow across hot-water pipes to distribute their warmth; other fans are incorporated in heaters installed on the smokestacks. Too much of the heat from a stove is lost up the stack. To capture it, one section of stovepipe is replaced by a piece of equipment that separates the ascending smoke into metal chambers. They become very hot, and a fan behind them will drive a blast of warm air out into the room. The effect is the same whether real or illusion: a lively circulation of heated air seems a barrier between us and the chilly walls.

Most houses in Nome have some insulation. In the newer ones some of the modern products were used. Houses that date from the gold rush have walls made of several layers of wood, with tar paper between, or walls filled with sand, sawdust, or ashes. Sand and sawdust were not effective; ashes were better except for one disadvantage. Last year a man in Nome bought and tore down an early-day structure in order to salvage the timbers. It had been insulated with ashes, and too late he learned that the lye in the ashes had eaten away most of the structural wood.

Is it a kind of fear, a mental block, that leads me to speak last of the stoves? A woman I know never mentions the subject because, she confided, if she discusses stoves she becomes hysterical. Another wife always goes to a hotel when her husband leaves town because, she says, "I wouldn't stay alone in the house with the stoves." During the winter I spent at Unalakleet the stove in my room exploded one evening. By morning the indoor temperature was 10° below zero, and everything in the room had frozen, including the ink and the hand lotion. Only one such experience is needed to give any woman, and some men, an irrational tension regarding the stoves.

A few houses in Nome have oil furnaces, but not many. The furnaces can't be installed easily in houses that were not planned for them, and since Nome is not growing at present, few new houses are built. Two kinds of stoves are used: the range, which not only must cook the food but heat the kitchen; and space-heaters in other areas of the house. Both kinds, if modern, are too well insulated for Northerners. The enameled sides of the cookstoves are cool to the touch, so that it's necessary to leave the oven door hanging open. Much of the time the cook's shins are bruised, and in winter some women do not bake potatoes or pies —the kitchen would get too cold. The old cast-iron ranges were better, those covered with bulges and curlicues, every one of which radiated welcome and lovely warmth. The space-heaters now being made are enclosed in trim metal boxes, boxes pierced, it is true, with slots and louvers, but more warmth got out through the old-fashioned screens made of sturdy wire mesh.

Eskimos as a rule do not have much money and therefore burn driftwood. There is no local supply of timber in Nome, no road to the groves where the last small spruces grow. Natural gas has been found in Alaska but so far is not available in the Northern cities, and coal is being mined but there is no coastal steamship line that will bring it out to the Bering Sea. The fuel used by white families is oil. Fuel bills average from $45 a month to $145 or higher—at Barrow four times as much.

The oil tanks are outside because of the dread of fire; a fire is a frightful experience up in these arctic temperatures. Since the tanks cannot be underground in the permafrost, they are placed up on racks and feed to the stoves by gravity. They are exposed to the ice and snow, of course, and these frequently block up the air vents. If one forgets to uncover the vents, as the oil level drops the vacuum inside sometimes causes the tanks to collapse. There is another threat: in the spring and fall, temperature changes are rather extreme, and moisture condenses inside the tank and collects in the bottom as water. Every tank has a trap with a petcock for draining the water off, but it does often get in the feedlines and freezes, and then stops the flow of oil.

With an outside tank it is not easy to keep other people from pilfering. I still have as souvenirs the equipment one neighbor used to siphon oil out of my air vent. He had left the gear hanging above my tank for his convenience.

The oil feedline runs under the house, where it branches to each of the stoves. The stoves burn well if all the conditions are quite ideal. But we live with the fearful knowledge that if anything stops the draft, if soot in the stove does or soot or snow in the stack, then the stove will explode. Stoves with electric blowers, the forced-draft type, soot up within minutes when power lines blow down. Stoves may also explode if they are lighted when they are warm.

The problems of Northern housekeeping are, therefore, numerous, but the truth is that maintaining a house is easier almost anywhere else in the North than at Nome. In the larger cities one can summon an expert mechanic. Nome has a few, only three or four, and at times they all vanish. Bad weather, the cause of most kinds of breakdowns, affects everyone. The mechanics are swamped with calls, until suddenly they may disappear, reportedly to some inaccessible room equipped with a deck of cards and a case of everybody-knows-what. In the larger towns there are more mechanics and pleas for help do not fall so heavily upon any one.

Although Fairbanks is colder than Nome in winter, through some ingenious engineering it does furnish modern utilities, and those greatly ease the problems. The Fairbanks municipal water circulates in a loop system, with pumps that prevent its freezing by keeping the water running at least three feet per second. Connections to customers are through double lines, one in and one out, and the water continually flows in these also. Each service line is insulated and, further, an electrical connection is provided to charge the line and thus thaw it if necessary.

The Fairbanks sewers are made of wood-stave pipe (concrete breaks in the permafrost), and they sometimes freeze up. Then the city sends out steam boilers on trucks, which will open the flow. Fairbanks generates its electricity by steam, and the steam is saved and piped through the downtown area to heat apartment and business buildings and a few homes. Everybody in Fairbanks wishes that he could live "on the steam line."

In the villages smaller than Nome few people try to have the more civilized comforts, except in the housing the missions and government furnish. But the white population of Nome aspire to have push-button households, and to a surprising extent they do create them. Perhaps they have the most satisfaction of any settlers, since they achieve comfort and strictly by their own efforts —gaining that feeling of competence which is one of the chief rewards of being a pioneer.

Sharing my house was Bobo, a blue-eyed Siberian husky. He was one of the compensations, part of what made the house seem such a warm and protective shelter. But any house in the North has the special meaning of holding away the cold. When Bobo and I would take our late-evening walk, each of the lighted homes we passed meant more to the owners, I thought, than homes do in most places. Beginning at about fifteen degrees below zero, the hot air from the stovepipes vaporizes and for some reason is luminous. In the usual winter wind from the North, the white plumes level down: "The smoke is lying on the roofs," people say of those nights. And the little houses of Nome are close and neighborly under this cover of driven and shining mist, which flows away into the night, over the icy width of the Bering Sea.

15

Supply Lines

"ALASKA" looks like a harmless word, not one to produce hypnosis or to cause a slip of the mind in anyone who is filling an order or writing a bill of lading. Yet we who live there and must depend on Stateside suppliers to do so, wonder sometimes if a kind of dizziness affects those who are shipping our goods. Such strange merchandise comes to us, by such amazing routes—if we get it at all. Many orders we send out are never acknowledged or filled. We mail them and that is the end of it. Maybe the ones who suffered the mental lapses were postal employees. We have had indications that they too can be thrown by the word "Alaska."

One summer when I was traveling, I found in Boston a desk set that I wanted to send to a friend in Nome.

"Please ship it by parcel post," I said to the clerk in the department store. She disappeared and when she came back and started to write up the sales check, she murmured,

"There's no post office in Nome. I looked in a book. But there's an express office. I'll send it up by express."

"Oh, there's a post office," I said. "I live in Nome, so I know. But there is no express office. So please mail the set."

The girl straightened up and I had a close view of that benumbed state of mind which causes us so much trouble.

"It will have to go by express," she said.

I asked for the manager of the department. He took the girl's side.

"Express goes everywhere," he said. "And if the book says that there is no post office in Nome, we can't mail a package there." I didn't believe there was any book. I thought the store had just found it easier to send out their long-distance shipments by express and they used the book story to silence customers who were sending packages to remote locations. I saw that the man and girl thought I simply lied when I said that I lived in Nome. (Instead of a piqué suit should I have been wearing fur *mukluks* and parki that hot July day in Boston?)

The desk set could actually have gone by express—to Anchorage. Then the department store would have had to write to Alaska Airlines in Anchorage, asking them to pick up the package and fly it to Nome and bill the store for the air freight. And to charge me for the air freight the girl and department-manager would have had to figure it out from some schedule that I was certain they didn't have. It would be easier, I decided, just to buy a thermometer that would register lower than 40° below zero, which my friend wanted, and carry it back myself. Such a thermometer proved hard to find, and the search reminded me that Alaskans do sometimes order outlandish things. The whole situation is quite chaotic. Meanwhile we sit up there on the arctic coast, with such needs and such longings. . . .

The mail-order houses do fairly well. At least they answer our letters—usually, though sometimes the replies seem to have little relation to questions asked. Typical was the case of my new refrigerator.

A number of order blanks come with each catalogue. There is a space on the blanks marked "Shipping Instructions." I not only wrote out my instructions there when I sent for the refrigerator, but I enclosed a letter in which I repeated them, explaining that Alaska shipments seem prone to go astray, but I was sure the refrigerator would reach me in Nome if the company sent it—

> *By ship to Valdez, Alaska*
> *By truck from Valdez to Anchorage*
> *By air from Anchorage to Nome*

From experience, I said, people in Nome knew that that was the quickest, surest way to get any heavy article like a refrigerator.

In a few days I received a card stating that my refrigerator was on the way; the company hoped that I would receive it promptly. It should have arrived in about three weeks. Six weeks passed. I sent an inquiry, which was not acknowledged. After ten weeks I wrote again and was answered by the company with a question: by what route had I wanted the refrigerator shipped? It was about that time that one of my neighbors, passing through Fairbanks, happened to see in the *railroad* freight office a crated refrigerator with my name on it. "She's waiting for that," he said to the agent. "Why don't you send it over?"

"We didn't know where she was," said the agent. "The refrigerator just landed here addressed to Sally Carrighar, Fairbanks." I never had lived in Fairbanks. I never had had any order shipped there. The mail-order company had by then sent me dozens of orders to Nome. And the railroad had not been mentioned in my original shipping instructions. When finally I learned the whereabouts of the refrigerator, I had Wien Alaska Airlines fly it to Nome from Fairbanks.

That was the same fall a friend of mine in Nome was trying to get from another mail-order firm a simple shipment, so it would seem: three plain white shirts of the best quality, via parcel post. He sent in his order, by air mail as usual. The month was October. In December the company wrote that they were out of those shirts and didn't know when they would have them. They were canceling his order, therefore, but if he didn't secure the shirts anywhere else, would he please reorder them at some future time?

Busy with preparations for Christmas, my friend let the shirt problem ride. In January the mail-order company wrote to him: his order for three plain white best-quality shirts that they had been holding could now be filled. Since he had been so patient, they were sending the shirts by air mail but would only charge him the parcel-post rates. He should have them in three or four days. With the shirts due so soon, he did not, of course, order others. When they hadn't arrived by March, he wrote a long letter summarizing the situation and asking, was he ever going to get the shirts? There was no answer, but a month later *six* shirts came by parcel post, six of the poorest grade and each equipped with a set of plastic tie clasp and cuff buttons in vivid colors. He gave them away and never was billed for them and never paid for them. Maybe, he said, they had not even come from the same company. Maybe somebody, somewhere, sent him a gift of shirts at a time when he'd ordered shirts. To Northern customers stranger things have happened.

Sometimes one can get action, though. One of the bush pilots was grounded, without income, for three months because a mail-order company failed to send him a simple mechanical part for his airplane and when it did come it was the wrong size. He dispatched a three-page collect telegram to the president of the company and within a week had the correct part in the correct size, by air mail.

Sharing troubles like these may help to cement arctic relationships. At least they do furnish subjects of conversation. Each time someone is sure to remember the case of the tropical oil.

It is the custom for one tanker to bring up the whole year's supply of fuel oil for all of northwest Alaska. To be sure that the ice will be gone from the coast off Kotzebue, the most northern stop, the ship comes late, only a few weeks before the new freeze-up. It was so that year. The tanker was seen, as it always is, with a slight sense of relief. In that tanker out there on the sea is our winter heat.

It anchors two miles off Nome, twelve miles off Kotzebue, for the tidelands are shallow, and up here there cannot be docks. They have been built a few times, but the winter ice always takes them out. And so the oil, and all water-borne shipments in summer, come ashore by barge. The oil is stored and delivered, 50 to 500 gallons at a time, to households and stores, most of which have outdoor tanks.

The tanks feed by gravity to the stoves inside through one-inch lead pipe or copper tubing about half that size. In that well-remembered year, as soon as the temperature dropped in the fall, the oil ceased to flow. For a few days the individual householders struggled with blowtorches, but then it was noticed that everybody was having trouble, and the terrible truth became known: the refinery had sent up the wrong kind of oil. It had sent tropical oil, which contains paraffine and will solidify in the Northern cold. By that time the sea had frozen, no other tanker could come, and since no roads or railroads connect with that country, and no tanker planes carrying fuel oil had been developed, that arctic area had to make do for the winter with solid oil.

"Make do"—it's a familiar phrase and a familiar skill in Alaska, and this is the meaning it had in that year. Every warm stove was surrounded at all times by buckets of solid oil being liquefied in the heat. As the oil in the stove burned out, it was replenished from these. Simple enough, except that somebody had to be watching and pouring constantly and refilling buckets, and a lot of carpets and floors were ruined, and arctic winters are very long.

A shipping mistake that could have been even more serious concerned flour, the year's supply for the village of Gambell on St. Lawrence Island. The schoolteacher had made up one order for all the natives and had listed "Flour—50-lb. sacks" in the number they wanted. What came, again too late to be replaced, were flour-sack dish towels, hundreds of them in the 50-lb. size. No flour at all was sent, and there would have been serious hunger in Gambell if people elsewhere in the North had not made contributions out of their own supplies.

Sometimes what arrives in amusing, like the saddle for a horse received by a man who had ordered a living-room chair.

Most families in Nome send for a year's supply of the staple groceries. By getting them in case lots from Seattle wholesalers, they partly defeat the high cost of living up on that coast. At least that is the theory. Considering all the things they get that they do not want, they are not so sure.

The groceries are brought ashore and piled in stacks in the lighterage company's warehouse. They have come C.O.D. because the wholesalers claim they cannot quote prices in advance of the shipping date; and to get any of them released, one must pay the entire bill, for both freight and merchandise, to the lighterage company. It usually amounts to several hundreds of dollars, often more than a thousand, and as you write out your check, you look at your heap of cartons and wonder, somewhat bemusedly, what will be in them.

As in the case of the tropical oil, this is the last boat. You can't return what you do not want for a year, and so you keep what you receive although sometimes it is pretty strange. One of my friends ordered an ounce of pink coloring-dye for her daughter's birthday cake and was sent a gallon. Another friend found a case of pistachio nuts but none of the olives she'd ordered, and I got a case of celery flakes instead of a case of soap flakes. You try to trade things around, but that is not always possible. It seems that nobody likes pistachio nuts very well, nor celery flakes in case lots, and the gallon of pink vegetable dye arrived before pink became such a popular color.

Once on a visit to Fairbanks I said to a man I had met that I didn't like to sound cynical but it was hard to believe that some of the shippers' mistakes were not deliberate. "Oh, they are," he replied in a tone which suggested that I should have known that. "I worked for a food company in Seattle once," he said, "and we had standing instructions to substitute slow-moving items for some of the articles on Alaska orders. Chutney for catsup was an example."

Even bills seem to have difficulty in reaching us. Most Alaskans keep a few charge accounts in the States, and bookkeepers as well as shipping clerks apparently suffer a kind of vertigo when they see "Alaska." But somehow their dunning letters always arrive on time.

It may be true that some Northern customers have been slow in paying. Since miners get all their income in summer and trappers in winter, Alaska stores often send out bills only once a year, or not at all, and Alaskans do pay—it's a part of their code—but *when* is another question. Stores in the States operate under a different system, and they may have been inconvenienced too many times. Anyway, some of them send their bills by surface mail and their dunning letters the tenth of the following month by air mail. Since surface mail comes to the North very slowly, the dunning letter often arrives before the bill, a situation that should be amusing but somehow isn't.

When we order from stores that don't often ship to Alaska, we are likely to get inquiries about customs, or letters which state that the store "does not accept orders from foreign countries." The lack of information about Alaska seems rather phenomenal, and we encounter it in other ways. A woman I know who was traveling last summer in Oregon was asked by a new acquaintance, "Who is your king up there now?" We would like to think that such a question would strike many Stateside readers as funny, but alas we know—if only from contact with shippers—that Alaska's status is a great mystery to many.

If we had a king, maybe he'd do something about those mail orders. Since we haven't, can anyone offer a recipe for a pink dessert, one that contains celery flakes and pistachio nuts and chutney?

Of course there are stores in Alaska. The owners and managers are our friends. They come to our homes, and sometimes a slightly embarrassed hostess must ask one of these guests to move so that she can get a can of tomato sauce, perhaps, from a crate that's behind the couch. To cache our personal stocks of supplies is always a problem, since few Northern houses have basements or attics. Crates of canned goods go under beds, in clothes closets, any place they will be out of sight and the contents won't freeze. The merchants, who know we have them, may think that these goods should be in their warehouses, but they don't complain.

Some customers buy only the extras locally, a habit that probably helps to keep prices high. As it is, three traders in arctic Alaska have told me their mark-up on merchandise is 100 per cent of the landed cost. It is, then, not surprising if consumers find it cheaper to send to the States for their orders. Perhaps both the stores and the customers would benefit if they could work out some compromise of the separate difficulties.

Some problems, however, are common to both. For the Alaska merchants, as well as consumers, shipments go astray often or don't arrive at all. A druggist showed me a letter he'd written to send with an order to a Seattle wholesaler: "These shipping instructions may sound peculiar to you, but I'd be grateful if you would just humor me in my wish to have the goods come this way." When I'd finished reading the letter, the druggist said, "They'll ignore that request," and then he just shook his head.

Increasingly Northern stores try to offer such foods as fresh vegetables, eggs only a few days instead of several months old (disappointing to sourdoughs, who complain that fresh eggs have no "strength"), and meat that has never been frozen. This freight, sent by air, when destined for most of the towns is transshipped at Fairbanks or Anchorage. Crates of lettuce may arrive at Fairbanks when the temperature is 40° below zero. They have to be carried from the incoming plane on the runway to a heated warehouse; later carried back out to another plane; and at Nome, for example, be trucked two miles to the store. In hauling around any vegetables in such cold, it is almost impossible to protect them so well that none will be frozen. Or quite often a shipment gets weather-bumped en route, and perishables stay for days at some transfer point.

"Warm storage" is one of the most familiar phrases Alaskans use. The fuel to keep stocks at above-freezing temperatures, fuel at Alaska prices, is an important item in merchants' overhead.

Another problem: usually, especially in the more isolated towns, a trader tries to have two warehouses and divide the essential items between them, because of the danger of fire. With most sources of water frozen all winter, with little fire-fighting equipment anywhere in the North, and with no roads to bring in substitute stocks of goods, there have been times when villages have faced starvation after a fire had consumed all a trader's supplies. Now, with planes operating more widely, the problem is not one of life and death, but to fly in all the food needed for several hundred people for several months would be an emergency to be avoided if possible.

A further handicap for some merchants is the size of the stock they must carry. Since a week, at least, would elapse before a druggist could get in an order by air, he must keep at all times all the medicines and equipment that people might need in a hurry. It is essential that other things, too, be quickly available. Stovepipe, kerosene for lamps, hardware items to repair plumbing: no one can wait very long for these. The small trading posts cannot carry them all, and every bush plane that comes to the larger towns brings in orders that tell of emergencies: "Quick, send me yeast. Dog got into mine and I cannot make bread." These are calls for help, and they are treated as such more than they are as orders.

In all parts of Alaska where freighters come via seas and rivers that freeze, stocks of most things are secured a year in advance of sales. To do that takes planning. And a trader must really know how to *trade*. Much of the time he will exchange civilized goods for animal pelts and for things whose value is harder to judge. Some Indians and Eskimos may have to get along for months without any money whatever. Then they offer the trader dried fish perhaps, a stoppered sealskin full of blubber, a carved trinket, or it may be an ancient harpoon head that one of the children kicked out of the sand on the beach. A knowledge of furs can be acquired, and also information about the fluctuating prices paid for them in the States. A successful trader will, too, learn what an Eskimo who does have money will pay for blubber and what a museum may pay for a fossil mastodon tooth. But how keep debits and profits straight? How make out an income-tax return?

I asked some of these questions of Mr. N. G. Hanson, who has been an Alaska trader for fifty years. His history is interesting, for he has had enterprises near Fairbanks and at Haines, a fox farm on an offshore island, a trapline out of McGrath, and stores at Platinum and now at Kotzebue. In all of these operations he has done his work methodically enough so that he is retiring soon, with his wife, Ruth, in comfort.

Mr. Hanson explained that every dried fish, every Eskimo spoon, carved ivory souvenir, and weasel hide he has taken in has been assigned a value and entered in his books to the native's credit, as well as being a record for the Internal Revenue Department. When these articles went out of his stocks, they were recorded again, and such is Mr. Hanson's experience that he can compute profits as between the spoon and some cans of baked beans, as between a mastodon tooth and cartridges for a native's rifle.

Mr. Hanson explained a special problem for any trader in Eskimo country: the natives' immemorial habit of sharing. With their philosophy it is natural for the Eskimos to think that a trader who has all that food on his shelves should give some to anyone who has the misfortune of being hungry. Patiently Mr. Hanson has conducted his education in the white-man's economics, showing his books to his Eskimo customers, explaining his own relationship with the Stateside wholesalers, and how he must make a profit to stay in business.

Like all traders, he does give credit. Sometimes these wilderness merchants will not only grubstake a hunter or trapper but also supply enough food for his family while he is away. In poor hunting seasons, or during epidemics of sickness, they may feed whole villages. Since they do stay in business, their prices have to reflect some inevitable losses: bigger credits require higher prices.

A fair number of traders have native wives; others, like Mr. Hanson, have brought families up from the States and in arctic settlements sometimes manage to lead almost conventional lives. The Hansons themselves look as if they belonged in New England. On their frequent Stateside vacations Mrs. Hanson has collected Early American glass. It amuses her when tourists, invited to her home at Kotzebue, say with surprise of the glass, "Why, you have some quite good pieces here!" When they were in McGrath, living in a log cabin, their teen-age daughter was rather unhappy because their surroundings seemed rough. Her mother said, "Don't look at the log walls. Look at that gate-legged table with the shelves of glassware behind it. Couldn't that corner be used as an illustration in any home-decorating magazine?" The Hansons have achieved contentment on the Alaska frontier, by enjoying the pioneer life and, when they were homesick for civilization, keeping their eyes on the gate-legged table.

The traders in the Alaska settlements are a very distinct class of Northerners. Many are about the same age as the gold-rush miners. They came at the same time and by now seem a little sharper in outlook; most are more prosperous than the average sourdough. They have missed something that many prospectors found besides gold, however, and the miners seem more self-sufficient.

The traders, able to grant or withhold credit, have had immense power in their tiny domains. Some have misused it, but more of those I have met have been friends to the natives. A few have been farsighted men and real benefactors.

Besides these individual traders there is a chain of stores across arctic Alaska and Canada, the Northern Commercial Company. They operate posts in some of the small settlements and also the cities, where they are like the general stores of rural Stateside communities. They do not carry everything. Once when I had been asked to show color slides at a church, I knew I should wear a hat and I didn't have any. There was not one woman's hat for sale at Nome, and I had to buy and wear a child's fur-lined

bonnet. "The N.C. Company," however, will order anything for
anyone and charge only the Stateside price plus the freight bills.
After I'd had such difficulty in getting up the refrigerator, I asked
the N.C. Company to send for a bed. It was so long in coming
that I suspected the company, too, were having difficulty with
the shipment—but they had the problem, not I. As years passed,
I stopped sending outside for my own winter stocks of food and
most other articles.

It's an unusual relationship that exists between the company
and their customers. They not only will send to the States for a
wanted item, but for people out in the bush the N.C. Company
in a town large enough to have other stores will shop locally. A
nurse in one of the Indian settlements, who was going to marry
the missionary, wanted a typical American wedding. She sent to
the Fairbanks branch of the company for her trousseau, flowers
and ribbons to decorate the church, and the food, dishes, candles,
and other supplies for the reception. They were all secured after
a search through a dozen shops and were sent to her on the day
she specified by a bush plane.

Special services would include gift-wrapping and shipping a
sweater that someone in a remote village had knitted; or having
steel runners handmade for an Eskimo's dog sled—and when the
runners go out on the plane the company will send screws
whether screws were ordered or not. Even now, but especially in
the early days, miners have sent their gold dust in to the Fairbanks store, which would weigh it, forward it to the Mint, and
credit the miner's account with its value. Today some of the
workers out on remote-site military construction jobs send the
store all their paychecks, using their credit for any supplies they
need and withdrawing their balance when they come back.

One such fellow was stationed up on the arctic coast at a
DEWline site. The contractor furnished his room and meals and
there was no place at the site to spend money—but he did want
a little to gamble with. Every week he would mail in his pay-
check, amounting to nearly $300, asking the store to credit it to

his account but send him back $30. They did that. Every Tuesday, whether his latest check had arrived or not, $30 of gambling money was put on a northbound plane. A customer had requested this service, and in the tolerant frontier spirit, the company didn't feel that they had any right to censor it.

The co-operation between the company and the arctic airlines deserves mention. Their joint service is illustrated by a birthday dinner delivered to one of the most distant Eskimo villages by Wien Alaska Airlines. The cake, as well as the roast and ice cream, were sent frozen and kept that way during a two-day wait for a bush plane at Kotzebue, while the potatoes, broccoli, and the salad ingredients were carefully not allowed to freeze.

Wien Alaska and the N.C. Company sponsor one of Alaska's most interesting radio programs. Called *Tundra Topics,* it is a program specifically for the bush people, but its human drama would give it a high rating anywhere. Such items as news about trapping regulations, or political moves that would affect the villages are told, but most of the program is made up of personal messages:

"To Tony Karmuk at Shungnak: your father had his frozen toes amputated today. He is going to be all right but he wishes he could see you. If it isn't snowing tomorrow, he says he would like to have you get the caribou that he cached on the mountain. . . . To Tom Turner at Nenana: Paul will be home tomorrow and he would appreciate it if you would have the dog sled out at the airstrip, because he is bringing a hundred-pound sack of flour. . . . To Rosie Johnson at Fort Yukon: your husband got a permanent job here yesterday. He will send your ticket on Friday's plane, and he would like to have you and the baby come on the plane. He will meet you. He says, be sure not to leave anything in the cabin that shouldn't freeze. He thinks you might give the rest of the canned goods to Phil and Flora."

The words are so human and real, and often desperate, that a heavy commercial announcement would be a jarring note, but these messages are kept short and light, being mostly about new shipments that have arrived at the N.C. Company, or about plane schedules—information the listeners need and are glad to have.

No merchandising is done in the North, in fact, in a very insistent way. The stores seem to assume that we'll buy what we want; all they should do is to let us know that they have it, and that sometimes they sell it at special prices. A Seattle grocer who moved to Fairbanks deplored the seeming lack of initiative, and he tried to wake up the merchants. He himself rebuilt an old store into a supermarket, staged many sales and promotions, took hours of time on radio and TV—and went broke. From the way people spoke of him, I think that the Northerners were put off by so much aggressiveness.

There have been others who came on brief trips to Alaska, saw a spot where some particular kind of store or service was needed, moved up to supply it, and charged quite outrageous prices because there was no competition. They did not need promotions; they discovered the secret of commercial bonanzas in Alaska— that the settlers will not count the cost, however great, if something they've wanted badly is made available to them.

However, these miners of people's pocketbooks are not readily taken into the hearts of Northerners, and they never seem very happy here, being neither builders nor adventurers for the fun of it. They are a class found on all frontiers, and after they've made a stake, sometimes a large one, they leave. Often they sell out to some permanent resident, who adjusts the prices more equitably into the frontier picture.

In arctic Alaska it still can be said that in most business transactions the human factors take precedence over any hard pressuring for profits.

16

Alaska Wages and Where They Go

It was an October day in Nome, when the whole winter's fury seemed compressed in one autumn storm. The ocean already had frozen, but the wild winds had broken up the young ice and were heaping it in insane confusion along the beach. Snow filled the air, driven too fast to fall. The house shook and rattled—but I heard the doorbell and found the chief of police on the steps. He came in and with a rather bemused look said,

"Down at the station we've got an old man without a dollar in his pocket. He's from Kentucky. He read an article of yours about mining gold in Alaska, so he took all the money he had and bought a plane ticket to Nome. He's come up to be a miner. What shall we do with him?"

If the man had had $100,000 and fifty years of experience in Alaska, he could not have done any mining for the seven or eight winter months. That he'd come was a startling problem—to me, but it was not unfamiliar to the welfare department, which helped to solve it. To some types of visionary people a frontier has so much appeal that suddenly and impulsively they will take off for the arctic without any clear idea of ways to support themselves there, or of the cost of living which makes a substantial income imperative. They are returned to the States, but it is more important to save them this disillusionment. For them and also the harder-headed who are considering moving North, some facts should be publicized about the types of employment available and the high prices here. In one of Fairbanks's largest and and busiest restaurants a man will have to pay 85 cents for a medium-sized bowl of canned tomato soup. With other prices proportionately high, he must not be encouraged to think that he can support himself by picking up a few dollars in odd jobs from time to time.

The following information applies chiefly to Fairbanks, but similar details for other cities will be supplied by the Alaska Territorial Employment Service. No one should hesitate to write to them. It is their responsibility to fill openings as well as to find employment for workers, and, like most of the Territorial agencies, they are efficient and interested to a degree not always found in Stateside government offices. They should be addressed at Fairbanks, Anchorage, Juneau, Ketchikan, or Petersburg—whichever city appeals to the applicant. The Nome jobs are handled through Fairbanks.

The agency's records show that in Fairbanks the largest single field of employment is in construction. It is seasonal, however— from May to October. In 1956 about 5,500 men were required for these jobs, placed through Fairbanks although some were sent out to remote sites for the military. Mining (coal and gold), the other activity confined chiefly to summer work, has places for about 1,500 men. Wages are low for the gold-mining employees, and most of the jobs are filled locally by natives. Coal-mining pays more but is limited in its opportunities.

The government-owned Alaska Railroad and the Alaska Road Commission employ some men throughout the year, although more in the summer months. These seasonal jobs often are filled by college boys, from both the States and the University of Alaska. Most other government jobs last through summer and winter. Some of them include special inducements, such as inexpensive government housing, and in federal civil-service jobs there is an extra, 25 per cent, tax-free, cost-of-living allowance.

At present the military employ about 1,500 civilians on bases at or near Fairbanks.

Besides the above categories there are the usual trade and service jobs, possibly 4,000 in number; and transportation, largely airlines, accounts for 1,200. Small factories employ about 400 in year-round work. In all there are more people who secure employment through Fairbanks than the total of those who live here —10,000. The explanation is that the population of the whole area, with suburbs, served by Fairbanks is estimated at 60,000.

As to other types of employment in Alaska, briefly, Anchorage and the Southeastern towns place some workers in fishing industries. Drilling for oil furnishes a few opportunities for men skilled in that field. They are sent out from Anchorage. Lumbering and logging work is expanding, most jobs being filled from the Ketchikan branch of the employment service. In Juneau, the capital of Alaska, are found the largest number of government employees.

It should be remembered that the above represent jobs, not job openings. In many cases there are more than enough local people to fill them. However, Alaska, like all frontiers, has sudden spectacular developments occasionally, and anyone who wants to move to the North should have his name and experience on file with at least one and perhaps all of the employment offices. As a substitute for a personal appearance in Alaska, he might write again from time to time to assure the employment people that he is still interested.

Nothing does take the place of coming oneself and with one's own initiative turning up something to do. So many have made that attempt with inadequate funds that officials suggest bringing money enough to live for six months, at Alaska prices, and then, if the job-hunt is unsuccessful, to pay one's way back to one's home town in the States. Though the land area of Alaska is large, its population is small; a little over 200,000 people is the estimate at the present time. Their taxes are high for Territorial services, especially since so many are Indians and Eskimos, many of whom pay no taxes at all, and the Territory cannot afford to support large numbers of strangers who have come hoping to find employment but have failed. The first step in a move to the arctic is, therefore, the accumulation of enough money to finance some exploring. As long as one has a return ticket, it does not really matter, of course, whether one stays for six months or six days. But six days would be a very short time in which to find permanent work in such an unfamiliar region.

Actually the best jobs in Alaska are often those that don't fit into the standard categories. An example would be the management of a native trading post. Most of the traders who own them are now too old to continue much longer. Some wish to retire but don't know where to find anyone to take over their posts. Much experience is required—knowledge of the climate and country, the local native ways, technical knowledge of furs and products of native skills and, not least important, of sources of supply. A young man with a family who can stand isolation might find an excellent opportunity in work like this if he would be willing to go into a post for a few years as an apprentice. No one who has even a trace of race prejudice should think of becoming a trader (if he has, he will be neither successful nor happy), but anyone who has an interest in, and sympathy for, primitive people could not only make a good living but also would have the satisfaction of helping his customers take the long step into civilization.

To find such an opportunity, one could go to one of the Northern airlines, find out where there might be a vacant trading post some time soon, fly out to the post, stay a few weeks, make friends with the trader, and not till the end of that time, perhaps, suggest coming to work. That would be an Alaska way of finding a job for oneself.

It is not recommended that any trappers come to the North. All the good traplines are already taken up, mostly by Indians and Eskimos, who certainly have a prior right to them, and who know the conditions. To do such work in the arctic is not for

On a flight from Anchorage to Nome,
Sally Carrighar rides with the freight.

A proud ram of the Dall species, only white mountain sheep in North America.

Largest since 1888: grizzly killed in Alaska by T. A. Miller in 1953.

Mother fur seal keeps a watchful eye on new-born pup.

Summer, and these caribou have sought mountain snows to escape insects.

Creamer's Field, a mile from the center of Fairbanks,
is a dairy farm in summer, a sports arena in winter.

Whether in modern homes or log cabins of gold-rush times,
the people of Fairbanks live comfortably.

Mount Shishaldin, one of Alaska's active volcanoes.

Sociable moose are familiar in Fairbanks.

Ben Gillette still works the gold mine described in Rex Beach's The Spoilers.

Bergman Sam, Indian from
Huslia, 1957 winner of Sled-Dog
Derby, with his two leaders.

Alfred Wells, Noorvik Eskimo,
brings home played-out dog and
finishes second.

Hillsides broken down by powerful water jets to reach gold also reveal prehistoric wildlife through fossil bones.

Kenai Lake, on the Sterling Highway.

Swimming at Camp Denali, near the 20,320-foot Great One.

even the very best woodsman who only has trapped in the States.

Besides the trading posts there are other niches not always filled in the economic structure of the Northern frontier. An example is laundries. At least until recently a laundry was needed at Kotzebue. Snack bars can sometimes prosper, even in native villages. Small roadhouses along lines of plane travel, stores to outfit the sportsmen, machine shops to repair marine engines: businesses such as these, when they fill a real need, offer the best security. But no employment office and no one person anywhere can give advice on the problem of finding them. A man has to be on the ground, stay long enough to fit into the Northern scene a little, and become friends with numbers of people before he will know where there might be such openings, and also whether he has the temperament to withstand the arctic difficulties.

At the time I left Nome, two years ago, there was a need for skilled mechanics who would settle there, learn the local conditions, be dependable, and, above all, stay sober. Wages were lower than in some other places, but not much, and the difference was made up in the reasonable rents. Good housing was hard to find, but a skilled mechanic probably would construct his own. There were a few summer jobs at the mining camps, for cooks as an example, male or female; and a man with a little capital probably could become a partner in a gold-mining venture already established by an owner with some experience. He should not hope that the ground would yield him a fortune, but he might make a good living out of it and have more than a little fun as he went along.

About farming I speak with great hesitation. In this field, perhaps more than any other, Northern experience is important, and also initial capital. A handicap is the fact that under the homestead laws one can only take up 160 acres, which are not sufficient to make a living unless the location is extremely favorable. Some settlers in the Matanuska Valley have sold out, enabling those who have stayed to increase their holdings. And in the Tanana Valley near Fairbanks a group of ambitious young men have filed for adjoining homesteads. They are helping one another to build their log cabins in a group and are clearing their acreage with equipment bought jointly. But the climate, the hardihood of local plant strains, the types of insect pests, and the peculiarities of the soil can't be learned in a day or a summer. I have heard a dairyman near Fairbanks say that no one can possibly get a start at Alaska farming without an original investment of at least $25,000—although it has been done. One of the skilled mechanics at Ladd Air Force Base, a civilian, has a new farm that seems to be promising. His wages support his family of several nearly grown children who, with his wife, are doing most of the farm work. The Agricultural Extension Service at College, Alaska, will send literature about Northern farming.

Professional people probably are the class who find placement most easily. A newspaper in Fairbanks ran an ad in the States describing an opening for a reporter. More than 100 answers arrived. Changes in employment occur with great frequency in Alaska, however, and those include newspaper jobs. People come up with enthusiasm, but then, suddenly, after a long spell of very cold weather perhaps, they may leave. One who is on the ground, though doing some other kind of work, can often jump into such a vacancy.

Doctors and nurses are always needed. The U.S. Public Health Service at Juneau would make suggestions about where to apply. There aren't enough dentists. Surveyors, geologists, assayers, experts in wildlife-management should not find it too hard to locate employment. They would know where to inquire— mostly through government agencies. Social workers are an important class of Alaska residents, and often there aren't enough of them.

Jobs for women, besides nurses and medical and dental technicians, include some kinds of work that are usually done by men elsewhere. Mrs. Pearl A. Scherer, for example, is a C.P.A., partner in the accounting firm of Hagelbarger & Co. Teaching in Indian

Bureau schools involves many other duties, as explained previously, and therefore often is done by men or teams of husbands and wives. The intangible rewards of working in native villages can be great, with good pay considering benefits such as low-cost government housing. The Juneau branch of the Bureau of Indian Affairs does the placing.

The Territorial schools of Alaska are excellent. No parents contemplating a move to Alaska need fear that their children will not be well taught. There is danger that, coming from some Stateside schools, they may be put back a grade when they reach Alaska. Teachers who like those tough-minded standards should apply to the Territorial Department of Education at Juneau. Salaries are higher than anywhere in the States.

Many office positions are filled by the wives of servicemen, sitting out husbands' Northern tours of duty. The girls are young, smart, and most have had recent office experience in the States. They will work for fairly low wages, and employers have adapted themselves to the frequent changes in personnel. For this class of workers, therefore, the supply is much greater than the demand. Waitresses and clerks in stores are usually residents with wide acquaintance among local people. The advantage to their employers is obvious.

Incidentally, in Alaska there seems to be little hesitancy about hiring older men and women. A surprising number of middle-aged women are bringing home paychecks, which often are needed in view of the high cost of living.

It is rare that there is any real shortage of workers. And most Alaska employers select new employees from among Northerners if they can—partly from loyalty, partly because the people already here "know the ropes." The "ropes" are many, and range all the way from being able to start a car at 40° below zero, morning after morning, to handling customers with an easy and natural friendliness. It is definitely, if intangibly, true that there is a Northern attitude which prevails not only within an organization but in its relationship with customers. Certainly it can be learned; but a little time may elapse during which a newcomer feels and seems strange in the North.

Suggestions like these are not intended to discourage anyone from moving up to the arctic frontier. Alaska needs every family who bring with them the pioneer spirit, and the arctic has much greater rewards than those that can be described in a book. The settlers and the country must find each other—but in a practical way. Many come, like the miner to Nome, depending on luck to see them through. Luck will be needed too, but luck alone isn't enough.

Money Matters

INDEED it does—especially in Alaska, where prices are high for other reasons besides the freight. The whole economy is inflated, way beyond that of the United States economy as a whole. The Alaska economy has always been inflated, however, and the important thing to know is: do wages keep pace with prices?

The following facts about the income of Alaskans are based on the 1950 census and represent incomes earned in 1949. It is not as unfortunate as it seems that the figures are not more recent. Wages are higher now, but are due largely to military spending, which can cease or be greatly curtailed without warning. Before missiles became so significant in the military situation, Alaska seemed to have grown into a permanent outpost of national defense. The DEWline installations along the far-Northern coast, and the so-called White Alice line, which boosts messages to the interior, were built since the more normal census year of 1950, and before 1957, when it became clear that an enemy attack probably would streak right over these expensive sites, perhaps undetected. Whether the military will continue to think of Alaska as so strategically important is open to question, but there will be people here. They will be developing the country, earning and spending money, and it seems better to consider their future economy as related to the years before the great influx of the military.

In 1949 the average income of all people in the continental United States was $1,917. In Alaska it was $2,064. The figures are misleading because the report for Alaska includes all the aboriginal people who hunt and fish and largely live off the land. If we consider only white male workers, both rural and urban, those in the United States had a median income of $2,572, in Alaska of $2,866. A very interesting figure is that of white females, whose median income in the States was only $1,137, and in Alaska was $1,923—a much larger spread than between the income of white males in the two places. In the U.S., that is, the average woman earned only 44.2 per cent as much as her masculine neighbors, but in Alaska she earned 67.09 per cent. Those differences are not surprising to anyone who has lived on a frontier, where women have a rather high standing as compared with that in communities longer established.

A white settler, wherever he lived in Alaska, could expect, thus, to be paid $294 more a year than he was in the States. But if he stayed in one of the cities, the increase would be very much greater. Stateside cities of 10,000 to 25,000 population compare roughly in size with the larger Alaska towns. The median income for all men in those small U.S. cities was $2,484. The men in comparable Alaska cities earned $4,131.

The women in U.S. cities smaller than 25,000 earned even less than the women's average for the entire country—only $926. But women in Alaska communities of the same size had a median wage of $2,044—more than twice as much.

The median wage for all who live in Alaska cities, men and women, white and non-white, was $3,438. The residents of Fairbanks earned a little more: $3,516. Those in Anchorage earned considerably more: $4,154. The residents of Juneau earned less, only $2,921, but that figure probably would be higher now, regardless of military spending, because of the new lumbering activity in Southeastern Alaska. The average Nome wage was very low, reflecting the fact that half the people in Nome are Eskimos and that few of them have any opportunity to work in year-round salaried jobs.

Breaking the wages down into classes of occupation, we find an amazing bit of information: in the U.S., farmers and farm-managers reported a median income of only $482; but in Alaska, where farming is considered so difficult, the same group earned an average of $1,979. Farmers are, of course, classed as experienced workers. In other occupations also listed as experienced, Alaska workers consistently earned about $1,000 more than they would in Stateside jobs. These are examples: professional, technical, and kindred workers, $5,150 in Alaska, $4,071 in the States; craftsmen, foremen, etc., $4,629 in Alaska, $3,601 in the States; managers, officials, and proprietors, $5,358 in Alaska, $4,143 in the States; public administrators, $4,705 in Alaska, and similar Stateside personnel, $3,565. Government workers are the largest single class of employees in Alaska, representing 17 per cent of the total labor force, 14 of the 17 per cent being on the payroll of the federal government.

The 1950 census figures for unskilled labor would have no meaning now, because the growth of unions in Alaska has wrought a very great change since that time. The beginning wage in construction, for example, is $3.48 per hour in both Fairbanks and Anchorage. As explained in a previous chapter, the overtime and bonuses for remote-site jobs boost the laborers' pay to heights that have little relationship to such work in the States, or to the income of other Alaskans.

If there is one comparison that would be most significant for families contemplating a move to Alaska, it probably would be the median wage of all male workers in small cities, both white and non-white: $4,131 in Alaska as against $2,484 in the States.

Almost exactly the same proportion of city women work in the North as in the States, 43 per cent of the Alaskans and 44 per cent of U.S. city women. There is always curiosity about the distribution of males and females in Alaska, not predominantly for economic reasons, but the ratio has some bearing on economics too. Even among the aboriginal population there are more males: they make up 53.2 per cent of the total. White men comprise 68.5 per cent of adult white Alaskans. They aren't all looking for wives, however, not even wives that work. Some of the excess men are the sourdoughs, most of whom seem satisfied with their single status; and some of the others have been frightened by these oft-quoted figures. They think every woman who comes to Alaska is here with romance on her mind. There might be a few instances in which they are correct, considering the number of inquiries sent to the North which begin: "I am a young divorcee, 23, attractive, with one child. What would be my chances of employment in Alaska?" Her chances are that she can and will support herself for a while, in Alaska as anywhere else, and in the meantime she will learn how to keep her child's toes from freezing, and where to find rose hips, and how to thaw frozen water pipes— skills worth acquiring. And she will stretch her rather high income over some prices that may make her gasp.

At Barrow I have paid 80 cents for a loaf of bread; at Nome, 65 cents a quart for milk, $1.35 for a stalk of celery, and $4.85 for a honeydew melon. And these are some prices I copied from the menu in a Fairbanks restaurant, not an elegant restaurant— I was sitting up at a counter:

Cold cereal with milk	$ .65
Toast and coffee	.60
French toast	1.35
2 eggs, fried or boiled	1.00
Cottage fried potatoes	.85
Plain omelet	1.60

It was breakfast time on a rainy morning—possibly one reason why the list seemed depressing. The date was July 25, 1953, but if the prices have changed since that time, they probably have gone up.

In August and September 1956, the Alaska Resources Development Board, assisted by Joseph B. Ward & Associates of Seattle, made a much needed survey of consumer prices in five Alaska cities. Their report contains information that will be useful in many ways, although one slight warning should be made: in formulating a consumer price index for Fairbanks and the other Alaska cities, Seattle was used as the U.S. city with which comparisons were made. But Seattle itself is an expensive city in which to live. In the two months of the survey, prices for the United States as a whole, as published by the Bureau of Labor Statistics in its regular Consumer Price Index, were 116.8, with the 1947–49 levels, as usual, as the 100 base. But at that time Seattle prices were two points higher: 118.8. Therefore when we learn that Fairbanks prices are 153.5 per cent of those in Seattle, it should be understood that they were 155.6 per cent of the U.S. average.[1]

Fairbanks prices were highest of the five Alaska cities surveyed, naturally, since it is the greatest distance from Stateside sources of supply. The index for Anchorage, as compared with Seattle, was 140.8; for Juneau 123.5; for Sitka 121.7; and for Ketchikan 122.2.

The survey reflects the fact that the basic necessities, food, housing, and fuel, take on special importance in an arctic climate. In the national averages established by the Bureau of Labor Statistics, 28.55 per cent of a family's budget goes for food. In Fairbanks the figure was 34.09 per cent. For housing, including fuel, the country-wide average was 21.73 per cent of the budget; in Fairbanks 28.49 per cent. To heat a Fairbanks home took nearly four times as much of the fuel share of a household budget as a family spent to keep warm in the States, a necessity that will puzzle no one. Some of the items on which Northerners spent a lower percentage of their budgets than most Americans—since there must be an evening-out process—were house-furnishings,

---

[1] The differential increases with every year. A recent cost-of-living survey by the Civil Service Commission shows that it now costs 41.7 per cent more to live in Juneau than in Washington, D.C., 56.7 per cent more in Anchorage, and 66.8 per cent more in Fairbanks.

apparel except children's clothes, medical care, and personal care, including visits to beauty and barber shops. Those shops are available, but most Alaska women give themselves permanents when they have them, and many have learned how to give their husbands their haircuts.

Partly because of the high price of bakers' bread, but also because they like to do it, many Alaska women make their own. In 1956 a five-pound sack of flour cost 57 cents in Seattle, 89 cents in Fairbanks. The cost of round steak in the two cities was 96 cents and $1.58. Bacon was 62 cents a pound in Seattle, 86 cents in Fairbanks; lamb, 70 cents as against $1.24; frying chickens 62 cents a pound versus 90 cents. Fluid milk cost 22 cents a quart in Seattle and 47 cents in Fairbanks.

Most fresh fruits and vegetables are imported from the States, even in summer, because the military stationed in Alaska buy a large proportion of the produce of Northern farms. Such airborne fruits and vegetables cost more than twice what they do in the States:

	Seattle prices per pound	*Fairbanks prices per pound*
Tomatoes	$.19	$.64
Lettuce	.11	.40
Celery	.08	.29

Fresh foods average 210.8 of the Seattle base price. Since canned and frozen fruits and vegetables cost only 163 per cent as much, Fairbanks women buy more of those.

For housing, the Fairbanks people have to count on 182.5 per cent of the cost in Seattle. A telephone is only about $1.00 a month more, but household water is twice as much, a situation to be expected from the scarcity of water everywhere in the North. Perhaps the high water bills also explain the high laundry bills: $5.30 in Fairbanks for a bundle that would cost $2.92 in Seattle.

The survey showed some curious discrepancies—a study of it might give ideas to someone who wanted to start an Alaska business. A living-room suite that sold for $310 in Seattle was priced at only $333 in Fairbanks, in spite of the crating and all that weight freighted so many hundreds of miles. But a bed sheet that would carry a Seattle price tag of $4.54 cost $6.76 in Fairbanks. If the freight on the living-room suite added only $23 to the price of the furniture, should it add $2.22 to a sheet's? A $136 water-heater cost only $6 more in the North than in Seattle, but a faucet for a sink cost $8.15 more.

There is a standard increase of $300 on one of the lower-priced cars; it represents the actual cost of the freight and can be avoided by having a friend drive a new car up the Alaska Highway for you—something that is done frequently. In Fairbanks a chassis lubrication cost $3.50, a job that averaged $1.81 in Seattle; and regular gasoline still has today about the same differential that it had in August 1956: 49 cents in Fairbanks and 31 cents in Seattle. Military personnel can buy at a very great reduction gasoline that comes through the new pipeline from Haines to Fairbanks.

Mortgage interest is high in the North—5.5 per cent in Seattle, 8 per cent in Fairbanks. And property insurance costs more than twice as much.

Fairbanks doctors and dentists keep their prices below the average mark-up. Perhaps they see intimately the unfortunate effects of money problems on their patients. An office call costs $5.00 in Fairbanks, a house visit, $10. Some surgical operations are less expensive than in the state of Washington, and so are dental extractions! The medical and dental skill available in the North is, moreover, excellent. Sometimes Fairbanks doctors have to send patients to the States for special types of care, but unless the physicians themselves think it necessary, few Alaskans go "outside" either for treatment or for operations.

It is time to bring these two sets of figures together: the higher incomes and the higher prices—do they come up to the same levels?

These again are the ratios of Alaska prices to Seattle prices:

Fairbanks	153.5
Anchorage	140.8
Juneau	123.5
Sitka	121.7
Ketchikan	122.2

It should be kept in mind too that in most of Alaska's rural places the prices are higher than in these cities—about as much higher as the freight from the nearest Alaska town, which may be 500 miles away, with the freight brought by plane. And even though the residents of the remote settlements are largely native, they would *like* to be able to buy the white-man's goods. It is very significant, then, that the median income of all Alaskans is only 107 per cent of the median income for all people in the United States, and therefore prices and incomes do not balance for Alaskans as a whole.

The situation is better, but only slightly, if we are considering only the white male workers in Alaska, both rural and urban. Their wages average 111 per cent of those earned by the same Stateside class. Things look much more comfortable, however, for the residents of Alaska *cities*. To pay the prices indicated by the above list of ratios, the men have incomes that average 165 per cent of those in towns of similar size in the States; and women's incomes average 220 per cent of similar U.S. women's. Even in Fairbanks, where prices are highest, these incomes would seem more than adequate. But there are other factors in balancing an Alaska budget.

For one thing, many of the less expensive forms of goods and services simply are not available in the North. There are no moderate-priced apartments in Fairbanks. It may be true that a Fairbanks apartment in a modern fireproof building, with electric stove and refrigerator and double-paned picture windows, rents for 182.5 per cent of what the same kind of apartment would in Seattle—and that the young divorcee, if she came to Fairbanks and if she earned the average wage, would be paid at 220 per cent of a woman's average wage in the States. She still would earn only $2,044 per year, or $170 per month, and so she could not pay the $140 to $200 a month charged for these modern apartments. In an older building I was shown a small, one-room apartment, so dingy that one would have to fight depression to live in it, and the rent was $45 *a week*. The high Alaska wages are not invariably high enough to absorb that kind of expense.

These remarks are not intended as an attack on the owners of the apartments. The rents reflect the prices paid on the imported materials of which the buildings were constructed. Concrete poured in the form costs $30 per cubic yard in Fairbanks, for example, as compared with $11.80 in Seattle—not 153.5 per cent of Seattle prices, as theoretically paid by consumers, but 255 per cent. And it takes a great many cubic yards of concrete to put up a ten-story building—or even a small store—wherefore most Fairbanks buildings are made of wood, and fire insurance is thereby boosted.

The highest median wage reported for Alaska was that of contractors, $7,027. Engineers, airplane-pilots, and construction foremen are some of the other workers who average over $6,000. Most construction workers make their money during the short summer season and leave for the rest of the year, but other classes of workers stay; they live in Alaska and are trying to raise families there.

Anyone with an income of $6,000 or less in the States will recognize that he would have difficulty if he tried to make ends meet with his expenses increased 53.5 per cent; he would especially in communities where the less expensive commodities often are not available. Most residents of Stateside towns have a much wider range of choices than Alaskans do, in all categories of merchandise. If they can't be found locally, it is not a long drive to a larger center. But Alaskans don't have that opportunity. And it may never be true that cheaper merchandise will be offered here. Houses have to be well built, with much insulation, to keep out the arctic cold; clothes have to be really warm, and food has to be really nourishing. In Northern Alaska no one can just "get by."

When the 1956 survey was made of Alaska prices, "It was assumed," the engineers stated, "that a theoretical family from each of the survey cities had $4200 per year to spend *at Seattle prices*": that is, the income of this theoretical family was $6,447 at Alaska prices. They were, therefore, in the highest-paid group. How do the others manage?

They do, but before I suggest the way they do, it should be pointed out that Alaskans have a much harder time financially than they would need to have if the national government were more sympathetic.

Freight rates, for example, are something most people never thought about till they came to Alaska. They are in everyone's consciousness here, and not chiefly because we live so far from the sources of supply—we would expect to pay the normal excess. But the excess is not normal. All along the route it includes special payoffs to groups who have been able to influence Washington, and those payoffs are plainly visible on the price tags in Alaska stores.

If two tractors are crossing the United States on a freight car, and one tractor is bound for Hong Kong and one for Fairbanks, the railroad freight on the Fairbanks tractor is about twice what it is on the other. For Alaska is not allowed to benefit from the so-called export-import tariffs. Any shipper who is sending goods into or outside the continental boundaries of the United States is given a large reduction in freight rates for the distance the goods travel on U.S. railroads—no, not any shipper. Those who are forwarding goods to and from foreign countries get it, and so also do shippers in Hawaii, a Territory like Alaska, but nobody in Alaska thus benefits. As well as tractors, such household items as cookstoves, bathtubs, and TV sets are carried by boat to some Alaska towns farther than if they went to Honolulu—but do not warrant the export-import rates.

In 1920 the late Senator Wesley L. Jones of Seattle had written

into the Maritime Act two other discriminations against Alaska.
According to that Act, any American shipper is allowed to use
either U.S. or foreign railroads or ships. Alaska, however, is excluded. All goods bound for Alaska are required by the Act to
cross the country on United States railroads and to come up from
Seattle in United States vessels. The western states—some Seattle
firms themselves—can and often do bring their freight from the
East on the less expensive Canadian railroads. And the same
firms can send their freight from Seattle to the Hawaiian Islands
on some of the lower-priced foreign freighters. Alaskans can't do
that. They are required by law to bring their goods up on American boats—until five years ago boats of the Alaska Steamship
Company, a monopoly which seemed only to limit its rates by the
danger that still higher rates would cause the whole Alaska economy to collapse.

Alaskans can't even ship their own products south on Canadian
carriers. A Juneau businessman found a midwest market for Sitka
spruce. He could send the lumber through Vancouver, B.C., for
$5.00 per thousand board feet—but the Jones Act prohibited.
Shipping through Seattle, the cost was $11 per thousand—more
than the operating costs justified—and so he went out of business.

He was one. There isn't a resident of Alaska whose living costs
are not higher because of this unfair legislation. Alaskans took
the matter to the United States Supreme Court, which ruled that
the Jones Act was indeed discriminatory against Alaska, but while
discrimination against a state would be unconstitutional, Congress can legally discriminate against a territory.

Most of Alaska's population live in Fairbanks or Anchorage, or
in the villages served by those cities. For three decades the bulk
of their freight has come by the Alaska Steamship Company
boats to Seward and then up the Alaska Railroad. The Alaska
Railroad is an operation wholly owned by the federal government. It is free of Interstate Commerce Commission control and
therefore sets rates arbitrarily. Except for four years the railroad

has made a profit continuously since 1940. In 1944 its net income was $5,242,924—profits added, of course, to the retail prices of goods shipped in. Ten years later the income of the railroad was less, but, according to an investigation by the Department of the Interior in 1953, "With certain improvements and greater effi- ciency, the line should earn a profit of $2,000,000 annually ap- parently without any increase in rates." Even after that report was published the Hoover Commission recommended that the rates be raised. And why should the line make a profit at all? Why should the government be in a business that takes money out of its pioneers' pockets?

The rates have been so exorbitant on the poorly run line that a group of energetic young men organized the Alaska Freight Lines, using barges to Valdez and trucks from there to Anchor- age and Fairbanks. Here at last was a little relief for Alaska con- sumers, for the barge-and-truck operation charged new, lower rates on freight that showed up immediately in reduced retail prices.

The Alaska Railroad first tried to wreck the new company by rate wars; and these continue. When the truck line still pros- pered, the railroad, in alliance with the Alaska Steamship Com- pany, brought a suit against Alaska Freight Lines in an attempt to prove that their business practices were unsound. The suit was dismissed for lack of evidence.

Besides burdens long since written into law, Alaskans are handi- capped by rules made by government bureaus and agencies. The Civil Aeronautics Board has seemed especially inconsiderate. A few years ago the board canceled all licenses of the private bush pilots, the courageous men who had pioneered arctic flying, and gave their routes to some scheduled airlines. Several of the pilots were put on the airlines' payrolls, but their new routes were circumscribed; they no longer could zigzag across the territory they served, as they had formerly, in order to check weekly or oftener on the well-being of isolated miners, trappers, and families homesteading out in the bush.

Alaskans sympathize with minorities that governments treat

unfairly. We are such a minority ourselves. When Washington finally secures the vote for all Southern Negroes, we would be pleased if attention would then be turned to the voteless Alaskans.

We cannot vote in any national election. We can elect a legislature, but any laws that it passes can be vetoed by the governor, who is appointed by the administration in Washington and takes his mandate from Washington, not from Alaskans. And yet we pay federal income taxes—more than Stateside citizens do, because, in Alaska's inflated economy, even to maintain a substandard living one must earn more than he would in the States, and is thus pushed up into a higher income-tax bracket.

With statehood Alaska could hope to have such injustices righted, for then we would have representatives and a senator who could trade votes. Our present delegate, the Hon. E. L. Bartlett, is extremely able and we hear that he is well liked in Washington, but without a vote he can do little. Long concerned about this unfair tax situation, he approached Representative Daniel A. Reed of the House Ways and Means Committee about the possibility of tax relief for Alaskans, but Representative Reed was cold to the idea. Though the federal government does give a tax-free cost-of-living allowance to its own employees, Representative Reed said: "I should think that Alaskans generally would wish to avoid being treated differently from the residents of the United States." Indeed we would wish it! We have little hope of it, since we can't even vote for a President.

It is not only tax relief for individuals that is needed; tax incentives for investment capital are even more important, for they would bring in new payrolls and help to develop the country. Canada furnishes such tax incentives in its Northern wilderness, but not the United States. Alaskans have a close view of humming industrial projects immediately on the other side of the Alaska-Canadian border—while on our side there have been only a few unimpressive efforts. Could it be otherwise, when any promotor can see the way that Washington treats its Northern Territory?

Mr. Ralph D. Paine, Jr., publisher of *Fortune,* made an extended tour through Alaska in 1954. He came with previous briefing on Alaska's problems, and he said in an address delivered to the Alaska Chamber of Commerce: "The publications of the Department of the Interior would persuade me to go to Canada, not Alaska. There is too much federal government in Alaska to tempt anyone with the pioneering spirit."

And on February 25, 1957, the influential *Fairbanks Daily News-Miner* said in an editorial:

> *We wonder if perhaps the Alaskans haven't been knocking too long on the wrong door. The Territory is some distance from the United States. It is cheek-by-jowl to Canada, though, and the ties between Canada and Alaska have been growing every day. We have an idea that the Canadians would be more than happy to have our valuable, strategically-vital northern outpost under the Maple Leaf.*
>
> *Washington couldn't very well delay Alaskans the right to a referendum on whether or not they would like to become a part of Canada, with the full rights and privileges of Canadian citizenship. But we have an idea that there would be a lot of startled looks and quick second-thoughts in Congress if the Alaskans were to ask for one. If the door in Washington refuses to open this year, perhaps the Alaskans should try knocking on another one.*

The statement about full rights and privileges of Canadian citizenship refers to the fact that Canada gives a full voting member of its national Parliament to the Yukon Territory's 10,000 people, whereas Alaska's population of more than twenty times that number have no voice whatever. All Alaskans are well aware that they were guaranteed better treatment in the treaty whereby the territory became a United States possession. Russia, from whom we bought Alaska in 1867, specified as much in this Article III of the treaty:

> *The inhabitants of the ceded territory, according to their choice, reserving their natural allegiance, may return to Russia*

within three years, but if they should prefer to remain in the ceded territory, they . . . shall be admitted to the enjoyment of all the rights, advantages and immunities of citizens of the United States.

It is important for our federal government to be able to point out cases in which the Soviet fails to keep its word. To do that without hypocrisy, Congress should not delay any longer its honoring of the treaty signed when Russia sold us Alaska.

Most adult Alaskans were born and grew up in the States. They came North with the music of Fourth-of-July bands still echoing in their ears, with pictures of Abraham Lincoln's compassionate face in their minds, and with belief in the ringing assurances made from the White House from time to time that the American government is fair-minded, that it wishes to treat all men, wherever they are, with justice. And Alaskans are patriotic. When they arrived, I think many of them had a vague idea that they were helping to conquer new territory for the United States. They found that the challenges were not limited to the climate. Cold winds also blow from Washington.

But Alaskans are pioneers—and they are on a frontier. A frontier means a wilderness stretching in every direction. When the exploitation by politicians makes it seem that some Alaskans cannot afford to live in the North, they shoulder axes and rifles, literally, and set out in a wilderness that may be in the arctic but still is generous.

The Bountiful Arctic Wilderness

THIS MORNING I CALLED my agent and asked about moose insurance. I'll be driving from Fairbanks to Anchorage soon, and motorists have been warned that moose and buffalo have appropriated the highway. It's an escape from deep snow for the animals, but they sometimes attack the cars. A moose recently smashed the windshield of one, punctured the roof, and bent a door so that it would not close. He broke his own neck, and the occupants of the car nearly lost their lives, for they had to drive on at a temperature of 55° below zero.

Collision insurance will cover assaults by moose, says the agent.

Moose frequently charge the Alaska Railroad trains in the winter. This year seventeen were killed by one train on a single trip. To disperse the animals, the railroad officials have tried fireworks, huge oscillating lights, supersonic whistles, and moose parking lots bulldozed along the right of way. The moose still haunt the rails. They seem to be drawn from miles away by the curious devices the men hope will frighten them.

Human activities in Alaska often attract other animals, partly of course because of stored food. The high-pole caches, structures in which Alaskans, both white and native, hang meat, were originated to keep it away from bears and wolverines, as well as wolves, as at Unalakleet. Sometimes polar bears are intruders. For

more than a week the supply plane could not land at an arctic
military installation because several polar bears, coming ashore
from the frozen sea, had discovered the nice smooth runway and
made it their own. Once at Barrow the congregation was held in
church by a polar bear at the entrance. The men had not brought
their rifles, and the threatening bear had no intention of giving
way for the people.

Incidents such as these, although inconvenient, have a very en-
dearing quality for Alaska residents. They point up the fact that
Northerners are surrounded by the most genuine, undepleted
wilderness anywhere on the continent. The inviting wild trails
are an emotional satisfaction to the kind of people who become
arctic settlers. But more, the wilderness helps to make it possible
for them to stay. It can furnish so many of the necessities that
Alaska's high prices can be, at least partly, defeated. It is a
bountiful wilderness; it would support any able-bodied pioneer
almost entirely, and there are few in this country who do not
turn to nature's resources for some supplies.

The land can, and does, give some of its residents—free of
charge—all their meat, fish, fruits, and green food. We need furs
to keep warm in winter, and anybody can shoot or trap animals
for their hides. Many Alaska houses are made of spruce logs, cut
without cost. Bear skins will cover the floors for the price of the
ammunition. When we want recreation, we almost invariably
turn to the out-of-doors.

The trees, the multitudes of animals, the berries, the herbs,
would not exist if the North were only an icy wasteland. That
picture, held widely, is a mistaken notion. Much of the time
Alaska is a land of inviting and brilliant color. Setting it off are
the sugar-white mountain ranges with fifteen peaks higher than
14,495-foot Mount Whitney, the loftiest in the States. Under the
glistening summits lie steep fiords and broad valleys that shimmer
with birch and aspen trees. Rivers are lacy cascades or long and
meandering, like the mile-wide Yukon. Lakes are everywhere,
large and small. Millions are muskeg ponds, some tinted bronze,

turquoise, and chartreuse by their algae growths. Flowers bloom
on their banks.

The mountains, the wilderness are in view from all the
Alaska towns. In a city like Fairbanks we have everything civilized people consider necessities; in the smaller settlements civilized comforts diminish, while the benefits of the wilderness come
right up to one's door. All of us have some of both, however;
the Eskimos have their gasoline washing-machines and the apart-
ment-dwellers hang bags of frozen wild game out their windows.

We all need and want the game, many kinds of it. Let us start
with moose. The problem in getting moose is not that of finding
it but of bringing it home. Six hundred pounds of meat are not
something that anyone can sling over his shoulder lightly, and
roads are few. I have heard it said that "shooting a moose at some
distance away from the road or boat is enough to make any man
a confirmed rabbit-hunter." Moose congregate in wet areas however, and Alaska has many of those. They can often be reached
by boat and always by plane. If we go by plane, we can take a
rubber boat, which can be inflated.

We search for a slough where the water is moving, but only
slightly. It will be one of those channels, drainage from thawed
permafrost, which loop off in endless series from most of Alaska's
rivers. The banks of the rivers are fragrant with dark-needled
spruces, but most of the sloughs are bordered by birches and willows. This will be fall, September. Alaska has had some hard
frosts by now, and the leaves of the birches are yellow, the willows
red-lavender, the cranberry bushes beneath, mahogany. Above
in the clean, fresh blue of the Northern sky stand mountains
eternally white. A sweep of their summits is visible.

The motor cut, we glide silently through a land primitive and
unpeopled, wild, impersonal, lovely. No breeze rumples the
birches. They are quiet and whole, their reflections advancing,
receding, as the boat slowly drifts down the curves of the slough.

These are wide curves, and so we can see far ahead the choco-
late-brown grotesque moose's bulk. Leaving the skiff, we creep

forward along the wet sand of the inner bank. We wait till the bull's head goes down in the water for some of his favorite aquatic plants. If his ears too are covered, we hurry, but pause again when his head comes up. Gradually we make progress.

Two other moose, cows, wade out into the slough. No wonder that moose meat is tender and free of muscle strings: the animals' motions all seem reluctant. Through much of their lives moose exercise only their jaws and necks.

But one of us slips on a wet root and snaps some willows. The antlers come up and the bull, with a lunge, has sprung towards the bank. We wait till he reaches it. As the last hoof comes out of the water then, with the crack of a rifle we have secured hundreds of pounds of delicious meat.

Ambitious families aspire to begin the winter with a moose, a caribou, and a mountain sheep. They may have more, since entire families often hunt, and each member is entitled to one of each kind of animal. As a naturalist I do not like to think of animals' lives being taken for sport, but it would not be wholesome to rebel against nature's program here, where we discover the timeless fact that human beings are only one species struggling, among all the rest, to exist.

The caribou range in loose herds, with the habit of making a major migration each spring and fall. They follow approximately the same routes in all years. In season the hunters seek them in bottlenecks such as river crossings and mountain passes. Eskimos used to corral them with barriers of willows, or sod dummies, or blocks of snow and ice. Now, like white men, the natives use guns. The Eskimos value not only the meat but the hides, for sleeping-robes, boots, and especially for parkis. (As fur is so prominent in the natives' lives, it is not surprising that surgeons find caribou hairs in Eskimos' appendixes—hairs rather than grape seeds.)

The herds are large: over 100,000 on the arctic slope and about 50,000 in one interior herd. Usually the lower herd crosses two highways, the Steese and the Taylor. Their progress is watched and reported by game-management officers, keeping track of the herd by plane.

This year the hunters who went by car were allowed to shoot as close as a hundred feet from the highway; and cows could be taken. The caribou missed the Steese road, but their Taylor crossing continued for almost two weeks. On October 15, the day the major crossing began, eighty-two per cent of the hunters took home a carcass.

The arrangement did not please many sportsmen. The very word *hunt* means *search*, and if the seeking element is not in it, the result is not very much more than a slaughter. Corrective measures are recommended, but it probably still will be true that any Alaska hunter who wants one can get a caribou. It dresses out to about 150 pounds of meat, not quite as tender and delicate as moose but less gamy and dry than Stateside deer. It tastes something like elk.

The *grand prix* of Alaska hunters is the Dall sheep, the only wild white sheep on the continent. One will yield less than a hundred pounds, but many people prefer it to any other kind of meat, wild or domestic.

Securing the sheep is not as easy for many hunters as it is for two friends of mine. They have a mining claim on a mountain where so many wild sheep graze that they call it their sheep ranch. When they see a few animals near the top of a ridge, they work their way to the opposite side, out of sight. As they creep up the slope then, they don't show themselves, but they are not quiet, inasmuch as the sheep always tend to run upward when they hear a suspicious noise. If the sounds and the sheep connect as the men hope they will, the sheep and the hunters meet at the top with the sheep running towards the rifles.

This procedure will often obtain meat but no spectacular heads, say the trophy-hunters. The old rams are too wary to be caught by such a ruse, and theirs are the most impressively curling horns. When the ram, with his binocular eyes, discovers a distant hunter, he gives the man a long look and walks off with a high-stepping gait until he is out of sight—when he bounds, uphill and upwind, which are the only clues for the hunter following. When the ram finally is spotted again, he is doubtless on some remote skyline cliff, and when shot he is likely to tumble down an inaccessible rock slide.

That is the kind of hunting enjoyed by the trophy men. Most are non-residents, here from the States. More Alaskans are meat-hunters, and the regulations protecting the animal populations are made with their needs in mind. The rules are generous enough so that game is available in what seems like excessive quantities—but only seems. Northerners crave meat instinctively, and now Dr. Kaare Rodahl, director of research at the Arctic Aeromedical Laboratory, has proved that much meat is indeed required here. It heightens the metabolic rate, even the skin temperature, and thus is a help in combating the cold.

In 1952 a survey was made of the food habits in 118 native Alaska villages. The total population involved was only 19,083 people, but they had eaten in one year 3,762,000 pounds of wild-animal meat. Seals topped the list at 1,202,000 pounds, with land animals next at 1,032,000. The total did not include fish, of which both Indians and Eskimos consume large amounts; but of the other animal products, the yearly supply averaged 197 pounds per person—well over a half-pound per day. My own appetite for meat increased after I came to the North. When I was living at Unalakleet and our meat supply had run out, hallucinations of big, juicy steaks kept drifting between my eyes and the typewriter, and at night, dreams of steaks woke me, aching with hunger.

Laws regarding the taking of waterfowl are unsatisfactory for the local residents. Most of the continent's ducks and geese breed in the arctic; it is Alaska's plants—and mosquitoes—that nourish the fledglings, but the laws regulating the shooting of waterfowl, made elsewhere, are designed for sports hunting in lower latitudes. The laws do not open the season until so late that many birds have long since left the North. "We supply the birds," say

Alaskans, "and we need them for food, but we cannot legally take them except a few stragglers."

Eskimo children often can shoot well by the age of eight and some white children when they are only a little older. In the fall of 1955, Fairbanks hunters were intrigued by the skill of Donnie Salisbury who, on his eleventh birthday, brought down a caribou with a spread of 71.5 inches—a freak head. The spread of the largest normal head ever recorded was 58.25 inches. Donnie shot from 150 yards with a Model 70 Winchester rifle. The next day he shot a moose at 250 yards.

One father of several sons, a physician, tells how he trains them: "Each boy has been given a twenty-two when he was ten years old. From the twenty-two's they advance to shotguns, and on to high-powered rifles. Meanwhile we have been studying game. I take the boys out to observe the animals, starting with caribou. We study moose next and then mountain sheep. My twin boys got their rams at the age of fourteen. It's a good experience for a boy to learn how to handle himself in a primitive wilderness, but we are not killers. We don't go around shooting everything that we see."

Such children learn more than woodcraft. When one little girl of eight was being taught to hunt by an elderly miner, she was told: "Never say you have shot a ptarmigan unless you have shot it in the head." A ptarmigan is a grouselike bird with a head about as wide as a fifty-cent piece. The advice she received can be applied to other situations besides hunting.

At the University of Alaska some of the students help to pay for their education by hunting and trapping. During caribou season they often are absent from classes for the justifiable reason that they are getting their winter's meat. For those who live in a dormitory, there is a gun room; and the coeds have their own rifle team.

The storage of all this game is a technique in itself. Cold-storage lockers are available in the cities, but even there some people use other methods, as of course they do in the smaller places. The favorite way is to put the meat in a high-pole cache, twenty feet off the ground. In the winter any place out-of-doors is a deep freeze, but some homes have inside storage. When I bought my Nome house, I was shown a neat little room, cross-ventilated and equipped with large shelves and numerous built-in boxes, all lined with linoleum. I was puzzled until the seller explained that this was "the game cache." The next winter my own moose meat was preserved in it quite satisfactorily.

The cooking of game is also of course a technique, or more—an art. Most Northern men are adept at it. For those who are not, there are Alaska cookbooks which tell what to do with beaver, muskrat, bear, and buffalo, as well as the more familiar game products. One book praises the meat of beaver and muskrat highly. It calls muskrat sweet, fine-grained, and palatable, but I have tried both and my stomach says no. I am not as adventuresome as members of the Wildlife Management Club at the University of Alaska. Once a year they attend a dinner at which are served many kinds of Alaska animals, even those as unlikely as wolf, wolverine, coyote, and mink.

Some women hunt with their families. Rifles are advertised on women's radio programs, right along with detergents and biscuit mix. When women go gathering wild greens and berries, they often carry their rifles into the berry patches. One couple separated last fall, the wife to pick blueberries, the husband to hunt their moose. The husband's search was a failure but when the day ended, the wife had a moose that had wandered among the berry bushes.

The natives use more of the wild greens than the settlers do; however homesteaders often depend on them, even preserving them for the winter. Farmers did not invent vitamins. The human race has been nourished a long time and on a diversified, even when a wild, diet.

I have found the spicy leaves of wild celery very appetizing. More familiar to white people are dandelion greens, sourdock, and willow leaves, which make good salad ingredients. The leaves of the willow, *salix pulchra,* are up to ten times as rich in vitamin C as oranges. A book on edible Northern plants, prepared by the nutritionist Christine Heller, lists thirty-four Alaska species whose leaves have food value: thirteen roots, eight plants whose stems are used, and twenty-three kinds of berries. Edible mushrooms abound in some areas.

Wild blueberries grow profusely. Also abundant, here and there, are wild red raspberries and strawberries, wild cranberries, salmonberries, cloudberries, thimbleberries, crowberries, and serviceberries—a mouth-watering crop, tangy and rich in flavor, perhaps because they mature in a sun that shines twenty-four hours a day.

Many species freeze well. Stored in ice cellars or caches, they may be used as late as the following spring with canned milk and sugar, or as a topping for shortcake. Blueberry pie is to Alaskans what apple pie is in the States. Berries are used in puddings and muffins, but the greatest quantities go into jam and jelly. Blueberry jam comes on the Northern breakfast tables like marmalade. Berry wine has enthusiasts.

More than a few of the early Alaska explorers died of scurvy, although they'd been pushing through wild-rose brambles much of their way. And the hips of Alaska wild roses, those bulbous capsules of seeds just below the flower, contain from five to thirty times as much vitamin C as the best of the citrus fruits; three rose hips furnish as much as an orange, says a publication of the University of Alaska Extension Service. Collecting rose hips is therefore another pleasant and urgent task. Thickets are acres wide in some regions. In the patch where I go, the wild-rose bushes grow so densely that I can stand in one place pulling hips off the stems for fifteen or twenty minutes. We preserve them in various ways.

Remove tails from rose hips and gently wash in sieve. Next, add enough water barely to cover, and boil for 20 minutes in enamelware pan. Remove seeds by rubbing through sieve or purée strainer.

To 2 qts. of purée add 2 lemons, rind and juice, and 3 lbs.
sugar. (First cook finely sliced lemon rind in a little water till
soft.)
  Boil purée, lemon, and sugar till thick and clear, and bottle
in sterilized jars. Can be used as a jam, or a spoonful can be
added to fruit drinks for extra vitamin C and sharpened flavor.

The berry-picking is always sociable. White, Eskimo, or Indian
women go out in groups, talking and laughing together as the
little buckets fill up. The small children go too, and help to pick,
or chase the late butterflies, or play with ptarmigan, which are
almost as tame as pigeons. Meanwhile the signs of the summer's
ending are all around us. Sometimes in the winter months we'll
come out on snowshoes to see our favorite ravine or meadow looking so different, but we won't have these long, relaxing days
under the open sky. And so, in the fall, there is a sense of fare-
well as we gather the berries.

We'll give glasses of jelly to friends as Christmas greetings. And
the pre-Christmas days bring us out of doors again temporarily,
for with spruces found almost everywhere but the tundra, most
families cut their own Christmas trees.

Last year I had two; and getting them was such fun that I felt
inspired to decorate one entirely with little trumpets. The drifts
were deep, up to our necks, and we hadn't worn snowshoes, but
we pushed into the silent white grove and excavated trees with
tops that looked promising. My dog, Bobo, plunged along on the
surface with leaping motions, the same way a wolf does, on bent
legs—strenuous exercise, so that he often stopped and lay on
the snow as if on a soft, down bed. It was not a very cold day as
Alaskans measure, 25° below zero. We snapped off our trees (they
are very brittle when frozen so hard) and held them over our
heads as we waded back to the road.

Alaska cabins, also some of the most pretentious houses, usually are made of logs. The building of them is often a long-term
project. Free permits are granted by the U.S. Forest Service to
take timber for personal use, and it may be one summer's program

to cut enough logs for the house and float them down to the homestead site on one of the numerous rivers.

The next summer, while the logs are still being seasoned, a family may construct a light, airy basement. They will live in it for a winter. The third summer the house takes shape.

One New Year's night I walked through a snowy spruce grove, on a dog-sled trail, with the moon's long, white aisles spreading widely around us. My friends and I were bound for a new log house, built by the owner in a forest clearing five miles from the center of Fairbanks. It is a snug, wide-eaved cabin. Eventually it will be the laboratory of Dr. William Pruitt, a scientist, but at present it is his home. In one of its two, generous-sized rooms we sat comfortably in front of a Franklin stove and ate a juicy moose roast, Alaska potatoes baked in the ashes, and Alaska blueberry pie. Meanwhile the tethered dogs of the team, sounding like moon-struck wolves, bayed outside.

Building a house can be thought of as labor—that is, doing the work oneself to save money—or it can just as well be described as fun. The same is true of our fishing: does a Northerner fish to secure nourishment or for recreation? The answer is, both.

There are but two ways to talk about the fishing in Alaska—with a paragraph or a book. Name your favorite cold-water fish: it is here, and the only thing that a sportsman could complain about is the fact that there are too many ("The rare species become too common"), and perhaps that there are so many good fishing-grounds that it's hard to choose where to go. But nobody will complain of the size, the fighting spirit, or table quality of the grayling, up to twenty-three inches long; rainbows nine inches longer; arctic charr (a Dolly Varden) a yard long . . . on through mammoth lake trout to the silver and king salmon, which are becoming interesting to salt-water fishermen. The record king weighed 126 pounds and was fifty-two inches long, forty-five inches in circumference, with a tail-spread of seventeen inches. That one was caught in a fish trap, but Alaskans take them by many methods, with seines, gillnets, fish wheels, rod and line, and, whatever the way, they taste equally good. In delicacy of flavor a fresh-caught king varies as much from canned, smoked, or cold-storage salmon as an avocado differs from mustard greens. There is one fish, however, that surpasses the kings in esteem. It is the shee, a Siberian "white salmon," found as well in northwest Alaska. It has been described as tasting not like fish but like fresh, sweet cream. Eskimos seine shee in arctic rivers during the summer and take them in winter by "jigging" through holes in the five-foot-thick ice on the sea. Most white settlers and visiting sportsmen like a gamier battle. They can have it at other seasons, since the fish will display up to eighty-five pounds of instantaneous fury. Mentioned too should be king crabs, taken from under the ice.

Besides the activities which have practical purposes, Alaskans turn to the out-of-doors, summer and winter, for play.

In summer we have regattas and excursions on the interior rivers, *kayak* and *umiak* races and exhibitions of boating skill by the Eskimos on the coast. We like target-shooting—sometimes we fire at bottles thrown into a river above us. We have baseball games; also other open-air sports, local in origin.

In winter come dog-sled racing and traveling, reindeer sledding, ski-sailing, hunting polar bears on the sea ice, snowshoeing, and some downhill skiing, mostly near the large cities. Festivals break out in all seasons, all over Alaska. Twice a year the Eskimos have a week of feasting and outdoor games, and there is an even more delirious celebration up on the arctic coast—the annual *Nalukutuk*, commemorating the killing of giant whales. After the trapping season the Indians stage a potlatch, with dog races and games and dances.

The white people also celebrate. Fairbanks, for example, has its Golden Days in the summer, Tanana Valley Fair in the fall, and the Ice Carnival every March. The world-championship dog-racing trophy is won at the Ice Carnival. Gatherings like conventions feature moose barbecues, the Eskimo skin-toss, and Eskimo and Indian dances. In the spring many go to Nenana for the break-up of the Tanana River and the winning of the world-famous Ice Classic.

Pleasures like these, which could be called simply a boiling up of high spirits, seem to appeal to Alaskans more than fiercely competitive sports. The average Northerner is not tense; he can tolerate things that are slow, having, himself, a tempo akin to nature's. While Stateside skiers may think that snowshoeing belongs with snail-watching, we enjoy getting out on top of the thick white cover and ambling around in a leisurely way, following tracks of foxes and hares till they come together, watching moose, a wolverine, or a lynx. We're just being outdoors, without any intensely sought goal.

But is the Alaska wilderness a Utopia? How about the mosquitoes?

Yes, indeed, the mosquitoes. Visitors who encounter them at the height of their summer abundance sometimes wonder why anyone lives in the North. Residents are more apt to talk of mosquitoes as funny. My own favorite among the jokes is the comment that if there were more mosquitoes they would have to be smaller.

One hears that people are sometimes driven insane, even killed by mosquitoes. I have authentic knowledge of only one case of each. An elderly Eskimo told with regret how a victim died when her tribe tied him outside among swarms of mosquitoes. A few years ago a headstrong newcomer declared he was going to walk from Kotzebue to Fairbanks, over some 500 miles of muskeg. Although many tried to discourage the man, he set out. A few weeks later a bush pilot discovered him wandering aimlessly, enclosed in a cloud of mosquitoes and completely out of his mind.

When I first encountered the famous hordes, I was fishing with Eskimos. They were wearing their cotton parki covers, with hoods and long sleeves but leaving the hands and faces exposed. The Eskimos were not bitten, and I asked a girl why. She said, "Mosquitoes don't bite if you don't get excited about them."

There does appear to be some such mechanism at work. Fear

of mosquitoes, like fear of dogs, seems to enrage the creatures, probably due to one's heightened scent. I once went on a bird-banding expedition on tundra made for the insects, with thousands of little unruffled ponds for their larvae to breed in. When we arrived, the batches of young were out, and the swarms were so thick that we could not complain—only laugh. I was camp cook, and when I would wash the dishes I frequently had to scoop a half-inch layer of mosquitoes off the top of the water. We drew them into our noses with every breath.

By then I had discarded such armor as headnets. Few Northerners bother with them. I did wear a ski cap and long sleeves, and I had a few bites near my eyebrows—those were all. The reason, I thought, was that the outing otherwise was absorbingly pleasant. After it ended I spent a few days loafing at Kotzebue, where, not having so much to think about, I was very conscious of the mosquitoes and was bitten from head to foot.

Alaska mosquitoes are not a great problem, even to the excitable, after mid-July. They are only a serious trial for about six weeks, at the time when millions of migrating birds are rearing their young and feeding many on a mosquito diet.

The frontier does make demands of us. It is not hard to endure mosquitoes when one can escape from them soon; but they are an ordeal to those who, day after day, are fishing to get in a food supply, to the lonely prospectors toiling over the flats, to the highway and railroad gangs, and the farmers. And the cold is not much to be dreaded in Fairbanks, where many services are available to keep one's house going; but the cold is a vast inconvenience, and can be menacing, to those living in wilderness cabins or following traplines.

However, for all of us, to a lesser or greater degree, there is a satisfaction in making the elemental adjustments. Old, basic instincts are wakened; there is fulfillment in fitting into the ageless scheme of the natural world. We miss some of the stimulations of Stateside cities, but for most Northerners they are outweighed by a curious tune-up of nerves.

Perhaps that is what Thoreau meant by the tonic of wildness.

PART

III

*Alaska Summons
Its Own*

>>>->>>->>> 18 <<<-<<<-<<<

One Man's Bonanza

AN UNNATURAL SILENCE seemed to lie over the land on the day I
went out to the hillside seven miles behind Nome where Ben
Gillette has his gold mine. Scattered over the face of the treeless
slope, also across on the opposite hill and below in the dry bed
of Anvil Creek, were the gray piles of tailings where thousands of
miners once worked with delirious haste to sluice out as much as
possible of their "noble metal" during the short arctic summer.
Their eagerness, what Rex Beach called the glad bright wine of
adventure, still seemed to spice the air. From the tailings came
none of the sounds that once echoed around the valley, the
clatter of winches, the clang of picks on rocks, the roar of cascades
from the pipelines, and, above all, the shouts, the exulting voices:
heard no more, they left an enormous hush. From a hummock
of moss came the small, sweet chirp of a plover. My dog bounded
towards it and even that sound was gone. In the Sunday stillness
the dog and I started farther along the ditch to find Ben Gillette.
Of the gold-rush miners on Anvil Creek he is the only one left,
the only one of an excited multitude who is still taking gold from
this famous ground.

Much of the gold is here yet, not in the quantities that made
millionaires in a single season, but Ben Gillette, in one clean-up,
has melted down gold worth $15,000. Others could do it if he
can, but few still alive have had his experience. Fewer still, per-

haps, have the ambition. For placer mining like this requires industry, an inventive mind, and some, though not a great deal of,
equipment. But Ben Gillette does not really drive himself. I
found him spading the moss out of his temporarily dry ditch,
and he was quite willing to stop for the day, though the time was
but half past two. As we were walking back to his cabin, he said,
"I'll admit I don't have to keep working this mine. I don't need
the money. But I love to find nuggets!" It was fifty-three years
ago that he first came to Nome. Inasmuch as he has been mining
ever since then, the novelty has had time to wear off. Yet his
voice had the ring of youthful high spirits: "I love to find nuggets!"

Later that day, while we stood at the side of his pit, he shoveled up some of the soil into a gold-pan and showed me the way
to rotate the pan in a tub of water. As the dirt, like a muddy mush,
is shaken, the heavier gold works its way to the bottom. I found
it surprisingly hard to do—the dirt wouldn't shift enough and the
water splashed out of the tub. Finally, when all but a cupful of
mud had washed over the edge of the pan, Gillette took it and
very skillfully, swishing the water into and out of it, drained away
everything except one little nugget attached to a pebble of quartz,
and a few gleaming grains of gold. He emptied my tiny clean-up
into a rusty coal shovel, carried it back to the cabin, and dried
out the gold in a granite saucer on top of his cookstove. Next,
stirring the grains with a magnet, he took out some slivers of iron
and, last, softly blew away traces of rock dust and weighed my
take. All this, he said, duplicated a large operation, even that on
a dredge. When he poured the grains from the saucer into an
envelope then, and gave it to me, his eyes were merry with private
amusement. He saw that another novice had caught the gold
fever, that eagerness which has kept him lively far past the age
when most men want to retire. He knew too that I would be like
the others who come and watch him and envy him and go away,
back to work that is probably both more hectic than his and more
humdrum. When he remembers such visitors I imagine his eyes

always twinkle, alone as he is out there on his beautiful hill, with his pet squirrel and the birds he enjoys, and the ingenious arrangements he has for recovering nuggets.

This mine is in the location that Rex Beach was writing about in *The Spoilers*. Rex Beach called it the Midas Mine. The Midas could have been Anvil Creek No. 9, a famous claim next to Ben Gillette's, or it could have been one of the four he now owns, adjoining Specimen Creek and called Specimen Nos. 1, 2, and 3, and Specimen Bench No. 7. Other claims are named more fantastically, such as Jumpers Fear, Whale, Lucky Six, Foggy Day, and Big Hurrah. The sober maps of the region record the exhilaration of the first white men who arrived. But this area where Specimen Creek enters Anvil Creek was so rich that the miners possessing it did not need to doctor their hopes with romance. If they could keep their mines working throughout the summer, if nobody jumped their claims and no dishonest judge, masking the theft with law, appropriated the treasure, the owners apparently did not care whether their mines bore names or numbers. But holding onto their mines was exactly what they were not able to do. In one of the biggest and boldest robberies ever plotted, the mines were taken away from them by what were proclaimed as legal procedures.

In *The Spoilers* Rex Beach described the dramatic events so accurately that his novel could be called history. They took place during the summer of 1900, and Gillette himself arrived just in time to become involved. He, one of 700 stampeders on a small steamer, the *Valencia*, came up from Seattle early in June. In the novel the hero sees two men kill each other on Front Street only a few hours after he has landed, and Ben Gillette witnessed that. The fighting was over a lot. In a year Nome had mushroomed from 400 people to 20,000, all of them living in tents when they did not live under the windy sky. Only the beach was habitable; 150 feet back from the water was spongy marsh. Therefore the tents were pitched on the shore, 20 deep on a five-mile stretch, in a scene of stupendous chaos: canvas households

set behind mountains of unidentified freight that the lighters had
dumped on the shore. Among the hams, cans of coal oil, the new
bar fixtures, tools, trunks, hay for pack-horses, bolts of mosquito
netting, timber, and crates of food, babies played and thousands
of miners shoveled the beach sand into their "sourdough rockers"
—rocking boxes not unlike those in which pioneer women made
butter. For these were "the golden sands of Nome," free to
everyone from the high-tide line back 60 feet. They were the richest poor-man's diggings—as the steamship companies advertised
—that the world ever had known. In 1899 the beach miners had
taken more than a million dollars out of the sands in two months.
The news touched off again the excitement fired by the Klondike
rush two years earlier, and by the following summer every kind of
ship that would float had been fitted up for the inevitable stampede. Now the people of Nome think they are fortunate if three
freighters come up in a summer; none carries passengers. In
June 1900, newcomers debarking at Nome averaged a thousand
a day.

Ben Gillette threaded his way through the jungle of freight on
the beach and talked to the men at the rockers. I think I know
how he looked, for he is a type that age does not greatly change.
He was of medium height, trimly built, quick in his movements
but patient, with interested blue eyes and a mouth, under his
reddish moustache, that often smiled, more in friendliness than
hilarity. His manner would have inspired confidence, and the miners no doubt were frank with him. From their reports he decided
the beach sands were running out and he would go somewhere
else.

First, though, he staked a claim only a little way back from the
shore, immediately behind town on the tundra flat. The several
prehistoric beach lines on the tundra also contain gold, which is
buried deep under muck and gravel, accessible to the buckets of a
large dredge but not to the pick and pan of a prospector. During
those first hectic weeks Gillette secured title to 20 of those unpromising acres; later he leased them to one of the dredge com-

panies for a share of the take. The take has been good. By such lucky hunches Gillette has proceeded, all the way.

The country beyond the flat is a tumbled terrain—winding valleys and mountains of moderate height. The most famous peak overlooks Nome: Anvil Mountain, so called because rocks on its summit form a crude anvil shape. Behind Anvil Mountain, Specimen Creek flows into Anvil Creek, and there near the junction were found the most fabulous gold deposits.

The claims around Specimen Creek were being worked by the Miocene Ditch Company. Water was then, as now, the prime need in gold-mining, and the Miocene men were building a ditch from the higher slopes—a ditch that still supplies water to gold-dredges down on the tundra flat. Ben Gillette took a job with the Miocene company. Today, when he is the owner of four of these claims, the ditch crosses his property, and its clear, swift flow is more than a little tantalizing, for its channel is held on a long-term lease, and it covers one of Gillette's finest pay streaks.

He did not stay many weeks with the ditch people. He and his partner, Jack Ferguson, went still farther inland, prospecting at first without luck but late in the season striking a pay that yielded them more than $1.00 a pan. Gillette says that he left Anvil Creek because he dislikes to work for a boss and, besides, the operation of all the most profitable Anvil Creek mines was disrupted, due to the fact that high-level robbers from Washington had arrived.

Historians state that Nome in its earliest years was the most lawless town that has ever existed. By 1900, thirty-three years had passed since Alaska was purchased from Russia, and yet Congress had made no provision for proper legal procedures in the new Territory. With the situation at Nome needing regulation so urgently, Congress did, in March of that year, pass a Civil Code for Alaska. Courts were to function in three places: Eagle City, Sitka, and Nome. A small military contingent at Nome had been enforcing some sanitary rules and was trying to curb an epidemic of smallpox, but the protection of life and property was left to the individual. It was, then, with great relief that the Nome citizens heard they finally would have a judge, marshal, prosecuting attorney, and staff of clerks. Law and order were due to reach Nome on July 19.

The judge, appointed in Washington, was a North Dakota man, Arthur Noyes. Alexander Mackenzie, a friend of his, arrived with him. Mackenzie said that he was the head of an eastern group called the Alaskan Gold Mining Company of New York. These two, Noyes and Mackenzie, proceeded to fleece the entire Nome community.

Under their scheme a false claimant would restake a mine already being worked—always one of the better mines. With the pretense, then, that the ownership of the mine was disputed, Judge Noyes would appoint Mackenzie as the receiver. They would throw the bona-fide owners off the property, with the help of the soldiers, whose commanding officer knew nothing of mining laws and did not challenge the judge. Noyes and Mackenzie said that the gold they were recovering from the mines in their control was being deposited in the banks till the question of ownership had been settled. But they would not tell the owners how much had been taken out. They would not let them be present at clean-ups.

In less than a week from the day they had landed, Noyes and Mackenzie had taken possession of most of the richest mines. Their game had been figured out by the local people, and, though the brief summer weeks were passing, the majority of the rest of the mines shut down. For the owners feared that if they were doing well, the corrupt pair would appropriate their claims. The dispossessed owners were of course protesting, but Judge Noyes paid no attention to them. Nor would he allow an appeal to be made to a higher court, which would have been the Ninth Circuit Court in faraway San Francisco. Finally, led by Charles D. Lane of the Wild Goose Mining Company, the owners sent lawyers to California. Judge Morrow granted them an appeal, and they brought back Morrow's orders that Judge Noyes must return all

the seized properties. Noyes, confident of his Washington back-
ing, refused. On the last-possible summer boat, Lane's attorneys
again went to San Francisco. Two U.S. marshals came back to
Nome with them. They arrested Mackenzie and took him out
immediately; by the following summer both he and Judge Noyes
had stood trial. Two of Noyes's staff members served prison sentences, but President McKinley secured the release of Mackenzie,
who also had been convicted. Noyes was let off with the payment
of a small fine.

That was the tale related accurately in *The Spoilers*. Rex Beach
hardly disguised the names: Arthur Noyes became "Arthur Still-
man," and Alexander Mackenzie "Alec McNamara." The author
was here himself. He was working a claim in Saturday Gulch,
near the location of the original gold strike, and he wrote with a
vividness that is only possible when one is stirred by some deep
conviction. All the old-timers still left in Nome, too, speak in-
dignantly of the daring plot that ruined the climactic year of the
gold rush. The miners had no way of knowing then, nor did they
ever learn, how much of their treasure was drained away by
"The Alaskan Gold Mining Company of New York."

The gold-production that was reported during the season of
1900 amounted to $4,750,000 for this Seward Peninsula. Between
that time and this, well over $100,000,000 in gold has been taken
out of the area. The production today could equal that of the
better years if there were more incentive to get the gold out of
the ground, if the mines could be worked more profitably. On the
whole of the Seward Peninsula during 1957, 254 men were employed in this glamorous occupation, producing approximately
$1,650,000 by methods as simple as panning by hand and as com-
plex as dredge operation. Many of the idle claims are held by
owners eager to open them up if and when the value of gold is
allowed to find its level according to market conditions.

Ben Gillette does not wait, and by working several months in
the summer, he takes a consistently handsome living out of his
property. That he can is due both to the curiously formed de-

posits he owns and to the efficient, if picturesque, way he re-covers them.

In a prehistoric age Anvil Creek was up near the top of this present slope. It was flowing through quartz that was generously combined and encrusted with gold, and it caused the rock to dis-integrate, as every stream does, thus releasing the precious metal. When the creek carried the rock particles off to the sea, most of the gold, the nuggets and heavier portions of fine gold, remained.

So far the process was similar to the formation of placer gold elsewhere. However, this arctic hillside was frozen. When the sur-face thawed out in summer, the top layer slid gradually downhill, sidewise, taking the creek with it. The creek at all stages was breaking up gold-bearing quartz, and as it slipped lower and lower, it left the gold strewn through the slope. In a warmer cli-mate it would not be true that an entire hillside would yield gold.

But there are pay channels in Ben Gillette's hill—streaks where the gold lies in denser deposits; at those levels the creek may have stayed for a longer time, or the rock formations be-neath may have trapped the metal. The Miocene Ditch, about 10 feet wide, lies almost on top of one of the pays. Yet the con-centration of gold does veer off to the side in some places, and when he finds one of those, Ben Gillette has impressive clean-ups.

The summer's work starts in the previous fall. Gillette's own small ditch, about two feet wide and two deep, extends up and around the hill for two and a half miles, dropping exactly three inches in each 100 feet. At the end of a season he clears it of weeds, meanwhile checking the 10-foot stakes that rise up at each turn in the ditch. Snow will cover the ditch nearly up to that height, and since the water won't run till the ditch is exposed, after the winter's last snowfall ashes and sand will be scattered along its course, with the stakes acting as guides. By attracting the heat of the sun, any such dark material will melt down the snow. The sand and ashes will be available because they will have been stockpiled in shallower snow near the cabin.

The ditch water comes from seepage, from melting snow higher along the slope. As it flows down the ditch, it collects in three basins Gillette has scooped out of the hillside. Small earthen dams and simple wood floodgates hold back or release the water. Below the dams the water enters a 14-inch pipe, which carries it to the "pit"—the excavation, wherever it is, that Gillette is currently working. All his pipe, incidentally, must be brought out of the pit in the fall because snow fills the pit to the rim and its weight would crush even the sturdy iron conduit. In summer the pipeline ends in two "giants," nozzles that hurl gushers of water upon whatever soil is to be moved. With water, it seems, earth can be put almost anywhere that one wants it. The water breaks down the sides of the pit and then pushes the earth and gravel along to the lower end, where two wooden "wings" funnel it into the sluice boxes.

The boxes are troughs of iron, 400 linear feet of them. They lead on down the hill at a grade very precisely calculated, for the water that brings the gravel and soil into the boxes must mix these materials as they are sluiced along, and allow the heavier gold to settle but must not sweep it away. In the bottom of the boxes, metal grids, riffles, hold back the fine sediment. The gold will be there. Gillette will have poured quicksilver, or "quick," as the miners call it, among the riffles, and this mercury picks up the gold almost as a magnet would, amalgamating the smaller particles that otherwise would be difficult to recover.

When the sluicing has gone on for a certain time—which might be a week or a summer, depending on the value of that particular soil—Ben Gillette has his clean-up. He lifts out the riffles, sloshing off any gold-bearing dirt that clings to them. Then, placing a tub at the end of the boxes, he works the sediment down, partly by shoveling, partly with a very slow stream of water. The concentrate in the tub will contain other heavy minerals besides gold, and some, such as scheelite, an ore of tungsten, are saved. The gold finally is separated from the rest of the concentrate by panning, which is done almost exactly as it was two thousand years ago and probably as far back as 4,000 B.C. Early accounts speak of it as "washing the gold in a bowl."

The mercury is recovered. Some is extracted by squeezing the amalgam in a chamois; Ben Gillette puts the rest in a retort, which is then heated in his handmade forge to a very high temperature, at which the mercury vaporizes. It is drawn off through a pipe into a pan of water, where, being cooled, it again becomes mercury. After the gold is weighed, it is brought to the Miners and Merchants Bank in Nome, where it is further refined and sent on its way to the United States government.

When I was buying some stamps at the Nome post office one day, William Haley, teller and assayer at the bank, came laboring up to the window with a package wrapped in burlap and obviously quite heavy. It weighed 84 pounds, although it was only the size, and about the shape, of a large beefsteak. It was gold from various mines, melted together at the bank, and was worth $47,040. Addressed to the U.S. Assay Office in Seattle, it would go down by registered air mail.

For handling the gold for the local mines, the bank makes a charge of 2 to 2.5 per cent of its gross value, depending on the amount. Besides the large dredges of the United States Smelting, Refining and Mining Company, and besides Ben Gillette's near-by mine, about 55 gold operations on the Seward Peninsula ship their take through Nome. These mines are scattered along the coast and back in the mountains. Since roads are so few in the area, most of them are reached only by plane. Bush pilots fly supplies and machinery to the mines and bring the gold out— very informally. Sometimes it is carried in the standard brown leather "pokes," bags about a foot long and two inches wide, inconvenient to get the gold into and out of, it seems; but as often the gold is transported in bottles or coffee cans.

In its color and form and the impurities it contains, the gold from each mine is so distinctive that in the case of a theft the bank can identify its origin. That happened once when Gillette's boxes were robbed. It is an unwritten law that no workman employed at a hydraulic mine shall look into the sluice boxes—perhaps on the principle that what he does not see won't tempt him. But apparently one young fellow helping Gillette broke the rule. A short time after his work was finished, he came back and asked to be taken on again. Gillette would have agreed, but he and his wife both had hunches, they say, that there would be trouble, and therefore Gillette turned him down. When some of the gold from the next clean-up disappeared, they suspected that he was the thief. However they had no real evidence, nothing except intuition. That was not enough, said the police, to justify getting out a warrant to search the boy's quarters. That night, in one of the frequent mining-town free-for-alls, the boy knocked another man down a flight of stairs. He was arrested, and then the police did go through his belongings. A poke with about $500 in gold was found, and the gold was identified beyond question as coming from Ben Gillette's mine.

Hunches play more than a small part in the finding of gold and in tracing the pay streaks. So too does luck, and Ben Gillette has respect for both. He is apt to speak of events in those terms, to discount his hard work and foresight and give most of the credit to fate and to intuition. Several years ago, very early in spring when the countryside was deserted, one of his giants fell off its tripod and knocked him down into a gully, breaking his leg. Logically he could not have expected anyone to come into the area for two weeks or more, but "something" told him that if he called help would arrive, and it did. Two men had come out from town to pick up some pipe they were going to buy from another miner. They heard Gillette call, and hauled him out to the road on a sled.

Mining is often hazardous, and Gillette has had other narrow escapes. Once he fell down a 60-foot shaft but chanced to be wearing a jacket which had got wet earlier in the day and had then frozen stiff. It checked his descent like a parachute.

Luck seems to be with him in finding his nuggets and pays,

and I wonder if part of his joy in his work is not the flattering sense that he is favored by fortune. Yesterday I looked out of a restaurant window and saw a dollar bill lying rain-soaked on the gravel inside the Nome breakwater. That small piece of good luck gave me more pleasure than any dollar I've ever got in a regular way; and when the nugget came up in the pan of dirt Ben Gillette was finishing for me, his chuckle was really delighted, as if we'd received a gift, one of considerable importance, worth far more than the little nugget.

He has been lucky too in his marriage, for Mrs. Gillette is a woman with a quietly sympathetic nature, greatly interested in what her husband is doing. She does not stay at the mine. She says, "My place is in Nome, keeping the house open, because Ben likes to come to town over the holidays, in a party mood, all dressed up, forgetting work, mud, water, and even gold." Some years they spend the winter in Nome, but more often fly down to a southern resort. Their favorite is Desert Hot Springs in California.

Their time in the States is always a sociable one, for Ben Gillette is no hermit by choice, and everyone finds his wife charming. And even his summer is not wholly solitary. About once a week Irene Gillette and a few friends drive out from Nome to the mine, bringing dinner. They appear, a string of heads bobbing up the slope as they walk single-file through the sluice boxes— treading on gold. When Ben Gillette greets them, his smile comes as easily as a tundra breeze, and he talks freely—about gold if he thinks that is what they would like. He is an excellent cook and generally contributes at least one dish to the meal, concocting it out of the staple supplies that a tractor pulls to the mine for him in the spring. I especially enjoyed his apple sauce, made with dried apples and with molasses as one ingredient. The conversation is good in the little cabin, but when the evening is over, there is no hint that Ben Gillette will have even a moment of loneliness as the voices die away down the hill. He will put out some scraps for his pet squirrel, look at his homemade weathervane—the end of a tin can nailed onto a rotating stick—and if it is late in the season will watch the sky to see if the first migrating cranes have begun to fly south. If they have, he believes that the freeze-up will come in two weeks. Then, at the end of his day, he may set some sourdough bread before he turns into his bunk, and it appears that he will feel only a keen impatience for morning—the new day with its bright and infallible nuggets.

He is something one seldom meets, a genuinely contented man. Both he and his wife have an unpretentious and friendly attitude that I have noticed in other owners of small Northern mines. So peaceful an outlook might seem almost dreamlike to men who require the stimulation of more intense activity. But four hundred years ago Agricola wrote: "The occupation of the miner is objectionable to nobody. For who, unless he be naturally malevolent and envious, will hate the man who gains wealth as it were from heaven?" Ben Gillette has similar words for the deeper satisfaction he finds in mining. As we started to leave, to make our way back to Nome through the wide notch in the hills with the shine of the Bering Sea on the other side, our host had this to say for his way of life:

"I'm not taking away anything somebody else wants. And I'm not bothering anybody."

19

The Mad Eskimo Woman
of Diomede

"IF I COULD I would squeeze out between the bars, then I would make myself small and slip through the little crack under the door. Because I would rather be outside, even if people would tear me to pieces, than locked up in that cell."

For months after those agonized words pierced the decorous air of the courtroom at Nome, they still pierced through my sleep. Womenga was speaking in Eskimo; yet her voice was so plainly desperate that we, the jury, had our composure shaken even before the interpreter had repeated the meaning in English. The interpreter, Mrs. Flora Oumauk, was beside the prisoner on one of the benches below the jury box. She was facing Womenga, and her posture as well as her tone seemed kind. Womenga's slight figure was nearly motionless. She has only one arm; when she was a child her left arm was shot off in a hunting accident. Her right hand lay in her lap, and only her eyes, not her shoulders or head, turned towards Mrs. Oumauk. She seemed more at our mercy because of her passive manner.

She still did not move when her outburst came—her frantic rebellion was all in her voice. It was sudden. We had been asking her questions, for this was no criminal trial. The charge was insanity; therefore the hearing was somewhat informal. In the beginning three affidavits were read, and then several witnesses testified. The jury, as well as the United States commissioner who was conducting the hearing, had questioned the witnesses. Now we were talking direct to Womenga. One of us asked, through Mrs. Oumauk, how Womenga had spent her time when she was at home. She replied that she worked. Grown stepchildren lived in her house, she said, but she was the cook for the family. Between meals she cleaned, and if there was time she did skin-sewing. She told us she liked to work, and she sounded as if that were a simple statement of fact, not one to make an impression. Unexpectedly then came her cry: "I would rather be outside, even if people would tear me to pieces, than locked up in that cell."

There was an audible gasp of sympathy, and one of the jurors, a banker, said in his gruff and impulsive voice, "I'd feel the same way myself." We had heard that Womenga was acting wild, up in the second-floor federal prison. The evidence made it seem doubtful that she was sane, till we realized how distressing confinement was to her. For all of the jury, I think, that was the point from which we discounted anything she had done in the jail.

It was not going to be simple to judge the sanity of this Eskimo with the beautiful name—Womenga K. Iyapana. She was one of the older, primitive type, as proved by the tattooed lines on her chin. In former times Eskimo girls were thus marked, by drawing fine strands of sinew, dipped in soot and seal oil, down through the flesh of their chins—the small center lines at the time they reached puberty, and the large lines at the sides later when they were married. That is a custom so long abandoned that only the elderly women have tattooed faces. Those women did not have schooling, most of them don't speak English, and therefore they largely observe the aboriginal ways of their race.

Womenga, moreover, had spent most of her adult life on Little Diomede Island. Her settlement is so hard to reach that very few white people have gone there. Womenga had left it from time to

time, but she still clung to her native culture, and we of the jury
were trying to judge her mental condition from her own point of
view. She might have done things that would seem crazy enough
to us, but logical to an Eskimo of her background. Or is there
some fundamental sanity of behavior that applies to all human-
kind? Could a sophisticated white man watch an uneducated native and say whether the native was rational? And if the roles
were reversed, could the native so judge the white man? Insanity
is in primitive experience too.

That was the jury's problem—one of the elemental situations
that make life in an arctic outpost so close-knit and human.
Indirectly, the whole town of Nome felt concerned. For nearly
everyone knew of Womenga's plight, and most people had formed
opinions as to whether she should be sent to an institution. Our
interest began about six weeks before she arrived, when reports
started coming over the radio, from the teacher on Little Diomede
Island, that one of the Eskimos there was insane and the rest of
the villagers wanted her taken away.

Here in northwest Alaska, winter all but isolates many settlements. But most are equipped with small radio transmitters, and
some responsible resident, often the teacher, talks to one of the
larger towns, Nome, Barrow, or Kotzebue, every day. Emergency
operations have been performed by a teacher, missionary, or
trader, with the doctor giving step-by-step instructions and people
in all other villages listening. Advice will be furnished in cases
of crime, shortage of food, village disputes, any such problem;
and personal news, as of births and deaths in the towns, is sent
out to the relatives. They are conversations in which human interest is packed very tight.

At the time for the broadcasts, late afternoon, the people in
Nome tune their radios to the short-wave band. One after another the more remote settlements come on the air. Those who
are busy may go on about their work, only half listening, but they
are apt to stop when the Little Diomede teacher begins to talk.
For the people on Little Diomede cannot reach the mainland

in winter except in the most desperate circumstances. The bush planes do go there, but not on a regular schedule, for it is considered the most dangerous flight in Alaska, perhaps in the world.

The island is one of two—Russia owns Big Diomede, three miles to the west—that huddle together in the tumultuous waters of Bering Strait. Little Diomede is but a mountaintop, tiers of rock ledges rising out of the water steeply. Thousands of birds such as auklets, murres, and cormorants arrive from the south every summer to nest on the barren slopes. And walrus, whales, and seals pass through the strait as the ice floes drift back and forth. These animals and the birds' eggs furnish most of the islanders' food. Their occupation is carving small souvenirs out of the walrus tusks. To sell them, some of the islanders journey to Nome and Kotzebue in their walrus-skin *umiaks* every summer.

In the fall, then, the ones who have made the trip all go home, usually on the *North Star*, a ship owned by the Indian Bureau, with their *umiaks* slung aboard. The assumption is that the island is cut off, without mail or supplies, without doctors or nursing care, till the next July. For the ice on the strait does not freeze in a quiet plain; the water is filled with a milling chaos of cakes and slabs plunging about in the almost unceasing gales. Normally no one could make his way over that ice, on foot or with dogs, and the possibility that he might crash in those floes is a nightmare of every pilot.

Between the two islands the current is slow enough so that a solid surface of ice does form. But it is always rough, covered with white spires and blocks, hard for a pilot to see in the racing fogs. In three situations, however, a pilot attempts to go: in the case of a broken bone or a ruptured appendix, also if one of the islanders goes insane.

The demented person may not need professional care very urgently, but it is felt that the other villagers should be aided in this predicament. There is no place in an Eskimo settlement to lock such a patient up, and at times they have been a menace. A few years ago on King Island, about 60 miles south of Little

Diomede and where landings are also difficult, a native was killed
by his demented wife. Since that time any case of insanity is considered an emergency, although some insane patients are harmless, and in other instances what seems insanity may not be that
at all. The people of Nome, understanding the difficulties but
always concerned for the safety of those who fly during the
Northern winter, were trying to diagnose this poor Eskimo's
symptoms.

Womenga was talking irrationally; at least that's what her step-
son reported to the teacher, Gerald F. Carlson. Sometimes in
the coldest weather she would go out with no parki on. She could
not sleep. Had she done anything threatening, anything to endanger the safety of others? There was no such report. But if she
was really insane, one never could tell what might happen.

There was one other consideration—the time was December.
As the islanders knew, Christmas mail was stacked up for them in
the Nome post office, mail they would not get till the following
summer unless in the meantime a plane were to come. In those
circumstances a mild case of dementia sincerely might seem like
a serious threat, justifying a plea that a plane be sent—and incidentally bring the Christmas packages.

The official in Nome who had been carrying on the radio conversations was Mr. Lawrence Williams, in charge of the local activities of the Indian Bureau. On December 18 he asked that a
warrant be issued for Womenga's arrest. The United States marshal must then try to secure a plane. Bill Munz was the pilot who
offered to go. A deputy marshal must also go as a guard, and
that was to be Maurice Kelliher.

On the day before Christmas they started. They flew the 110
miles to Cape Prince of Wales, passing en route the York Mountains, where snow streaked the vertical rocky walls. From Wales
they proceeded west over the strait. The plane, a single-engined
Stinson, had carried them out about 20 miles when the oil pressure suddenly dropped. In order to stay aloft Munz cut the oil
supply to the propeller. The pressure rose in the engine, but then

the plane would not climb. Munz returned to Wales, landed there on the icy beach, and found that the lowered pressure was due to the frigid, congealing weather. No pilot could remedy that. Nevertheless, the two men decided to risk trying to cross the strait again. As they approached the island they found that the landing conditions would be too hazardous in a badly functioning plane. They flew back to the mainland. There, with the lowered pressure, they had difficulty in getting over the mountains. But finally, with their fuel nearly gone, they were able to pass the peaks and reach Nome.

The next time they tried was the day after New Year's. It was a beautiful morning, frozen mist near the ground but the sky filled with a rose-tinted moonlight. My dog Bobo and I had set out for a walk on the road to the city airfield. The road passes the school, a group of white Cape Cod houses for government workers, some Eskimo cabins ingeniously put together, like Robinson Crusoe's, out of flotsam and jetsam, and last, on the right, a comforting solid structure of yellow cement, the hospital. Beyond it the road makes a dip to cross Dry Creek, and then lifts to a tundra flat rimmed with a semicircle of mountains. The airstrip bisects the flat, and all the way out one may watch the small planes skim down and rise, seeming most birdlike in winter when they are equipped with skis, shaped like the webs of ducks and geese spread for a landing.

On that morning no planes were flying. I thought I knew why, for the mist was whitening Bobo's black coat with frost. In a mist like that flying might be unwise, as Munz must have decided, for his new blue jeep passed us, returning to town. His face was immobile, set as usual in an expression of stubborn patience. He is one of Nome's most courageous and skillful pilots, expecting as much hardihood of his passengers as of himself, but no one complains of that, for he keeps his aircraft, himself, and his flying technique in nearly a state of perfection. In a town where last names are discarded almost universally, few call him Bill, few indeed know him well enough for a greeting. But some of the town's most colorful legends concern him, his narrow escapes in thick weather, and his daring rescues of sick and wounded out in the villages.

But perhaps he was flying that day after all, for his jeep passed again, heading towards the field, with Maurice Kelliher on the seat beside him. Maurice, tall, with a lean, handsome face and an unfailing Irish friendliness, waved and smiled. Soon then I heard the roar of Munz's airplane engine, and just before Bobo and I started into the gully, the green Stinson rose into the air and began to bank, one of Munz's typical turns, as smooth as a seagull's.

I said to Bobo, "You look like a silver fox," and I stooped to brush some of the frost from his fur. When I glanced up, Munz's plane was falling. It was plunging to earth in a swift, sagging drop like a shot plover's. A crash—then a sickening silence.

From the creek I could not see the plane hit the ground. By the time I was up on the tundra flat, Munz and Maurice were out of it. Maurice was feeling one of his arms; the pilot was walking around the plane. Before Munz had come back into town, he had cleaned the plane's surfaces, but enough frost had formed on the wings in the short time he was gone to destroy the plane's lift. The men fell from an altitude of about 150 feet and would not have survived if the plane had not landed in willows heavily padded with snowdrifts.

Later that afternoon I had occasion to stop at the marshal's office. Maurice, who did not hear me enter, was talking to his small son on the telephone. When he hung up, his hand rested on the receiver a moment longer, and he continued to smile, tenderly, thoughtfully.

Would the men make a third attempt? Most people hoped that they wouldn't. Nothing new was reported over the radio. Womenga still did not sleep at times, and she still had a strong urge to escape from walls. She was watched "so she would not hurt herself or anyone else," Mr. Carlson said. He did not tell anything that would indicate she was a menace.

Womenga had been to Nome and was remembered here, and we who were listening to the radio had exchanged bits of information about her. The first thing to come out was the fact that she had been brought in before for a hearing, and more than one jury had judged her insane. The procedure then was that a patient was taken to Portland, Oregon, to the Morningside Hospital, which for many years had contracted with the Department of the Interior to give custodial care to Alaska's mentally ill. Custodial care does not imply an extensive effort to cure a patient; nevertheless, some do improve, and Morningside never had kept Womenga long. They had released her each time, and she had made her way back to Nome.

Those who had met her here spoke of a quality some described as cleverness, some as personality. She was a woman you did not forget. She had had a dramatic history, born in Siberia and perhaps with white blood in her background—a Russian explorer? For her hair, although nearly black, was said to be softer than that of a typical Eskimo, and her skin not so dark. She was about ten years old when her left arm was injured; it was amputated without any anaesthetic. She had been married four times. Her first husband had been a Siberian. After he died, she had married one of the Little Diomede men who had come to her village to trade. She had gone to live on his Alaska island, but they were not happy and separated. Her third husband was one of the most intelligent, most respected men on Little Diomede, Karipari by name. Mrs. Emily Boucher remembers that when he came to town he would walk around with his elbows crooked back over a stick. He died a few years ago. Womenga had borne several children, herself. None was now living.

After so many tragedies most people, of any race, would give up the attempt to be happy. Not so Womenga, who, whatever else she had, did have spirit apparently. In the summer of 1951 she and a widower, Tom Iyapana, came to Nome with an *umiak*-load of islanders to be married—properly, by the white-man's law. Tom was said to be fond of her, proud of her.

That was Womenga, who now might or might not be insane. Munz and Maurice took off again on the 6th of January. This time they reached Little Diomede and came down on a large ice field attached temporarily to the island's north shore. Maurice has told me how, as soon as the plane landed, several of the villagers, including her husband, began helping Womenga out over the ice. It was heaved into the usual ridges and hummocks, and the plane was a mile and a half from shore. Munz was impatient to leave, for a mist in the air was again turning to frost on the wings. But it was necessary for Maurice to go to the village. Mr. Williams at Nome had told the Diomede teacher to have signed affidavits ready, legal proof that the islanders had recently seen Womenga acting in a demented manner. Such affidavits were necessary in order to conduct a sanity hearing away from her home. Maurice went to the teacher's house, but no affidavits had been prepared, for the radio reception had been so poor in the previous few days that Mr. Carlson had not understood the instructions. Hastily Maurice secured three brief signed statements.

The return trip was made without mishap. There was a second passenger, a young neighbor, Jacob Ahkinga. When Womenga first heard of the trip, she had refused to come, but Jacob told her they both were going to see the doctor, and that the doctor would help her to sleep. He felt guilty, he said to me later, to lie to her. He had known her since he was a boy, and he spoke of her with affection. He implied that he did not think she should have been brought to Nome. He said there had always been times when she "talked funny"—her sisters did too, periodically; but he said that she never had harmed anybody, and that she was a tireless worker. He intimated that among the stepchildren, one was antagonistic to her.

On the plane Womenga was quiet, sitting beside her young friend and from time to time talking with him. The plane was met by a taxi, and a few minutes later Womenga was in a locked cell.

I had been following the case without expecting to be involved in it. But a few days later a deputy marshal brought a summons:

"To Sally Carrighar, Greeting: You are hereby commanded to be and appear in the United States Commissioner's Court at . . . Nome, Alaska . . . at the hour of 2:00 o'clock p.m. on the 12th day of January 1954 for service as a juror in the matter of the inquiry into the mental condition of Womenga K. Iyapana. Hereof fail not." The quaint language pointed up the rather intense, almost old-fashioned sincerity with which this case was to be examined. The jurors in such a hearing are not chosen by lot; they were personally selected by Mrs. Helen Bochman, the commissioner, and besides myself included Mrs. Emily Boucher, publisher of the *Nome Nugget*; Mrs. Della Goshaw, a housewife; Mr. Boyd Harwood, druggist; Mr. G. R. Jackson, the Nome banker; and Mr. Mike Walsh, a mining executive. It was a jury experienced in far-Northern matters, for I was the only one who had not lived in Alaska for decades.

On January 12 we assembled in the Nome courtroom. A new federal building is planned; it will be more modern, but the courtroom will not have a more homely dignity than the present high-ceilinged room, paneled in golden oak, where the judge sits in his high oaken box and the jury in theirs. The spectators watch from the pewlike benches.

The commissioner acted as judge, and the six jurors waited on the front bench till she motioned for us to enter the jury box. As we did so, the prisoner—for she was that—was brought in and led to the seat we had vacated; to make room for her, someone had to remove my coat from the bench. The change of places was slightly startling. It made us realize our good fortune that the arrangement was not reversed. Perhaps now, subconsciously, we were even more anxious to do what was right for Womenga.

Four people accompanied her, a deputy marshal, a jail matron, another prisoner who was to be a witness, and Mrs. Emma Willoya, a reputable Eskimo woman employed by the court, like an attorney, to see that Womenga was given justice. These are all rather tall. Among them, there, was the small defenseless figure of the accused, neat and clean in a fresh pink house dress with one empty sleeve. Her hair was cut in a tapering bob, with long bangs smoothly brushed to the sides.

I was almost reluctant to look at her face, but I needn't have dreaded it, for it aroused only sympathy. It was a tragic face, so pale it was almost green-white, and with muscles as limp as though they were drained of every capacity to express anything except suffering. "She is not sane," I thought, till I noticed her eyes— every juror was struck by them, as we found during our later discussion. They were calm, clear, knowing eyes, and they remained so throughout the session. They seemed to show that she understood why she was in this room and what could come out of the hearing. She could not know what we were saying, in our strange tongue—and that seemed rude of us—but could she be conscious of undercurrents the rest of us were not aware of? Intuitive feeling is characteristic of primitive people, and with it goes a detached and observant look. Womenga had it.

With sedateness but a kind of humane informality, Mrs. Bochman opened the hearing. She first read the statements that Maurice Kelliher had secured on the island.

> *James Iyapana, a stepson:* "*I have seen Womenga Iyapana acting crazy since November 1953. She has gone outdoors without her parka and complained of the cold. She has been talking funny.*"

> *Joseph Iyahuk, a neighbor:* "*I have seen Womenga Iyapana acting crazy since November. She talks a lot of silly talk. She has had to be watched so she would not harm herself.*"

> *Gerald F. Carlson, the teacher:* "*I have had numerous requests by the Iyapana family to administer sedatives to enable the patient, Womenga Iyapana, to sleep. She has gone for as much as two days without sleep. I have been informed that she talks funny.*"

We jurors were not as restrained as we might have been; after Mrs. Bochman had read the affidavits, there were murmurs of dissatisfaction because of the sketchiness and the generalities.

The next witness called was Mr. Williams, who gave a résumé of the radio conversations. He reported the same three complaints: that Womenga was said to talk like a crazy person; that she did not sleep well, which was a hardship on her family because someone sat up with her; and that she went out of doors without wearing her parki. It had been said, Mr. Williams continued in a subdued and reticent voice, that once she had gone out with no clothes on at all. Mrs. Bochman informed us that we could question Mr. Williams, and one of the jurors asked whether Womenga actually had injured or threatened anyone. He did not have anything definite to report on that.

Our physician at Nome was the next one to take the stand. He testified that he had examined Womenga, that she had had schizophrenic tendencies at some time in the past, but at present he did not consider that her mental condition warranted placing her in an institution. He stressed the fact that she came from a primitive and uncomplicated environment, but a very difficult one. I asked him if he would consider Womenga likely to be a menace to people around her, and he said no.

The prisoner who was to be a witness is a Nome Eskimo who was serving a sentence for drunk and disorderly conduct. She told how Womenga would rush for the door every time that she had a chance. She also described how Womenga climbed up the bars of her cell—with her single arm; how she scrambled all over it.

There were no other witnesses, but we were to be allowed to question Womenga. The interpreter, Mrs. Oumauk (she has since remarried and is now Mrs. George Washington), came forward and sat at Womenga's side. She was a plump little native, carefully dressed and with trim gray hair. She was sworn to interpret truthfully.

Mrs. Bochman asked the first question: would Womenga tell us more about how she felt when she was sick? Mrs. Oumauk phrased it in Eskimo, while Womenga turned her dark eyes to the interpreter's face and listened, concentrating on what was said. Before she answered she hesitated, now as she did each time, as though considering carefully what she would say. And then she began to talk, in an appealing, sad, quiet voice.

Mrs. Oumauk, who speaks good if not perfect English, reported: "She say she feels light. When she feels light, she wants to get out, she wants to go away quick. At the same time she feels light, she always has sounds in her chest, on both sides. That's when she can't sleep, too." Did Womenga know she'd been acting bad in the prison upstairs, Mrs. Bochman asked. The two Eskimo women conferred. Yes, Mrs. Oumauk said, she knew. But the noise in the jail kept her from sleeping, the other prisoners always walking, walking on the bare floor. Even after the footsteps stopped she could hear them, and then she would feel light and it was terrible that she could not escape. Mrs. Bochman asked why, when she was on the island, she had gone outside in the cold with no parki on. Mrs. Oumauk said that Womenga told her, "because she get sweat."

Now the jury might have their turn. Mrs. Boucher began; she asked, "Does Womenga know why she is here?" Womenga replied, with a hand touching her chest, "because of her lights." I inquired whether Womenga remembered going to Morningside Hospital in the past. Mrs. Oumauk informed us she did remember. Were the people there kind to her? Womenga replied that, yes, they were kind. It had occurred to me that perhaps she was wishing to go again, that she might be faking this illness in order to be returned to the hospital. I asked whether she had enjoyed the plane ride. She seemed puzzled by that. Did she want to go to the States, did she want to go back to the hospital? Her response was brief; she asked, "Would it be forever?"

Would it indeed be forever if we committed Womenga to Morningside now? Would this be the last time? Transportation for a patient and guards costs almost $1,000. If Womenga were to continue to have her lapses, it might appear cheaper to keep her in Oregon for the rest of her life—if, that is, there were no way that she could be given care in Alaska. But now she was talking again, in a distressed, tragic voice. "She would not want to leave her native people forever," said Mrs. Oumauk.

Possibly thinking of the alternative, one of the jurors asked what Womenga did with her time when at home on the island. She told us about her cooking and cleaning and sewing, her liking for work, and then she broke suddenly into her protest: "If I could I would squeeze out between the bars, then I would make myself small and slip through the little crack under the door. Because I would rather be outside, even if people would tear me to pieces, than locked up in that cell."

Having lived in an Eskimo village, I was remembering the peacefulness and the silence: no cars or trucks of course, and no shouts and no yelling. Womenga's ears would be tuned to that silence, broken in winter only by winds brushing over the mountainside and in summer by cries of the sea birds, and waves sucking and ploshing along the rocks—all errant and casual sounds. They do not demand of anyone that he do anything, even listen.

I was remembering that the Eskimos live impulsively. They come in and go out, rest, get up, work, or amuse themselves as they feel moved; follow no routine, have no sense of time, it seems, and in jail, where their whole day is scheduled, the loss of their free way is so nearly unbearable that they are treated rather well otherwise. But apparently nothing, not good meals and warmth and radio music, could compensate for the regularity and the noise for Womenga, who had committed no crime. At Morningside too she would be confined.

No one had any more questions, and Mrs. Bochman dismissed the court. When the room was cleared, the six of us gathered around a table below the judge's stand. "Your decision will not be easy," said Mrs. Bochman, and left.

Mr. Walsh commented, first, that we were not to judge whether Womenga was sane intermittently, nothing concerning her past mental condition, only whether she was sane now; second, that we had two kinds of evidence, what we had learned from others and what was indicated by Womenga's behavior during the hearing. It took but one quick unanimous vote to decide that her words and manner in court had not proved her to be demented.

It was a little strange for her to say she felt light, or had lights. But could her lights be the bright spots before the eyes that come with some headaches? She might also have meant the dizziness that we sometimes describe as lightheadedness. Her phrase, anyway, was poetic, and so was her statement that she would make herself small if she could, and slip under the door. Writers say things like that, or at least they would like to. I offered the thought that maybe Womenga's colorful talk was the evidence on which her neighbors decided that she was crazy. She talked funny— funny by whose standards? To some people, I know, I talk funny, while to me others talk very funny indeed. Perhaps on the island Womenga had been describing her far-off Siberian childhood; maybe she was relating nightmares. Maybe the things she said were funny only in view of the undelivered Christmas packages. They did arrive, on the plane that was sent for Womenga.

We dismissed her wild actions while she was in jail, even the fact that she climbed up the bars of her cell. Regarding that, someone recalled that a resident of her perpendicular island would be more accustomed to climb than to walk. All the accusations boiled down, in the end, to the fact that she went out of doors with no parki on, and once with no clothes on at all. Northern houses are so well sealed, to keep out the cold, that they become very warm and sometimes suddenly seem unbearably stuffy. In the most frigid weather I have often stepped out with no coat to snatch a quick breath of air. Probably all of us had. But no clothes at all? That was a truly irrational act—or was it? We all understood that the older Eskimos were not self-conscious about nakedness. It was not immoral to them, it was simply of no significance. Especially in Siberia, travelers had found that the natives, accustomed to wear only fur clothing, might take it all off when they entered a dwelling. For Womenga, who had grown up in Siberia, would that be crazy? She was old, or soon would be. Perhaps she was reverting to childhood ways. That was nothing to lock her up for. We decided to judge her sane.

To this verdict we added a recommendation. It seemed certain Womenga was not very stable, and her health obviously needed building up. Let her be kept in Nome for a while. Let her be boarded with some quiet, kindly family. Let the doctor prescribe a nutritious diet and, observing her over a period of time, discover her real condition. We suggested that program, which would cost very much less than to send her to Oregon. Since she was here in Nome without family or money, some help must be given her, and it surely would. The jurors went home feeling satisfied that this elderly primitive Eskimo, with her terrible difficulties, was having humane and fair treatment. Yet, as sometimes does happen, a distant government agency had the last word in Womenga's case.

It was not easy to find the right foster home for her. Some families were afraid of her. One did take her, but they had eight young children and more confusion than she could stand. Then Nome's informal and practical way of doing things went to work. It was decided that Womenga could receive the same care as the men with DT's. They are not insane, except temporarily, but the hospital has no facilities for them, and so they are put in jail, treated kindly, and when they recover they are released without coming to trial. It was explained to Womenga that she would go back to prison, but only because that was a place to be warm and fed. The well-behaved prisoners are not locked in their cells. The women can spend their time in a central room, sewing, talking, listening to the radio. Womenga could be there too. She was admitted to jail on a technical charge.

The prospect of being a prisoner again was very disturbing to her, and for a few days at the start Womenga was difficult. Later she quieted down. A week passed, and two weeks. The matrons could manage her. One told me they liked her. She was so eager to work that when all the tasks had been finished, she continued to dust.

The federal jail operates under the Bureau of Prisons at Washington. Its director in Nome was a comparative newcomer in the North. There is a glass panel between his office and the quarters of women inmates. Through this window he watched the prisoner who did not technically belong in his jail. The job of the daytime matron had been abolished, in spite of the fact that—contrary to regulations—the female prisoners were left with no female guard for a part of each day. And one-armed Womenga did need assistance at times. The female guard who had left might have had to be reinstated. Womenga was endangering an economy program.

We heard suddenly that she was gone. The jailer was also gone, and all we could learn at Nome was that they had departed for Anchorage. I was going to Anchorage soon myself, and two or three of the other jurors asked me to find out what had happened to our Womenga.

By the time I arrived there, she was at Morningside Hospital. The details of her speedy commitment and transportation to Oregon were as follows.

Womenga, in custody of the Nome jailer, arrived in Anchorage at six o'clock Monday evening, February 8. A second sanity hearing took place at one o'clock the next day. According to law, a warrant may be issued for a person's arrest "if he is insane and at large in the commissioner's district." Womenga was not at large in the district of the Anchorage commissioner. But the warrant stated that she "for some time prior to the present is an insane person within the Anchorage Precinct." The description would seem to imply that she was a resident, but the "some time" was less than 18 hours.

After the warrant was issued, a jury had to be chosen, and the six jurors notified to appear in court. Preceding the issuance of the warrant, a complaint had to be made. The complaint was signed by a psychiatrist in the employ of the Territorial Department of Health. If he examined Womenga, it could not have been very thoroughly, during that hurried morning. He had not been in Alaska long and could hardly know, in anything like detail, the life and customs of the Siberian Eskimos. And no interpreter could be found in Anchorage who understood the Diomede dialect.

I was curious as to the evidence. The files in a case like this are public property, and I asked for Womenga's file in the office of the Anchorage U.S. commissioner. It contained no report by the psychiatrist, other than the complaint. As to her past behavior or her condition at home there were no affidavits, no signed statements. The only information of that kind the jury heard was presented in court by one witness, the Nome jailer. Indeed, no one else was there who could furnish facts as to her history, and no record was made, or at least was kept, of the statements the jailer made.

After the jury brought in their verdict, the United States marshal at Anchorage had no choice but to send Womenga to Morningside Hospital. That he did, with two guards, a trip that cost about $800. I talked to him, and learned that the money came out of his budget for handling bona-fide Anchorage matters. He complained of this drain on his limited funds.

The bald fact seemed to be that Womenga was railroaded into an institution. She might be insane at times. Until Alaska has its own psychiatric hospital, Morningside might be the best available place for her. We of the Nome jury did not think so, and residents of the patient's precinct were the proper ones to decide.

Womenga is still, in 1958, at Morningside—considered rational by the staff there but not well enough physically to be sent back to Alaska unless there is assurance that care will be provided for her. As her health declines it becomes more doubtful that she will find her own people again, more certain that this illegal commitment will indeed be forever.

On a frontier like Alaska "the law" is viewed somewhat liberally. It is seen in its primary meaning, of neighbors and friends taking hold of a situation when something goes wrong. One of the stead-

iest men in Nome says he doesn't believe in laws at all; he thinks
every citizen ought to carry a gun and use it when justified—
"Pretty soon all the hoodlums would be disposed of," he says,
forgetting that the hoodlums might be the first on the draw. In
Nome someone was stealing the oil from my outdoor tank. When
I went to the chief of police, he said: "You keep a watch out for
the thief yourself, but remember, he wouldn't be taking the oil
if he could afford to buy it. He's probably cold."

In regard to midwinter murders the attitude is decidedly
lenient. For most people have had a touch of that madness called
"cabin fever." They know how distorted a situation can seem after
one has been confined for several months by the arctic cold. Last
winter in Fairbanks there were six rather dreadful killings. And
the judge was so tolerant in his sentences that there was a saying
in town: "If you are going to shoot somebody, be sure he isn't
standing in front of a moose, because if the bullet goes through
and kills the moose, then you've had it!"

In this civic climate it didn't seem out of the way for Womenga
to be boarded at the Nome jail without any charge against her.
Her stay there was not strictly legal, but important parts of her
Anchorage hearing were not legal either. The law was waived at
Nome for Womenga's sake—at Anchorage for the convenience
of officials in the Bureau of Prisons.

It is only on humane grounds that Northerners think the ir-
regularities may be justified.

20

Closing Night

WHAT CLOSES, at midnight on some spring date about April first, is the chance to estimate at what day, hour, and minute a small patch of ice on the Tanana River in front of the town of Nenana, Alaska, will start to move downstream. Between closing night and April 20, the earliest that the ice has gone out, a post painted in black and white stripes will be erected out there on the ice and connected by wire to a clock in the watchmen's shack on the riverbank. The clock will stop when the pylon has drifted about 100 feet. And then radio telegraph will carry the news all over the continent, but especially to the more than 100,000 people (in 1951, 150,000) who will have registered guesses.

This event is of course the famous Ice Classic, and it is more than a guessing contest for its own sake, such as estimating the number of beans in a jar. Intrinsically no one cares how many beans, but the date when the ice goes out would be newsworthy in any event, for that is the time when Northerners switch to a new way of living. Give the rivers a few days to sweep their loads of ice to the sea, then the barges can begin delivering much-needed freight to the river villages; the uncounted Alaskans who own big and little boats can take off for their summer camps and the wilderness fishing-grounds; the natives can put out their fish wheels and start hauling in salmon. The rivers are highways in this

Northern territory which has so few roads, and the date when we can begin using them is probably the most welcome day in the year.

The guessing is not a mere matter of chance, either, because natural laws regulate the break-up, and if one were observant enough it almost should be possible to predict the day accurately. The break-up depends less on the weather at the immediate time than on the kind of winter it's been. The ice at Nenana will be perhaps thirty or forty inches thick on the first of April. It will be frozen tight to the banks. As the river starts to rise, then, the ice breaks along the edges, and the more water under it, the more turbulent the stream and the more quickly the ice will crack. If it has been a mild and "dry" winter, the break-up often is late, because there isn't enough snow to make a sudden, tremendous run-off.

The Tanana (pronounced *"Tan*-a-naw") is the chief tributary of the Yukon, and its headwaters are over on the Canadian border. As the important date draws near and the ice buckles and channels open, *cheechakos* talk about the temperature and wind at Nenana (pronounced "Nee-*nan*-ah"), but the old-timers tell them that the time of the break-up depends on "what is happening hundreds of miles away." It depends not only on the amount of run-off, but on how fast the snow melts on the banks of the headwaters. If a warm spell should cause flash floods up there in the mountains, the water would pick up a lot of silt, and extra silt in the river can gnaw the underside of the ice away very fast. The ice in the Tanana has been known to lose fifteen inches of thickness a day because the water beneath it carried a sudden load of abrasives. All these factors are discussed with absorbed interest through March, as Alaskans work out the times of their guesses.

The advice of the old-timers is sought, especially of river men, and the talk goes on everywhere. Headquarters for the excitement, however, is the lobby of the Nordale Hotel in Fairbanks. It is not excitement, exactly, until closing night. Before then it is more a dreamy preoccupation, with everyone trying to be, or at least feel

like, an oracle. But on closing night the interest becomes electric.
In an alcove off the lobby, amid flowers and a flurry of souvenirs—
calendars, an Alaska flag, figurines, plaques, one of Josephine
Crumrine's talented paintings of huskies, and a discarded scarf
or two—sits Fairbanks's much loved Eva McGown, presiding
over the wishing wells. These are two large tin cans, painted red,
with slots in the top. Eva gives out the little white cards on which
the guesses are registered, and her Irish effervescence is the perfect
expression of what everyone else is feeling.

Exactly at midnight Eva will seal the cans. All evening people
drop in, more as midnight approaches, till the gathering seems
like a party, held for old-time Alaskans. Newcomers aren't there,
nor the military, although they would be welcome. The Ice Classic
belongs most to those who know personally what the break-up
means, those who have lived through ten to fifty arctic winters, and
each time have experienced the release from tension that comes
in the spring. Although most Alaskans prefer winter to summer,
fall is a time of quieter anticipation. Spring is indeed a freeing of
energies, and in the Nordale lobby on closing night buoyant
spirits swell up like the flood soon to swell the river.

Alaska has hotels more luxurious than the Nordale, but Alaskans
know what they want, and they congregate here as they do at the
Anchorage Hotel in Anchorage, and the New Washington in
Seattle. This is just the right atmosphere for their kind of people,
they think—no self-consciousness and no swank, year after year the
same, and always keyed to the mood of Northerners. You come
in from the bush or back from the States, and you will be known
here, and however crowded the hotel is, there will be room for you.

It is told that once, when only one room was available, a Stateside governor and a sourdough from the hills walked up to the desk
at the same time and the sourdough "of course" got the room.
The men behind the desk are old-timers themselves: Arne Lee,
the manager, and the trio who share the shifts: Jim Wood, Frank
Nigro, and Ole Iverson. Their greeting will be a real welcome but
not effusive; it will be understated a little. It is better for guests

if they too can fit into the casual atmosphere. I have seen travelers turned away when there were vacant rooms, and not through ill-temper. It was just that the Nordale Hotel was not the right place for their kind of egos.

And here comes Eva—one always knows when she is coming, by the lilting voice of this pretty colleen with white hair and fresh, delicate skin. As she swings through the lobby, high heels a-click, the old-timers' eyes follow her with affection, for she is a friend to all of them—and to newcomers too. Eva McGown is the official city hostess of Fairbanks, who finds rooms for the surplus of visitors when hotels are full, and her kind Irish heart prompts her to do much more than that when it is needed. A girl came to Fairbanks to marry her GI fiancé, only to find that he had been sent away on manoeuvers. Eva took charge and, unknown to the girl, arranged a big church wedding for the time when the boy returned. The guests were all friends of Eva's, and the flowers came from their gardens. Eva has been one of the celebrities on the TV *This Is Your Life* program.

E. J. Rusing, one of the bankers of Fairbanks, is sure to come into the Nordale on closing night, and that probably will be one of the times when he says, as he often does, "Aren't we illogical? We live in the North because we like the simplicity and rugged-ness, and we're destroying the frontier atmosphere just as fast as we can."

He will smile when he says it, for he smiles much of the time, not to make an effect, it seems, but only because he is deeply enjoying life. His bank, too, has an affable air, with oil paintings lining the walls and a huge Kodiak bear mounted in a front corner behind a row of low plants. One can enter the bank with as easy a mind as one enters a hardware store.

Rusing was reared in Alaska and is one of those most active in trying to turn the North into a well-rounded area. He is working on plans for a 10,000-acre wheat ranch near Fairbanks; and as soon as legislation permits, his bank plans to expand into the native Alaska villages. At that point banking becomes sociology, for one of the greatest needs among the Indians and Eskimos is a chance to handle their money, especially to save it, in normal ways. Rusing is now chairman of the Territorial Banking Board. He made the point at a recent bankers' convention that the Alaska Railroad keeps its account, totaling up to $20,000,000, in Washington, D.C., whereas it would seem that Alaskans, who provide the revenue for the railroad, should have the privilege of banking its funds.

For most Northerners, however, Alaska does not yet mean banks and large farming and business developments as much as it does country, and people, and the things people do more than the things they have.

It is people like Bob and Olivia Westcott and the life they lead. The Westcotts' interest is dogs and dog racing, and as they walk through the lobby on closing night, they have especially warm greetings for most of the sourdoughs, for the sourdoughs too were mushers.

The Westcotts grew up in a small town in Missouri. Bob majored in journalism at the University of Missouri and became the youngest newspaper editor in the state. That career ended abruptly when a member of the school board was thrown in jail and Bob reported the fact, although Bob's sister taught in the local school. The next year she taught somewhere else and Bob had decided that editing wasn't for him. He now owns one of the largest photo-processing plants in Alaska.

Bob has wide-set eyes and a quick but reticent smile. Libby is one of those tiny girls, as feminine as a pink bow, who have a wonderful way with animals. At the time she was married, Libby was training and gaiting saddle horses. When Bob proposed, he added one special condition: that she agree to love, honor, and obey, *and never complain about how many dogs he had*. He had fourteen at the time, not because he raised dogs to sell— he just liked them. He still does, and so does Libby. She found it easy to switch from horses.

For a few years after the Westcotts came to Fairbanks, in 1946, they kept a kennel of more than 100 dogs. "But that's too many," Libby says, "because it takes so much time to feed them that you don't have time to work them." To "work dogs" means to hitch them up to a sled and take off over the beautiful snowy landscape. Ostensibly you are training the dogs to race, and the Westcotts are good at that; Bob came in first the second time that he ever entered a team, and in each Winter Carnival Libby is up there close to the top. But it isn't the winning that interests either one as much as the pleasure of riding the sled behind spirited dogs.

The Westcotts are two of the most active members in the Fairbanks Dog Mushers' Association, the group that is most responsible for the Winter Carnival every March. The Carnival is just over at the time the Ice Classic guesses are sealed, and the talk around Eva's desk is as likely to turn to dog racing as to ice.

In the Carnival are included a curling tournament, fancy ice skating, an art show, a photo contest, dancing by Eskimos brought from the coast, and other activities, but no event can compete with the North American Championship Sled Dog Derby. For women the races consist of two twenty-mile heats, run on consecutive days. For men an extra thirty-mile heat is added. The 1957 winner was Bergman Sam, a young Indian from the trapping village of Huslia, with a total elapsed time of 4:48:26 over seventy miles of a sloppy and muddy trail. As a boy Bergman Sam spent four years in the hospital with a tubercular spine, and he still has a steel plate in his back. The drivers of racing teams run more than they ride, but Sam paced himself, he said, and when the last race was over he did not drop onto his sled dramatically as some of the racers do; he finished with seeming ease and faced the cameramen with a slight, remote smile. The 1956 winner was Jim Huntington, a cousin of Sam's, and forty-one years old. At the end of that Derby it was found that Huntington had infectious hepatitis when he ran, and yet he pushed himself into first place. Stamina must be a family trait.

To win, as Bob Westcott says, takes everything that a man

and each of his dogs can give. Teams and drivers come to the Derby from all over Northern Alaska: Eskimos, Indians, and white men, and it is usually a native who takes the cup. The races are very close. One year the top eight finished, after the three-day heats, within seconds of one another.

The races start and end on the snow-covered Creamer's Field, in summer a wide, spacious dairy farm within a mile of the center of Fairbanks. While the races are being run, members of the Midnight Sun Sky-Divers, a club of parajumpers, drop from planes overhead, and there are skijoring contests, dog-sled rides for spectators, an Eskimo skin-toss, and food and coffee. But the dogs are the stars, quite as much as the men—the dogs who don't know about showmanship, they just try terribly hard to run as fast as the driver wants them to. Their effort is touching, and most of the thousands who watch are dog-lovers anyway. Spectators are allowed in the space at the end of the chute where the handlers hitch up the dogs, and they pet them and endlessly photograph them, and over the whole affair there is a gentleness rare in competitive sports.

Team-leaders are known by name, and though the Westcotts' famed leader, Chena, is too old to race now, he often is spoken of. Part wolf, he is perhaps the most celebrated leader of modern racing—a dog with such authority in his nature that he could maintain peace at the Westcotts' kennel even when it included over 100 dogs. Other strong leaders are still content to run behind Chena, and no team ever disputes his turn on a trail. The Westcotts have developed a blue-eyed strain of pure huskies. They sell a few dogs and board a few, but they don't want to make money, only to try to help pay for the dog food.

The Dog Mushers' Association has about forty members, half of whom like to race. Others own teams, sometimes of as few as three to five dogs, with no purpose except that of getting out on the trail on a winter day. Bob Westcott says, "Having three to five dogs is no chore, and no more expensive than partying, and a lot healthier." Dogs are used in the bush for trapping, and races are held in the smaller towns. But many dog teams are kept for diversion only, and there is no question but that the average Northerner rates working a team of dogs as his favorite sport.

Closing night is preceded by a long day's work for Eva. Most people wait till the final day, or near it, to estimate when the ice will go out. They want to see if there is going to be much more snow—called water by those who are thinking about the break-up.

On most years Eva does not leave her desk and the guarding of those red tin boxes all day. Someone brings her a cup of coffee and piece of pie occasionally. But by mid-evening she needs a short rest, and the one who relieves her is likely to be her good friend Mrs. Lydia Fohn-Hansen.

Mrs. Fohn-Hanson has made an interesting career for herself—that of expert in wilderness housekeeping. Born in Iowa, where she had her college home-economics training, in 1925 she came to teach at the young University of Alaska. Two years later she married Hans Christian Fohn-Hansen, a miner. Her own experience showed her that most pioneers need help with the problems of meals while camping, trapping, prospecting, homesteading, or just "living out on the creeks" for a season. Some of the special problems are the transporting of food, keeping it without refrigeration, cooking it on stoves often improvised out of tin cans—and yet having meals that taste good and satisfy ravenous outdoor appetites.

Mrs. Fohn-Hansen helped to organize a U.S. Department of Agriculture co-operative extension program; she has written nearly 500 bulletins, circulars, and project books for 4-H Club members. These are packed with practical information, such as the fact that vinegar, hard to transport, can be doubled in volume at the camp end by diluting with water and adding brown sugar, which ferments to form acid. After she explains how to make soap, using such wilderness materials as reindeer fat and seal oil, she tells how to reclaim the batch if the inexperienced soap-cook finds that her product is crumbly or greasy.

Would anyone like to know how to make jellied moose's muffle, or nose? Mrs. Fohn-Hansen tells you to parboil it for forty-five minutes, cool, scrub away the hairs, and wash. Boil gently in fresh water with onion, a little garlic, and pickling spices. Cool overnight. There will be two kinds of meat: the bulb of the nose, which will be white, and dark strips along the bone and jowls. Slice thin and pack in jars, covering with the juice, which will jell.

A friendly woman with a quiet helpful manner, Mrs. Fohn-Hansen has hundreds of grateful Alaskans as friends. She is a widow now, but she keeps house in Fairbanks where, with the city's modern conveniences, it means nothing to her to cope with sub-sub-zero temperatures. She is a fellow of the Arctic Institute of North America (only six women hold that honor) and in 1957 was given the superior-service award of the U.S. Department of Agriculture.

The Nordale lobby is ringed with sofas and big easy chairs. In a fireplace at one end a lazy fire smolders even as late as the first of April. It is flanked by a television set. Since the set was installed the lounge is usually rather dark, but on closing night all the lights are up, and no one is watching the musical-comedy stars capering on the screen.

Many men from the bush have come into town and have gathered here, men for whom weather and ice and rivers have been their lifelong business. One is Gus Benson of Manley Hot Springs, who grows forty-two-pound watermelons, and twenty-pound Hubbard squashes, and cucumbers in six weeks "from seed to eating," in earth warmed gratuitously by nature's springs. Also sure to be present is Charlie Wilson, retired from his job as engineer on the Alaska Railroad, and now a member of the Territorial Road Commission. He looks frail, but you won't see any eyes keener, or kinder, than Charlie's blue eyes in the younger faces.

Through this crowd of sourdoughs, and stopping for hand-shakes, come Dr. Arthur Schaible and his wife, Druska. Dr. Schaible is formal in a black Homburg, and, since they have just left a dinner party, Druska wears an imported gown of royal red velvet, topped by a silver mink cape, and a little tiara of pearls on her ash-blond hair. These are people whose very movements show them to be connoisseurs in most choices they make, and yet they are at home on the edge of the arctic, and this is the place they prefer to live. The social life here in Fairbanks is often, in fact, quite cosmopolitan. A few years ago two or three hosts combined efforts to give a Hawaiian dinner. They brought from Honolulu, by air, all the food, and an orchestra, and a group of Hawaiian dancers.

Dr. Schaible and his partner, Dr. Paul Haggland, have the oldest clinic in Alaska, established in 1932 by Dr. F. B. Gillespie. With a medical and surgical staff of at least six specialists, the clinic treats patients from all over the North. Probably no two men, therefore, know more about arctic life, its hazards and all the details of its difficulties, than Dr. Schaible and Dr. Haggland.

There is nothing rigid about the clinic. Both partners will treat anybody for almost anything, but Dr. Schaible is said with affection to be "a wonderful belly surgeon," while Dr. Haggland, an orthopedic specialist, is so skilled that several times he has constructed workable elbows from splinters of bone picked up off a dirty street. Dr. Haggland is a free-wheeler, intuitive in his contacts with patients; Dr. Schaible has an intense, almost a researcher's absorption in every medical problem that comes to him. His hands, now, as he fills out his Ice Classic cards, and later tamps tobacco into a pipe, have a touch so fine that they could be splicing a nerve.

Dr. Schaible was born in South Africa, of a missionary father and an English mother. When he was fourteen the family moved to Michigan, and the boy, who already knew that he wanted to be a physician, began preparing to take his degree at Northwestern University. His internship was followed by a year at Walter Reed Hospital, but he found that the military set-up was not what he liked and he volunteered to take over the management of an Indian Bureau hospital at the little town of Tanana on the Yukon River. For several years he not only ran the hospital but traveled vast distances up and down the Yukon, ministering to the native villages. Such a practice of course had disadvantages, and during World War II he moved to Fairbanks and joined Dr. Haggland as partner.

His wife, Druska, is a small, delicate-featured woman with a manner as exquisite as her face. Very logically, it seems, she is married to this man of precise and civilized talents. And yet— the kind of surprise that is typical of Alaska—she is the capable head of the biology department at the University of Alaska, and is part-owner of a profitable baby shop. She was born in Antibes, France, of an English artist father and a mother of aristocratic Dutch and Russian ancestry. When Druska's mother was widowed she came to America, where she met and married one of the early deans at the University of Alaska. Druska by then was teaching, specializing in biological sciences, and she too came to the university. She is a gay and generous person. To hear of anyone needing help is enough to inspire her to give it—always inconspicuously, for she belongs to the noble tradition that prompts the finest courtesies.

Dr. Schaible is one of the more accomplished members of the Fairbanks Curling Club, and both Schaibles are hi-fi fans: many-sided people and examples of what everyone hopes will be the more cultured society that the North is developing.[1]

No Alaskans do more, and in a practical way, to bring it about than the David Adlers, who are owners of the oldest bookstore in the Territory. David walks with a cane because of arthritic difficulties, but his mind is alert and agile, as one can surmise from the way his eyes dart from face to face. His wife seems a little reluctant to be here; perhaps she thinks guessing on river ice a bit foolish, or perhaps this is only her manner, which is always sedate —so reserved, it is unexpected to hear that she was born in Wales, reared in the midwest states, and set out when she was grown to see the world via a teaching career. Her first stop was Montana,

[1] Druska Schaible perished in a fire at Fairbanks during the winter of 1957–58.

Alaska her second. She had planned to go on to the Philippines, but she liked Fairbanks, where she taught high-school English, and then in 1936 she married and gave up her ambition to travel farther.

Many Alaskans, like this group at the Nordale, have come from the earth's distant corners, and it always seems interesting to know what has brought them so far. Very rarely does one meet a white inhabitant born here, and in the process of getting acquainted the question is apt to arise: "And why did *you* come to the North?" Many say that they came to join an older brother, or uncle, or friend. David Adler was one of the younger brothers.

He was born in New York. As a young man his hobby was magic. By the time of the First World War he was giving public performances, as he did for the soldiers in France. During the war he was in the remount service, replacing cavalry horses with fresh mounts. In the early twenties he came to Alaska and, like most pioneers of the time, "did any and every kind of work" until his own longing for books suggested that others on the frontier needed a bookstore. In 1929, therefore, he went into the book business.

The Adlers never have sold any comic books or cheap paper-backed fiction, and they stock—and sell—an amount of poetry that seems surprising on a frontier: not only the standard poets, Byron, Shelley and Keats, but moderns like e. e. cummings. Shakespeare moves well, right along with the modern fiction and nonfiction that is being discussed in reviews at the moment. Perhaps few bookstores would carry as large a proportion of technical titles. In the North, where in so many situations you do it yourself or it isn't done, there is a big demand for books on electrical wiring, plumbing, carpentry, as well as the more complex subjects like electronics and engineering. Dave Adler's particular interests are heraldry now, and ancient Chinese history and literature. It is fairly certain that the copy of *Burke's Peerage* which he keeps within reach of his easy chair is the only copy in Fairbanks of that directory to the English aristocrats.

In this distant and still very primitive land it is fascinating to see the grassroots urge to create a richer cultural life. Fairbanks people can hear four concerts with imported artists each winter, but no lecture series, and no troops of actors come with new or old plays. A circus visited Fairbanks once, but went broke here. Fairbanks has a public library but no art museums. The two movie theatres and two radio and two television stations bring in filmed and recorded shows. Most periodicals are on sale. Some years ago the National Geographical Society reported that membership, in proportion to population, was higher in Alaska than anywhere else in the world.

Alaskans are well informed about current happenings—but that is not enough. They want the stimulation of great art and thought. If no one brings it to them, they can find it themselves, however, and that is what they do. Great Books discussion groups, clusters of people listening to fine music together, reading plays, and staging their own theatrical productions don't feel themselves cut off from cultural sources. Fairbanks has two art associations, and a camera club. Folk dancing, ceramics and other handicrafts have their practitioners, and the Toastmasters, both the men's and women's clubs, choose for their speeches subjects that seem imaginative and stimulating, to a degree that reflects perhaps the intellectual hunger.

One of the two organizers of the Golden Heart Toastmasters Club was Tom Miklautsch, a pharmacist, bachelor, and good-looking in a bright and warm, human way. Tom has a knack for sparking other people with the wish to exert themselves, and the Fairbanks Little Theatre coveted his several talents. They persuaded him to take one part in a play, in which he did so well that he was appointed director of the next play, *Outward Bound*. Tom now is deep in Little Theatre activities, and, knowing his eager creative mind, one is not surprised that he and his group are performing Shaw and see as their aim nothing less than a school of acting, with a playhouse of its own, bringing classics as well as amusing plays to the Fairbanks audience. The first step in this program is now under way, a junior little theatre for training children who will act in grown-up plays with adult members.

It is rather inspiring to hear Tom talk about Alaska, how this is the place where individuals can fulfill themselves because individuality is respected here. "In the North," he says, "people are conscious of others as people too, even while we are conscious that we're all standing together against the isolation and difficulties of Northern living." Tom himself is an individual, in the sense of a man who is reaching to find the talents that are innately his, and then developing them.

He was the only boy among seven sisters, born in North Dakota of Yugoslavian heritage. He took his degree in pharmacy at the University of Washington, and then found his way to Alaska—in his case, because he was offered work in Fairbanks.

The University of Alaska, whose campus is five miles from Fairbanks, had its start as a college of mines and agriculture and has now added courses in arts and letters and sciences. It is supported generously. The Legislature spends *more than half* of the total tax revenues of the Territory on education—surely commendable on a frontier where so much else is needed, and perhaps reflecting the fact that, up in this wilderness, college graduates form a larger percentage of the population than in the United States as a whole. The university receives money for everything that is essential, but Alaskans are still waiting for the time when it will catch up with their vision for it. New buildings are going up and are needed, but the administration puts so much emphasis on the physical plant that in the spring of 1957, when detailed plans for new dormitories were announced, the students themselves revolted, saying they wanted better teaching rather than mahogany paneling in their rooms.

Many young Northerners whose families can afford to send them go to the States for their college years. Of the University of Alaska students, ninety per cent work to pay for their training. They are a very inspiring group of young people, about 600 of them at present, who themselves spearhead the campaign for higher standards in the curriculum. Any time students will campaign for a chance to work harder, they certainly are entitled to the best kind of leadership.

Formally part of the university now is the world-renowned Geophysical Institute, which commenced in 1929 to study the Aurora with a grant from the Rockefeller Foundation and was expanded by the Congress of the United States twenty years later to include arctic research in other natural phenomena. The staff at the Institute have been among the most prominent scientists carrying on the investigations of the Geophysical Year.

The university also inherited the Navy's Arctic Research Center at Barrow.

Some very sound work is being done at the university by scientists who have affiliations with other educational institutions. Such is the collecting of fossils that spell out Alaska's past, which have been assembled since 1929 with the assistance of the Frick Laboratories of the American Museum of Natural History of New York. Almost all this important contribution has been made by one man, Dr. Otto Geist.

Many times fossils appear during the hydraulic washing-down of hillsides of frozen silt by gold-mining companies, especially the United States Smelting, Refining and Mining Company. As the huge streams of water are poured onto cliffs, bones of prehistoric animals and sometimes almost complete carcasses, including the hair and flesh, are exposed. Dr. Geist stands by to retrieve these fossils, which have appeared in such numbers that he knows by now what life in the Pleistocene period was like over most of Alaska.

Some of the animals here today were common then also: wolves, caribou, and moose. Bison were "most common," and many remains of wild horses are found. Others were musk oxen, lions, and saber-tooth tigers. Among the surprises are the giant sloth—and camels! But the fossils that most intrigue everyone are those of the mammoth and mastodon, huge elephants that are believed to have lost their lives when they walked into marshes and their enormous weight carried them down into a stratum of silt beneath. Mastodons browsed, whereas mammoths grazed—grass, sedges, and some of today's boreal flowers have been found in the mammoth stomachs. One whole head, intact, was shipped in ice to New York, where it may be seen at the Natural History Museum. The animals' ivory tusks, which sometimes grew ten feet long, are by now greenish in color. Beads, earrings, and other jewelry made of them are among the more valuable of Alaska souvenirs.

Before he started this work, Dr. Geist was an archeologist who worked with Froelich G. Rainey at St. Lawrence Island on the Eskimo artifacts there. They published their findings in *Archeological Excavations at Kukulik,* issued by the U.S. Government Printing Office, Washington, D.C.

Archeology was the special interest of Dr. Geist's father, who was principal of the school at Eiselfing, Germany, where Dr. Geist was born. Otto accompanied his father on some of his expeditions. There were fifteen children in the family, however, and it was necessary for some of them to strike out on their own. Otto came to Alaska—he, too, following a brother.

He has lectured on paleontology throughout Europe and has been made an honorary citizen of Eiselfing, as his father was also —the only two men to receive that award in the town's 800 years of history.

As he walks through the lobby with his somewhat rolling gait, no one would guess that Dr. Geist is so eminent. Instead of expecting homage of you, he is more likely to leave you with the memory of one of his stories, of which he has hundreds after all these years in a dramatic land. One concerns a keg of whisky that had been taken in some illegal operation in Southeastern Alaska and was going to be dumped. Otto asked for it as a preservative for specimens in the field, and the authorities gave it to him, but he had to add strychnine before they would release it. He took it to St. Lawrence Island, and warned his

Eskimo helper there that he must not drink the whisky, as it was poisoned. Otto had a bad time one day when the helper got drunk and confessed that he had been sampling the preservative. Otto warned him again, this time more strongly. When he was ready to leave the island however, he found the keg nearly empty. His helper was still alive, and when Otto got back to the mainland, he learned why: strychnine is not soluble in alcohol. It had all sunk to the bottom.

Just as cities like Rome, Athens, and Jerusalem are especially interesting because we can visualize their distant past, knowledge about the still more distant past of a wilderness gives it a new dimension. We look out on the Tanana Valley and marvel to think of exotic animals that we know were there once. The present Alaska wildlife is amazing enough, however, and three people who spend their winters on the outskirts of Fairbanks have made a career of showing that wildlife to residents and to Stateside travelers. In Mount McKinley National Park is the most extraordinary concentration of animals and birds on the continent. The wildlife cannot be hunted there, but for that very reason it can be seen more often and intimately. With the purpose of making it possible to live out among the animals, Morton and Virginia Wood and their friend Celia Hunter have established Camp Denali, ninety miles west of the Park Hotel.

The camp, consisting of cabins and tents and a central lodge and store, is on a ridge that faces the utterly white and unbelievable mass of The Great One. In the foreground is Wonder Lake, and a smaller pond is within the camp. Fishing for arctic grayling in Moose Creek and for Mackinaw trout in Wonder Lake are a sport that wouldn't seem tame to many, but more of the guests at the camp prefer to observe and photograph at close range animals that are almost legendary, they are so rare.

On the ninety-mile ride to the camp from the park entrance, through a wilderness untouched by man except for the road, these are some of the animals that stop to watch the cars go by and see the curious actions of human travelers getting out to take

pictures: grizzly bears, moose, lynx, wolves, foxes, marmots, the
miniature "rabbits" called conies; and pure-white Dall sheep look
down from their rocky ledges. Ptarmigan slip away from the road
and into the brush, but not in great haste, since they never have
heard a gun. Here wolverines are not the "almost extinct species"
they are called in the States; they are fairly common. Even the
mysterious and lovely golden plovers often are photographed.
All these creatures, their lives and habits, are described in *The
Wolves of Mount McKinley*, by Adolph Murie, and information
on how to trail them is given in Olaus J. Murie's *Field Guide to
Animal Tracks*.

One evening when he was driving alone from the Park Hotel
to the camp and his truck broke down, "Woody" got out and lay
on the moss at the side of the road to sleep. He woke up feeling
a warm, soft tongue licking his face. Knowing that frightened
animals are unpredictable, he did not move until he heard the
slight, brittle rustling that told him the creature was going away.
It was a porcupine.

Such an experience would be startling to the timid, but the
three young owners of Camp Denali are so familiar with the
ways of the wild ones that visitors feel secure in their care, and no
one need explore alone if he doesn't wish to.

The trio would be extraordinary in any place but Alaska. The
two girls met about 1942 when they were flying as WASP's for
the Air Force. Celia had flown for two years before the war. She
says she became a pilot because of a book she had read: *I'll Take
the High Road*, by Wolfgang Langewiesche. Virginia learned to
fly in a pilot-training program at the University of Washington.
After the war the two girls were commissioned to fly a rickety
plane to Alaska. They followed the Alcan Highway and had so
many mishaps en route that the trip took twenty-seven days.

Woody, son of a prosperous family in Maine, had discovered
that he liked mountain wilderness when he trained with the 10th
Mountain Infantry in Colorado and fought later in Italy. It is a

little hard to keep track of these three in their next adventurous years. Woody, a forestry major, was a ranger at Mount McKinley National Park and Katmai National Monument for a while, but he also studied in France. The girls had gone to the university at Stockholm after their introduction to Alaska. They spent some time in Finland with the American Friends' Service Committee, and then they toured France and went with Woody to ski in Switzerland. They had met him in Alaska, and their paths continued to cross. Now they have log-cabin homes in a birch and spruce grove, part of a little community ten miles from Fairbanks. Woody and Virginia, married somewhere along the way, have a baby daughter appropriately named Romany.

Celia has her own plane, and so do the Woods. They also have jeeps and a bus for the camp guests—*mobility* is the word that would best characterize the three of them.

As one meets them in Fairbanks in April they probably will be wearing ski pants and their colorful Swedish sweaters. Tanned and red-cheeked even in winter, when they still spend much time out of doors, on skis or working their dog team, they are a healthy and handsome trio and quite civilized really, for all that Woody feels enough at home in the wilderness to lie quietly while a porcupine licks his face.

Eva's clock is now showing 11:45 . . . 11:50. The sourdoughs all have made their decisions. Each has put in his pocket the memorandum of times he has guessed and has dropped his white cards into one of the cans. Perhaps he has had to work them in, with the cans now so full. One of the newer Alaskans put in fifty guesses, all for the same time. He'd had a dream, he says, that revealed when the ice would go out. (It was wrong.) I personally have known two who guessed right: one a miner named Carl Anderson, and Ben Mozee, marshal of Nome—both old-timers who guessed from experience. Both listed mid-afternoon as the time of day. The most common date for the pylon to move is during the first two weeks of May.

Eva's hands fly above her desk as she helps some late-comers. Her telephone rings and a shrill woman's voice says: "Don't seal the cans! I've sent my cards down by taxi."

And here are the very last visitors to the alcove. They had got their cards earlier, filling them out at home, and they are not hurrying now, for there still are four or five minutes to spare. Bill and Virginia never do anything in a breathless way. Rushing is not in their program.

Bill is tall, slim, and muscular. He has a relaxed manner, but an exuberant voice, for he is young, he is free, he knows what he wants and knows it is good, and that he is getting it. Few can say as much.

Virginia, his wife, has a face piquant and sensitive under her dark-blond hair. Bill's remarks, which often are humorous, touch off her laugh, which has a half-smothered catch in it, very infectious.

Married in midwinter, the Bacons went to a most unlikely place, Barrow, to spend their honeymoon. There they stayed several months in a cabin rented from Eskimos. When other Eskimos asked where they lived, they would say, "That white house over there by the hill," and wonder why the Eskimos always looked puzzled. When the snow and ice fell off the house the next summer, they found it was green, and the hill melted into the ground.

Bill went whale-, seal-, and walrus-hunting, and both the Bacons made dog-sled trips. They were collecting not only colorful memories but the stories without which no one should call himself an Alaskan:

"That ship, the *Chimo*, that was abandoned because it got caught in the ice, was only fifty miles off the coast a few years ago. The sea was frozen all the way out to it, and some Barrow Eskimos went with their dog teams and boarded it. They loaded themselves down with things that the crew had left, binoculars, guns, clothing. But all one Eskimo wanted was a great, big, fancy birthday cake that stood on the table, uncut, when pressuring ice made it necessary for the crew to leave in a hurry.

"After the Eskimos started back to shore they were hungry, and the men teased the owner of the cake to let them have some. At last he agreed—but even with fists the men couldn't break it. It was like a cake made of plaster of Paris."

The Bacons are settled in Fairbanks now, in a house that Bill himself built. It's on skids so that when the town starts to nudge them, they can hitch up their house and move farther out, where again they can have blueberries growing around the door, and moose peering in at the windows, and waterfowl nesting around whatever pond is near. The house, white with blue trim, suggests a neat little ship.

Beyond a few well-chosen comforts the Bacons do not believe in owning things, nor in "wasting time" making money. Some of the money they do have Bill earns, in spurts, it may be in construction, mining, or cannery jobs; Virginia says, "When a stranger asks what my husband does, I say, 'Do you mean yesterday or today or tomorrow?' " She is only being amusing, for Bill is one of the best photographers in the profession and could be one of the highest-paid. But then he'd be tied to a routine, and that, he thinks, would be deadening. Ever since he first came to Alaska however, he has been assembling negatives of the Northern country, the land and activities of the people, and he is now known as a source of such pictures. Clean, sharp, and effective, his work shows particularly well the delicate brilliance of arctic light.

William W. Bacon III is a member of one of the oldest families in Philadelphia, and his name is still in the *Social Register,* but no one learns that fact from him. When he and Virginia were married, some of the family silver and a framed replica of their crest were sent to them up at Barrow, where they were given places among Eskimo knives and harpoon heads and a fossil milk tooth from a baby mammoth. Bill conformed to the conservative life of his family quite well until he was graduated from the Eagle Brook School in Deerfield. Then he went into the Navy.

When he got out, he decided to enter, not Yale, Harvard, or Princeton, but Utah State. By that time his course had been set in a different direction from that of his ancestors.

Virginia's mother came up to Alaska to teach in 1913; her father was assistant regional forester until his retirement. Just before Virginia was born, "We," says Virginia, "rode twenty miles on a dog sled from Klukwan to Haines, then by boat to Juneau," from where her mother expected to fly to the States, but the doctors decided there wasn't time. Virginia therefore was born an Alaskan.

The Bacons live very simply, catching game and fish, using some of the wild plants the natives do, and even grinding their own flour. They are happiest when they are out of doors. Virginia has an informal career in promoting a love of nature in small children who come her way, and they always do come. About six of them live in her shadow now, children so young they have garbled her name and call her Mr. Baker. She has had the reward of hearing a small girl plead with a playmate: "Don't kill that bug! That's Mr. Baker's bug."

Sir Arthur Quiller-Couch said: "The roots are always the roots, and we can only reinvigorate our growth through them." The Bacons know what those words mean, and they have decided to live by them.

Midnight has come and gone. The boxes are sealed, and Eva's friends have taken her out to celebrate. The cards will be sped to Nenana by bush plane, not only from Fairbanks but from all other parts of the Territory. Almost everyone in Nenana will devote the next two weeks to sorting the cards and listing them, with the entrants' names, by date, hour, and minute, in a mimeographed book inches thick. Copies will be distributed before break-up to the principal cities, where anybody can check his own record and see how many others guessed the same times.

Someone, or more likely several, will have chosen the right minute—and all who take part will have won something: the renewed sense of being the people who are especially committed to frontier living. The contest has little besides a financial meaning to strangers, but for the real Northerners it is more, a kind of tribute to the country that holds them here and that makes so many of the rules, including the time when they can begin to use rivers again.

Most of these people one meets in the Nordale on closing night have spent all their adult lives in the arctic and will be here to the end. They are the permanent Northerners sifted out, so to speak—permanent as are Ben Gillette, Bob Murphy, Bill Munz, and other sourdoughs and bush pilots, and the officials genuinely concerned about the welfare of neighbors such as Womenga. From many places Alaska summoned them—and it must also have put its imprint on them. It would be pleasant to think that one could become like them by staying here long enough. "An extraordinarily friendly and natural people," Robert Shaw, guest conductor at the Anchorage Festival of Music, described them. "Bach wrote his music for people like this." Seeing them as an outsider, but a perceptive one, he said that what seemed most moving about the Northerners was "this openness and lack of pretension. It must be that people who are familiar with first-hand experience are better equipped by aptitude and hunger to know the real thing."

Life on a frontier does attract—and repel—certain kinds of people. This is a circumstance so well recognized that generalizing seems permissible. No one who values security highly ever would choose to live in the arctic. No one who is much concerned about other people's opinion of him will be in surroundings so unconventional. No one with real criminal tendencies will be here, except natives who may be born with them; there have been a few of those, not many. Most frontiers have been the hideouts of scoundrels but, happily for Alaska, few scoundrels are winter types.

Some crimes are, of course, committed in arctic communities, chiefly petty thefts and what could be called crimes of tension.

For the percentage of neurotic temperaments is rather high. Frontiers attract not only explorers and builders, but escapists. I never have heard Northerners complain about the less stable neighbors who at times may need special kindness. The attitude is more likely to be: "They have to live somewhere, and perhaps they are happiest here." Anyway, some of the most constructive settlers are escaping too, consciously, from hopeless family situations, or climates that don't agree with them, or from a mechanistic civilization that doesn't give them much personal satisfaction.

These, then, are the Alaska settlers, here for various reasons but especially the challenges. Some of them probably came for the same reason that Sir Edmund Hillary wanted to climb Mount Everest: because it was there—as Alaska is here, and the farthest place.

It is the residents' North that I've tried to picture, the North visitors seldom see—an Eskimo settlement off the tourist track and the larger cities in winter when, sad to us, few travelers come.

Strangers, we hear, think of it as our "long, cold, dark winter." That is the season now. It is January, 38° below zero today, and the windows high in one of the Fairbanks apartments are framing a scene that, yes, could be called dark.

Ice fog covers the city, a fog composed of the minute crystals formed from the steam of warm walls, doors opening, and the people's breaths. It comes only up to the seventh floor of the building, and so I look down on the top of it, which is level and smooth, like the top of a lake composed not of water but crystal motes.

The fog is thin enough so that the roofs can be seen, vaguely, and blurred frosty points of color: lights in windows, neon signs in red, orange, and yellow, and blue sodium-vapor street lights. They are like jewels decorating a drowned city.

Today there is no Aurora, but overhead are the clear, steady stars of the North and a moon which is full and therefore will not set during all the twenty-four hours. It silvers the top of the ice fog and puts a sheen on the snow-covered mountains along the horizon.

And the time? Close to midday, now in the depths of our cold, dark winter.

The ice fog comes to an end at the city limits. Beyond that are none of the man-made lights, but there still is the moonlight, shimmering and unearthly across the wide, white, silent land.

The human life in the North is like that illumination the moon is casting. The tolerance, decency, even tenderness of the relationships are such a bright source of comfort that the long winter does not seem too cold to us, or too dark.

NOTE

➤➤➤➤➤➤➤➤➤➤➤➤➤➤➤➤➤➤➤➤➤➤➤➤➤➤➤➤➤➤➤➤➤

Those who need special kinds of information
about Alaska may secure it from the following:

Travel in Alaska
by tourists, sportsmen, or others—

Alaska Visitors Association
Juneau, Alaska

Investment opportunities—

Alaska Resources Development Board
Juneau, Alaska

Employment—

Alaska Employment Service
Anchorage, Fairbanks, Juneau,
Ketchikan, or Petersburg, Alaska

Housing—

Local Chambers of Commerce

Publications on Alaska

and Other Sources Quoted in This Book

⤏⤏⤏-⤏⤏⤏-⤏⤏⤏-⤏⤏⤏-⤏⤏⤏-⤏⤏⤏-⤏⤏⤏-⤏⤏⤏-⤏⤏⤏-⤏⤏⤏⤘-⤛⤛⤛-⤛⤛⤛-⤛⤛⤛-⤛⤛⤛-⤛⤛⤛-⤛⤛⤛-⤛⤛⤛-⤛⤛⤛-⤛⤛⤛

Brooks, Alfred Hulse: *Blazing Alaska's Trails* (published jointly by the University of Alaska and the Arctic Institute of North America; 1953).

Bynner, Witter: *The Way of Life According to Laotzu* (New York: The John Day Company; 1944).

Geist, Otto William, and Rainey, Froelich G.: *Archaeological Excavations at Kukulik.* University of Alaska Misc. Publ., Vol. II (Washington, D.C.: U.S. Government Printing Office; 1936).

Gruening, Ernest: *The State of Alaska* (New York: Random House; 1954).

Hinz, Rev. John, of The Society of the United Brethren for Propagating the Gospel Among the Heathen: *Grammar and Vocabulary of the Eskimo Language* (Green Bay, Wisconsin: Reliance Publishing Company; 1944).

Hoffman, Walter James: *Graphic Art of the Eskimos.* Report of U.S. National Museum, 1895 (Washington, D.C.: U.S. Government Printing Office; 1897).

Hulley, Clarence C.: *Alaska, 1741–1953* (Portland, Oregon: Binfords & Mort; 1953).

Huxley, Julian: *Man Stands Alone* (New York: Harper & Brothers; 1941).

Jenness, Diamond: *Life of the Copper Eskimos:* Report of the Canadian Arctic Expedition, 1913–18, XII (Ottawa: E. Cloutier, King's Printer; 1922).

Miller, Herman P.: *Income of the American People* (New York: John Wiley & Sons; 1955).

Murie, Adolph. *The Wolves of Mount McKinley.* Fauna of the National Parks of the U.S., Fauna Series No. 5 (Washington, D.C.: U.S. Government Printing Office; 1944).

Murie, Olaus J.: *A Field Guide to Animal Tracks* (Boston: Houghton Mifflin Company; 1954).

Nelson, E. W. *The Eskimo About Bering Strait.* Bureau of American Ethnology, 18th Annual Report, Part 1 (Washington, D.C.: U.S. Government Printing Office; 1899).

Rainey, Froelich G.: *The Whale Hunters of Tigara* (New York: Anthropological Papers of The American Museum of Natural History, Vol. 41, Part 2; 1947).

Rasmussen, Knud: *Across Arctic America* (New York: G. P. Putnam's Sons; 1927).

Rodahl, Kaare: *North* (New York: Harper & Brothers; 1953).

Soothill, William Edward and Hodous, Lewis: A *Dictionary of Chinese Buddhist Terms* (London: Kegan Paul, Trench, Trubner & Co., Ltd.; 1937).

United Nations, UNESCO: *Cultural Patterns and Technical Change*, a manual prepared by The World Federation for Mental Health and edited by Margaret Mead (1955).

United States Department of Commerce, Bureau of the Census: *United States Census of Population: 1950*, Vol. II, Part 51 (Washington, D.C.: U.S. Government Printing Office; 1952).

United States Department of Commerce, Coast and Geodetic Survey: *United States Coast Pilot, Alaska Part II* (Washington, D.C.: U.S. Government Printing Office; 1947).

United States Department of Labor, Bureau of Labor Statistics: *Monthly Labor Review*, December 1956, Vol. 79, No. 12 (Washington, D.C.: Government Printing Office; 1956).

United States House of Representatives, Committee on Government Operations: *Alaska Native Loan Program:* House Report No. 1821, 85th Congress, 2nd Session (Washington, D.C.: Government Printing Office; 1958).

Weiss, Paul: *Nature and Man* (New York: Henry Holt and Company; 1947).

Weyer, Edward Moffat, Jr.: *The Eskimos* (New Haven: Yale University Press; 1932).

INDEX

>>>->>>->>>->>>->>>->>>->>>->>><<<-<<<-<<<-<<<-<<<-<<<-<<<-<<<-<<<

A NOTE ABOUT THE AUTHOR

Sally Carrighar was born in Cleveland, Ohio, attended Wellesley College, wrote radio dramas and feature articles, and edited a financial monthly before she embarked, in 1937, on the career for which she is now so well known—that of an eloquent chronicler of wildlife. Her own biological research and firsthand experiences provided the rich material for her three previous books: *One Day on Beetle Rock* (1944), about animals in the Sierra Nevadas; *One Day at Teton Marsh* (1947), about the amazing variety of wildlife in Jackson Hole, Wyoming; and *Icebound Summer* (1953), an account of the struggle for survival by animals, birds, and human beings on the northwest coast of Alaska.

She went to Alaska for only two years, but the arctic captured her so completely that she stayed for nearly ten.

A NOTE ON THE TYPE

This book is set in Electra, a Linotype face designed by W. A. Dwiggins (1880–1956), who was responsible for so much that is good in contemporary book design. Although much of his early work was in advertising and he was the author of the standard volume *Layout in Advertising*, Mr. Dwiggins later devoted his prolific talents to book typography and type design, and worked with great distinction in both fields. In addition to his designs for Electra, he created the Metro, Caledonia, and Eldorado series of type faces, as well as a number of experimental cuttings that have never been issued commercially.

Electra cannot be classified as either modern or old-style. It is not based on any historical model, nor does it echo a particular period or style. It avoids the extreme contrast between thick and thin elements which marks most modern faces, and attempts to give a feeling of fluidity, power, and speed.

This book was composed, printed, and bound by Kingsport Press, Inc., Kingsport, Tenn. The paper was manufactured by P. H. Glatfelter Company, Spring Grove, Penn. The typography and binding are by Guy Fleming.

Date Due

MAR 15 '60			
MAR 29 '60			
MAR 13 '6|			
MAY 12 61			
MAY 12 61			
MAY 16 '61			
MAY 15 '62			
AUG 13 '6|			
⊨			
DEC 14 '66			
2 0 '67			
FEB 2 0 '67			
JUL 12 '68			
DEC 7 '70			
MAY 5 79			
OC 14 '86			
FEB 6 '89			
	PRINTED	IN U. S. A.	